Lecture Notes in Computer Science 14534

The series Lecture Notes in Computer Science (LNCS), including its subseries Lecture Notes in Artificial Intelligence (LNAI) and Lecture Notes in Bioinformatics (LNBI), has established itself as a medium for the publication of new developments in computer science and information technology research, teaching, and education.

LNCS enjoys close cooperation with the computer science R & D community, the series counts many renowned academics among its volume editors and paper authors, and collaborates with prestigious societies. Its mission is to serve this international community by providing an invaluable service, mainly focused on the publication of conference and workshop proceedings and postproceedings. LNCS commenced publication in 1973.

Mark Manulis · Diana Maimuţ ·
George Teşeleanu
Editors

Innovative Security Solutions for Information Technology and Communications

16th International Conference, SecITC 2023
Bucharest, Romania, November 23–24, 2023
Revised Selected Papers

Springer

Editors
Mark Manulis 🆔
Universität der Bundeswehr München
Munich, Germany

Diana Maimuţ 🆔
Technology Innovation Institute
Abu Dhabi, United Arab Emirates

George Teşeleanu 🆔
Advanced Technologies Institute
Bucharest, Romania

ISSN 0302-9743   ISSN 1611-3349 (electronic)
Lecture Notes in Computer Science
ISBN 978-3-031-52946-7   ISBN 978-3-031-52947-4 (eBook)
https://doi.org/10.1007/978-3-031-52947-4

This Springer imprint is published by the registered company Springer Nature Switzerland AG
The registered company address is: Gewerbestrasse 11, 6330 Cham, Switzerland

Paper in this product is recyclable.

Preface

SECITC (International Conference on Security for Information Technology and Communications) is an annual international conference held in Romania focusing on all theoretical and practical aspects related to information technology and communications security. Its primary goal is connecting security and privacy researchers as well as professionals from different communities and providing a forum that allows informal exchanges necessary for the emergence of new scientific and industrial collaborations. Since 2015 the post-proceedings of the conference have been published in Springer LNCS. The Program Committee also became international. This was a turning point for Romania as it represented the alignment to the international standards in terms of research.

The 16th edition of the conference, SECITC 2023, took place (both in person and online) from 23rd to 24th November, 2023, in Bucharest. It was organised jointly by the Bucharest University of Economic Studies, the Military Technical Academy, and the Advanced Technologies Institute, the latter being the main organizer of this edition.

SECITC 2023 received 57 submissions. Each Program Committee (PC) member was assigned an average of three submissions for review. Each paper was assigned to at least three reviewers. The PC was helped by the reports and opinions of ten external reviewers. The submission process was anonymous and author names were not visible to the reviewers. Received reviews were anonymised to the paper's authors. The review process was organized and managed through EasyChair. The reviewers were asked to declare any conflicts of interest for all submissions in the beginning of the process, and the EasyChair system was configured to ensure that PC members (including PC chairs) could see neither reviewer assignments nor reviews of papers for which they had a confict of interest. For several papers, one PC Co-chair had a conflict of interest, and the discussion on each of the papers was held, and the decision was made, between the other two PC Co-chairs without a conflict of interest. The selection process was competitive and after highly interactive discussions and a careful deliberation, 14 full papers (24.6%) were selected by the PC for presentation at the conference.

SECITC 2023 programme featured three invited talks given by Bart Preneel from KU Leuven, Ahmad-Reza Sadeghi from TU Darmstadt, and Ivan Visconti from the University of Salerno. All invited speakers were offered an opportunity to publish extended abstacts of their talks in the post-proceedings of the conference.

SECITC 2023 PC was co-chaired by Mark Manulis, Diana Maimuţ, and George Teşeleanu, who selected the PC members and led their efforts in selecting papers that appear in this volume.

We would like to thank everyone who contributed to the success of SECITC 2023. We are grateful to all PC members and external reviewers for their commitment and enthusiasm, which ensured that each submitted paper went through a thorough and fair review process. We thank all members of the Organizing Committee of SECITC 2023 for their professional work and support. Last but not least, we also wish to thank all authors who submitted to SECITC 2023 and all conference participants for making the conference an enjoyable experience.

November 2023   Mark Manulis
                                                              Diana Maimuţ
                                                            George Teşeleanu

Organization

Program Committee

Claudio Ardagna	Università degli Studi di Milano, Italy
Lasse Berntzen	University of South-Eastern Norway, Norway
Ion Bica	Military Technical Academy, Romania
Cătălin Boja	Bucharest University of Economic Studies, Romania
Guillaume Bouffard	National Cybersecurity Agency of France (ANSSI), France
Samia Bouzefrane	CEDRIC Lab, Conservatoire National des Arts et Métiers, France
Jeremy Chamboredon	Technology Innovation Institute, UAE
Christophe Clavier	Université de Limoges, France
Otto Csanyi	Sappi Europe, Austria
Paolo D'Arco	University of Salerno, Italy
Roberto De Prisco	University of Salerno, Italy
Eric Diehl	Sony Pictures, USA
Mihai Doinea	Bucharest University of Economic Studies, Romania
Vlad Drăgoi	LITIS, France
Mohamed Amine Ferrag	Technology Innovation Institute, UAE
Eric Freyssinet	LORIA, France
Dieter Gollmann	Hamburg University of Technology, Germany
Rémi Géraud-Stewart	Ecole Normale Supérieure, France
Gerhard Hancke	City University of Hong Kong, China
Helena Handschuh	Rambus, USA
Shoichi Hirose	University of Fukui, Japan
Mehmet Sabir Kiraz	De Montfort University, UK
Miroslaw Kutylowski	Wroclaw University of Technology, Poland
Giovanni Livraga	University of Milan, Italy
Diana Maimuţ	Technology Innovation Institute, UAE
Mark Manulis	Universität der Bundeswehr Munchen, Germany
Stig Mjølsnes	Norwegian University of Science and Technology, Norway
David Naccache	Ecole Normale Supérieure, France
Svetla Nikova	KU Leuven, Belgium
Andrei-George Oprina	Advanced Technologies Institute, Romania

Victor Patriciu	Military Technical Academy, Romania
Marius Popa	Bucharest University of Economic Studies, Romania
Joachim Posegga	University of Passau, Germany
Peter Roenne	University of Luxembourg, Luxembourg
Peter Y. A. Ryan	University of Luxembourg, Luxembourg
Damien Sauveron	XLIM (UMR University of Limoges/CNRS 7252), France
Emil Simion	University Politehnica of Bucharest, Romania
El Mamoun Souidi	University Mohammed V in Rabat, Morocco
Riccardo Spolaor	Shandong University, China
Pantelimon Stanica	Naval Postgraduate School, USA
Rainer Steinwandt	University of Alabama in Huntsville, USA
George Teşeleanu	Advanced Technologies Institute, Romania
Norbert Tihanyi	Technology Innovation Institute, UAE
Ferucio Laurenţiu Ţiplea	Alexandru Ioan Cuza University of Iasi, Romania
Mihai Togan	Military Technical Academy, Romania
Cristian Toma	Bucharest University of Economic Studies, Romania
Denis Trcek	University of Ljubljana, Slovenia
Alin Zamfiroiu	Bucharest University of Economic Studies, Romania
Lei Zhang	East China Normal University, China

Additional Reviewers

Aragon, Nicolas	Lazar, Constantin-Sebastian
Aziz, Rezak	Neacsu, Eugen
Berger, Christian	Xiao, Yucheng
Hristea, Cristian	Xu, Lin
Kelesidis, Evgnosia-Alexandra	Ye, Yangyue

Contents

x   Contents

BASS: Boolean Automorphisms Signature Scheme

Dima Grigoriev[1], Ilia Ilmer[2], Alexey Ovchinnikov[3], and Vladimir Shpilrain[4(✉)]

[1] CNRS, Mathématiques, Université de Lille, 59655 Villeneuve d'Ascq, France
Dmitry.Grigoryev@univ-lille.fr
[2] Department of Computer Science, CUNY Graduate Center,
365 5th Avenue, New York, NY 10016, USA
i.ilmer@icloud.com
[3] Department of Mathematics, Queens College, City University of New York,
Queens, NY 11367, USA
alexey.ovchinnikov@qc.cuny.edu
[4] Department of Mathematics, The City College of New York,
New York, NY 10031, USA
shpilrain@yahoo.com

Abstract. We offer a digital signature scheme using Boolean automorphisms of a multivariate polynomial algebra over integers. Verification part of this scheme is based on the approximation of the number of zeros of a multivariate Boolean function.

Keywords: digital signature · multivariate polynomial · Boolean function

1 Introduction

Due to the concern that if large-scale quantum computers are ever built, they will compromise the security of many commonly used cryptographic algorithms, NIST had begun in 2016 a process to develop new cryptography standards and, in particular, solicited proposals for new digital signature schemes [5] resistant to attacks by known quantum algorithms, such as e.g. Shor's algorithm [6]. In particular, there is an interest in signature schemes whose security is based on new assumptions.

One possible way to avoid quantum attacks based on solving the hidden subgroup problem (including the attacks in [6]) is *not* to use one-way functions that utilize one or another (semi)group structure. The candidate one-way function that we use in our scheme here takes a private polynomial automorphism φ as the input and outputs $\varphi(P)$ for a public multivariate polynomial P.

To avoid any parallels with the encryption scheme of [4], we say up front that since ours is just a signature scheme (i.e., is not a spin-off of any encryption scheme), we do not need our candidate one-way function to have a trapdoor because the private key holder does not need to invert the function. Also, in [4],

M. Manulis et al. (Eds.): SecITC 2023, LNCS 14534, pp. 1–12, 2024.
https://doi.org/10.1007/978-3-031-52947-4_1

the candidate one-way function was φ itself, and the private (decryption) key was φ^{-1}. In contrast, in our signature scheme φ^{-1} does not play any role and does not have to be computed.

The main novelty of our signature scheme is manifested in the verification part. First, note that any polynomial P has as many zeros as $\varphi(P)$ does, where φ is any automorphism of the polynomial algebra. To balance between security and efficiency, we do not want the number of zeros to be either too small or too large. To that end, we use polynomials over integers, but we count zero values on Boolean tuples only. Since the number of Boolean tuples is exponential in the number of variables, it can still be too large to process deterministically. Instead, we use a non-deterministic (Monte Carlo) method to estimate the number of zero (or nonzero) values of a polynomial in question. We note that the accuracy of the Monte Carlo method for estimating the number of zeros of a multivariate polynomial was studied and quantified in [1].

2   Scheme Description

Let $K = \mathbb{Z}[x_1, \ldots, x_n]$ denote the algebra of polynomials in n variables over the ring $\mathbb{Z}$ of integers, and let $B(K)$ denote the factor algebra of K by the ideal generated by all polynomials of the form $(x_i^2 - x_i)$, $i = 1, \ldots, n$. Informally, one can call $B(K)$ the "Booleanization" of K. We note that the ring $B(K)$ is isomorphic (as a ring) to the direct sum of 2^n copies of the ring $\mathbb{Z}$.

The signature scheme is as follows.

Private: an automorphism φ of the algebra $B(K)$. We note that φ is defined by the polynomials $y_i = \varphi(x_i)$, $i = 1, \ldots, n$.

Public:

- 3 sparse polynomials $P_i = P_i(x_1, \ldots, x_n)$ with coefficients ± 1.
- 3 polynomials $\varphi(P_i)$, where φ is a private automorphism of the algebra $B(K)$. We note that $\varphi(P_i) = P_i(y_1, \ldots, y_n)$, where $y_i = \varphi(x_i)$.
- a hash function H with values in the algebra $B(K)$ and a (deterministic) procedure for converting values of H to sparse polynomials from the algebra $B(K)$.
- a set $\mathbb{G}$ of polynomials. This set includes, in particular, all monomials and all polynomials of the form (1-monomial). See Sect. 4) for more details.

Remark 1. We emphasize that the automorphism φ, the 3 sparse polynomials P_i, and the 3 polynomials $\varphi(P_i)$ are all generated/computed in the offline phase. The hash function H is one of the standard hash functions (we suggest SHA3-256), with values converted to a polynomial in $B(K)$ (see Sect. 3.3).

Signing a message m:

1. Apply the hash function H to the message m. Convert $H(m)$ to a polynomial $Q = Q(x_1, \ldots, x_{n+1})$ with integer coefficients using a deterministic public procedure (see Sect. 3.3). That is, the polynomial Q has an extra variable compared to the polynomials P_i.

2. The automorphism φ is extended to the "Booleanization" of the algebra $\mathbb{Z}[x_1, \ldots, x_{n+1}]$ by taking x_{n+1} to $x_{n+1} + r(x_1, \ldots, x_n) - 2x_{n+1} \cdot r(x_1, \ldots, x_n)$, where $r(x_1, \ldots, x_n)$ is a random polynomial from the set $\mathbb{G}$ of polynomials (see Sect. 4). This extended automorphism we denote by the same letter φ. (The fact that this is, indeed, an automorphism of the "Booleanization" is part of Proposition 1 in Sect. 4.)

3. The signature is $\varphi(Q)$.

Remark 2. The reason why we extend the automorphism φ by adding an extra variable x_{n+1} at Step 2 is to prevent the forger from accumulating many pairs $(Q, \varphi(Q))$ with the same φ. Now, with each new signature, we have a different φ because of a random choice of the polynomial $r(x_1, \ldots, x_n)$ at Step 2. We note that after extending φ, polynomials $\varphi(P_i)$ do not change since all P_i depend on $x_1, \ldots, x_n$ only.

Verification:

1. The verifier computes $H(m)$ and converts $H(m)$ to $Q = Q(x_1, \ldots, x_{n+1})$ using a deterministic public procedure.

2. The verifier selects a random 4-variable polynomial $u(x, y, z, t)$ from $B(\mathbb{Z}[x, y, z, t])$ with coefficients 0, 1, -1, 2, or -2, and computes $u(\varphi(P_1), \varphi(P_2), \varphi(P_3), \varphi(Q))$. Note that this is equal to $\varphi(u(P_1, P_2, P_3, Q))$. Denote the polynomial $\varphi(u(P_1, P_2, P_3, Q))$ by S.

3. The verifier also computes $u(P_1, P_2, P_3, Q)$. Denote this polynomial by R. (Note that S should be equal to $\varphi(R)$ if the signature is valid.)

4. The verifier then compares the proportion of positive values on Boolean tuples for the polynomials R and S. That is, the proportion of positive values on $(n+1)$-tuples $(x_1, \ldots, x_{n+1})$, where each x_i is 0 or 1. These proportions are estimated using a non-deterministic (Monte Carlo) method.

The verifier accepts the signature if and only if these proportions for R and S are different in no more than 3% of the total number of trials in the Monte Carlo method. (See Sect. 4 for an explanation of why these proportions should be exactly the same when computed deterministically if S is an automorphic image of R.)

Remark 3. With suggested parameters, the number of Boolean $(n+1)$-tuples is quite large (2^{n+1}, to be exact). Given that counting zeros (or non-zeros) on Boolean tuples is #P-hard, see [7], it is computationally hard to count the number of positive values on Boolean tuples *precisely*, which is why the verifier has to use a non-deterministic method. We explain the method in the following subsection.

Correctness. While it is obvious that polynomials P and $\varphi(P)$ have the same number of zeros, it is not at all obvious why they have the same number of positive values on Boolean tuples. Indeed, this may not be true for an arbitrary automorphism φ, so we have a special algorithm for sampling φ. This is explained in Sect. 4, and correctness is formally proved in the Appendix.

2.1 Monte Carlo Method for Counting Positive Values of a Polynomial on Boolean Tuples

Our non-deterministic method for estimating the proportion of positive values on Boolean tuples for a given polynomial P is pretty standard. Just plug in a large number of random Boolean tuples into P and count how many of them yield a positive value of P. Then divide the obtained number by the total number of Boolean tuples used; this is your proportion.

We note that the accuracy of the Monte Carlo method for counting *zeros* of Boolean polynomials was studied and quantified in [1]. See our Sect. 6.1 for more details on the accuracy.

3 Key Generation

First we note that, since the algebra $B(K)$ is the factor algebra of K by the ideal generated by all polynomials of the form $(x_i^2 - x_i)$ and since we only count values of a polynomial on Boolean tuples, when we generate the public polynomials P_i it makes sense to only generate monomials where no x_j occurs with an exponent higher than 1. Then generating P_i will look as follows.

3.1 Generating a Random t-Sparse Polynomial

1. Select, uniformly at random, an integer d between 1 and b (where b is one of the parameters of the scheme). This integer will be the degree of our monomial. (Note that the degree of a monomial cannot be higher than n since our monomials are square-free because of factoring by the ideal generated by all polynomials of the form $(x_i^2 - x_i)$.)
2. To select a monomial of degree d, do a selection of x_i, uniformly at random from $\{x_1, \dots, x_n\}$, d times, avoiding repetition of x_i. Then build the monomial as a product of the selected x_i.
3. Finally, build a t-sparse polynomial as a linear combination of t selected monomials with coefficients ± 1, selected at random.

3.2 Generating a Random Polynomial from the Set $\mathbb{G}$

The set $\mathbb{G}$ of polynomials in $\mathbb{Z}[x_1, \dots, x_n]$ will play a crucial role in generating automorphisms of the algebra $B(K)$, see Sect. 4. This set can be defined recursively as follows. Assign all variables $x_1, \dots, x_n$ to $\mathbb{G}$. Then keep adding more polynomials to $\mathbb{G}$ using the following rules: (1) if a polynomial P belongs to $\mathbb{G}$, then $1 - P$ belongs to $\mathbb{G}$, too; (2) if both polynomials P_1 and P_2 belong to $\mathbb{G}$, then their product $P_1 P_2$ belongs to $\mathbb{G}$, too.

Remark 4. The number of multiplications in the above procedure for generating a polynomial from the set $\mathbb{G}$ (see Step 3 in the procedure below) is one of the parameters of our scheme; denote it by r.

Note that the set $\mathbb{G}$ consists of polynomials P such that $P(x_1, \ldots, x_n) = 0$ or 1 for any Boolean n-tuple $(x_1, \ldots, x_n)$. This easily follows by induction from the above recursive definition of the set $\mathbb{G}$. In other words, any polynomial from $\mathbb{G}$ induces an n-variable Boolean function and, conversely, any n-variable Boolean function is induced by a polynomial from $\mathbb{G}$.

Based on this description, we suggest the following procedure for sampling a polynomial, depending on variables from a subset X of the set of variables, from the set $\mathbb{G}$. We emphasize again that in our scheme, this is done in the offline phase.

1. Select a random monomial as in the previous Sect. 3.1, except that the degree d should be really small, 1 or 2. Denote this monomial by M.
2. With probability $\frac{1}{2}$, select between M and $1 - M$. Denote the result by M'.
3. Select, uniformly at random, a variable x_i not from the subset X of variables. Then, with probability $\frac{1}{2}$, multiply M' by either x_i or $1 - x_i$.
4. Repeat steps (2) through (3) r times for some small r (one of the parameters of the scheme).

3.3 Converting $H(m)$ to a Polynomial

We suggest using a hash function H from the SHA-3 family, specifically SHA3-256. We assume the security properties of SHA3-256, including collision resistance and preimage resistance. Below is an ad hoc procedure for converting a hash $H(m)$ to a polynomial. We assume there is a standard way to convert $H(m)$ to a bit string of length 256.

Let B be a bit string of length 256. We will convert B to a polynomial from the factor algebra of $K = \mathbb{Z}[x_1, \ldots, x_{n+1}]$ by the ideal generated by all polynomials of the form $(x_i^2 - x_i)$, $i = 1, \ldots, n + 1$. We note that this process is deterministic.

(1) Split 256 bits in 32 8-bit blocks. The 5 leftmost bits will be responsible for a coefficient of the corresponding monomial, while the 3 rightmost bits will be responsible for a collection of variables x_i in the monomial.
(2) After Step (1), we have 32 3-bit blocks corresponding to monomials of degree 3 that we now have to populate with 3 variables each. Enumerate 96 bits in these 32 3-bit blocks by $x_1, \ldots, x_{32}, x_1, \ldots, x_{32}, x_1, \ldots, x_{32}$ (in this order, going left to right). Now each 3-bit block is converted to a monomial that is a product of x_i corresponding to the places in the bit string where the bit is "1". In particular, each monomial will be of degree at most 3.
(3) Now we have to use 5 remaining bits in each 8-bit block to obtain an integer coefficient for each monomial of degree ≤ 3 obtained at Step 2. This is done as follows. First, we compute the sum of these 5 bits. Then, we reduce it modulo 3. If the result is 0, then the coefficient is 0. If the result is 1, then the coefficient is 1. If the result is 2, then the coefficient is -1.
(4) Combine all monomials and coefficients obtained at Steps (2), (3) into a polynomial.

4 Generating an Automorphism φ

An automorphism φ is generated offline, as follows.

Recall that the set $\mathbb{G}$ consists of polynomials P such that $P(x_1, \ldots, x_n) = 0$ or 1 for any Boolean n-tuple $(x_1, \ldots, x_n)$, see Sect. 3.2.

Then we have:

Proposition 1. *Let $h = h(x_1, \ldots, x_n)$ be a polynomial from the set $\mathbb{G}$. Suppose h does not depend on x_k. Let α be the map that takes x_k to $x_k + h - 2x_k \cdot h$ and fixes all other variables. Then:*

(a) *α defines an automorphism of $B(K)$, the factor algebra of the algebra $\mathbb{Z}[x_1, \ldots, x_n]$ by the ideal generated by all polynomials of the form $(x_i^2 - x_i)$, $i = 1, \ldots, n$. Denote this automorphism also by α.*

(b) *The group of automorphisms of $B(K)$ is generated by all automorphisms as in part (a) and is isomorphic to the group of permutations of the vertices of the n-dimensional Boolean cube.*

(c) *For any polynomial P from $\mathbb{Z}[x_1, \ldots, x_n]$, the number of positive values of P on Boolean tuples $(x_1, \ldots, x_n)$ equals that of $\alpha(P)$.*

For the proof of Proposition 1, see the Appendix.

4.1 Generating Triangular Automorphisms

Our (private) automorphism φ will be a composition of "triangular" automorphisms and permutations on the set of variables. Below is how we generate an "upper triangular" automorphism α.

(1) Let $k = 1$.
(2) With probability $\frac{1}{2}$, either take x_k to itself or take x_k to $x_k + h(x_1, \ldots, x_n) - 2x_k \cdot h(x_1, \ldots, x_n)$, where $h(x_1, \ldots, x_n)$ is a random t-sparse polynomial from the set $\mathbb{G}$ not depending on any x_j with $j \leq k$ (see Sect. 3.2). Fix all other variables.
(3) If $k < n$, increase k by 1 and go to Step (2). Otherwise, stop.

Generating a "lower triangular" automorphism β is similar:

(1) Let $k = n$.
(2) With probability $\frac{1}{2}$, either take x_k to itself or take x_k to $x_k + h(x_1, \ldots, x_n) - 2x_k \cdot h(x_1, \ldots, x_n)$, where $h(x_1, \ldots, x_n)$ is a random t-sparse polynomial from the set $\mathbb{G}$ not depending on x_j with $j \geq k$. Fix all other variables.
(3) If $k > 1$, decrease k by 1 and go to Step (2). Otherwise, stop.

4.2 Generating φ as a Composition of Triangular Automorphisms and Permutations

Having generated an upper triangular automorphism α and a lower triangular automorphism β, we generate our private automorphism φ as a composition $\alpha\beta\pi$, where π is a random permutation on the set of variables. Here α is applied first, followed by β, followed by π.

At the end of the whole procedure, we will have n polynomials $y_i = \varphi(x_i)$ that define the automorphism φ.

5 Suggested Parameters

For the hash function H, we suggest SHA3-256.

For the number n of variables, we suggest $n = 31$.

For the number t of monomials in t-sparse polynomials, we suggest $t = 3$.

For the bound b on the degree of monomials in t-sparse polynomials, we suggest $b = 3$.

For the degree d of the monomial M in the procedure for generating a polynomial from the set $\mathbb{G}$ (Sect. 3.2), we suggest $d = 2$.

For the number r of the number of multiplications in the procedure for generating a polynomial from the set $\mathbb{G}$ (Sect. 3.2), we suggest $r = 1$.

For the number of trials in Monte Carlo method for counting positive values of a polynomial on Boolean tuples, we suggest 3,000.

6 Performance and Signature Size

For our computer simulations, we used Apple MacBook Pro, M1 CPU (8 Cores), 16 GB RAM computer. Julia code is available, see [2].

With the suggested parameters, signature verification takes about 0.3 s on average, which is not bad, but the polynomial $\varphi(Q)$ (the signature) is rather large, almost 4 Kb on average.

The size of the private key (the automorphism φ) is about 1.5 Kb, and the size of the public key is about 12.5 Kb.

We note that we have measured the size of a signature, as well as the size of private/public keys, as follows. We have counted the total number of variables that occurred in relevant polynomial(s) and multiplied that number by 5, the number of bits sufficient to describe the index of any variable (except x_{32}). To that, we added the number of monomials times 3 (the average number of bits needed to describe a coefficient at a monomial in our construction(s).

As usual, there is a trade-off between the size of the private key φ and its security. The size of φ can be reduced to just a few hundred monomials, but then security becomes a concern since some of $\varphi(x_i)$ may be possible to recover more or less by inspection of the public pairs $(P_i, \varphi(P_i))$.

In the table below, we have summarized performance data for most reasonable (in our opinion) parameter sets. Most columns are self-explanatory; the last column shows memory usage during verification.

Performance metrics for various parameter values

# mono-mials in P_i	max degree of P_i	max degree of mono-mials M	parameter r	verification time (sec)	signature size (Kbytes)	public key size (Kbytes)	private key size (Kbytes)	memory usage (Mbytes)
3	3	1	1	0.3	4.3	17.5	1.2	5.7
3	3	2	1	0.3	3.7	12.6	1.6	5.7
3	4	1	1	0.5	4.3	25	1.2	5.8
4	3	1	1	4.1	4.2	38	1.25	7.1
5	3	1	1	6.2	6	46	1.3	8.2
3	3	1	2	2	20	56	5.5	6.3

6.1 Accuracy of the Monte Carlo Method

We have run numerous computer simulations to estimate the probability of a "false positive" result, in particular accepting a forged signature from somebody who knows only some of $\varphi(x_i)$. In our experiments, the difference between the number of positive values of u and u' for a u' obtained by using a wrong private key φ was always above 9%. Recall that the threshold difference for accepting a signature in our scheme is 3%.

"False negative" results (i.e., rejecting a valid signature because the difference was more than 3%) are not as critical as "false positive" results are, but it is still better to avoid them. Increasing the number of trials in the Monte Carlo method obviously reduces the probability of false negative (as well as false positive) results. To quantify this statement, one can use the formula from [1, Theorem 1]:

$$N \geq C \cdot \frac{4 \log(\frac{2}{\delta})}{\epsilon^2} \tag{1}$$

for some constant C. Here δ is the probability that the Monte Carlo method gives a wrong answer, and ϵ is the accuracy we want. (In our case, $\epsilon = 3\% = 0.03$.) Then, N is the number of trials needed to provide the desired accuracy with the desired probability.

According to our computer simulations, in 1000 trials there is one false negative result on average. This suggests that the constant C in our situation is about 0.02.

Therefore, with the recommended 3000 trials the probability of a false negative result will be about 2^{-33}.

Thus, it is not surprising that with 3000 trials, we did not detect any false negative or false positive results in any of our computer simulations.

7 What is the Hard Problem Here?

Recall that the candidate one-way function that we use in our scheme takes a private polynomial automorphism φ as the input and outputs $\varphi(P)$ for a public multivariate polynomial P. Thus, the (allegedly) hard problem here is: given a public pair (or several pairs) $(P, \varphi(P))$, recover φ. We note that such a φ does not have to be unique, although most of the time it is.

The problem of recovering φ from a pair $(P, \varphi(P))$, as well as the relevant decision problem to find out whether or not, for a given pair of polynomials (P, Q), there is an automorphism that takes P to Q, was successfully addressed only for two-variable polynomials [3]. For polynomials in more than two variables the problem is unapproachable at this time, and there are no even partial results in this direction. This is, in part, due to the fact that there is no reasonable description of the group of automorphisms of $\mathbb{Z}[x_1, \ldots, x_n]$ when $n > 2$, so even a "brute force" approach based on enumerating all automorphisms is inapplicable.

Of course, in a cryptographic context one is typically looking not for general theoretical results, but rather for practical ad hoc, often non-deterministic, attacks. The most straightforward non-deterministic attack that comes to mind here is as follows. Recall that monomials in the polynomial P have low degree (bounded by 3). Thus, given a monomial, say, $x_1 x_2 x_3$ in the polynomial P, one can try to replace each x_i by a hypothetical $\varphi(x_i)$ of the form $\sum(c_i x_i + c_{ij} x_i x_j + c_{ijk} x_i x_j x_k)$, with indeterminate coefficients c_i, c_{ij}, c_{ijk}. Given that φ is "sparse", this may yield a number of equations in the indeterminate coefficients that is not huge. However, these equations will include not just linear equations, but also equations of degree 2 and 3 (since $\varphi(x_1 x_2 x_3) = \varphi(x_1)\varphi(x_2)\varphi(x_3)$), and given a large number (hundreds) of unknowns c_i, c_{ij}, c_{ijk}, there is no computationally feasible way known to solve such a system.

In the next Sect. 8, we offer a "linearization" of this attack where all equations become linear, at the expense of making the number of unknowns and the number of equations very large.

8 Linear Algebra Attack

One can attempt to recover the private automorphism φ from the public pairs $(P_i, \varphi(P_i))$ by using linear algebra, more specifically by trying to replace φ by a linear transformation of the linear space of monomials involved in P_i and in the polynomials $\varphi(x_i)$. The latter polynomials are not known to the adversary, but at least the degrees of monomials in those polynomials can be bounded based on the public polynomials $\varphi(P_i)$.

Let us compute the dimension of the linear space of monomials of degree at most 27 in 31 variables. This is because a polynomial P_i has monomials of degree at most 3, and in the polynomials $\varphi(x_i)$ there can be monomials of degree up to 9 (with the suggested parameters), so in $\varphi(P_i)$ there can be monomials of degree up to 27.

By a well-known formula of counting combinations with repetitions, the number of monomials of degree at most 27 in 31 variables is equal to $\binom{57}{30}$ $\approx 1.4 \cdot 10^{16} > 2^{53}$. This is how many variables the attacker will have should (s)he use a linear algebra attack. The number of equations will be about triple of this number.

Solving a system of linear equations with that many variables and equations would require more than $2^{53 \cdot 2.3} \approx 2^{122}$ arithmetic operations, according to our understanding of the state-of-the-art in solving systems of linear equations.

We note that increasing the number of variables in the polynomial algebra will not seriously affect efficiency as long as the bound on the degrees of monomials remains the same. At the same time, the more variables the less feasible the linear algebra attack is.

9   Security Claims

The linear algebra "brute force" attack amounts to solving a system of linear equations (over $\mathbb{Z}$) with about 2^{53} variables and at least as many equations.

There could be ad hoc attacks on the public key aiming at recovering some of the $\varphi(x_i)$, but recovering only some of $\varphi(x_i)$ does not make the probability of passing verification non-negligible, according to our computer simulations.

We have not been able to come up with any meaningful ideas of forgery without getting a hold of the private key.

As for quantum security, we do not make any general claims, just mention that since there are no abelian (semi)groups in play in our scheme, Shor's quantum algorithm [6] cannot be applied to attack our scheme.

10   Conclusion: Advantages and Limitations of the Scheme

10.1   Advantages

1. A novel mathematical idea used for signature verification.
2. Efficiency of the signature verification (about 0.3 s on average).

10.2   Limitations

1. The main limitation is the size of the public key (about 15 Kbytes with suggested parameters).

   The private key (the automorphism φ) is not too small either, about 1.5 Kbytes on average. There is a trade-off between the size of φ and its security. The size of φ can be, in principle, reduced to just a few hundred monomials, but then security becomes a concern since some parts of $\varphi(x_i)$ may be possible to recover more or less by inspection of the public pairs $(P_i, \varphi(P_i))$.

   The signature size is about 4 Kb on average, which is decent but not record-breaking.

2. Another limitation is that using non-deterministic methods, such as a Monte Carlo type method, may result in errors, more specifically in false negative or even false positive results of the signature verification, although so far, with suggested parameters, we did not detect any false negative or false positive results ("False negative" means rejecting a valid signature.)

Appendix

Here we give a proof of Proposition 1.

Proposition 1. Let $h = h(x_1, \ldots, x_n)$ be a polynomial from the set $\mathbb{G}$. Suppose h does not depend on x_k. Let α be the map that takes x_k to $x_k + h - 2x_k \cdot h$ and fixes all other variables. Then:

(a) α defines an automorphism of $B(K)$, the factor algebra of the algebra $\mathbb{Z}[x_1, \ldots, x_n]$ by the ideal generated by all polynomials of the form $(x_i^2 - x_i)$, $i = 1, \ldots, n$. Denote this automorphism also by α.

(b) The group of automorphisms of $B(K)$ is generated by all automorphisms as in part (a) and is isomorphic to the group of permutations of the vertices of the n-dimensional Boolean cube.

(c) For any polynomial P from $\mathbb{Z}[x_1, \ldots, x_n]$, the number of positive values of P on Boolean tuples $(x_1, \ldots, x_n)$ equals that of $\alpha(P)$.

Proof. (a) Let B^n denote the Boolean n-cube, i.e., the n-dimensional cube whose vertices are Boolean n-tuples. The map α leaves the set of vertices of B^n invariant. Indeed, α fixes all x_i except x_k, and it is straightforward to see that if $x_k = 0$, then $\alpha(x_k) = h(x_1, \ldots, x_n)$, and if $x_k = 1$, then $\alpha(x_k) = 1 - h(x_1, \ldots, x_n)$. Since on any Boolean n-tuple $(x_1, \ldots, x_n)$, one has $h(x_1, \ldots, x_n) = 0$ or 1 (see Sect. 3.2), we see that α is a bijection of the set of vertices of B^n onto itself.

Next, observe that for any polynomial h from the set $\mathbb{G}$, one has $h^2 = h$ modulo the ideal generated by all polynomials of the form $(x_i^2 - x_i)$; this easily follows from the inductive procedure of constructing polynomials h, see Sect. 3.2. Therefore, α leaves the ideal generated by all $(x_i^2 - x_i)$ invariant since α takes x_i to $x_i + h - 2x_i \cdot h$, and then $\alpha(x_i^2 - x_i) = (x_i + h - 2x_i \cdot h)^2 - (x_i + h - 2x_i \cdot h) = (x_i^2 - x_i) + (h^2 - h) + 2x_ih - 4x_i^2h - 4x_ih^2 + 4x_i^2h^2 + 2x_ih = (x_i^2 - x_i) + (h^2 - h) + 4h(x_i - x_i^2) + 4h^2(x_i^2 - x_i)$.

(b) Consider the automorphism α again. Fix a particular Boolean n-tuple $(x_1, \ldots, x_n)$. Suppose that $h(x_1, \ldots, x_n) = 1$. Suppose $x_k = 0$ in this tuple. Then α takes this tuple to the tuple where all x_i, except x_k, are the same as before, and $x_k = 1$, i.e., just one of the coordinates in the tuple was flipped. Therefore, an appropriate composition of different α (with different x_k) can map any given Boolean n-tuple to any other Boolean n-tuple.

(c) This follows immediately from the argument in the proof of part (a). More specifically, since the set of vertices of B^n is invariant under α, there is a bijection between the sets of values of P and $\alpha(P)$ on Boolean n-tuples.

References

1. Grigoriev, D., Karpinski, M.: An approximation algorithm for the number of zeroes of arbitrary polynomials over GF[q]. In: Proceedings 32 IEEE Symposium FOCS, pp. 662–669 (1991)
2. Julia code for the BASS. https://drive.google.com/file/d/1z3RWV9SRhSAxbBOtTXu w_HEIZhNFyB3a/view
3. Makar-Limanov, L., Shpilrain, V., Yu, J.-T.: Equivalence of polynomials under automorphisms of $K[x, y]$. J. Pure Appl. Algebra **209**, 71–78 (2007)
4. Moh, T.T.: A public key system with signature and master key functions. Comm. Algebra **27**, 2207–2222 (1999)
5. NIST: Post-Quantum Cryptography: Digital Signature Schemes. https://csrc.nist. gov/csrc/media/Projects/pqc-dig-sig/documents/call-for-proposals-dig-sig-sept-2022.pdf
6. Shor, P.: Polynomial-time algorithms for prime factorization and discrete logarithms on a quantum computer. SIAM J. Comput. **26**, 1484–1509 (1997)
7. Valiant, L.: Complexity of computing the permanent. Theor. Comput. Sci. **8**, 189–201 (1979)

Using Page Offsets for Detecting Control-Flow Anomalies

Engincan Varan[2]([✉])[iD], Khadija Hanifi[1,2][iD], Aysegul Rana Erdemli[2][iD],
Musa Unal[2][iD], Yunus Emre Tat[2][iD], Dilara Tekinoglu[2][iD], Orcun Cetin[2][iD],
Ramin Fuladi[1][iD], and Cemal Yilmaz[2][iD]

[1] Ericsson Research Turkey, Istanbul, Turkey
{khadija.hanifi,ramin.fuladi}@ericsson.com
[2] Sabanci University, Istanbul, Turkey
{evaran,aysegulrana,musa,tatyunus,dilara.tekinoglu,orcun.cetin,
cyilmaz}@sabanciuniv.edu

Abstract. In this study, we introduce an approach that leverages memory-page offsets as an abstraction mechanism for real-time detection of control-flow-affecting cyberattacks. We, in particular, leverage page offsets for a number of reasons. First, being a part of the memory addresses, they can efficiently be monitored by using some of the features directly supported by modern CPUs, such as Intel Processor Trace (intel PT). Second, they are not affected by the presence or absence of address space layout randomization (ASLR). Finally, they can be extracted from the system binaries statically without the need for historical program executions for analysis. At runtime, we monitor the sequences of page offsets being processed, mark the "suspicious" sequences, and raise alarms as needed. In the experiments, which we carried out on real-life, document-based malware instances for Adobe PDF Reader and MS Word, the proposed approach successfully detected the malicious executions with F-measures of 0.9903 and 0.9771, respectively.

Keywords: runtime detection of cybersecurity attacks · control-flow hijacking attacks · malware · dynamic program analysis

1 Introduction

An important class of cyberattacks, including control-flow hijacking attacks and certain types of malware, modifies the control flow of a system, such that a malicious payload is carried out by executing some instructions that, from the end-user's perspective, are not supposed to be executed in the given context. We collectively refer to these attacks as *control-flow affecting attacks*. Due to their flexibility, control-flow affecting attacks are one of the most prevalent types of attacks today [9].

Numerous control-flow integrity schemes [1], such as address space layout randomization (ASLR) [20], stack canaries [6], and non-executable stacks [8], have

M. Manulis et al. (Eds.): SecITC 2023, LNCS 14534, pp. 13–25, 2024.
https://doi.org/10.1007/978-3-031-52947-4_2

been developed to prevent control-flow affecting attacks. At a high level, ASLR randomly arranges a process's address space, so that its parts are placed at different memory addresses each time the process is spawned [17]. This randomization makes it difficult for an attacker to predict the target memory addresses needed to carry out the attack. In contrast, stack canaries aim to detect and prevent stack buffer overflows by employing special tokens that are checked right before every return instruction [29]. If the token values are incorrect, the processes are terminated. Since the tokens are randomly determined each time a process is spawned, it is challenging for an attacker to predict the tokens, preventing the attacker from gaining control of the return pointers and the instruction pointers. Finally, non-executable stacks prohibit the execution of the stack memory region, which forces the attacker to use more sophisticated techniques to place the malicious payload in a non-protected memory region [7].

Despite the widespread deployment of the control-flow integrity schemes in production environments, control-flow affecting attacks remain a reality. One reason is that as these approaches do not monitor the actual control flows of programs, they may fail to detect the potentially suspicious system behavior.

To alleviate these issues, many dynamic program analysis-based approaches have been proposed [10, 27, 30]. These approaches monitor the memory addresses, to which the control is transferred during the executions, so that the suspicious transfers and/or the transfers that are previously known to be malicious can be detected. One important downside of these approaches, however, is that they generally do not provide an efficient and effective means of taking ASLR into account. Indeed, some of these approaches completely ignore ASLR and use the actual memory addresses for the analysis [27, 30].

Given that the memory addresses would change from one execution to another in the presence of ASLR and that ASLR is widely deployed in the field, the practicality of these approaches is significantly hindered. Other approaches, namely the *control-flow integrity* (CFI) approaches, check the memory addresses encountered at runtime to see if they follow the statically determined control-flow graph (CFG) of the program [10]. Since these approaches map the memory addresses to the CFG nodes at runtime, they are not affected by the presence (or the absence) of ASLR. However, to reliably construct the CFGs, many of the CFI approaches require to have the source code and/or the binaries with the debug information, which is often not available for the commercial software systems. Furthermore, regardless of how the CFGs are constructed, the CFI approaches typically impose excessive runtime overheads as the CFGs are to be constructed, the memory addresses are required to be dynamically mapped to the CFG nodes, and the paths taken need to be determined at runtime. One commonly employed approach to reduce the overhead is to use a looser notion of the control-flow integrity. It is, however, known that looser notions of control-flow integrity are typically susceptible to certain types of control-flow affecting attacks [10].

In this work we propose an ASLR-agnostic abstraction mechanism for program executions, along with an accompanying anomaly-based approach to detect control-flow affecting attacks, including the zero-day attacks, at runtime. The proposed abstraction mechanism leverages the page offsets, rather than the actual memory addresses, to model the control flows. Since ASLR only modifies the start addresses of memory pages but leaves the offsets within each page intact, our solution is not affected by the presence or absence of ASLR.

At a high level, our approach works by analyzing the sequences of page offsets encountered at runtime to detect the presence of the "suspicious" sequences, i.e., those that never appear in benign executions. If suspicious sequences are detected, an alarm is raised, allowing the countermeasures, which are beyond the scope of this work, to be taken in time.

We evaluated the proposed approach by using some real-life instances of document-based malware. In particular, we experimented with a total of 1450 benign and 1918 malicious (i.e., infected) PDF and MS Word documents. The proposed approach correctly determined the malicious documents with F-measures of 0.9903 and 0.9771 for PDF and MS Word, respectively.

The remainder of the paper is organized as follows: Sect. 2 introduces the proposed approach; Sect. 3 presents the empirical studies carried out and analyzes the results obtained; Sect. 4 discusses related work; and Sect. 5 concludes with potential future work ideas.

2   Approach

The proposed approach leverages the page offsets to detect "suspicious" paths taken by the executions. Memory management in computer systems typically operates at the level of memory pages, which are fixed-size contiguous blocks of memory, representing the smallest unit of interest from the perspective of memory management. In particular, the processes' memory spaces are divided into memory pages that can individually be loaded into or swapped from the physical memory. In the presence of ASLR, although the start addresses of the pages are randomized, the page offsets (i.e., the relative addresses) within the pages remain intact. Consequently, the page offsets, which are a part of the actual memory addresses, are not affected by the presence or absence of ASLR.

We, in particular, monitor a system to obtain the memory addresses, thus the page offsets, processed by the system at runtime (Fig. 1). One way to obtain these memory addresses is through software instrumentation, which requires to

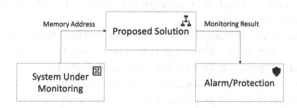

Fig. 1. A high-level view of the proposed approach.

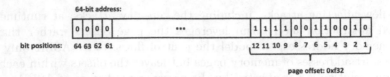

Fig. 2. For a general-purpose computing platform, which uses memory pages of size 4 KB, the right-most 12 bits of the address typically constitute the page offset.

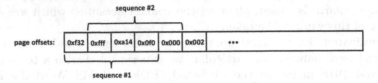

Fig. 3. An example scenario where sliding windows of size 4 with a lag of 1 are used with the page offsets.

instrument the source code and/or the binaries of the systems. To significantly reduce the runtime overheads, we, on the other hand, push the majority of the monitoring tasks onto the hardware, by using some of the features directly supported by the CPU, namely Intel Processor Trace (Intel PT) [15].

At a very high level, Intel PT is an extension of the x64 architecture, allowing an efficient tracing of the executions. More specifically, every trace is represented in the form of a stream of packages, each of which captures information about various aspects of the execution, including the branch addresses taken and the clock cycles elapsed. Consequently, the exact sequence of all the instructions executed, thus the exact path taken, by a process can reliably be reconstructed for analysis. Furthermore, as the monitoring tasks are carried out by the CPU and the traces are collected by bypassing the cache hierarchy, the runtime overheads are reduced to the extent possible. The software developer's manual published by Intel indicates that collecting the PT traces generally impose less than 5% runtime overhead. Intel PT has, indeed, been extensively used for debugging and profiling [18]. We, however, use them to determine the memory addresses, to which the control is transferred at runtime by the branch instructions. Note further that, although we use an Intel-specific feature to monitor the executions in this work, the same (or similar) features are also supported by other general-purpose CPUs, such as AMD [5]. Consequently, the proposed approach is readily applicable to other platforms.

From each memory address observed, we first extract the page offset (Fig. 2). Page offsets are a part of the actual memory addresses, but the way they need to be extracted may depend on the underlying hardware. For example, in today's general-purpose computing platforms, the memory pages are typically of size 4 KB each and the page offsets are stored in the rightmost 12 bits of the addresses (i.e., 2^{12} bytes is 4 KB).

We then analyze the sequences of page offsets encountered to determine the presence of "suspicious" sequences at runtime (Fig. 3). For this work, we define a *suspicious sequence* as a sequence of page offsets, which has not been observed in any of the historically known benign executions, i.e., the ones that are known not to be affected by any attack.

To this end, we use a sliding window-based approach with two hyperparameters, namely *window size* and *lag*. Figure 3 illustrates an example where sliding windows of size 4 with a lag of 1 are used. That is, the first 4 page offsets encountered at runtime constitute the first window and the window is shifted to right by one offset to form the subsequent window.

In the training phase, we use a collection of benign executions as the training set (Fig. 4). For each execution, the memory addresses are captured, the page offsets are extracted, and the sliding windows are formed for the given values of hyperparameters. We then express all the distinct sequences of page offsets observed in the training set as a hash set, which will simply serve as the basis of the anomaly detection model used in the deployment phase.

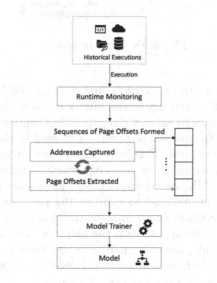

Fig. 4. Training phase.

In the deployment phase (Fig. 5), the sliding windows of page offsets are computed in exactly the same manner with the training phase. For each window encountered, we check to see if the same window is observed in the training set. If not, the window is marked as *suspicious*. In the remainder of the document, these decisions, which are made individually for each window of offsets, will be referred to as *first-level decisions*.

Rather than making binary decisions (e.g., suspicious or not), we could have made probabilistic decisions by, for example, computing the likelihood of observ-

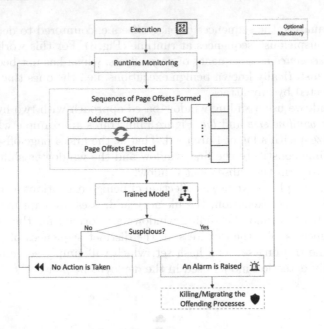

Fig. 5. Deployment phase.

ing a page offset given a window of preceding page offsets. We, however, deliberately opt to evaluate the accuracy of the binary decisions in this work, because, as a feature work, we plan to extract the page-offset sequences from the binaries in a static manner. Note that the page offsets present in the binaries do not get changed during the executions. This helps us cope with the difficulties of having a representative set of samples for training, which is a common issue with all the machine learning (ML)-based approaches. This issue is, indeed, magnified when the ML models are trained to capture the program behavior as finding representative set of program executions for training is quite challenging.

One way to raise an alarm is to emit the alarm as soon as the first suspicious window is observed. This, however, may increase false positive rates [24]. An alternative approach, which we employ in this work, is to analyze the sequences of first-level decisions made over a period of time before raising the alarm. This is because a number of suspicious windows encountered during a brief period of time is typically a better sign for the presence of an attack, compared to a single, isolated suspicious window [24].

We, therefore, analyze the first-level decisions, i.e., the suspicious or not suspicious decisions that are made on a per window of page offsets, by again using a sliding window-based approach before raising an alarm.

To this end, we define three hyperparameters, namely *window size*, *lag*, and *threshold*. The first two parameters are, indeed, semantically similar to the hyperparameters used for the first-level decisions, but they are applied to the sequences of first-level decisions, rather the sequences of page offsets. The threshold parameter, on the other hand, is defined as the cutoff ratio of the "suspicious" first-level decisions to the total number of first-level decisions made in a window. In particular, if the ratio is above the threshold, then an alarm is raised.

When an alarm is raised, preventive and protective actions can be taken against the potential attacks (Fig. 1). Such actions include, but are not limited to, killing the offending processes, migrating the offending processes to a different machine, closely monitoring the offending processes with the goal of collecting further information about a potential attack, disconnecting the offending machines from the network, taking a snapshot of the system for post-mortem analysis or as a backup, and reporting the issue to the registered stakeholders. These countermeasures (except for raising an alarm) are, however, beyond the scope of this work.

3 Experiments

To evaluate the proposed approach, we have carried out a series of experiments.

3.1 Subjects

In these experiments, we used the Intel PT traces collected for the real-world, document-based malware instances embedded in PDF and MS Words documents. More specifically, we experimented with 200 benign and 379 malicious PDF documents and 1250 benign and 1539 malicious MS Word documents. The traces for the documents were obtained from Adobe PDF Reader version 9.3 and MS Word version 2010, which ran on the same platform consisted of an Intel $i7 - 6700K$ CPU and an Nvidia 1080-Ti GPU, running a 64-bit Windows operating system. We, indeed, utilized the same traces used in [30].

3.2 Operational Framework

As the platform used in the experiments utilized memory pages of size 4 KB where the page offsets were stored in the right-most 12 bits of the addresses, we extracted the aforementioned bits from the memory addresses and used them as the page offsets. Furthermore, since the control-flow affecting attacks typically affect the conditional branches [30], we filtered out all the remaining types of addresses in the traces before the windows of page offsets were computed.

For the first-level decisions, we used sliding windows of size 4 with a lag of 1 on the sequence of page offsets encountered. For finalizing the decisions, i.e., for deciding whether an alarm should be emitted or not, we used sliding windows of size 3000 with a lag of 1 on the first-level decisions. Furthermore, the threshold parameter was set to 0.3, i.e., an alarm was emitted when 30% or more of the first-level decisions in a window of 3000 decisions indicated potentially suspicious sequences of page offsets.

Note that optimizing the settings of these hyperparameters is beyond the scope of this work. Our ultimate goal in this work is rather to demonstrate that there is at least one set of settings for these hyperparameters, which support the claims of the paper. To determine the settings we used in the experiments, we, indeed, carried out small-scale experiments where we systematically varied the hyperparameters until we encountered a tipping point, which did not necessarily represented a global optimum.

3.3 Evaluation Framework

In the experiments, we created separate models for the PDF and MS Word documents. In particular, we randomly created 10 different training and test set pairs for each subject application. In each pair, while the test set consisted of all the malicious traces and 10% of the benign traces, the training set consisted of the remaining 90% of the benign traces.

For each training set, we trained a model, i.e., figured out the collection of subsequences of page offsets appearing in the benign traces included in the training set, and used the test set to evaluate the proposed approach. In particular, if an alarm indicating the presence of a potential malware was emitted for a given trace, we marked the trace as malicious. Otherwise, that is when no alarm was raised, we marked the trace as benign. We then computed the accuracy as well as the precision, recall, and F-measure metrics for both malicious and benign traces. The accuracy of the approach is computed as the ratio of the correctly predicted traces. The precision of detecting malicious traces is then computed as the ratio of correctly predicted malicious traces over all traces predicted as malicious. And, the recall is computed as the ratio of correctly predicted malicious traces over all truly malicious traces. Finally, F-measure is computed by giving equal importance to both precision and recall. Furthermore, the evaluation metrics for predicting the benign traces are also computed in the same manner. Note that all these metrics assume a value between 0 and 1, inclusive. The higher the value, the better the proposed approach is.

Table 1. Results obtained in the experiments.

		PDF Documents	MS Word Documents
accuracy		98.22%	95.71%
malicious	F1-score	0.9903	0.9771
	precision	0.9979	0.9894
	recall	0.9829	0.9651
benign	F1-score	0.8859	0.6548
	precision	0.8129	0.5519
	recall	0.9735	0.805

3.4   Results and Discussions

All told, we created an evaluated 20 models by using a total of 1450 benign and 1918 malicious executions. Table 1 presents the results we obtained.

We first observed that the proposed approach detected the malicious documents with high F-measures. More specifically, the F-measures for successfully detecting the malicious documents were 0.9903 and 0.9771 for PDF and MS Word, respectively (Table 1).

We next observed that the results obtained for the PDF documents were generally better than those obtained for the MS Word documents (Table 1). This was also reflected on the F-measures of detecting the benign documents.

We believe that this was mainly due to the significantly fewer samples (i.e., documents) we had for training the model for MS Word. In particular, while we had 1125 benign documents for training the PDF model, we had only 180 documents for training the MS Word model. As we have already discussed, this is, in fact, a common issue with any statistical- and machine learning-based approaches in that the quality of the models typically depends on both the size and the representativeness of the data used for training/analysis. Indeed, finding a representative set of program executions for training is quite challenging due to the sheer sizes of the input spaces that area present even for simple software systems.

These results together with our choice of the first-level hyperparameter settings, therefore, further justify the importance of this work as a preliminary work towards having a more reliable approach by reducing the need for finding representative samples of program executions. More specifically, since we mark any window of page offsets, which are not seen in the training set, as suspicious in this work and since the runtime page offsets do not differ from the page offsets present in the system binaries, a large fraction of the benign sequences of page offsets can directly be extracted from the binaries statically without requiring any program executions. This is, indeed, the hypothesis that we plan to evaluate as a future work.

The sizes of the models used in the experiments, i.e., those of the hash sets used for storing the sequences of page offsets observed in the training sets, were 30 and 25 MB for PDF Reader and MS Word, on average. Note that these sizes include the redundant spaces that need to be maintained to keep the load factors of the hash sets less than 0.5. Furthermore, we report the sizes without any attempt to minimize them by, for example, using compression.

Note, however, that the size of a model depends on the window size to be used for the first-level decisions as the maximum number of sequences, in theory, grows exponentially with the window size. However, as not all of these sequences may be valid, only a fraction of them typically need to be stored in the models. For example, our models included only a $4.19e-07\%$ (1.18 million out of 4096^4) and $3.5e-07\%$ ($984,276$ out of 4096^4) of all possible sequences page offsets of size 4, on average, for the PDF and MS Word applications, respectively. From this perspective, reducing the window sizes for the first-level decisions is important, which was, indeed, the case in our experiments where we used windows of size

4. If, however, longer sequences need to be used, then one way to cope with it could be to make statistical decisions based on the embeddings created for the sequences by using deep learning models, such as LSTMs [11].

4 Related Work

At a very high level, program analysis approaches are classified into two primary groups: static analysis and dynamic analysis. Static analysis approaches operate by analyzing the source code and/or binaries of the applications without ever executing them. These approaches are widely used by the third-party analysis tools to detect vulnerabilities and defects in the implementations [4]. However, static analysis has its own limitations as not all the dynamic behavior of the application under analysis can statically be determined, typically resulting in high false positive rates [2]. Consequently, some research specifically focus on reducing the false positive rates of static analyzers [12,25,33]. A comprehensive analysis presented in [14] investigates the effectiveness of these studies, offering valuable insights, lessons, and guidelines for evaluating false alarm detectors.

In contrast, dynamic program analysis involves executing the programs, collecting information from inside the executions, and analyzing the information collected to further improve the quality of the systems [22,34]. Consequently, while the static analysis approaches reason about what might happen during the executions, the dynamic analysis approaches focus on what has actually happened in the executions.

To overcome the limitations of static and dynamic analysis, some studies focus on developing hybrid approaches, which combine both types of analyses [16,21,28,35]. The ultimate goal of such an analysis is to detect a wider range of issues with the systems, while reducing the false positive rates, compared to using either of the analysis approaches in isolation. Consequently, hybrid approaches include leveraging static analysis results to guide dynamic analysis, using dynamic analysis to validate and refine the static analysis results, and integrating the results of both types of analyses to provide more detailed insights and recommendations for quality improvements.

Other approaches for improving the security of the software systems, such as malware detectors, employ machine learning (ML) and/or statistics to train models capturing the normal behaviors of the systems and/or the previously known malicious behaviors [3,13,19,26,31]. The observed system behaviors are then compared to these models to identify the similarities (with the malicious behavior models, for example) and/or the deviations (from the normal behavior models, for example). The fundamental assumption behind these approaches is that there are repeatable and identifiable patterns in program executions, and deviations from these patterns and/or similarities to them is typically an indicative of a potentially malicious behavior [23,32]. One downside of these approach, however, is that they require to have a representative set of training data, so that the models being trained could capture the actual patterns, rather than the superficial ones. Indeed, finding representative samples of program executions is quite challenging due to the sheer volume of the input spaces even for simple software systems.

In this work, we used page offsets for detecting the presence of control flow-affecting attacks at runtime, which cause suspicious deviations in the control flows of systems. From this perspective, the proposed approach, as it is presented in this work, can be classified as a dynamic analysis approach employing a simple ML/statistical model. However, the reason behind our choice of using the page offsets as an abstraction mechanism as well as the choice of the hyperparameter values we used for the first-level decisions in the experiments, was to demonstrate the potentials of utilizing the proposed abstraction mechanism in a hybrid approach employing ML/statistical models by extracting the page offsets statically from the binaries, reducing the need of having representative set of historical program executions.

5 Conclusion

In this paper, we presented an approach, which leverages sequences of page offsets encountered at runtime, to detect the presence of control-flow affecting attacks. We used page offsets, which are embedded in the actual memory addresses, as an abstraction mechanism for three main reasons. First, they can efficiently be collected by using some of the features that are directly supported by modern CPUs, such as Intel PT. Second, they are not affected by the presence or absence of ASLR. Finally, they can be extracted from the binaries statically without the need for historical program executions for analysis.

The results of the empirical studies strongly support our basic hypothesis that sequences of page offsets can, indeed, be used to distinguish malicious executions (e.g., malicious paths taken) from benign executions. We have arrived at this conclusion by observing that the proposed approach with the same hyperparameter settings, detected the malicious PDF and MS Word documents with F-measures of 0.9903 and 0.9771, respectively.

One avenue for future research is to develop hybrid approaches where the benign sequences of page offsets can be learned both via static analysis of the binaries and via dynamic analysis of the historical executions. Another avenue is to evaluate the performance of other anomaly detection models, including LSTMs [11], by conducting comparative studies. Yet another avenue is to apply the approach to a wide range of control-flow affecting attacks.

References

1. Abadi, M., Budiu, M., Erlingsson, U., Ligatti, J.: Control-flow integrity principles, implementations, and applications. ACM Trans. Inf. Syst. Secur. (TISSEC) 13(1), 1–40 (2009)
2. Amankwah, R., Chen, J., Song, H., Kudjo, P.K.: Bug detection in Java code: an extensive evaluation of static analysis tools using Juliet test suites. Softw. Pract. Experience 53(5), 1125–1143 (2023)

3. Arp, D., et al.: Dos and don'ts of machine learning in computer security. In: 31st USENIX Security Symposium (USENIX Security 2022), pp. 3971–3988 (2022)
4. Bardas, A.G., et al.: Static code analysis. J. Inf. Syst. Oper. Manag. 4(2), 99–107 (2010)
5. Costan, V., Devadas, S.: Intel SGX explained. Cryptology ePrint Archive (2016)
6. Cowan, C., et al.: StackGuard: automatic adaptive detection and prevention of buffer-overflow attacks. In: USENIX Security Symposium, San Antonio, TX, vol. 98, pp. 63–78 (1998)
7. De Groef, W., Nikiforakis, N., Younan, Y., Piessens, F.: JITSec: just-in-time security for code injection attacks. In: Benelux Workshop on Information and System Security (WISSEC 2010), Nijmegen, The Netherlands (2010)
8. Designer, S.: Getting around non-executable stack (and fix) (1997). http://ouah.bsdjeunz.org/solarretlibc.html
9. Dessouky, G., et al.: LO-FAT: low-overhead control flow attestation in hardware. In: Proceedings of the 54th Annual Design Automation Conference, pp. 1–6 (2017)
10. Göktas, E., Athanasopoulos, E., Bos, H., Portokalidis, G.: Out of control: overcoming control-flow integrity. In: 2014 IEEE Symposium on Security and Privacy, pp. 575–589. IEEE (2014)
11. Goodfellow, I., Bengio, Y., Courville, A.: Deep Learning. MIT Press (2016). http://www.deeplearningbook.org
12. Hanam, Q., Tan, L., Holmes, R., Lam, P.: Finding patterns in static analysis alerts: improving actionable alert ranking. In: Proceedings of the 11th Working Conference on Mining Software Repositories, pp. 152–161 (2014)
13. Jha, A., Reddy, C.K.: CodeAttack: code-based adversarial attacks for pre-trained programming language models. arXiv preprint arXiv:2206.00052 (2022)
14. Kang, H.J., Aw, K.L., Lo, D.: Detecting false alarms from automatic static analysis tools: how far are we? In: Proceedings of the 44th International Conference on Software Engineering, pp. 698–709 (2022)
15. Kleen, A., Strong, B.: Intel processor trace on Linux. Tracing Summit 2015 (2015)
16. Lacombe, G., Féliot, D., Boespflug, E., Potet, M.L.: Combining static analysis and dynamic symbolic execution in a toolchain to detect fault injection vulnerabilities. J. Cryptographic Eng. 1–18 (2023)
17. Lee, B., Lu, L., Wang, T., Kim, T., Lee, W.: From zygote to morula: fortifying weakened ASLR on Android. In: 2014 IEEE Symposium on Security and Privacy, pp. 424–439. IEEE (2014)
18. Liu, Y., Shi, P., Wang, X., Chen, H., Zang, B., Guan, H.: Transparent and efficient CFI enforcement with intel processor trace. In: 2017 IEEE International Symposium on High Performance Computer Architecture (HPCA), pp. 529–540. IEEE (2017)
19. Marcelli, A., Graziano, M., Ugarte-Pedrero, X., Fratantonio, Y., Mansouri, M., Balzarotti, D.: How machine learning is solving the binary function similarity problem. In: 31st USENIX Security Symposium (USENIX Security 2022), pp. 2099–2116 (2022)
20. Marco-Gisbert, H., Ripoll Ripoll, I.: Address space layout randomization next generation. Appl. Sci. 9(14), 2928 (2019)
21. Navas, J.A., Gehani, A.: OCCAM-v2: combining static and dynamic analysis for effective and efficient whole-program specialization. Commun. ACM 66(4), 40–47 (2023)
22. Or-Meir, O., Nissim, N., Elovici, Y., Rokach, L.: Dynamic malware analysis in the modern era-a state of the art survey. ACM Compu. Surv. (CSUR) 52(5), 1–48 (2019)

23. Ozcelik, B., Yilmaz, C.: Seer: a lightweight online failure prediction approach. IEEE Trans. Softw. Eng. **42**(1), 26–46 (2015)
24. Ozcelik, B., Yilmaz, C.: Seer: a lightweight online failure prediction approach. In: 2017 IEEE 41st Annual Computer Software and Applications Conference (COMPSAC), vol. 1, pp. 624–625 (2017). https://doi.org/10.1109/COMPSAC.2017.210
25. Shen, H., Fang, J., Zhao, J.: EFindBugs: effective error ranking for findbugs. In: 2011 Fourth IEEE International Conference on Software Testing, Verification and Validation, pp. 299–308. IEEE (2011)
26. Srinivasan, R., Subalalitha, C.: Sentimental analysis from imbalanced code-mixed data using machine learning approaches. Distrib. Parallel Databases 1–16 (2021)
27. Tian, D., Ying, Q., Jia, X., Ma, R., Hu, C., Liu, W.: MDCHD: a novel malware detection method in cloud using hardware trace and deep learning. Comput. Netw. **198**, 108394 (2021)
28. Tzermias, Z., Sykiotakis, G., Polychronakis, M., Markatos, E.P.: Combining static and dynamic analysis for the detection of malicious documents. In: Proceedings of the Fourth European Workshop on System Security, pp. 1–6 (2011)
29. Wagle, P., Cowan, C., et al.: StackGuard: simple stack smash protection for GCC. In: Proceedings of the GCC Developers Summit, vol. 1 (2003)
30. Yagemann, C., Sultana, S., Chen, L., Lee, W.: *Barnum*: detecting document malware via control flow anomalies in hardware traces. In: Lin, Z., Papamanthou, C., Polychronakis, M. (eds.) ISC 2019. LNCS, vol. 11723, pp. 341–359. Springer, Cham (2019). https://doi.org/10.1007/978-3-030-30215-3_17
31. Yerima, S.Y., Alzaylaee, M.K., Sezer, S.: Machine learning-based dynamic analysis of android apps with improved code coverage. EURASIP J. Inf. Secur. **2019**(1), 1–24 (2019)
32. Yilmaz, C., Porter, A.: Combining hardware and software instrumentation to classify program executions. In: Proceedings of the Eighteenth ACM SIGSOFT International Symposium on Foundations of Software Engineering, pp. 67–76 (2010)
33. Yüksel, U., Sözer, H.: Automated classification of static code analysis alerts: a case study. In: 2013 IEEE International Conference on Software Maintenance, pp. 532–535. IEEE (2013)
34. Zaazaa, O., El Bakkali, H.: Dynamic vulnerability detection approaches and tools: state of the art. In: 2020 Fourth International Conference on Intelligent Computing in Data Sciences (ICDS), pp. 1–6. IEEE (2020)
35. Zhauniarovich, Y., Ahmad, M., Gadyatskaya, O., Crispo, B., Massacci, F.: StaDynA: addressing the problem of dynamic code updates in the security Analysis of android applications. In: Proceedings of the 5th ACM Conference on Data and Application Security and Privacy, pp. 37–48 (2015)

Elementary Remarks on Some Quadratic Based Identity Based Encryption Schemes

Paul Cotan[1,2] and George Teşeleanu[1,2(✉)]

[1] Advanced Technologies Institute, 10 Dinu Vintilă, Bucharest, Romania
{paul.cotan,tgeorge}@dcti.ro
[2] Simion Stoilow Institute of Mathematics of the Romanian Academy,
21 Calea Grivitei, Bucharest, Romania

Abstract. In the design of an identity-based encryption (IBE) scheme, the primary security assumptions center around quadratic residues, bilinear mappings, and lattices. Among these approaches, one of the most intriguing is introduced by Clifford Cocks and is based on quadratic residues. However, this scheme has a significant drawback: a large ciphertext to plaintext ratio. A different approach is taken by Zhao *et al.*, who design an IBE still based on quadratic residues, but with an encryption process reminiscent of the Goldwasser-Micali cryptosystem. In the following pages, we will introduce an elementary method to accelerate Cocks' encryption process and adapt a space-efficient encryption technique for both Cocks' and Zhao *et al.*'s cryptosystems.

Keywords: identity based encryption · quadratic residues · optimizations

1 Introduction

The development of identity based encryption (IBE) began in 1984 when Shamir formulated its basic principles in [23]. However, he left the practical construction of such a scheme as an open problem. In 2001, the first IBE schemes were proposed by Boneh and Franklin [6], who used bilinear mappings, and by Cocks [11], who utilized quadratic residues, respectively.

The Cocks' encryption scheme processes messages on a bit-by-bit basis, where each encrypted bit is represented as a pair of two integers. Decryption involves calculating the Jacobi symbol of one of the two integers in each pair. Therefore, Cocks' IBE has a large ciphertext to plaintext ratio, and thus is efficient only for small messages. A space-efficient IBE based on quadratic residues was introduced in [7]. Unfortunately, their solution is based on a quartic deterministic time-complexity algorithm, and thus is infeasible to use in practice. To address this issue, Jhanwar and Barua [4,18] introduced an efficient probabilistic algorithm. However, their scheme, along with several other variations [13,14], have been shown to be insecure [22]. A different approach was taken in [24]. Their proposal

© The Author(s), under exclusive license to Springer Nature Switzerland AG 2024
M. Manulis et al. (Eds.): SecITC 2023, LNCS 14534, pp. 26–34, 2024.
https://doi.org/10.1007/978-3-031-52947-4_3

resembles the Goldwasser-Micali [16] cryptosystem. Their solution also has a large ciphertext to plaintext ratio: to encrypt a bit we need four integers.

Our paper focuses on Cocks' and Zhao *et al.*'s IBE schemes [11,24]. In the first part of the paper we introduce a different method for generating the special random numbers t required by Cocks' encryption algorithm. The generation method bears similarity to the Goldwasser-Micali encryption, with the primary distinction being the distribution of one of the public parameters. While this method may seem obvious, it is worth noting that all previous papers dealing with Cocks' IBE have relied on a trial-and-error method based on Jacobi symbols to generate the t values. Therefore, our method lowers the complexity of generating t values from at least $\mathcal{O}(M(2\lambda)\log 2\lambda)$ to $\mathcal{O}(M(2\lambda))$, where λ is a security parameter and $M(\cdot)$ denotes the complexity of a multiplication.

In the second part of our work, we use some elementary remarks to reduce the bandwith requirements for both Cocks' and Zhao *et al.*'s IBE schemes with 2 and 4 bits per ciphertext, respectively. The changes made to achieve this improvement, do not introduce any additional overhead to the encryption process. It is worth noting that both IBEs have been recommended for symmetric key encapsulation. Consequently, the additional bits can serve various purposes, such as authenticating the encapsulation package. Since our changes involve only comparison operators and differences, coupled with our reduced bit usage per encapsulation, we believe that our proposal is preferable when compared to the original schemes.

Structure of the Paper. In Sect. 2, we introduce the fundamental notions used throughout the paper. In Sect. 3, we present a computationally efficient variant of Cocks' IBE. Section 4 discusses two space-efficient IBEs. Finally, we conclude in Sect. 5.

2   Preliminaries

Notations. Throughout the paper, λ denotes a security parameter. The action of selecting a random element x from a sample space X is denoted by $x \xleftarrow{\$} X$, while $x \leftarrow y$ represents the assignment of value y to variable x.

The Jacobi symbol of an integer a modulo an integer n will be represented by $J_n(a)$. We consider the sets QR_n and QNR_n of quadratic and, respectively, non-quadratic residues modulo an integer n. J_n denotes the sets of integers modulo n with Jacobi symbol 1.

2.1   Identity-Based Encryption

An IBE scheme [5] comprises four probabilistic polynomial-time (PPT) algorithms, denoted as *Setup*, *KeyGen*, *Enc*, and *Dec*. The first algorithm takes the security parameter as input and produces the master secret key along with the system's public parameters as output. The subsequent algorithm takes an identity id, the master secret key, the public parameters as input, and yields a private key associated with id as output. The third algorithm, labeled Enc, accepts a message m, an identity id, and the public parameters as input, encrypting m using a key derived from id to produce the ciphertext c. The final algorithm, Dec, decrypts the ciphertext c using the private key associated with id, yielding the original message m.

Cocks' IBE Scheme. The first IBE based on the QR assumption[1] was introduced in [11]. The original scheme was defined for primes of type $p \equiv q \equiv 3 \bmod 4$. Later on, this scheme was generalized in [19] to any prime numbers p and q. We further present the IBE scheme provided in [19].

$Setup(\lambda)$: Given a security parameter λ, generate two primes $p, q > 2^\lambda$ and compute their product $n = pq$. Randomly generate an integer $u \in J_n \setminus QR_n$. The public parameters are $pp = \{n, u, H\}$, where $H : \{0, 1\}^* \to J_n$ is a cryptographic hash function. The master secret key is $msk = \{p, q\}$.

$KeyGen(pp, msk, id)$: Let $R = H(id)$. If $R \in QR_n$, then compute $r \equiv R^{1/2} \bmod n$. Otherwise, computes $r = (uR)^{1/2} \bmod n$. The private key is r.

$Enc(pp, id, m)$: On inputting pp, an identity id and a message $m \in \{-1, 1\}$, compute the hash value $R = H(id)$ and randomly choose two values $t_1, t_2 \xleftarrow{\$} \mathbb{Z}_n$ such that $J_n(t_1) = J_n(t_2) = m$. Also, calculate

$$c_1 = t_1 + \frac{R}{t_1} \bmod n \quad \text{and} \quad c_2 = t_2 + \frac{uR}{t_2} \bmod n.$$

Return the ciphertext $C = (c_1, c_2)$.

$Dec(pp, r, C)$: On input pp, a secret key r and a ciphertext C, compute

$$m = \begin{cases} J_n(c_1 + 2r) & \text{if } r^2 \equiv H(id) \bmod n; \\ J_n(c_2 + 2r) & \text{otherwise.} \end{cases}$$

Remark 1. Cocks' IBE scheme does not provide anonymity [7]. As a result, several techniques have been introduced to address this issue [2, 19–21]. Among these, the most efficient method is the one described in [20], which is a simplified version of the approach presented in [19].

Zhao *et al.*'s IBE Scheme. An alternative IBE scheme relying on the QR assumption was presented in [24]. Specifically, the scheme operates with polynomials modulo n, where the primes p and q are selected such that $p \equiv -q \bmod 4$. This scheme was subsequently extended and generalized in [12] to accommodate arbitrary values of p and q. We further provide the scheme's description as given in [12].

$Setup(\lambda)$: Given a security parameter λ, generate two primes $p, q > 2^\lambda$ and compute their product $n = pq$. Randomly generate two integers $u, y \in \mathbb{Z}_n$ such that $J_p(u) = J_q(u) = -1$ and $J_p(y) = -J_q(y)$. The public parameters are $pp = \{n, u, y, H\}$, where $H : \{0, 1\}^* \to J_n$ is a cryptographic hash function. The master secret key is $msk = \{p, q\}$.

---

[1] This assumption states that an adversary trying to decide if a random element is from $J_n \setminus QR_n$ or QR_n has a negligible success probability.

KeyGen(pp, msk, id): Let $R = H(id)$. If $R \in QR_n$, then compute $r \equiv R^{1/2}$ mod n. Otherwise, computes $r = (uR)^{1/2}$ mod n. The private key is r.

Enc(pp, id, m): On inputting pp, an identity id and a message $m \in \{0,1\}$, compute the hash value $R = H(id)$ and randomly choose two polynomials $f(x), \overline{f}(x)$ of degree 1 from $\mathbb{Z}_n[x]$. Also, calculate

$$g(x) = f(x)^2 \bmod (x^2 - R) \quad \text{and} \quad \overline{g}(x) = \overline{f}(x)^2 \bmod (x^2 - uR).$$

Return the ciphertext $C = (y^m \cdot g(x), y^m \cdot \overline{g}(x))$.

Dec(pp, r, C): On input pp, a secret key r and a ciphertext $C = (c(x), \overline{c}(x))$, compute

$$m' = \begin{cases} J_n(c(r)) & \text{if } r^2 \equiv H(id) \bmod n; \\ J_n(\overline{c}(r)) & \text{otherwise.} \end{cases}$$

Remark 2. Although Zhao *et al.*'s IBE scheme is not anonymous [24], it can be made so by using the anonymization technique described in [9,10].

3   Computational Efficient IBE

In this section, we present an efficient method for generating the random t values used in Cocks' IBE. Although the method employed is elementary, it is worth noting that all the papers built upon Cocks' work, generate t values until the Jacobi symbol reaches the desired value.

3.1   Cocks' IBE Efficient Version

We further present the proposed encryption algorithm. To make the proposed scheme work, we incorporate a public element $e \in \mathbb{Z}_n \setminus J_n$ into the setup algorithm. Note that the t values can be interpreted as a Goldwasser-Micali ciphertext [16].

Enc(pp, id, m): On inputting pp, an identity id and a message $m \in \{-1, 1\}$, compute the hash value $R = H(id)$ and randomly choose two values $x_1, x_2 \xleftarrow{\$} \mathbb{Z}_n$. Set $t_i \equiv e^{(1-m)/2} x_i^2 \bmod n$ for $i \in \{1, 2\}$. Also, calculate

$$c_1 = t_1 + \frac{R}{t_1} \bmod n \quad \text{and} \quad c_2 = t_2 + \frac{uR}{t_2} \bmod n.$$

Return the ciphertext $C = (c_1, c_2)$.

3.2   Performance Analysis

To determine the efficiency of our proposal, we consider the following complexities for μ-bit integers

- Multiplication [17]: $M(\mu) = \mathcal{O}(\mu \log \mu)$,
- Jacobi symbol [8]: $\mathcal{O}(M(\mu) \log \mu)$.

Without loss of generality, we further assume that $p \bmod 8 \leq q \bmod 8$. To further accelerate the encryption process, we can select e as follows

$$
e = \begin{cases}
-1 & p \equiv -q \bmod 4, \\
2 & p \equiv 1 \bmod 8 \text{ and } q \equiv 5 \bmod 8, \\
2 & p \equiv 3 \bmod 8 \text{ and } q \equiv 7 \bmod 8, \\
\bar{e} & \text{otherwise,}
\end{cases}
$$

where $\bar{e}$ is random element from $\mathbb{Z}_n \setminus J_n$. Therefore, generating t values comes down to

$$
t = \begin{cases}
n - x^2 & e = -1, \\
x^2 + x^2 & e = 2, \\
\bar{e}x^2 & \text{otherwise.}
\end{cases}
$$

In the original scheme, generating a t value amounts to computing at least an Jacobi symbol. Therefore, we obtain a complexity of at least $\mathcal{O}(M(2\lambda) \log 2\lambda)$. In our proposal, we obtain the following complexity

$$
\begin{cases}
\mathcal{O}(M(2\lambda)) & e = -1, \\
\mathcal{O}(M(2\lambda)) & e = 2, \\
\mathcal{O}(2M(2\lambda)) & \text{otherwise.}
\end{cases}
$$

We further provide the reader with benchmarks for Cocks' original scheme and for our proposal. We ran the encryption algorithm for both schemes on a CPU Intel i7-8700 3.20 GHz and used GCC to compile it (with the O3 flag activated for optimization). Note that for all computations we used the GMP library [1]. To calculate the running times we used the native C++ function *clock()*. To obtain the average running time in seconds we chose to encrypt 1000 128/192/256-bit messages. According to NIST [3], the modules of size 3072/7680/15360 offer 128/192/256-bit security. Therefore, we wanted to simulate a key distribution scenario.

The results are provided in Table 1. Please take note that the percentages represent the time improvement relative to the original version. We can clearly see that our proposal significantly reduces encryption time by at least 50%.

Table 1. Average Encryption Time (ms)

Key	Original			Proposal		
Length	$e = -1$	$e = 2$	$e = \bar{e}$	$e = -1$	$e = 2$	$e = \bar{e}$
128 bits	27.2190	23.1005	25.9760	10.1901 (62.56%)	8.55514 (62.96%)	10.1151 (61.06%)
192 bits	118.701	114.695	115.931	50.6101 (57.36%)	48.9982 (57.28%)	52.1820 (54.99%)
256 bits	360.541	355.493	354.617	167.129 (53.64%)	164.818 (53.63%)	173.592 (51.04%)

4 Space Efficient IBEs

In [19], the author introduces a variant of Cocks' IBE that allows one to derive the encryption of $-m$ from the original ciphertext. Additionally, the author presents a bandwidth-saving approach for this variant. In this section, we show that this technique can be easily adapted to Cocks' and Zhao *et al.*'s IBE schemes.

We further impose the restriction $p \equiv q \bmod 4$. This implies that $J_p(-1) = J_q(-1)$, and therefore $J_n(-1) = 1$. Using this restriction, we are able to restrict the ciphertexts interval from $\{1, \ldots, n-1\}$ to $\{1, \ldots, (n-1)/2\}$.

4.1 Cocks' IBE Compact Version

We remind the reader that Cocks' ciphertext takes the following form

$$c_1 = t_1 + \frac{R}{t_1} \bmod n \quad \text{and} \quad c_2 = t_2 + \frac{uR}{t_2} \bmod n.$$

We can see that

$$J_n(-c_1 + 2r) = J_n(-t_1 - R \cdot t_1^{-1} + 2r)$$
$$= J_n(-(t_1 - r)^2 \cdot t_1^{-1}) = J_n(t_1),$$

and $J_n(-c_2 + 2r) = J_n(t_2)$. Thus, the decryption algorithm works as intended with any ciphertexts of the form $(\pm c_1, \pm c_2)$. Therefore, we propose the following encryption algorithm aimed at minimizing the bandwith overhead.

$Enc(pp, id, m)$: On inputting pp, an identity id and a message $m \in \{-1, 1\}$, compute the hash value $R = H(id)$ and randomly choose two values $t_1, t_2 \xleftarrow{\$} \mathbb{Z}_n$ such that $J_n(t_1) = J_n(t_2) = m$. Also, calculate

$$c_1' = t_1 + \frac{R}{t_1} \bmod n \quad \text{and} \quad c_2' = t_2 + \frac{uR}{t_2} \bmod n.$$

Define

$$c_1 = \min(c_1', n - c_1') \quad \text{and} \quad c_2 = \min(c_2', n - c_2'),$$

and return the ciphertext $C = (c_1, c_2)$.

Remark 3. Remark that the technique outlined in this section does not interfere with the security proofs of Cocks' IBE provided in [15,19]. Furthermore, the methods of anonymization outlined in [2,19–21] can be effectively applied to this variant as well.

4.2   Zhao *et al.*'s IBE Compact Version

Using the trick presented in Sect. 4.1, we can also make Zhao *et al.*'s IBE scheme more compact. Let $f(x) = a \cdot x + b$ and $\overline{f}(x) = \overline{a} \cdot x + \overline{b}$. When we compute $c(x)$ and $\overline{c}(x)$ we obtain

$$c(x) = c_0 \cdot x + c_1 = [2y^m a] \cdot x + [y^m(a^2 R + b^2)]$$
$$\overline{c}(x) = \overline{c}_0 \cdot x + \overline{c}_1 = [2y^m \overline{a}] \cdot x + [y^m(\overline{a}^2 uR + \overline{b}^2)]$$

Therefore, when $r^2 \equiv H(id) \bmod n$ we obtain that

$$J_n(c_0 \cdot r + c_1) = J_n(y^m \cdot (2ar + a^2 R + b^2)) = J_n(y^m \cdot (ar + b)^2) = J_n(y)^m,$$
$$J_n(c_0 \cdot r - c_1) = J_n(y^m \cdot (2ar - a^2 R - b^2)) = J_n(-y^m \cdot (ar - b)^2) = J_n(y)^m,$$
$$J_n(-c_0 \cdot r + c_1) = J_n(y^m \cdot (-2ar + a^2 R + b^2)) = J_n(y^m \cdot (ar - b)^2) = J_n(y)^m,$$
$$J_n(-c_0 \cdot r - c_1) = J_n(y^m \cdot (-2ar - a^2 R - b^2)) = J_n(-y^m \cdot (ar + b)^2) = J_n(y)^m,$$

since $J_n(-1) = 1$. Similarly, for the case $r^2 \equiv uH(id) \bmod n$ we obtain

$$J_n(\overline{c}_0 \cdot r + \overline{c}_1) = J_n(\overline{c}_0 \cdot r - \overline{c}_1) = J_n(-\overline{c}_0 \cdot r + \overline{c}_1) = J_n(-\overline{c}_0 \cdot r - \overline{c}_1).$$

Hence, the decryption algorithm works as intended with either of the following ciphertext versions

$$(\pm c_0 \cdot x \pm c_1, \pm \overline{c}_0 \cdot x \pm \overline{c}_1).$$

Therefore, we can use the following encryption algorithm to save bandwith.

Enc(pp, id, m): On inputting pp, an identity id and a message $m \in \{0,1\}$, compute the hash value $R = H(id)$ and randomly chooses two polynomials $f(x), \overline{f}(x)$ of degree 1 from $\mathbb{Z}_n[x]$. Also, calculate

$$g(x) = f(x)^2 \bmod (x^2 - R) \quad \text{and} \quad \overline{g}(x) = \overline{f}(x)^2 \bmod (x^2 - uR)$$

and let

$$(c_0' \cdot x + c_1', \overline{c}_0' \cdot x + \overline{c}_1') = (y^m \cdot g(x), y^m \cdot \overline{g}(x)).$$

Define

$$c_0 = \min(c_0', n - c_0') \quad \text{and} \quad c_1 = \min(c_1', n - c_1')$$
$$\overline{c}_0 = \min(\overline{c}_0', n - \overline{c}_0') \quad \text{and} \quad \overline{c}_1 = \min(\overline{c}_1', n - \overline{c}_1'),$$

and return the ciphertext $C = (c_0 \cdot x + c_1, \overline{c}_0 \cdot x + \overline{c}_1)$.

Remark 4. Note that this space-saving technique does not interfere with the security proof of Zhao *et al.*'s IBE provided in [24]. Additionally, the anonymization technique described in [9,10] can also be applied to this version.

5 Conclusion

In this paper, we have introduced a method for accelerating the Cocks IBE scheme. Additionally, through the application of elementary operations, we managed to reduce the bandwidth requirements of both the Cocks and Zhao *et al.* IBEs.

References

1. The GNU Multiple Precision Arithmetic Library. https://gmplib.org/
2. Ateniese, G., Gasti, P.: Universally anonymous IBE based on the quadratic residuosity assumption. In: Fischlin, M. (ed.) CT-RSA 2009. LNCS, vol. 5473, pp. 32–47. Springer, Heidelberg (2009). https://doi.org/10.1007/978-3-642-00862-7_3
3. Barker, E.: NIST SP800-57 Recommendation for Key Management, Part 1: General. Technical report, NIST (2016)
4. Barua, R., Jhanwar, M.P.: On the number of solutions of the equation $Rx^2 + Sy^2 = 1 \pmod{N}$. Indian J. Stat. **72-A**, 226–236 (2010)
5. Boneh, D., Di Crescenzo, G., Ostrovsky, R., Persiano, G.: Public key encryption with keyword search. In: Cachin, C., Camenisch, J.L. (eds.) EUROCRYPT 2004. LNCS, vol. 3027, pp. 506–522. Springer, Heidelberg (2004). https://doi.org/10.1007/978-3-540-24676-3_30
6. Boneh, D., Franklin, M.: Identity-based encryption from the Weil pairing. In: Kilian, J. (ed.) CRYPTO 2001. LNCS, vol. 2139, pp. 213–229. Springer, Heidelberg (2001). https://doi.org/10.1007/3-540-44647-8_13
7. Boneh, D., Gentry, C., Hamburg, M.: Space-efficient identity based encryption without pairings. In: FOCS 2007, pp. 647–657. IEEE Computer Society (2007)
8. Brent, R.P., Zimmermann, P.: An $O(M(n)\log n)$ algorithm for the Jacobi symbol. In: Hanrot, G., Morain, F., Thomé, E. (eds.) ANTS 2010. LNCS, vol. 6197, pp. 83–95. Springer, Heidelberg (2010). https://doi.org/10.1007/978-3-642-14518-6_10
9. Clear, M., Hughes, A., Tewari, H.: Homomorphic encryption with access policies: characterization and new constructions. In: Youssef, A., Nitaj, A., Hassanien, A.E. (eds.) AFRICACRYPT 2013. LNCS, vol. 7918, pp. 61–87. Springer, Heidelberg (2013). https://doi.org/10.1007/978-3-642-38553-7_4
10. Clear, M., Tewari, H., McGoldrick, C.: Anonymous IBE from quadratic residuosity with improved performance. In: Pointcheval, D., Vergnaud, D. (eds.) AFRICACRYPT 2014. LNCS, vol. 8469, pp. 377–397. Springer, Cham (2014). https://doi.org/10.1007/978-3-319-06734-6_23

11. Cocks, C.: An identity based encryption scheme based on quadratic residues. In: Honary, B. (ed.) Cryptography and Coding 2001. LNCS, vol. 2260, pp. 360–363. Springer, Heidelberg (2001). https://doi.org/10.1007/3-540-45325-3_32
12. Cotan, P., Teşeleanu, G.: Generalized Galbraith's test: characterization and applications to anonymous IBE schemes. Mathematics 9(11), 1184 (2021)
13. Elashry, I., Mu, Y., Susilo, W.: An efficient variant of Boneh-Gentry-Hamburg's identity-based encryption without pairing. In: Rhee, K.-H., Yi, J.H. (eds.) WISA 2014. LNCS, vol. 8909, pp. 257–268. Springer, Cham (2015). https://doi.org/10.1007/978-3-319-15087-1_20
14. Elashry, I., Mu, Y., Susilo, W.: Jhanwar-Barua's identity-based encryption revisited. In: Au, M.H., Carminati, B., Kuo, C.-C.J. (eds.) NSS 2014. LNCS, vol. 8792, pp. 271–284. Springer, Cham (2014). https://doi.org/10.1007/978-3-319-11698-3_21
15. Goldwasser, S.: Cocks' IBE scheme, bilinear maps. MIT Lecture Notes: "6876: Advanced Cryptography" (2004)
16. Goldwasser, S., Micali, S.: Probabilistic encryption. J. Comput. Syst. Sci. 28, 270–299 (1984)
17. Harvey, D., Van Der Hoeven, J.: Integer multiplication in time $\mathcal{O}(n \log n)$. Ann. Math. 193(2), 563–617 (2021)
18. Jhanwar, M.P., Barua, R.: A variant of Boneh-Gentry-Hamburg's pairing-free identity based encryption scheme. In: Yung, M., Liu, P., Lin, D. (eds.) Inscrypt 2008. LNCS, vol. 5487, pp. 314–331. Springer, Heidelberg (2009). https://doi.org/10.1007/978-3-642-01440-6_25
19. Joye, M.: Identity-based cryptosystems and quadratic residuosity. In: Cheng, C.-M., Chung, K.-M., Persiano, G., Yang, B.-Y. (eds.) PKC 2016. LNCS, vol. 9614, pp. 225–254. Springer, Heidelberg (2016). https://doi.org/10.1007/978-3-662-49384-7_9
20. Nica, A.M., Tiplea, F.L.: On anonymization of cocks' identity-based encryption scheme. Comput. Sci. J. Moldova 81(3), 283–298 (2019)
21. Schipor, G.A.: On the anonymization of cocks IBE scheme. In: Ors, B., Preneel, B. (eds.) BalkanCryptSec 2014. LNCS, vol. 9024, pp. 194–202. Springer, Cham (2015). https://doi.org/10.1007/978-3-319-21356-9_13
22. Schipor, A.G.: On the security of Jhanwar-Barua identity-based encryption scheme. In: Lanet, J.-L., Toma, C. (eds.) SECITC 2018. LNCS, vol. 11359, pp. 368–375. Springer, Cham (2019). https://doi.org/10.1007/978-3-030-12942-2_28
23. Shamir, A.: Identity-based cryptosystems and signature schemes. In: Blakley, G.R., Chaum, D. (eds.) CRYPTO 1984. LNCS, vol. 196, pp. 47–53. Springer, Heidelberg (1985). https://doi.org/10.1007/3-540-39568-7_5
24. Zhao, X., Cao, Z., Dong, X., Zheng, J.: Anonymous IBE from quadratic residuosity with fast encryption. In: Susilo, W., Deng, R.H., Guo, F., Li, Y., Intan, R. (eds.) ISC 2020. LNCS, vol. 12472, pp. 3–19. Springer, Cham (2020). https://doi.org/10.1007/978-3-030-62974-8_1

SDVS Sender-Privacy in the Multi-party Setting

Jeroen van Wier[✉][iD]

Interdisciplinary Centre for Security, Reliability and Trust,
University of Luxembourg, Esch-sur-Alzette, Luxembourg
jeroen.vanwier@uni.lu

Abstract. Strong designated verifier signature schemes rely on sender-privacy to hide the identity of the creator of a signature to all but the intended recipient. This property can be invaluable in, for example, the context of deniability, where the identity of a party should not be deducible from the communication sent during a protocol execution. In this work, we explore the technical definition of sender-privacy and extend it from a 2-party setting to an n-party setting. Afterwards, we show in which cases this extension provides stronger security and in which cases it does not.

Keywords: Designated-Verifier · Digital Signatures · Sender-Privacy · Undeniable Signatures

1 Introduction

Digital signatures have many useful applications in our everyday lives, from message authentication to software updates. In many cases, they provide a publicly verifiable way of proving the authenticity of a message. However, sometimes it is desired to prove authenticity only to the intended receiver, or designated verifier, of a message. Designated verifier signature (DVS) schemes were constructed for this reason, to allow for the signing of a message in such a way that the receiver would be fully convinced of its authenticity, but to third-party observers, the validity of the signature could be denied. Strong designated verifier signature (SDVS) schemes are the refinement of this idea, with the additional restraint that no one but the creator and the designated verifier should be able to deduce from a signature who was the creator. While this concept has been studied extensively and is interpreted intuitively in the same way by many, the technical definitions for the property separating DVS schemes from SDVS schemes, known as sender-privacy, vary. In this work we analyze and generalize the definitions in current literature and aim to provide a universally applicable way to define this property, particularly focusing on the n-party setting. Furthermore, we prove that our general form of sender-privacy can be achieved by combining weaker forms of sender-privacy with non-transferability or unforgeability.

© The Author(s), under exclusive license to Springer Nature Switzerland AG 2024
M. Manulis et al. (Eds.): SecITC 2023, LNCS 14534, pp. 35–50, 2024.
https://doi.org/10.1007/978-3-031-52947-4_4

1.1 Related Work

Chaum and van Antwerpen first introduced undeniable signatures in [3], which required interaction between the signer and verifier. In 1996 this requirement was removed by Chaum [2] and by Jakobsson et al. [6] separately, who introduced designated verifier signatures. These formal definitions were later refined by Saeednia et al. [9]. Rivest et al. introduced ring signatures in [8], which can be interpreted as DVS when a ring size of 2 is used, although not SDVS.

An important step was made when Laguillaumie and Vergnaud formalised *sender-privacy*, the property separating DVS from SDVS, in [7]. The notion of SDVS was further refined to Identity-Based SDVS by Susilo et al. [10], where all private keys are issued using a master secret key (i.e. central authority). For this setting, sender-privacy was later formalized in a game-based manner by Huang et al. [5].

1.2 Summary of Contributions

The main objective of the paper is to present a definition of sender-privacy that is usable in the multi-party setting without requiring additional proofs. To achieve this, we first survey the definitions of sender-privacy that are present in the literature in Sect. 2. Here we also show how the definition of designated verifier signatures got split into non-transferability and sender-privacy.

In Sect. 3 we show how the definitions from the literature differ from each other and what their potential shortcomings are. Here we also present the multi-party sender-privacy definition and go deeper into which oracles are used.

Definition 9 (Simplified). *A designated verifier signature scheme is n-party sender-private if an adversary interacting with n parties with oracle access to the signing, simulating and verification procedures has negligible advantage in deducing who the signing party of a challenge signature is. Here the challenge signing party is always one of two fixed parties known to the adversary.*

In Sect. 4 we show that a number of alternative definitions are equivalent to the one above.

Definition 10 (Simplified). *A designated verifier signature scheme is n-party random-challenge sender-private if an adversary interacting with n parties with oracle access to the signing, simulating and verification procedures has negligible advantage in deducing who the signing party of a challenge signature is. Here the challenge signing party is always one of the n parties known to the adversary.*

Definition 11 (Simplified). *A designated verifier signature scheme is n-party adversarial-challenge sender-private if an adversary interacting with n parties with oracle access to the signing, simulating and verification procedures has negligible advantage in deducing who the signing party of a challenge signature is. Here the challenge signing party is always one of two parties chosen by the adversary.*

Theorem. *Definitions 9, 10, and 11 are equivalent up to polynomial differences in the advantages.*

In order to integrate our definition with the current literature, we present in Sect. 5 some settings in which definitions with different oracles or numbers of parties coincide.

Theorem 4 (Simplified). *For any scheme that is strongly unforgeable, the definitions of sender-privacy with or without access to a verifications oracle are equivalent.*

Theorem 5 (Simplified). *For any scheme that is strongly unforgeable and computationally non-transferable, the definitions of 2-party sender-privacy and n-party sender-privacy are equivalent.*

2 Preliminaries

We denote with $\kappa \in \mathbb{N}$ the security parameter of a scheme and implicitly assume that any algorithm that is part of a scheme is given input 1^κ, i.e. the string of κ 1's, in addition to its specified inputs. We implicitly assume that all adversaries are probabilistic polynomial-time Turing machines (PPT). We write $[n]$ for the set $\{0, \dots, n\}$. We call a function $\varepsilon(n)$ negligible (denoted $\varepsilon \leq \mathrm{negl}(n)$) if for every polynomial p there exists $n_0 \in \mathbb{N}$ such that for all $n \geq n_0$ it holds that $\varepsilon(n) < \frac{1}{p(n)}$. We reserve $\perp$ as an error symbol.

Definition 1. *A designated verifier signature scheme (DVS scheme) is a tuple* (Setup, KeyGen, Sign, Verify, Simulate) *of* PPT *algorithms such that:*

- Setup: *Produces the public parameters of a scheme,* params. *It is implicitly assumed that these parameters are passed to the following algorithms.*
- KeyGen: *Produces a keypair* (pk, sk).
- $\mathsf{Sign}_{S \to V}(m) := \mathsf{Sign}(\mathsf{sk}_S, \mathsf{pk}_S, \mathsf{pk}_V, m)$: *produces a signature σ if all keys are valid and $\perp$ otherwise.*
- $\mathsf{Verify}_{S \to V}(m, \sigma) := \mathsf{Verify}(\mathsf{sk}_V, \mathsf{pk}_V, \mathsf{pk}_S, m, \sigma)$: *outputs the validity of σ (a boolean value) if all keys are valid and $\perp$ otherwise.*
- $\mathsf{Simulate}_{S \to V}(m) := \mathsf{Simulate}(\mathsf{sk}_V, \mathsf{pk}_V, \mathsf{pk}_S, m)$: *produces a simulated signature σ'.*

2.1 Current Definitions

The original definitions for strong verifier designation are a combination of what we currently distinguish as *non-transferability* and *sender-privacy*. The following definitions are the initial attempts at defining strong verifier designation, and in their respective papers, they are accompanied by definitions for (non-strong) verifier designation, which are very much in line with the intuition behind non-transferability. To distinguish them from the later definitions, we name them JSI and SKM strong designated verifier schemes respectively, after the names of the authors that proposed them.

Definition 2 ([6]). *Let* $(\mathcal{P}_A, \mathcal{P}_B)$ *be a protocol for Alice to prove the truth of the statement* Ω *to Bob. We say that Bob is a* JSI *strong designated verifier if, for any protocol* $(\mathcal{P}_A, \mathcal{P}_B, \mathcal{P}_C, \mathcal{P}_D)$ *involving Alice, Bob, Cindy, and Dave, by which Dave proves the truth of some statement* θ *to Cindy, there is another protocol* $(\mathcal{P}_C, \mathcal{P}'_D)$ *such that Dave can perform the calculations of* $\mathcal{P}'_D$*, and Cindy cannot distinguish transcripts of* $(\mathcal{P}_A, \mathcal{P}_B, \mathcal{P}_C, \mathcal{P}_D)$ *from those of* $(\mathcal{P}_C, \mathcal{P}'_D)$*.*

Definition 3 ([9]). *Let* $\mathcal{P}(A, B)$ *be a protocol for Alice to prove the truth of the statement* Ω *to Bob. We say that* $\mathcal{P}(A, B)$ *is a* SKM *strong designated verifier proof if anyone can produce identically distributed transcripts that are indistinguishable from those of* $\mathcal{P}(A, B)$ *for everybody, except Bob.*

In later work, we see the definition for strong verifier designation split. Non-transferability captures the notion that the verifier can produce signatures from anyone designated to himself, thus ensuring that no signature provides proof of signer-verifier interaction for third parties. Sender-privacy adds to this that, from a signature, one cannot deduce the sender, thus allowing no third-party observer to use a signature to plausibly deduce that an interaction between two parties happened.

Definition 4. *A* DVS *scheme* $\Pi = (\mathsf{KeyGen}, \mathsf{Sign}, \mathsf{Verify}, \mathsf{Simulate})$ *is computationally non-transferable if for any adversary* $\mathcal{A}$*,*

$$\mathsf{Adv}_{\Pi,\mathcal{A}}^{\mathsf{NT}}(\kappa) = \Pr_{b \in \{0,1\}}\left[\mathsf{G}_{\Pi,\mathcal{A}}^{\mathsf{NT}}(\kappa, b) = b\right] - \frac{1}{2} \leq \mathsf{negl}(\kappa),$$

where the game $\mathsf{G}_{\Pi,\mathcal{A}}^{\mathsf{NT}}$ *is defined as follows:*

Game 1: $\mathsf{G}_{\Pi,\mathcal{A}}^{\mathsf{NT}}(\kappa, b)$

---
1   params $\leftarrow$ Setup
2   $(\mathsf{pk}_S, \mathsf{sk}_S) \leftarrow$ KeyGen
3   $(\mathsf{pk}_V, \mathsf{sk}_V) \leftarrow$ KeyGen
4   $(m^*, ,) \leftarrow \mathcal{A}(1, \mathsf{params}, \mathsf{pk}_S, \mathsf{sk}_S, \mathsf{pk}_V, \mathsf{sk}_V)$
5   **if** $b = 0$ **then**
6   $\quad \lfloor \;\; \sigma^* = \mathsf{Sign}(\mathsf{sk}_S, \mathsf{pk}_S, \mathsf{pk}_V, m^*)$
7   **else**
8   $\quad \lfloor \;\; \sigma^* = \mathsf{Simulate}(\mathsf{sk}_V, \mathsf{pk}_V, \mathsf{pk}_S, m^*)$
9   $b' \leftarrow \mathcal{A}(2, , \sigma^*)$
10 Output b'

Definition 5. *A* DVS $\Pi = (\mathsf{KeyGen}, \mathsf{Sign}, \mathsf{Verify}, \mathsf{Simulate})$ *is statistically non-transferable if for all* S*,* V*, and* m*,* $\mathsf{Sign}_{S \to V}(m)$ *and* $\mathsf{Simulate}_{S \to V}(m)$ *are statistically indistinguishable distributions.*

For sender-privacy, many slightly different definitions are presented in the literature. Many follow the form of Game 2, but with different oracles presented to the adversary. Note that this game is a generalized definition designed to be instantiated with a set of oracles $\mathcal{O}$ to form the specific definitions found in the literature. For each $i \in [n]$, party i is denoted P_i. P_n is designated as the verifier for the challenge. In much of the literature, this game is played with 3 parties: S_0, S_1, and V, who would here correspond with P_0, P_1, and P_2 respectively in the $n = 2$ setting.

Game 2: $\mathsf{G}_{\Pi,\mathcal{A},\mathcal{O}}^{\mathsf{SendPriv}}(\kappa, n, c)$, the generalized game for sender-privacy.

---

1 params $\leftarrow$ Setup
2 $(\mathsf{pk}_{P_0}, \mathsf{sk}_{P_0}) \leftarrow$ KeyGen; $\ldots$; $(\mathsf{pk}_{P_n}, \mathsf{sk}_{P_n}) \leftarrow$ KeyGen
3 $(m^*,) \leftarrow \mathcal{A}^{\mathcal{O}_{sign}^{(1)}, \mathcal{O}_{veri}^{(1)}, \mathcal{O}_{sim}^{(1)}}(1, \mathsf{params}, \mathsf{pk}_{P_0}, \ldots, \mathsf{pk}_{P_n})$
4 $\sigma^* = \mathsf{Sign}_{P_c \to P_n}(m^*)$
5 $c' \leftarrow \mathcal{A}^{\mathcal{O}_{sign}^{(2)}, \mathcal{O}_{veri}^{(2)}, \mathcal{O}_{sim}^{(2)}}(2, , \sigma^*)$
6 Output c'

Definition 6 ([5]). *A DVS $\Pi =$ (KeyGen, Sign, Verify, Simulate) is a Hua-strong DVS if it is statistically non-transferable and for any PPT adversary $\mathcal{A}$,*

$$\mathsf{Adv}_{\Pi,\mathcal{A}}^{\mathsf{SendPriv}}(\kappa) = \Pr_{c \leftarrow \{0,1\}} \left[\mathsf{G}_{\Pi,\mathcal{A}}^{\mathsf{SendPriv}}(\kappa, 2, c) = c \right] - \frac{1}{2} \le \mathsf{negl}(\kappa),$$

where $\mathsf{G}_{\Pi,\mathcal{A}}^{\mathsf{SendPriv}}$ is played with the following oracles:

- $\mathcal{O}_{sign}^{(1)}$: *Upon input (m_i, d_i) returns $\mathsf{Sign}_{P_{d_i} \to P_2}(m_i)$ if $d_i \in \{0, 1\}$ and $\perp$ otherwise.*
- $\mathcal{O}_{sign}^{(2)}$: *Upon input (m_i, d_i) returns $\mathsf{Sign}_{P_{d_i} \to P_2}(m_i)$ if $d_i \in \{0, 1\}$ and $m_i \ne m^*$, and $\perp$ otherwise.*
- $\mathcal{O}_{veri}^{(1)}$: *Upon input (σ_i, m_i, d_i) returns $\mathsf{Verify}_{P_{d_i} \to P_2}(m_i)$ if $d_i \in \{0, 1\}$ and $\perp$ otherwise.*
  $\mathcal{O}_{veri}^{(2)}$: *Upon input (σ_i, m_i, d_i) returns $\mathsf{Verify}_{P_{d_i} \to P_2}(m_i)$ if $d_i \in \{0, 1\}$, $\sigma_i \ne \sigma^*$, and $m_i \ne m^*$, and $\perp$ otherwise.*
- $\mathcal{O}_{sim}^{(1)} = \mathcal{O}_{sim}^{(2)} = \emptyset$

In [5], Huang et al. define signer-privacy for identity-based-SDVS, a similar type of DVS where all keypairs are issued by a central authority. Here, they allow signing queries from any party to any party, and the adversary is allowed to choose the two signer and the verifier parties. We explore this option for SDVS in Definition 11.

3   Bringing Sender-Privacy to the Multi-party Setting

Sender-privacy is meant to provide security in the setting where an eavesdropping adversary is trying to detect the identity of the sender of a signature. In the previously presented definitions, this is modelled by a coin flip between two senders, with a fixed verifier. This way of defining sender-privacy is similar to key-privacy in public-key cryptography [1]. The key difference here is that public-key ciphertexts are only related to one keypair, the receiver's. However, designated verifier signatures are bound to two parties, the signer and the designated verifier. This creates the problem that the naive way of defining sender-privacy does not cover any attacks that require multiple parties. In key-privacy, any adversary requiring n parties for their attack can perform this attack in the two-party setting by simulating the other $n - 2$ parties themself. However, in the case of SDVS schemes, this is not necessarily possible. The adversary could be unable to create signatures signed by one of the two challenge parties with their simulated parties as the verifier We explore settings where this is a non-issue in Sect. 5.

3.1   Oracles

Many different interpretations exist in the literature of what oracles the adversary should be given access to. The key choices here are whether (1) a simulation oracle should be provided, (2) a verification oracle should be provided, and (3) whether the adversary should still have access to the oracles after the challenge has been issued. Whereas the precise attacker model might depend on the context and our framework allows us to capture this, we here choose to focus on the strongest level of security, by providing the adversary with as much as possible without trivially breaking the challenge.

Definition 7. *For any n, let the* standard n-sender SendPriv-oracles *denote:*

- $\mathcal{O}_{sign}^{(1)} = \mathcal{O}_{sign}^{(2)}$*: Upon input (m_i, s, v) returns $\sigma_i := \mathsf{Sign}_{P_s \to P_v}(m_i)$ if $s, v \in [n]$ and $\perp$ otherwise.*
- $\mathcal{O}_{sim}^{(1)} = \mathcal{O}_{sim}^{(2)}$*: Upon input (m_i, s, v) returns $\sigma_i := \mathsf{Simulate}_{P_s \to P_v}(m_i)$ if $s, v \in [n]$ and $\perp$ otherwise.*
- $\mathcal{O}_{veri}^{(1)}$*: Upon input (m_i, σ_i, s, v) returns $\mathsf{Verify}_{P_s \to P_v}(m_i, \sigma_i)$ if $s, v \in [n]$ and $\perp$ otherwise.*
- $\mathcal{O}_{veri}^{(2)}$*: Upon input (m_i, σ_i, s, v) returns $\mathsf{Verify}_{P_s \to P_v}(m_i, \sigma_i)$ if $s, v \in [n]$ and $\sigma_i \neq \sigma^*$, and $\perp$ otherwise.*

Note that the oracles make use of an implicit ordering of the parties. This makes no difference in any real-world application, but for constructing proofs we also define a set of oracles that allows this ordering to be hidden by a permutation.

Definition 8. *For any set of oracles for $\mathsf{G}^{\mathsf{SendPriv}}$ and any permutation π define the permuted oracles as follows, where $b \in \{0, 1\}$:*

- $\mathcal{O}_{sign}^{(\pi,b)}$: On input (m_i, s, v) output $\mathcal{O}_{sign}^{(b)}(m_i, \pi(s), \pi(v))$
- $\mathcal{O}_{sim}^{(\pi,b)}$: On input (m_i, s, v) output $\mathcal{O}_{sim}^{(b)}(m_i, \pi(s), \pi(v))$
- $\mathcal{O}_{veri}^{(\pi,b)}$: On input (m_i, σ_i, s, v) output $\mathcal{O}_{veri}^{(b)}(m_i, \sigma_i, \pi(s), \pi(v))$

3.2   Definition

Taking all these things into consideration, we can now craft a definition of sender-privacy. This definition is more in line with current research in ID-based-SDVS research such as [4].

Definition 9. *A DVS scheme Π is n-party sender-private with respect to $\mathcal{O}$ if for any adversary $\mathcal{A}$,*

$$\mathsf{Adv}_{\Pi,\mathcal{A},\mathcal{O}}^{\mathsf{SendPriv}}(\kappa, n) = \Pr_{c \leftarrow \{0,1\}} \left[\mathsf{G}_{\Pi,\mathcal{A}}^{\mathsf{SendPriv}}(\kappa, n, c) = c \right] - \frac{1}{2} \le \mathrm{negl}(\kappa).$$

A DVS scheme is n-party sender-private if it is n-party sender-private with respect to the standard n-sender SendPriv-oracles.

4   Alternative Definitions

In this section, we look at possible alternative definitions that one could consider equally valid generalizations of the 2-party setting to the n-party setting. For example, in the 2-party setting, we pick the challenge uniformly at random between the two possible senders, thus one could consider picking uniformly at random from n senders in the n-party setting.

Definition 10. *A DVS scheme is n-party random-challenge sender-private with respect to $\mathcal{O}$ if for any adversary $\mathcal{A}$,*

$$\mathsf{Adv}_{\Pi,\mathcal{A},\mathcal{O}}^{nr\mathsf{SendPriv}}(\kappa, n) = \Pr_{c \leftarrow [n-1]} \left[\mathsf{G}_{\Pi,\mathcal{A},\mathcal{O}}^{\mathsf{SendPriv}}(\kappa, n, c) = c \right] - \frac{1}{n} \le \mathrm{negl}(\kappa).$$

A DVS scheme is n-party random-challenge sender-private if it is n-party random-challenge sender-private with respect to the standard n-sender SendPriv-oracles.

Furthermore, one could strengthen the definition even more by allowing the adversary to choose which two senders the challenge is chosen from and which party is the verifier.

Definition 11. *A DVS scheme is n-party adversarial-challenge sender-private with respect to $\mathcal{O}$ if for any adversary $\mathcal{A}$,*

$$\mathsf{Adv}_{\Pi,\mathcal{A},\mathcal{O}}^{\mathsf{ChosenSendPriv}}(\kappa, n) = \Pr_{c \leftarrow \{0,1\}} \left[\mathsf{G}_{\Pi,\mathcal{A}}^{\mathsf{ChosenSendPriv}}(\kappa, n, c) = c \right] - \frac{1}{2} \le \mathrm{negl}(\kappa).$$

A DVS scheme is n-party adversarial-challenge sender-private if it is n-party adversarial-challenge sender-private with respect to the standard n-sender SendPriv-oracles.

Game 3: $G_{\Pi,\mathcal{A},\mathcal{O}}^{\mathsf{ChosenSendPriv}}(\kappa, n, c)$

1 params $\leftarrow$ Setup
2 $(\mathsf{pk}_{P_0}, \mathsf{sk}_{P_0}) \leftarrow \mathsf{KeyGen}; \ldots; (\mathsf{pk}_{P_n}, \mathsf{sk}_{P_n}) \leftarrow \mathsf{KeyGen}$
3 $(m^*, s_0, s_1, r,) \leftarrow \mathcal{A}^{\mathcal{O}_{sign}^{(1)}, \mathcal{O}_{veri}^{(1)}, \mathcal{O}_{sim}^{(1)}}(1, \mathsf{params}, \mathsf{pk}_{P_0}, \ldots, \mathsf{pk}_{P_n})$
4 $\sigma^* = \mathsf{Sign}_{P_{s_c} \to P_r}(m^*)$
5 $c' \leftarrow \mathcal{A}^{\mathcal{O}_{sign}^{(2)}, \mathcal{O}_{veri}^{(2)}, \mathcal{O}_{sim}^{(2)}}(2, , \sigma^*)$
6 Output c'

4.1   Relations

As one might expect, the above-defined alternative definitions relate strongly to the main definition, Definition 9. In fact, in this section, we show that they are equivalent up to polynomial differences in the advantages.

For the universally random challenge, this can be done by simply only considering the cases where the challenge is P_0 or P_1, which will be the case 2 out of n times, giving us a loss in the advantage of a factor $\frac{2}{n}$.

Theorem 1. *For any adversary* $\mathcal{A}$, *DVS scheme* Π, *and set of oracles* $\mathcal{O}$,

$$\frac{2}{n} \cdot \mathsf{Adv}_{\Pi,\mathcal{A},\mathcal{O}}^{\mathsf{SendPriv}}(\kappa, n) \leq \mathsf{Adv}_{\Pi,\mathcal{A},\mathcal{O}}^{nr\mathsf{SendPriv}}(\kappa, n).$$

Proof. $\mathsf{Adv}_{\Pi,\mathcal{A}}^{nr\mathsf{SendPriv}}(\kappa, n)$

$$= \Pr_{c \leftarrow [n-1]}\left[G_{\Pi,\mathcal{A}}^{\mathsf{SendPriv}}(\kappa, n, c) = c\right] - \frac{1}{n}$$

$$= \frac{2}{n} \Pr_{c \leftarrow [1]}\left[G_{\Pi,\mathcal{A}}^{\mathsf{SendPriv}}(\kappa, n, c) = c\right] + \frac{n-2}{n} \Pr_{c \leftarrow [2,n-1]}\left[G_{\Pi,\mathcal{A}}^{\mathsf{SendPriv}}(\kappa, n, c) = c\right] - \frac{1}{n}$$

$$= \frac{2}{n}\left(\Pr_{c \leftarrow [1]}\left[G_{\Pi,\mathcal{A}}^{\mathsf{SendPriv}}(\kappa, n, c) = c\right] - \frac{1}{2}\right) + \frac{n-2}{n} \Pr_{c \leftarrow [2,n-1]}\left[G_{\Pi,\mathcal{A}}^{\mathsf{SendPriv}}(\kappa, n, c) = c\right]$$

$$= \frac{2}{n} \cdot \mathsf{Adv}_{\Pi,\mathcal{A}}^{\mathsf{SendPriv}}(\kappa) + \frac{n-2}{n} \Pr_{c \leftarrow [2,n-1]}\left[G_{\Pi,\mathcal{A}}^{\mathsf{SendPriv}}(\kappa, n, c) = c\right]$$

$$\geq \frac{2}{n} \cdot \mathsf{Adv}_{\Pi,\mathcal{A},\mathcal{O}}^{\mathsf{SendPriv}}(\kappa, n),$$

where $[2, n-1] = \{2, \ldots, n-1\}$. $\square$

Theorem 2. *For any adversary* $\mathcal{A}$, *set of oracles* $\mathcal{O}$ *and* DVS *scheme* Π, *there exists an adversary* $\mathcal{B}$ *such that*

$$\frac{1}{2}\mathsf{Adv}_{\Pi,\mathcal{A},\mathcal{O}}^{nr\mathsf{SendPriv}}(\kappa, n) \leq \mathsf{Adv}_{\Pi,\mathcal{B},\mathcal{O}}^{\mathsf{SendPriv}}(\kappa, n).$$

Simplified. We define an adversary $\mathcal{B}$ that randomly permutes the parties to avoid a bias for the $0, 1$ parties in $\mathcal{A}$. We then run $\mathcal{A}$ and use its guess if it outputs the original 0 or 1 party, otherwise we guess 0. This transfers the guessing advantage of $\mathcal{A}$ in the chosen cases. The full proof is available in Appendix A. $\square$

Corollary 1. *For any $n \in \mathbb{N}$, an* SDVS *scheme is n-party random-challenge sender-private if and only if it is n-party sender-private.*

Similarly, we can show an equivalence up to polynomial factors for the adversarial-chosen challenges.

Theorem 3. *For any adversary $\mathcal{A}$ and set of oracles $\mathcal{O}$, there exists an adversary $\mathcal{B}$ such that*

$$\frac{2}{n^3 - n} \cdot \mathsf{Adv}_{\Pi,\mathcal{A},\mathcal{O}}^{\mathsf{ChosenSendPriv}}(\kappa, n) \leq \mathsf{Adv}_{\Pi,\mathcal{B},\mathcal{O}}^{\mathsf{SendPriv}}(\kappa, n)$$

Simplified. We could try to simply consider only the cases where the adversary chooses P_0 and P_1 as the challenge senders and P_n as the challenge verifier. However, an adversary could be crafted to never choose this exact combination of parties. Thus, we again hide the indexation of the parties under a random permutation. This is done only for the proof and has no impact on the actual definition, as all parties' keypairs are i.i.d. samples. Since the adversary does not know this permutation, the chance of them picking these parties is in the order of n^{-3} and thus a loss of this order is incurred in the advantage. The detailed proof can be found in Appendix B.   □

Corollary 2. *For any $n \in \mathbb{N}$, an* SDVS *scheme is n-party adversarial-challenge sender-private if and only if it is n-party sender-private.*

Proof. Theorem 3 shows that if a scheme is sender-private then it is also adversarial-challenge sender-private since the advantage differs by a factor $\mathcal{O}(n^3)$. The other direction is trivial, as any adversary for sender-privacy can trivially be transformed into an adversary for adversarial-challenge sender-privacy, always outputting $s_0 = 0, s_1 = 1, r = n$, which gives both adversaries the exact same winning probability.   □

5   Alternative Oracles

In this section we show that one can use other properties of SDVS schemes, e.g. non-transferability and unforgeability, to provide equally strong sender-privacy while giving the adversary weaker oracles. This allows us to more easily prove that existing schemes satisfy our definition. Note that in this section we only consider the cases where the security advantages are negligible. First, we will focus on the verification oracle, showing that they can be removed without impacting the quality of the security when the scheme is unforgeable. Then, we show that the number of parties can be limited to 3 ($n = 2$) when a scheme is both unforgeable and non-transferable.

Definition 12. *A* DVS *scheme $\Pi = (\mathsf{KeyGen}, \mathsf{Sign}, \mathsf{Verify}, \mathsf{Simulate})$ is n-party strongly-unforgeable with respect to $\mathcal{O}$ if for any adversary $\mathcal{A}$,*

$$\mathsf{Adv}_{\Pi,\mathcal{A},\mathcal{O}}^{\mathsf{UF}}(\kappa, n) = \Pr\left[\mathsf{G}_{\Pi,\mathcal{A},\mathcal{O}}^{\mathsf{UF}}(\kappa, n) = \top\right] \leq \mathsf{negl}(\kappa),$$

Game 4: $\mathsf{G}^{\mathsf{UF}}_{\Pi,\mathcal{A},\mathcal{O}}(\kappa, n)$

1 params ← Setup
2 $(\mathsf{pk}_{P_0}, \mathsf{sk}_{P_0}) \leftarrow \mathsf{KeyGen}; \ldots; (\mathsf{pk}_{P_n}, \mathsf{sk}_{P_n}) \leftarrow \mathsf{KeyGen}$
3 $(m^*, \sigma^*, s, v) \leftarrow \mathcal{A}^{\mathcal{O}_{sign}, \mathcal{O}_{veri}, \mathcal{O}_{sim}}(\mathsf{params}, \mathsf{pk}_{P_0}, \ldots, \mathsf{pk}_{P_n})$
4 **if** $\mathsf{Verify}_{P_s \to P_v}(m^*, \sigma^*) = 1$ *and* $\forall i : \sigma^* \neq \sigma_i$ **then**
5 | Output $\top$.

6 **else**
7 | Output $\bot$.

---

where the game $\mathsf{G}^{\mathsf{UF}}_{\Pi,\mathcal{A},\mathcal{O}}$ is defined in Game 4. A DVS scheme is n-party strongly-unforgeable *if it is n-party strongly-unforgeable with respect to* $\mathcal{O}^{(1)}_{sign}$, $\mathcal{O}^{(1)}_{sim}$, $\mathcal{O}^{(1)}_{veri}$ *from the standard n-sender* SendPriv-*oracles.*

Theorem 4. *Let $n \in \mathbb{N}$ and $\mathcal{O} = \{\mathcal{O}^{(1)}_{sign}, \mathcal{O}^{(2)}_{sign}, \mathcal{O}^{(1)}_{sim}, \mathcal{O}^{(2)}_{sim}, \mathcal{O}^{(1)}_{veri}, \mathcal{O}^{(2)}_{veri}\}$ be the n-sender standard oracles. Any DVS scheme that is n-party sender-private with respect to $\mathcal{O}' = \{\mathcal{O}^{(1)}_{sign}, \mathcal{O}^{(2)}_{sign}, \mathcal{O}^{(1)}_{sim}, \mathcal{O}^{(2)}_{sim}, \mathcal{O}'^{(1)}_{veri} = \emptyset, \mathcal{O}'^{(2)}_{veri} = \emptyset\}$ and strongly unforgeable is n-party sender-private (with respect to $\mathcal{O}$).*

Proof. Fix $n \in \mathbb{N}$. Suppose DVS scheme Π is n-party sender-private with respect to $\mathcal{O}' = \{\mathcal{O}^{(1)}_{sign}, \mathcal{O}^{(2)}_{sign}, \mathcal{O}^{(1)}_{sim}, \mathcal{O}^{(2)}_{sim}, \mathcal{O}'^{(1)}_{veri} = \emptyset, \mathcal{O}'^{(2)}_{veri} = \emptyset\}$ and strongly unforgeable, but not n-party sender-private with respect to $\mathcal{O}$. Then there exists an adversary $\mathcal{A}$ such that $\mathsf{Adv}^{\mathsf{SendPriv}}_{\Pi,\mathcal{A},\mathcal{O}}(\kappa) \not\leq \mathsf{negl}(\kappa)$. Let $\mathcal{A}'$ be $\mathcal{A}$, except every query $\mathcal{O}^{(b)}_{veri}(m_i, \sigma_i, s, v)$ is replaced with $\top$ if (m_i, σ_i) was the result of a signing or simulating oracle query and $\bot$ otherwise. Since $\mathcal{A}'$ no longer uses the verification oracles, we have $\mathsf{Adv}^{\mathsf{SendPriv}}_{\Pi,\mathcal{A}',\mathcal{O}} = \mathsf{Adv}^{\mathsf{SendPriv}}_{\Pi,\mathcal{A}',\mathcal{O}'} \leq \mathsf{negl}(\kappa)$, i.e. $\mathcal{A}'$ has the same advantage with respect to $\mathcal{O}$ and $\mathcal{O}'$, as they only differ in the verification oracles.

Now consider the adversary $\mathcal{B}$, who intends to create a forged signature. $\mathcal{B}$ runs $\mathcal{A}$, recording all signing and simulating queries. Whenever $\mathcal{A}$ makes a verification query for a valid signature that was not the result of a signing or simulating query, $\mathcal{B}$ outputs this signature and halts. Note that the only difference in the behaviour of $\mathcal{A}$ and $\mathcal{A}'$ can occur when $\mathcal{A}$ makes such a query. Since the difference between $\mathsf{Adv}^{\mathsf{SendPriv}}_{\Pi,\mathcal{A}',\mathcal{O}}$ and $\mathsf{Adv}^{\mathsf{SendPriv}}_{\Pi,\mathcal{A},\mathcal{O}}$ is more than negligible, we have that such a query occurs with more than negligible probability, giving $\mathcal{B}$ a more than negligible probability of constructing a forgery. This contradicts the fact that Π is strongly unforgeable. □

Theorem 5. *Any DVS scheme Π that is 2-party sender-private, strongly unforgeable, and computationally non-transferable is n-party sender-private for any $n \geq 2$.*

Proof. Suppose a DVS scheme Π is 2-party sender-private, strongly unforgeable, and computationally non-transferable. Assume towards a contradiction that Π

is not n-party sender-private for some fixed $n > 2$. By Theorem 4, this means Π is also not n-party sender-private with respect to

$$\mathcal{O}' = \{\mathcal{O}_{sign}^{(1)}, \mathcal{O}_{sign}^{(2)}, \mathcal{O}_{sim}^{(1)}, \mathcal{O}_{sim}^{(2)}, \mathcal{O}_{veri}^{'(1)} = \emptyset, \mathcal{O}_{veri}^{'(2)} = \emptyset\}.$$

Thus, there exists and adversary $\mathcal{A}$ such that $\mathsf{Adv}_{\Pi,\mathcal{A},\mathcal{O}'}^{\mathsf{SendPriv}}(\kappa, n) \not\leq \mathsf{negl}(\kappa)$. Let $\mathcal{A}'(1, \mathsf{params}, \mathsf{pk}_{P_0}, \mathsf{pk}_{P_1}, \mathsf{pk}_{P_2})$ be as follows: First, sample $n - 2$ keypairs $(\mathsf{sk}'_{P_2}, \mathsf{pk}'_{P_2}) \ldots (\mathsf{sk}'_{P_{n-1}}, \mathsf{pk}'_{P_{n-1}})$ representing parties $P_2' \ldots P_{n-1}'$ and set $P_0' = P_0$, $P_1' = P_1$, $P_n' = P_2$. Then, run $\mathcal{A}$ with the oracles $\mathcal{O}''$ defined as follows, with $b = 1, 2$:

- $\mathcal{O}_{veri}^{''(b)} = \emptyset$.
- $\mathcal{O}_{sign}^{''(b)}(m_i, s, v)$:
  - If $s, v \in \{0, 1, n\}$, return $\mathcal{O}_{sign}^{(b)}(m_i, \max(2, s), \max(2, v))$.
  - If $s \in \{2, \ldots, n-1\}$ and $v \in [n]$, return $\mathsf{Sign}_{P_s' \to P_v'}(m_i)$.
  - If $s \in \{0, 1, n\}$ and $v \in \{2, \ldots, n-1\}$, return $\mathsf{Simulate}_{P_s' \to P_v'}(m_i)$.
  - Else, return $\perp$.
- $\mathcal{O}_{sim}^{''(b)}(m_i, s, v)$:
  - If $s, v \in \{0, 1, n\}$, return $\mathcal{O}_{sim}^{(b)}(m_i, \max(2, s), \max(2, v))$.
  - If $v \in \{2, \ldots, n-1\}$ and $s \in [n]$, return $\mathsf{Simulate}_{P_s' \to P_v'}(m_i)$.
  - If $v \in \{0, 1, n\}$ and $s \in \{2, \ldots, n-1\}$, return $\mathsf{Sign}_{P_s' \to P_v'}(m_i)$.
  - Else, return $\perp$.

Note that these oracles make use of the fact that one can simulate or sign a signature without, respectively, the sender's or verifier's secret key. Thus we circumvent the issue mentioned in Sect. 3. In the oracles, max is used here to map n to 2, as n and 2 are the challenge verifiers in the n- and 2-party respectively.

Since Π is 2-party sender-private, we have $\mathsf{Adv}_{\Pi,\mathcal{A}',\mathcal{O}''}^{\mathsf{SendPriv}}(\kappa, 2) \leq \mathsf{negl}(\kappa)$. When we replace all oracle calls by their respective functionality, then $\mathsf{G}_{\Pi,\mathcal{A},\mathcal{O}'}^{\mathsf{SendPriv}}(\kappa, n, c)$ and $\mathsf{G}_{\Pi,\mathcal{A}',\mathcal{O}''}^{\mathsf{SendPriv}}(\kappa, 2, c)$ differ, up to relabeling of the parties, only in one way: some Sign executions in $\mathsf{G}_{\Pi,\mathcal{A},\mathcal{O}'}^{\mathsf{SendPriv}}(\kappa, n, c)$ have been replaced by $\mathsf{Simulate}$ in $\mathsf{G}_{\Pi,\mathcal{A}',\mathcal{O}''}^{\mathsf{SendPriv}}(\kappa, 2, c)$ and vice versa. Suppose $i \in \mathbb{N}$ such replacements have been made, then for $0 \leq j \leq i$ let $\mathsf{G}_j(\kappa, c)$ be $\mathsf{G}_{\Pi,\mathcal{A},\mathcal{O}'}^{\mathsf{SendPriv}}(\kappa, n, c)$ with only the first j such replacements made, which means $\mathsf{G}_0(\kappa, c) = \mathsf{G}_{\Pi,\mathcal{A},\mathcal{O}'}^{\mathsf{SendPriv}}(\kappa, n, c)$ and $\mathsf{G}_i(\kappa, c) = \mathsf{G}_{\Pi,\mathcal{A}',\mathcal{O}''}^{\mathsf{SendPriv}}(\kappa, 2, c)$. Since, by construction, $\Pr[\mathsf{G}_0(\kappa, c) = c] - \frac{1}{2} \not\leq \mathsf{negl}(\kappa)$ and $\Pr[\mathsf{G}_i(\kappa, c) = c] - \frac{1}{2} \leq \mathsf{negl}(\kappa)$, we can fix a lowest k such that $\Pr[\mathsf{G}_k(\kappa, c) = c] - \frac{1}{2} \not\leq \mathsf{negl}(\kappa)$ and $\Pr[\mathsf{G}_{k+1}(\kappa, c) = c] - \frac{1}{2} \leq \mathsf{negl}(\kappa)$. G_k and G_{k+1} differ only in one replacement. Without loss of generality, assume one $\mathsf{Sign}_{P_s \to P_v}(m)$ was replaced by $\mathsf{Simulate}_{P_s \to P_v}(m)$

Now define an adversary $\mathcal{B}$ for G^{NT} as follows: $\mathcal{B}(1, \mathsf{params}, \mathsf{pk}_S, \mathsf{sk}_S, \mathsf{pk}_V, \mathsf{sk}_V)$ picks a $c \in \{0, 1\}$ and runs $\mathsf{G}_k(c, \kappa)$, replacing pk_s with pk_S, sk_s with sk_S, pk_v with pk_V, and sk_v with sk_V. This replacement is only a relabeling. The execution of G_k is stopped at the one difference with G_{k+1}, then outputs $(m, (\mathsf{state}, c))$, where state is the current state of G_k and m the message in the replaced Sign.

$\mathcal{B}(2, (\text{state}, c), \sigma)$ then continues the execution of G_k with σ as the result of the replaced Sign until G_k outputs c'. $\mathcal{B}$ then outputs 0 if $c = c'$ and 1 otherwise.

Note that in $G^{NT}_{\Pi,\mathcal{B}}(0, \kappa)$, i.e. the case where a Sign is used in the non-transferability game, $\mathcal{B}$ plays $G_k(c, \kappa)$ and in $G^{NT}_{\Pi,\mathcal{B}}(1, \kappa)$, $\mathcal{B}$ plays $G_{k+1}(c, \kappa)$. Thus we have that

$$\Pr_b\left[G^{NT}_{\Pi,\mathcal{B}}(b, \kappa) = b\right] = \frac{1}{2}\Pr_c\left[G_k(c, \kappa) = c\right] + \frac{1}{2}\Pr_c\left[G_{k+1}(c, \kappa) \neq c\right].$$

This directly implies that

$$\mathsf{Adv}^{NT}_{\Pi,\mathcal{B}}(\kappa, n) = \frac{1}{2}\left(\Pr_c\left[G_k(c, \kappa) = c\right] - \Pr_c\left[G_{k+1}(c, \kappa) = c\right]\right) \not\leq \mathsf{negl}(\kappa).$$

This contradicts our assumption that Π is computationally non-transferable, thus Π must be n-party sender-private.   □

6   Conclusion

In this paper, we provided a way of defining sender-privacy in the n-party setting that is novel for DVS schemes, a generalization of existing definitions and in line with definitions for other types of schemes in the multi-party setting, in particular, ID-based SDVS schemes. We explored the effects of choosing the challenge differently and observed that this induces only polynomial differences in the advantage the adversary has. Furthermore, we showed how other properties of a SDVS scheme can be used to boost the sender-privacy of a scheme from an alternative definition to our definition. In particular, we have proven that under the assumption of strong unforgeability and computational non-transferability, a 2-party sender-private scheme is n-party sender-private. The proven relations are important since the SDVS schemes are often meant to be employed in an n-party setting and we give sufficient conditions for this to be secure.

We would like to stress that the objective of this paper is to formulate sender-privacy in such a way that it can be invoked in proofs that require this property and deal with a multi-party setting. Our last theorem shows that in almost all schemes the two-party sender-privacy will extend to the multi-party setting, as most schemes are unforgeable and non-transferable. As such we do not provide separating examples of schemes that satisfy one definition but not another, as any such case would be extremely artificial. Instead, the definitions in this work and their equivalence should be used to simplify proofs where sender-privacy property is used.

Acknowledgements. Jeroen van Wier was supported by the Luxembourg National Research Fund (FNR), under the joint CORE project Q-CoDe (CORE17/IS/11689058/ Q-CoDe/Ryan) and the CORE project EquiVox (C19/IS/13643617/EquiVox/Ryan).

A Full Proof of Theorem 2

Theorem 2. *For any adversary $\mathcal{A}$, set of oracles $\mathcal{O}$ and DVS scheme Π, there exists an adversary $\mathcal{B}$ such that*

$$\frac{1}{2}\mathsf{Adv}_{\Pi,\mathcal{A},\mathcal{O}}^{nr\mathsf{SendPriv}}(\kappa,n) \leq \mathsf{Adv}_{\Pi,\mathcal{B},\mathcal{O}}^{\mathsf{SendPriv}}(\kappa,n).$$

Proof. Here, we omit the subscripts Π and $\mathcal{O}$ for Adv and G for simplicity. Let $\mathcal{B}$ be defined as in Games 5 and 6. The permutationis used here to hide the indexation of the parties from the adversary. Note that applying a permutation π in this fashion is equivalent to generating the keypairs in the order $\pi^{-1}(0)\ldots\pi^{-1}(n)$ and since these are i.i.d. samples the order of their generation does not affect the winning probability of $\mathcal{A}$. However, it guarantees that the winning probability of $\mathcal{A}$ is the same for every c. Note that here we use Pr_π to indicate the uniform probability over all $\pi : [n] \mapsto [n]$ such that $\pi(n) = n$.

Game 5: $\mathcal{B}^{\mathcal{O}_{sign}^{(1)},\mathcal{O}_{veri}^{(1)},\mathcal{O}_{sim}^{(1)}}(1, \mathsf{params}, \mathsf{pk}_{P_0}, \ldots, \mathsf{pk}_{P_n})$

---

1 Pick a random permutation $\pi : [n] \mapsto [n]$ such that $\pi(n) = n$
2 $(m^*,) \leftarrow \mathcal{A}^{\mathcal{O}_{sign}^{(\pi,1)},\mathcal{O}_{veri}^{(\pi,1)},\mathcal{O}_{sim}^{(\pi,1)}}(1, \mathsf{params}, \mathsf{pk}_{P_{\pi(0)}}, \ldots, \mathsf{pk}_{P_{\pi(n)}})$
3 Output $(m^*, (\pi,))$

Game 6: $\mathcal{B}^{\mathcal{O}_{sign}^{(2)},\mathcal{O}_{veri}^{(2)},\mathcal{O}_{sim}^{(2)}}(2,{}',\sigma^*)$

---

1 Parse $'$ as $(\pi,)$
2 $c' \leftarrow \mathcal{A}^{\mathcal{O}_{sign}^{(\pi,2)},\mathcal{O}_{veri}^{(\pi,2)},\mathcal{O}_{sim}^{(\pi,2)}}(2,,\sigma^*)$
3 **if** $\pi(c') \in \{0,1\}$ **then**
4   $\lfloor$ Output $\pi(c')$
5 **else**
6   $\lfloor$ Output 0

$\mathsf{Adv}_{\mathcal{B}}^{\mathsf{SendPriv}}(\kappa,n)$

$$= \Pr_{c\leftarrow[1]}\left[\mathsf{G}_{\mathcal{B}}^{\mathsf{SendPriv}}(\kappa,n,c) = c\right] - \frac{1}{2}$$

$$= \Pr_{c\leftarrow[1],\pi}\left[\mathsf{G}_{\mathcal{A}}^{\mathsf{SendPriv}}(\kappa,n,\pi^{-1}(c)) = \pi^{-1}(c)\right]$$

$$\quad + \frac{1}{2}\Pr_{\pi}\left[\mathsf{G}_{\mathcal{A}}^{\mathsf{SendPriv}}(\kappa,n,\pi^{-1}(0)) \notin \{\pi^{-1}(0),\pi^{-1}(1)\}\right] - \frac{1}{2}$$

$$= \Pr_{c\leftarrow[n-1]}\left[\mathsf{G}_{\mathcal{A}}^{\mathsf{SendPriv}}(\kappa,n,c) = c\right]$$

$$-\frac{1}{2}\Pr_{\pi}\left[\mathsf{G}_{\mathcal{A}}^{\mathsf{SendPriv}}(\kappa,n,\pi^{-1}(0))\in\{\pi^{-1}(0),\pi^{-1}(1)\}\right]$$

$$=\frac{1}{2}\Pr_{c\leftarrow[n-1]}\left[\mathsf{G}_{\mathcal{A}}^{\mathsf{SendPriv}}(\kappa,n,c)=c\right]-\frac{1}{2}\Pr_{\pi}\left[\mathsf{G}_{\mathcal{A}}^{\mathsf{SendPriv}}(\kappa,n,\pi^{-1}(0))=\pi^{-1}(1)\right]$$

$$=\frac{1}{2}\left(\Pr_{c\leftarrow[n-1]}\left[\mathsf{G}_{\mathcal{A}}^{\mathsf{SendPriv}}(\kappa,n,c)=c\right]-\frac{1}{n-1}\Pr_{c\leftarrow[n-1]}\left[\mathsf{G}_{\mathcal{A}}^{\mathsf{SendPriv}}(\kappa,n,c)\neq c\right]\right)$$

$$=\frac{1}{2}\left(\frac{n}{n-1}\Pr_{c\leftarrow[n-1]}\left[\mathsf{G}_{\mathcal{A}}^{\mathsf{SendPriv}}(\kappa,n,c)=c\right]-\frac{1}{n-1}\right)$$

$$=\frac{n}{2(n-1)}\mathsf{Adv}_{\mathcal{A}}^{nr\mathsf{SendPriv}}(\kappa,n)\geq\frac{1}{2}\mathsf{Adv}_{\mathcal{A}}^{nr\mathsf{SendPriv}}(\kappa,n)$$

$\square$

B   Full Proof of Theorem 3

Theorem 3. *For any adversary $\mathcal{A}$ and set of oracles $\mathcal{O}$, there exists an adversary $\mathcal{B}$ such that*

$$\frac{2}{n^3-n}\cdot\mathsf{Adv}_{\Pi,\mathcal{A},\mathcal{O}}^{\mathsf{ChosenSendPriv}}(\kappa,n)\leq\mathsf{Adv}_{\Pi,\mathcal{B},\mathcal{O}}^{\mathsf{SendPriv}}(\kappa,n)$$

Proof. Fix $\mathcal{A}$. Let $\mathcal{B}$ be defined as in Game 7 and Game 8.

Game 7: $\mathcal{B}^{\mathcal{O}_{sign}^{(1)},\mathcal{O}_{veri}^{(1)},\mathcal{O}_{sim}^{(1)}}(1,\mathsf{params},\mathsf{pk}_{P_0},\ldots,\mathsf{pk}_{P_n})$

---

1 Pick a random permutation $\pi:[n]\mapsto[n]$

2 $(m^*,s_0,s_1,r,)\leftarrow\mathcal{A}^{\mathcal{O}_{sign}^{(\pi,1)},\mathcal{O}_{veri}^{(\pi,1)},\mathcal{O}_{sim}^{(\pi,1)}}(1,\mathsf{params},\mathsf{pk}_{P_{\pi(0)}},\ldots,\mathsf{pk}_{P_{\pi(n)}})$

3 **if** $\pi(s_0)=0\wedge\pi(s_1)=1\wedge\pi(r)=n$ **then**

4 $\quad\lfloor$ Output $(m^*,(0,))$

5 **else if** $\pi(s_0)=1\wedge\pi(s_1)=0\wedge\pi(r)=n$ **then**

6 $\quad\lfloor$ Output $(m^*,(1,))$

7 **else**

8 $\quad\lfloor$ Output $(m^*,(2,))$

The permutation is used here to hide the indexation of the parties from the adversary. Note that applying a permutation π in this fashion is equivalent to generating the keypairs in the order $\pi^{-1}(0)\ldots\pi^{-1}(n)$ and since these are i.i.d. samples the order of their generation does not affect the winning probability of $\mathcal{A}$. When playing game $\mathsf{G}_{\Pi,\mathcal{B}}^{\mathsf{SendPriv}}$, we can now distinguish two cases:

1. $\{\pi(s_0),\pi(s_1)\}=\{0,1\}$ and $\pi(r)=n$. Since π is random and unknown to $\mathcal{A}$, this happens with probability $\frac{2(n-2)!}{(n+1)!}$. In this case, $\mathcal{A}$ has chosen P_0 and P_1 as the possible signers and P_n as the verifier, making $\mathsf{G}_{\Pi,\mathcal{A}}^{\mathsf{ChosenSendPriv}}$ and $\mathsf{G}_{\Pi,\mathcal{B}}^{\mathsf{SendPriv}}$ equivalent.

Game 8: $\mathcal{B}^{\mathcal{O}^{(2)}_{sign},\mathcal{O}^{(2)}_{veri},\mathcal{O}^{(2)}_{sim}}(2,',\sigma^*)$

---

1 Parse $'$ as $(b,)$

2 $c' \leftarrow \mathcal{A}^{\mathcal{O}^{(2)}_{sign},\mathcal{O}^{(2)}_{veri},\mathcal{O}^{(2)}_{sim}}(2,,\sigma^*)$

3 **if** $b = 0$ **then**

4 $\quad\lfloor$ Output c'

5 **else if** $b = 1$ **then**

6 $\quad\lfloor$ Output $1 - c'$

7 **else**

8 $\quad\mid\quad c'' \leftarrow \{0,1\}$

9 $\quad\lfloor$ Output c''

---

2. Otherwise, $\mathcal{A}$ has chosen different signers or verifiers, in which case $\mathsf{G}^{\mathsf{SendPriv}}_{\Pi,\mathcal{B}}$ becomes equivalent to a random coin flip, with probability $\frac{1}{2}$ of guessing c.

Combining this, we get that

$$\Pr_{c \leftarrow \{0,1\}} \left[\mathsf{G}^{\mathsf{SendPriv}}_{\Pi,\mathcal{B},\mathcal{O}}(\kappa,n,c) = c \right] =$$

$$\frac{2(n-2)!}{(n+1)!} \Pr_{c \leftarrow \{0,1\}} \left[\mathsf{G}^{\mathsf{ChosenSendPriv}}_{\Pi,\mathcal{A},\mathcal{O}}(\kappa,n,c) = c \right] + \left(1 - \frac{2(n-2)!}{(n+1)!} \right) \frac{1}{2}.$$

Thus,

$$\mathsf{Adv}^{\mathsf{SendPriv}}_{\Pi,\mathcal{B},\mathcal{O}}(\kappa,n) = \frac{2(n-2)!}{(n+1)!} \cdot \mathsf{Adv}^{\mathsf{ChosenSendPriv}}_{\Pi,\mathcal{A},\mathcal{O}}(\kappa,n).$$

$\square$

References

1. Bellare, M., Boldyreva, A., Desai, A., Pointcheval, D.: Key-privacy in public-key encryption. In: Boyd, C. (ed.) ASIACRYPT 2001. LNCS, vol. 2248, pp. 566–582. Springer, Heidelberg (2001). https://doi.org/10.1007/3-540-45682-1_33
2. Chaum, D.: Private signature and proof systems. US Patent No. 5,493,614, February 1996
3. Chaum, D., van Antwerpen, H.: Undeniable signatures. In: Brassard, G. (ed.) CRYPTO 1989. LNCS, vol. 435, pp. 212–216. Springer, New York (1990). https://doi.org/10.1007/0-387-34805-0_20
4. Huang, Q., Yang, G., Wong, D.S., Susilo, W.: Identity-based strong designated verifier signature revisited. J. Syst. Softw. **84**(1), 120–129 (2011). https://doi.org/10.1016/j.jss.2010.08.057
5. Huang, X., Susilo, W., Mu, Y., Zhang, F.: Short (identity-based) strong designated verifier signature schemes. In: Chen, K., Deng, R., Lai, X., Zhou, J. (eds.) ISPEC 2006. LNCS, vol. 3903, pp. 214–225. Springer, Heidelberg (2006). https://doi.org/10.1007/11689522_20

6. Jakobsson, M., Sako, K., Impagliazzo, R.: Designated verifier proofs and their applications. In: Maurer, U. (ed.) EUROCRYPT 1996. LNCS, vol. 1070, pp. 143–154. Springer, Heidelberg (1996). https://doi.org/10.1007/3-540-68339-9_13
7. Laguillaumie, F., Vergnaud, D.: Designated verifier signatures: anonymity and efficient construction from *any* bilinear map. In: Blundo, C., Cimato, S. (eds.) SCN 2004. LNCS, vol. 3352, pp. 105–119. Springer, Heidelberg (2005). https://doi.org/10.1007/978-3-540-30598-9_8
8. Rivest, R.L., Shamir, A., Tauman, Y.: How to leak a secret. In: Boyd, C. (ed.) ASIACRYPT 2001. LNCS, vol. 2248, pp. 552–565. Springer, Heidelberg (2001). https://doi.org/10.1007/3-540-45682-1_32
9. Saeednia, S., Kremer, S., Markowitch, O.: An efficient strong designated verifier signature scheme. In: Lim, J.-I., Lee, D.-H. (eds.) ICISC 2003. LNCS, vol. 2971, pp. 40–54. Springer, Heidelberg (2004). https://doi.org/10.1007/978-3-540-24691-6_4
10. Susilo, W., Zhang, F., Mu, Y.: Identity-based strong designated verifier signature schemes. In: Wang, H., Pieprzyk, J., Varadharajan, V. (eds.) ACISP 2004. LNCS, vol. 3108, pp. 313–324. Springer, Heidelberg (2004). https://doi.org/10.1007/978-3-540-27800-9_27

Software Mitigation of RISC-V Spectre Attacks

Ruxandra Bălucea[1] and Paul Irofti[1,2(✉)]

[1] LOS-CS-FMI, University of Bucharest, Bucharest, Romania
ruxandra.balucea@unibuc.ro
[2] Institute for Logic and Data Science, Bucharest, Romania
paul@irofti.net

Abstract. Speculative attacks are still an active threat today that, even if initially focused on the x86 platform, reach across all modern hardware architectures. RISC-V is a newly proposed open instruction set architecture that has seen traction from both the industry and academia in recent years. In this paper we focus on the RISC-V cores where speculation is enabled and, as we show, where Spectre attacks are as effective as on x86. Even though RISC-V hardware mitigations were proposed in the past, they have not yet passed the prototype phase. Instead, we propose low-overhead software mitigations for Spectre-BTI, inspired from those used on the x86 architecture, and for Spectre-RSB, to our knowledge the first such mitigation to be proposed. We show that these mitigations work in practice and that they can be integrated in the LLVM toolchain. For transparency and reproducibility, all our programs and data are made publicly available online.

Keywords: side-channel attacks · hardware security · system security

1 Introduction

The introduction of Spectre [12] and Meltdown [16] attacks in 2018 opened up a new field of research exploiting side-effects that are spilled by speculation techniques inside the micro-architecture of modern processors [5,8,11,13,22,26]. Spectre attacks proved to be the hardest to mitigate [4,18,26], even though it was attempted via both software [1,9,20,21,24] and hardware [8,14,17] patches. These attacks mainly targeted the popular x86 architecture, but Spectre was later shown to affect multiple other architectures [8,19,22,23].

RISC-V is a new open-standard instruction set architecture (ISA) [25] recently proposed by University of California, Berkeley that has seen wide academic and industry adoption [17]. In this paper we focus on reproducing and mitigating Spectre attacks on the RISC-V architecture.

Even if the RISC-V cores are written from scratch in order to research new efficient hardware methods, they must also keep up with existing performance-inducing technologies. Speculation is one of them and it is present on all modern

Supplementary Information The online version contains supplementary material available at https://doi.org/10.1007/978-3-031-52947-4_5.

M. Manulis et al. (Eds.): SecITC 2023, LNCS 14534, pp. 51–64, 2024.
https://doi.org/10.1007/978-3-031-52947-4_5

processors. Despite recent speculation attacks, unfortunately, for mainstream architectures such as x86, there are few hardware mitigations and even these seem to not be sufficient [4]. On RISC-V, the few proposed hardware implementations [8,17,27] are mostly combinations or adaptations of the x86 ones. So, even if they seem to be quite efficiently in the present, as the RISC-V community grows, we expect the same problems as on x86. In this context, despite the fact that the same performance can not be achieved as with hardware solutions, software mitigations remain the most practical and safe ones.

To our knowledge, currently on RISC-V there are implemented the following variants of Spectre: Spectre on Conditional Branches (Spectre v1), Spectre Branch Target Injection (Spectre-BTI or Spectre v2) [8] and Spectre Return Stack Buffer (Spectre-RSB or Spectre v5) [23].

In this paper we propose software mitigations for the Spectre-BTI variants and also for Spectre-RSB. As far as we know, this is the first time that Spectre-RSB mitigations are proposed.

Retpoline [24] is such a mitigation for x86 that targets only Spectre-BTI. As far as we know, no software mitigation is known for the RISC-V architecture and in fact, for any other RISC architecture. We assume that this is also due to the fact that for the RISC-V ISA things are not as straight-forward as on x86 because the prologue and the epilogue of a function are more complex. The stack frame requires saving of a really important callee-saved register - the return address `ra`. Retpoline is influenced by the calling-convention and how function return is achieved. Therefore, for RISC-V, it can not be applied. In this paper we propose a new software mitigation method for RISC-V that addresses and circumvents these issues.

Revisiting the main idea behind x86 Retpoline, we note that this mitigation can be applied for Spectre v2 because speculation also appears in the context of a call instruction. Thus, we defend against this type of attack by applying a defense technique derived from another speculation attack - Spectre v5. The idea is that the indirect jump to an address from a register (x86 `jmp`, RISC-V `jalr`) can be replaced with a direct call to a function (`call`, `jal`) where the return address can be overwritten with the value of that register. At the return phase, the execution will continue at the address from the register. At the same time, speculatively there will be executed the instructions under the call. Thus, in order to trap the speculation, we add an infinite loop after the indirect jump.

Focusing on RISC-V, this defense can not be applied in the same manner. If we modify the return address with the desired register value, the function called indirectly will also have as return address the beginning of the function and the execution will be caught in an infinite loop (we describe this in detail around Listings 3 and 6). This is because the return is not dictated by the value from the top, but by the return address register which is saved on the stack and restored at the end (we describe this behavior in detail around Listing 4). Nevertheless, this mitigation can be applied as described above in specific contexts: for indirect jumps there is no stack frame created and there is no dependency on the value of the return address register.

Contribution. Our main contribution is the proposal of software mitigations on RISC-V against Spectre attacks. To this end we provide an implementation of the proposed defense that handles Spectre-BTI, for both indirect jumps and calls, and Spectre-RSB. To our knowledge, this is the first time that Spectre-RSB mitigation is proposed. The distinction can be made directly in the assembly code and the defense can be applied by replacing the jump/call instructions with specific code. To prove this, we provide a publicly available LLVM feature that can be activated at compilation time through enabling the mitigations via a single flag. The resulting executable can be run on the RISC-V speculative core BOOM. Spectre-BTI and Spectre-RSB will be no longer reproduced. Another contribution is the adaptation of the existing Spectre variants for the RISC-V speculative cores that we implement in practice and make publicly available. We also provide the steps necessary to reproduce our research together with our test programs and data.

Outline. In Sect. 3, we revisit and adapt the Spectre attacks needed in order to prove that RISC-V is vulnerable to this type of attacks, which are also required in part for our proposed mitigations. Next, in Sect. 4, we introduce the proposed defenses against Spectre-RSB and two types of Spectre-BTI attacks. We test our attack and mitigations attacks and provide experiments along with ways of reproducing our results in Sect. 5. In the next section we conclude and make publicly available our implementation and data.

2   Berkeley Out of Order Machine

Berkeley Out of Order Machine (BOOM) [3,7,28] is an open-source RV64GC core written in Chisel. It is superscalar, out-of-order and speculative, being an ideal candidate for our work. The speculation is dictated by a two-level branch predictor composed of a Next-Line Predictor (NLP) and a Backing Predictor (BPD). The predicted address is chosen based on two other structures incorporated in the NLP - Branch Target Buffer (BTB) and Return Address Stack (RAS). The taken/not taken decision is up to the BPD, but as we do not address an attack based on branches, we will not present more information here.

BTB is a table with 64×4 entries, set-associative which stores a mapping from a PC address to a target address. A tag search is initiated in this table, whenever a prediction for an indirect jump is needed.

RAS is a stack which maintains in the top the following address after the last call. This value is popped when a `ret` instruction is met. The stack structure was chosen in order to handle nested calls. However, this was a problem in the second version of BOOM because the stack was not updated correspondingly in case of a mispredict. This was solved in SonicBoom, the third version of BOOM.

3   RISC-V Spectre Attacks

This section presents Spectre-BTI (Branch Target Injection) [12] and Spectre-RSB (Return Stack Buffer) [13] in the RISC-V context [8] along with the side-channel technique Evict&Reload [10] which is a prerequisite for these attacks. Both attacks are illustrated by reading memory from the same process, in-place, referred to as BTB-SA-IP and RSB-SA-IP accordingly to the threat model presented in [6].

3.1 Spectre-BTI

Spectre-BTI was reproduced on RISC-V on the experimental speculative core BOOM. In this variant, arbitrary locations in the allocated memory of a program can be read exploiting the indirect branch instructions - `jalr` for calls and `jr` for jumps. Each jump/call to an indirect address, loaded in a register, creates a speculation window during which essential information can be brought into the cache memory. As on other architectures, in case of a mispredict, the cache is not cleared and the information can be retrieved by an attacker.

The attack is illustrated by reading memory from the same process, having a role-play between an attacker and a victim. In our experiments we use this approach due to the limitations imposed by the simulator (as will be later described). The time needed to execute is quite long, so we prefer to use a single binary. In the first phase, the attacker mistrains the Branch Target Buffer (BTB) jumping for a large number of times to a valid fixed address. The valid jump is taken to a segment of code that discloses information from a certain memory region. This step makes the predictor assume that the jump will always be taken. In the second stage, the attacker makes the victim execute an indirect jump to another (normally illegal) address, where the disclosed information is of interest to the attacker, and, due to the training phase and speculation, the predictor assumes the jump will be taken and the pipeline proceeds with the memory access. Thus, the second phase can create side-effects into the cache, side-effects that provide unauthorized information to the attacker. In the end, even if the jump is made to the correct address, the data from cache can still be read by the attacker.

We will present here only the main aspects of this attack in order to introduce our work. The implementation details can be found in the Supplementary Material and also in the original paper [8]. Spectre authors present an attack based on the indirect calls having two pieces of code similar to the functions presented in Listing 1. Spectre-v2 was presented by the authors only for indirect calls that appear, for example, when we are talking about virtual functions. We extended this example and add a new one for the indirect jumps when the register keeps the address of a snippet of code, such as for a switch case. Thus, in the new example, we took the assembly code generated for this function, removed the instructions related to the stack frame and used the global variable `passInIdx` to access the desired memory. Even if for the calls we could have maintained `passInIdx` as a parameter, we also kept it as a global variable for linearity.

As presented above, the BTB is trained in the first stage to predict the `victimFunc` address. The jump to that function was repeated 40 times, each time assigning different valid values to the `passInIdx` variable. The 41st time, as it can be seen in line 15, the attacker assigned to this variable a convenient value, for example, the index corresponding to the beginning of the secret. In

```
1   uint64_t passInIdx;
2   uint8_t array1[10] = {1,2,3,4,5,6,7,8,9,10};
3   uint8_t array2[256 * L1_BLOCK_SZ_BYTES];
4   char* secretString = "BOOM!";
5
6   void wantFunc(){
7       asm("nop");
8   }
9
10  void victimFunc(){
11      temp &= array2[array1[passInIdx] * L1_BLOCK_SZ_BYTES];
12  }
13
14  int main() {
15      uint64_t attackIdx =
16          (uint64_t)(secretString - (char*)array1);
17      ...
18      //victimFunc address is loaded in %[addr]
19      //    for the training phase
20      // wantFunc addrees is loaded in %[addr]
21      //    by the victim
22      "jalr ra, \%[addr], 0\n"
23      ...
24  }
```

Listing 1. Spectre v2

the second phase, in line 22, the victim tries to call via an indirect instruction wantFunc, but speculatively victimFunc is called again. So, in line 11, array2[array1[attackIdx] * L1_BLOCK_SZ_BYTES] is brought in the cache (i.e. array2['B' * L1_BLOCK_SZ_BYTES]). Having this value in the cache and access to array2, the attacker can retrieve the first character from the password with a side-channel attack method such as Evict & Reload [10]. For your convenience, we review this in the Supplementary Material.

For more details, the reader is advised to consult the full attack provided in the Supplementary Material. There, the code presented in Listing 9 is for an attack on indirect calls (see the called functions from Listing 10). For indirect jumps, at line 73, we should have a jump instruction: jalr x0, %addr, 0. Also, for the return from the snippets of code presented in the assembly file from Listing 11, we added at the end a jump back to a label from the source file. This label should be added after the indirect jump at line 74 and declared as global before main (asm(".global end\n")).

3.2   Spectre-RSB

Spectre-RSB [13], known as Spectre-v5, was reproduced on SonicBoom, the third generation of BOOM which added as a feature a functional RAS. In this variant, the vulnerability is based on the RAS hardware stack where the most probable return addresses are pushed for each call instruction. Based on these values, the return from a function is speculatively computed and, as before, a speculation execution window is created. Although, if the value of the return address register ra is manipulated during the function, the program will continue the execution on a different path and the information brought into the cache by the instructions

```
1  __asm__ (
2      "frameDump:";
3      "# Pop off stack frame and get main RA"
4      "ld ra, 56(sp)";
5      "addi sp, sp, 64";
6      "ld fp, -16(sp)";
7      ...
8      "ret");
9  void specFunc(char *addr){
10     extern void frameDump();
11     uint64_t dummy = 0;
12     frameDump();
13     char secret = *addr;
14     dummy = array2[secret * L1_BLOCK_SZ_BYTES];
15     dummy = rdcycle();
16 }
```

Listing 2. Spectre v5

executed speculatively will not be erased. In this context, again, an attacker can retrieve the information using the Flush & Reload technique.

For BOOM, the implementation of RAS generates a new stack entry: the address of the next instruction after the `call`. In Listing 2 we illustrate the attack. As can be seen, it is enough to add a function which modifies the return address and add relevant code after the call to this function (lines 13–15). To accomplish this, the function `frameDump` (line 2) loads in `ra` the value of the return address of the function `specFunc` (line 4) and the stack frame is popped (line 5), so the execution will continue directly in the calling function of `specFunc`.

Similar to what we discussed in the previous attack, the attacker can set the parameter to `specFunc` as the desired address (line 9), in this case the address of the secret string. The value from `array2` (line 14) corresponding to the first character will be brought into memory and the attacker will be able to retrieve the information using Flush & Reload. By repeating the attack for all characters, the secret will be revealed.

4   RISC-V Spectre Mitigations

Given the attacks from Sect. 3, we now propose two Spectre-BTI mitigation strategies for the RISC-V architecture, inspired by the x86-specific software mitigation Retpoline [24] and a new Spectre-RSB mitigation, the first in the field as far as we know. In the current section we present and discuss ways of replacing indirect jumps and calls with a sequence of instructions that will provide the same behavior while removing the speculation attack.

4.1   Spectre-BTI: Indirect Jumps

Indirect jumps are realized using the `jr` instruction which is in fact an assembly pseudo instruction for `jalr` with the first operand set as register X0.

$$jr \ rd, \ rs1 \rightarrow jalr \ x0, \ rs1, \ 0$$

```
1   jr        a5
```

```
1   jal set_up_target
2   capture_spec:
3      j capture_spec
4   set_up_target:
5      addi ra, a5, 0
6      jr ra
```

Listing 3. RISC-V mitigation - indirect jump

```
1   addi sp, sp, -16    # add space on the stack
2   sd ra, 8(sp)        # save the return address
3   sd fp, 0(sp)        # save the frame pointer
4   addi fp, sp, 16     # modify the stack frame base
```

```
1   ld fp, 0(sp)        # restore the frame pointer
2   ld ra, 8(sp)        # restore the return address
3   addi sp, sp, 16     # reduce the size of the stack
4   jr ra               # return in the caller
```

Listing 4. Current general function prologue (top) and epilogue (bottom)

This register is hardwired zero. So, its presence on that position indicates that no register will take the value of the following instruction address.

The mitigation is summarized in Listing 3; the first block represents the original indirect jump and the second its replacement. To replace the jr instruction (first block, line 1), we use the Spectre v5 vulnerability and rewrite it as a direct call to a pseudo-function with no calling-convention applied (second block, line 1). In this function we store in ra the value of the register from the indirect jump (line 5). At the end we do a ret - an indirect jump to the return address register jr ra (line 6). During this time the speculation will be caught in an infinite loop that takes place after the call instruction (lines 2–3).

Remark 1. Regarding line 6, it may seem that the original problem from line 1 was only moved below due to the usage of the same instruction (the unconditional jump jr). In fact this is not the case because this new jump has a special property - it is a return instruction. The unconditional jumps having as operand the register ra are marked as SPSVERBc6s and are used only to remove the RAS entry added by the calls. It would make no sense to predict a target of a ret as it depends on the location of the associated call. This behavior was also confirmed by our experiments from Sect. 5.

4.2   Spectre-BTI: Indirect Calls

For the indirect calls, the transformation is not so simple. The indirect calls are reflected in the jalr single-operand pseudo-instruction which is an alias for the instruction with the same name, but more operands.

$$jalr\ rs1 \rightarrow jalr\ ra,\ rs1,\ 0$$

The first operand which is the operand that will take the value of the following instruction address is in this case set by default to ra. In this way, the return from the called function is right after the call instruction and now it is quite clear why this value is chosen as a RAS entry.

$$ra \leftarrow pc + 4$$
$$pc \leftarrow rs1 + 0$$

```
1 addi sp, sp, -32
2 sd ra, 24(sp)
3 sd fp, 16(sp)
4 addi fp, sp, 16
5 sd s1, 8(sp)
6 sd s2, 0(sp)
```

```
1 addi sp, sp, -16
2 sd ra, 8(sp)
3 sd fp, 0(sp)
4 addi fp, sp, 0
5 addi sp, sp, -16
6 sd s1, 8(sp)
7 sd s2, 0(sp)
```

Listing 5. Prologue mitigation for function **f1**: top block represents the original prologue and the bottom block presents the proposed mitigation.

In order to achieve the same behavior as for the indirect jumps we need to find a way not to overwrite the return address for the functions called through the register. We want to maintain the idea of overwriting the return address for the **set_up_target** function with the address of the beginning of the function stored in the register. Thinking about where does the called function return, we discover that in fact that address is not represented by the value from **ra**, but by the value from the stack restored at the end in **ra**. Thus we can replace the return address register with the value of the register from the indirect call, but with one condition: we can not store this new address on the stack. Instead, we need to save the legitimate one - the address after the indirect call.

Remark 2. If during the function execution the return address register **ra** is modified, for example when handling an error via an early return inside an if-clause, our mitigation will not affect the normal program behavior.

In Listing 4 we present an usual prologue and epilogue for a 64-bit RISC-V core. In the Prologue (top block), in order to meet the condition presented above, we need to jump over the instruction that adds space on the stack by default (line 1) and over the instruction that stores the value of **ra** on the stack (line 2). In order to do this, we need to recreate these instructions in the body of the **set_up_target**.

In practice the first lines in the prologue are not always the ones presented in the top block of Listing 4. These lines are changed by adding the callee-saved registers on the stack. These are resizing the stack and the space added becomes dependent on their number. For example, for a given function **f1**, registers **s1** and **s2** must be saved on the stack so the allocated space is increased to 32 bytes. Another function **f2**, that is also called indirectly, requires a single register to be saved and the allocated space is only of 24 bytes. Our goal is to replace the indirect call with the same code all the time no matter of the function at hand.

Thus the first measure to be taken is one that offers consistency to the instructions used by the prologue. We propose to accomplish this in two separate phases. The idea here is to modify the prologue of all functions such that in the first phase, the memory is allocated only for the registers saved all the time - **ra** and **fp**. In the second stage, the stack size can be adjusted by the initial value minus 16 bytes (in case of a 64-bit architecture). From then on, the compiler can continue to emit the stores for the other callee-saved and the rest of the function

```
1 jalr    a5
```

```
1 jal set_up_target
2 capture_spec:
3   j capture_spec
4 set_up_target:
5   addi ra, a5, 4
6   addi sp, sp, -16
7   la a5, end
8   sd a5, 8(sp)
9   jr ra
10 end:
```

Listing 6. RISC-V mitigation - indirect call

```
1 call    frameDump
```

```
1 jal set_up_target
2 capture_spec:
3   j capture_spec
4 set_up_target:
5   la ra, frameDump
6   jr ra
```

Listing 7. RISC-V mitigation - Spectre RSB

body. Therefore, the initial part of the prologue is replaced by one with the same behavior which keeps the first instructions constant.

As an example, the transformation for the f1 function is presented in Listing 5. In the first frame, the stack allocation is the usual one, similar to the one exposed in Listing 4, adapted for the f1 function. In the second frame, the prologue is changed as previously described. The stack size is initially increased only by 16 bytes (line 1) in order to allocate space for the storage of ra and fp (lines 2–3). Now, the frame pointer is modified to point to the value of the old fp by taking the value of sp (line 4). As a last step, at line 5, the value of sp is decreased again with the necessary amount of space for the callee-registers - 16 bytes for s1 and s2 (the stack grows downwards).

We generalize this approach and introduce the resulting instructions in the body of the set_up_target function. The full implementation is depicted in Listing 6: the top block contains the original indirect call instruction and the bottom block our proposed mitigation. On line 5, in order to jump over the first two instructions, we need to add in ra the value from the register plus 4. For this, we remind the reader that we use RV64GC - the default target for the existing compilers. In this case, some instructions like addi and sd are compressed on 2 bytes each. After that, on line 6, we need to add the instruction which allocates space for the registers ra and fp and store on the stack (lines 7–8) the address at the end of the snippet of code (line 10). In our LLVM implementation we computed the offset for the relative jump, but here, for clarity, we store the address of a pre-added label (line 10). Other than that, the idea is the same as for the indirect jump, the call to the function is realized using the value from the ra register (line 9) and the speculation is trapped after the call (lines 2–3).

Remark 3. The transformation presented in 6 is applied in case of using the compressed extension. Also, the function and the call should be in files compiled with the same option (with or without the compressed extension activated).

4.3 Spectre-RSB

The idea behind this mitigation is similar to the one presented for the two variants of Spectre-BTI. We need to avoid a `call` instruction which will add into the RAS an address that will be used for speculation.

A call does not have as an operand a register, but a relocated symbol whose address is either known, either will be computed at link time. Either way, there is no reason not to use the symbol in a different instruction. So, similar to moving the value of the register used for indirect jumps in `ra`, we can use the symbol for a load in `ra`.

As a result, we propose a mitigation where, as per Listing 7, we maintain the idea of catching the speculation in an infinite loop (lines 2–3) and make a call to the `set_up_target` function (line 1). In this function with no prologue and no epilogue, we load the address of the symbol in the `ra` register(line 5) and return basically at the beginning of the function that we need to call (line 6).

5 Experiments[1]

To run our experiments we used a superscalar, speculative, out-of-order core named BOOM (Berkeley Out-of-Order Machine). For this project we used the latest version of BOOM named SonicBoom. BOOM can be also integrated in a SoC using the majority of hardware structures from Rocket Chip by loading them like a library. BOOM can be used as a part of a larger project named Chipyard which includes a number of different cores, tools, accelerators and simulators. From this project, different configurations of a chip can be generated with different numbers of cores, with vectorization support or different number of inputs for certain components. In our experiments, we used the smallest available configuration - `SmallBoomConfig`.

These configurations can be used directly on FPGAs or using the VCS simulator. They can also be executed on the open-source simulator Verilator which was our choice as well. Being a software simulated environment, execution times can take a really long time. Nevertheless, the results are reliable and the behavior is similar as for the other options. Even though we reached out to other vendors that offer RISC-V chips with speculation enabled, in our case this was the only testbed available that we could run our attacks and test our proposed mitigations on. To reproduce our experiments, we created a minimal configuration in the `Spectre-v2-v5-mitigation-RISCV` repository. The interested reader should also consult the official documentation of BOOM [28] and Chipyard [2].

The mitigations for the scenarios presented in Sect. 4 were adapted and integrated in the LLVM toolchain. In the future, we hope to get our work integrated in the official LLVM project. The patchset and the full tree of the modified LLVM version is also made available online in our repository. To reproduce our results, it is necessary to download the updated version of LLVMand build it following

---

[1] Programs, code and data available at https://github.com/riscv-spectre-mitigations.

```
 1 ./simulator-chipyard-SmallBoomConfig bin          1 ./simulator-chipyard-SmallBoomConfig bin
     /indirectBranchFunction.riscv                       /indirectBranchFunction.riscv
 2 The attacker guessed character B 8 times.          2 The attacker guessed character  1 times.
 3 The attacker guessed character O 8 times.          3 The attacker guessed character  1 times.
 4 The attacker guessed character O 7 times.          4 The attacker guessed character  1 times.
 5 The attacker guessed character M 8 times.          5 The attacker guessed character  1 times.
 6 The attacker guessed character ! 9 times           6 The attacker guessed character  1 times.
 7 The guessed secret is BOOM!                        7 The guessed secret is
 8 ./simulator-chipyard-SmallBoomConfig bin          8 ./simulator-chipyard-SmallBoomConfig bin
     /indirectBranchSwitch.riscv                         /indirectBranchSwitch.riscv
 9 The attacker guessed character B 7 times           9 The attacker guessed character  1 times.
10 The attacker guessed character O 6 times          10 The attacker guessed character  1 times.
11 The attacker guessed character O 7 times          11 The attacker guessed character  1 times.
12 The attacker guessed character M 6 times.         12 The attacker guessed character  1 times.
13 The attacker guessed character ! 8 times          13 The attacker guessed character  1 times.
14 The guessed secret is BOOM!                       14 The guessed secret is
15 ./simulator-chipyard-SmallBoomConfig bin         15 ./simulator-chipyard-SmallBoomConfig bin
     /returnStackBuffer.riscv                            /returnStackBuffer.riscv
16 The attacker guessed character B 9 times          16 The attacker guessed character  0 times.
17 The attacker guessed character O 8 times          17 The attacker guessed character  1 times.
18 The attacker guessed character O 6 times          18 The attacker guessed character  0 times.
19 The attacker guessed character M 6 times.         19 The attacker guessed character  1 times.
20 The attacker guessed character ! 10 times         20 The attacker guessed character  0 times.
21 The guessed secret is BOOM!                       21 The guessed secret is
```

Listing 8. Attacks (left) and mitigations (right): spectre attack is repeated 10 times for each memory read. Left block recovers the secret "BOOM!" via three Spectre attacks; right block attempts to do the same but with mitiagtions enabled but fails.

the recommendations on their official page. Additionally, GNU toolchain version 2.32 for RISC-V needs to be installed in the same directory as LLVM.

Our repository also contains programs testing for and, if possible, reproducing the attacks for the two variants of Spectre v2, on indirect jumps (see indirectBranchSwitch), and indirect calls (see indirectBranchFunction) and also for Spectre v5 (returnStackBuffer). These can be compiled and executed using the Makefile. To activate the mitigation it is necessary to add the parameter RETPOLINE=1 to the make command. For both cases, there are also some variants of the tests that do not need the updated compiler. Here, the attack is mitigated directly from the code, using inline assembly and manually replacing the unsafe sections as described in Sect. 4.

We present an instance of our experiments in Listing 8 where the left block reproduces the Spectre attacks and the right block tries to reproduce them with mitigations enabled thus failing to retrieve the secret. As customary with Spectre attacks, due to the empirically chosen cache hit threshold, the confidence level of the retrieved data is increased by running the attack for ten times on each character from the secret. As we can see in Listing 8 in the left block, on an unpatched system, the characters are guessed in the majority of times. After adding the LLVM compiler option that includes our mitigations, in the right block of Listing 8, the characters are no longer guessed. Nothing will be printed in the console, as each time a different non-printable character from the ASCII code is guessed. Other times no character is guessed at all (denoted "0 times" in the figure) as nothing was found in the cache. This is why we do not see a character in the output and this is also why for each character we get that it was guessed only a single time.

Table 1. Size difference for each change created by the mitigation for the standard ISA (RV64G) and standard ISA with the compressed extension (RV64GC).

	RV64G	RV64GC
Indirect jumps	12 bytes	10 bytes
Indirect calls	28 bytes	22 bytes
Function Prologue	4 bytes	2 bytes
Direct calls	16 bytes	14 bytes

Regarding the performance impact of our proposed mitigations, unfortunately, using the simulator as our only option, did not permit us to obtain a reliable execution time performance analysis. Of course, the code size will be increased by the instructions depicted in Listings 3 and 6, but we argue that this small increase is acceptable.

The code size depends on the usage of the compressed extension (RV64GC). Also, the size difference is influenced by the number of indirect jumps, indirect calls, direct calls, and functions. The number of bytes for each case is presented in Table 1. For indirect jumps and calls, the difference results from adding extra instructions as presented in Listings 3 and 6. For functions, only one supplementary instruction is added by splitting the stack allocation in two phases. Future research can help reduce this code size increase by employing static or dynamic analysis to identify and replace only the vulnerable paths. Given that our mitigations have a similar approach to that of the x86 Retpoline implementation which is in use by most users today, we expect this to also be the next step for RISC-V development and to become the default on this platform. Nowadays kernels on x86 are compiled with this mitigation for both Windows [1] and Linux (since 4.15) [21] operating systems. Also, the Retpoline authors showed that this mitigation does not cause significant performance degradation for x86 [15].

6   Conclusions

In this paper we reproduced Spectre-BTI and Spectre-RSB attacks on the RISC-V speculative core BOOM. Our main contribution represents the proposed software mitigations for Spectre-RSB, to our knowledge the first mitigation for this attack, and for Spectre-BTI indirect jumps and indirect calls. We demonstrate that these mitigations are effective against Spectre variants as depicted by our experiments. The resulting work is integrated in the LLVM toolchain for ease of use and reproducibility.

References

1. Allievi, A.: Retpoline: the anti-spectre (Type 2) mitigation in windows. In: BlueHat v18 Security Conference (2018)
2. Amid, A., et al.: Chipyard: integrated design, simulation, and implementation framework for custom SoCs. IEEE Micro **40**(4), 10–21 (2020)

3. Asanovic, K., Patterson, D.A., Celio, C.: The Berkeley out-of-order machine (boom): an industry-competitive, synthesizable, parameterized RISC-V processor. Technical report, University of California at Berkeley, Berkeley, United States (2015)
4. Barberis, E., Frigo, P., Muench, M., Bos, H., Giuffrida, C.: Branch history injection: on the effectiveness of hardware mitigations against cross-privilege spectre-v2 attacks. In: USENIX Security, vol. 11 (2022)
5. Bhattacharyya, A., Sánchez, A., Koruyeh, E.M., Abu-Ghazaleh, N., Song, C., Payer, M.: SpecROP: speculative exploitation of ROP chains. In: 23rd International Symposium on Research in Attacks, Intrusions and Defenses RAID 2020), pp. 1–16 (2020)
6. Canella, C., et al.: A systematic evaluation of transient execution attacks and defenses. In: 28th USENIX Security Symposium (USENIX Security 2019), pp. 249–266 (2019)
7. Celio, C., Chiu, P., Nikolic, B., Patterson, D.A., Asanovic, K.: BOOMv2: an open-source out-of-order RISC-V core. In: First Workshop on Computer Architecture Research with RISC-V (CARRV) (2017)
8. Gonzalez, A., Korpan, B., Younis, E., Zhao, J.: Spectrum: classifying, replicating and mitigating spectre attacks on a speculating RISC-V microarchitecture. Technical report, University of California at Berkeley (2019)
9. Gruss, D., Lipp, M., Schwarz, M., Fellner, R., Maurice, C., Mangard, S.: KASLR is dead: long live KASLR. In: Bodden, E., Payer, M., Athanasopoulos, E. (eds.) ESSoS 2017. LNCS, vol. 10379, pp. 161–176. Springer, Cham (2017). https://doi.org/10.1007/978-3-319-62105-0_11
10. Gruss, D., Spreitzer, R., Mangard, S.: Cache template attacks: automating attacks on inclusive Last-Level caches. In: 24th USENIX Security Symposium (USENIX Security 2015), pp. 897–912 (2015)
11. Kiriansky, V., Waldspurger, C.: Speculative buffer overflows: attacks and defenses. arXiv preprint arXiv:1807.03757 (2018)
12. Kocher, P., et al.: Spectre attacks: Exploiting speculative execution. In: 2019 IEEE Symposium on Security and Privacy (SP) (2019)
13. Koruyeh, E.M., Khasawneh, K.N., Song, C., Abu-Ghazaleh, N.: Spectre returns! Speculation attacks using the return stack buffer. In: 12th USENIX Workshop on Offensive Technologies WOOT 2018) (2018)
14. Koruyeh, E.M., Shirazi, S.H.A., Khasawneh, K.N., Song, C., Abu-Ghazaleh, N.: SPECCFI: mitigating spectre attacks using CFI informed speculation. In: 2020 IEEE Symposium on Security and Privacy (SP), pp. 39–53. IEEE (2020)
15. Linton, M., Parseghian, P.: More details about mitigations for the CPU speculative execution issue. https://security.googleblog.com/2018/01/more-details-about-mitigations-for-cpu_4.html. Accessed 28 May 2022
16. Lipp, M., et al.: Meltdown: reading kernel memory from user space. In: 27th USENIX Security Symposium (USENIX Security 2018) (2018)
17. Martinoli, V., Teglia, Y., Bouagoun, A., Leveugle, R.: CVA6's data cache: structure and behavior. arXiv preprint arXiv:2202.03749 (2022)
18. Milburn, A., Sun, K., Kawakami, H.: You cannot always win the race: analyzing the LFENCE/JMP mitigation for branch target injection. arXiv preprint arXiv:2203.04277 (2022)

19. Miles, S., McDonough, C., Michael, E.O., Shankar Kumar, V.S., Lee, J.J.: Simulating modern CPU vulnerabilities on a 5-stage MIPS pipeline using node-RED. In: Verma, P., Charan, C., Fernando, X., Ganesan, S. (eds.) Advances in Data Computing, Communication and Security. LNDECT, vol. 106, pp. 707–716. Springer, Singapore (2022). https://doi.org/10.1007/978-981-16-8403-6_65

20. Nikolaev, R., Nadeem, H., Stone, C., Ravindran, B.: Adelie: continuous address space layout re-randomization for Linux drivers. arXiv preprint arXiv:2201.08378 (2022)

21. Poimboeuf, J.: Static calls. Linux Weekly News (2018)

22. Ravichandran, J., Na, W.T., Lang, J., Yan, M.: PACMAN: attacking ARM pointer authentication with speculative execution. In: Proceedings of the 49th Annual International Symposium on Computer Architecture, pp. 685–698 (2022)

23. Sabbagh, M., Fei, Y., Kaeli, D.: Secure speculative execution via RISC-V open hardware design. In: Fifth Workshop on Computer Architecture Research with RISC-V (2021)

24. Turner, P.: Retpoline: a software construct for preventing branch-target-injection. https://support.google.com/faqs/answer/7625886. Accessed 28 May 2022

25. Waterman, A., Asanovi, K.: The RISC-V instruction set manual, volume I: user-level ISA. RISC-V Foundation (2014)

26. Wieczorkiewicz, P.: The AMD branch (mis)predictor part 2: where no CPU has gone before (CVE-2021-26341). grsecurity Blog (2022)

27. Wistoff, N., Schneider, M., Gürkaynak, F.K., Heiser, G., Benini, L.: Systematic prevention of on-core timing channels by full temporal partitioning. arXiv preprint arXiv:2202.12029 (2022)

28. Zhao, J., Korpan, B., Gonzalez, A., Asanovic, K.: SonicBOOM: the 3rd generation Berkeley out-of-order machine. In: Fourth Workshop on Computer Architecture Research with RISC-V, vol. 5 (2020)

Pinky: A Modern Malware-Oriented Dynamic Information Retrieval Tool

Paul Irofti[1,2]([envelope])

[1] LOS-CS-FMI, University of Bucharest, Bucharest, Romania
[2] Institute for Logic and Data Science, Bucharest, Romania
paul@irofti.net

Abstract. We present here a reverse engineering tool that can be used for information retrieval and anti-malware techniques. Our main contribution is the design and implementation of an instrumentation framework aimed at providing insight on the emulation process. Sample emulation is achieved via translation of the binary code to an intermediate representation followed by compilation and execution. The design makes this a versatile tool that can be used for multiple task such as information retrieval, reverse engineering, debugging, and integration with anti-malware products.

Keywords: binary analysis · dynamic analysis · information retrieval

1 Introduction

In this paper we present the design and implementation of a new security tool called Pinky. Although an emulator at its core, Pinky comes with its own instrumentation framework, intermediate representation, coupled with a set of translators and compilers, and platform emulation (filesystem, memory, libraries) thus allowing samples from multiple operating systems to be analyzed and executed on any platform or machine. For example, its platform independence allows it to analyze a Windows 32-bit executable on a Linux distribution running on a MIPS-64 platform.

The instrumentation framework is designed such that the emulation process can be stopped at any point in order to provide data on the state it is in. For example we can peak and change mapped memory, registers, stack, executable code and data sections, and the filesystem. At the same time, we can also enable, set, or disable various information points. The instrumentation framework has no performance impact on the emulation process. Through instrumentation, Pinky can put on various hats. It can act as a tracer for system and library calls. Suspending and resuming emulation allows it to create memory dumps at various execution points, making it an universal unpacker. With more abstract instrumentation points, the tool can also become a reverse engineering debugger. And finally, it can act as anti-malware engine enabling the setup for static and dynamic signatures through its callback mechanism.

M. Manulis et al. (Eds.): SecITC 2023, LNCS 14534, pp. 65–78, 2024.
https://doi.org/10.1007/978-3-031-52947-4_6

Pinky is designed as an opaque tool providing a clear and simple interface that allows it to be integrated and controlled by third-party applications in a non-intrusive way. Thus it can be used inside datacenters (e.g. as an automated information retrieval tool or scanner), together with other software (e.g. existing IDS or anti-malware solutions), or as a stand-alone reverse engineering tool inside a laboratory.

Existing Work. We focused our work on recent studies regarding dynamic binary analysis. Our main inspiration for the intermediate representation and the compiler-translator coupling has been the work on UQBT [6,24,25] but also others like [10,17,18].

We differentiate ourselves from existing tools such as generic emulation tools such as QEMU [4] or Bochs [14] through performance, customization and instrumentation. The goals are different, we do not plan on being a generic virtualisation solution. This is important, especially in the anti-malware scenario, because speed difference and low-memory footprint sets us apart from generic solutions. More sophisticated tools like Valgrind [18] or rr [20] are more advanced in some regards, but they do not offer platform customization, a file system, instrumentation, nor cross platform emulation.

In the examples displayed in this paper we will see that, through instrumentation, Pinky can act as many well known tools. For example, it can give traces of system calls and native APIs (such as ntdll.dll, kernel32.dll, advapi32.dll and so on) much like `strace` and `ltrace` do in Linux. But while it does that, at the same time it can provide much more functionality.

2   Emulator Schematics

Following the work on intermediate representation languages we seek to obtain a fast and performant emulator through our virtual machine (VM) implementation coupled with just-in-time (JIT) compilation strategies and efficient caching. The main emulation performance is gained by tiered compilation through threshold-based mixins of JIT compilation and VM emulation. Every codeblock that gets processed is also cached and will be reused the next time it's encountered. Currently there are two caching strategies to choose from. More aggressive optimizations can occur when a codeblock is frequently enough. If a platform is missing JIT support, it will always fallback on the VM.

Instrumentation is done by dynamically enabling and disabling information retrieval points throughout the emulation process. Data points can adhere to dictated caller-callee protocols and exchange data structures that influence the sample control and data flows. The instrumentation points have no performance impact when they are disabled.

The emulation callback system is designed with the anti-malware engines in mind. For example a common issue that comes up in the field is handling polymorphic routines in static unpackers and coping with the different versions and variations in the wild. This can get to a point where the static routine gets so complex and has to deal with so many cases that it slowly becomes a dynamic analysis tool on its own. In this scenario, a solution would be to let the static unpacking process run until the offending polymorphic routine is reached, stop and handle things over to the emulator which will dynamically unpack it and then give control back to the static routine.

When used as a reverse-engineering tool, it can act as a debugger by setting breakpoints, watches, single-stepping at different granularity (e.g. codeblocks or instructions), setting different instrumentation points at runtime, tracing system calls and library APIs, enabling different logs at various verbosity levels for discrete periods of time, and many other similar useful features. As a tool in the laboratory, it can also be used in bulk scans to craft generic or specific reports. The generated data can include sample geometry, memory dumps, classification criteria, profiling data and other custom data retrieved through instrumentation.

Reproducible results are made possible through the ability to stop the emulation process in a coherent and platform agnostic fashion. This implies reproducibility no matter of the processor frequency, memory size or type, disk input-output throughput or other machine dependent factors.

Pinky is written in C++ with a focus on the C-subset with portability in mind. The interface is simple and intuitive. It consists of three parts: the emulator interface, the configuration interface and the instrumentation interface. It is implemented through abstract virtual classes that make it easy to decouple from the rest of the project. In the following sections we will describe each tool component and go into more details about its design and implementation.

3 Design and Implementation

3.1 Intermediate Representation

The goal of the intermediate representation (IR) was to have a small and reusable instruction set architecture (ISA) that would cater to all existing hardware and software computer models. In order to keep the instruction set small we designed an orthogonal ISA [19], thus allowing us to separate addressing modes and opcode functionality [12]. Existing hardware examples are the PDP-11, VAX, and ARM11 architectures. Orthogonality also allowed us to enforce fixed size instructions which in turn made it easier for us to enforce aligned access. Our architecture address resolution is 32-bits, and its instruction size is identical to its word size. Each of our instructions has the following fixed form: `opcode size dest src imm flags`. This is unlike most hardware implementations [5] which have variable instruction size and permit unaligned access. The x86 family [11] is particular famous in this regard as it permits constructs like

```
Before:                                          After:
407F1A E834000000 CALL sample.407F53
...
407F4F 20978CEAF873 AND BYTE PTR DS:[EDI+73F8EA8C],DL    407F53 F8 CLC
407F55 020F ADD CL, BYTE PTR DS:[EDI]                    407F54 7302 JNB SHORT sample.407F67
```

The `call` instruction at address `1A` jumps in the middle of the `and` instruction at address `4F` which is interpreted as a legitimate but entirely different instruction.

Note that the entire program flow is affected by this and that the attacker relied on the fact that a legitimate hidden instruction exists at address 53.

Stability was another key aspect because once we will start having consumers of our architectures (also called translators), it would become difficult to make large changes in the initial choice. This is also true for compilers and interpreters that will use the resulting intermediate representation to target code and execute it. The ARM architecture is infamous for its frequent ISA changes. A small and stable ISA meant that we had to ensure that we can reduce CISC architectures to it. We did and we provide a few examples of difficult instruction subsets (such as SSE and FPU) that we were successfully able to emulate with our ISA in the following sections. With that in mind, we are now able to define our cross intermediate representation (XIR). In Table 1 we present the entire instruction set. The control instructions handle jumps, function returns, and flag manipulations, while for memory manipulations we only have load, store and move instructions. The arithmetic and logic operations consist of the usual suspects with the note that the some have a c-suffix denoting an extra carry operation. Shifts and rotation are supported also.

Table 1. Instruction set

Control	jmp, ret, fsave, frestore
Memory	ld, st, mv
Arithmetic	add, addc, sub, subc, mul, div
Logical	and, or, xor, not, cmp
Shifts	rl, rr, sl, sr
Special	syscall

When designing such a tool, if going after full CPU and thus ISA support one of a few hard choices has to be made: design only for a specific platform (e.g. IA-32-based only), sprinkle hacks throughout the codebase thus ensuring multiple layer violations (the translator reaches into the intermediate representation, or even directly into the compiler), or, in academic spirit, we can just ignore them and have a toy example working only on an instruction subset. In this article we propose an alternative approach which is able to deal with all special architecture specific instruction set extensions. That is why at the end of Table 1 we introduced a special instruction syscall that maintains modularity and solves the issue by calling out to the emulator for help. We have implemented and tested its usefulness with multiple extensions such as Intel's FPU, MMX, SSE instructions. We consider this to be fully extensible to others and also consider it future proof. Of course, this instruction is slower.

When picking registers we went with 256 word-sized 32-bit registers with 8-bit access. Further, we partitioned them into groups: upper range mapped to the registers of the emulated architecture, lower range reserved for compiler internal use, plus other special registers for interrupts, flags and initialization.

In terms of stack choices, while most architectures have a word-sized stack or worse, a multiple granularity stack like x86, we choose no stack at all. This avoids multiple security issues Even though the ISA has no concept of a stack nor does it emulate it in any way, the stack of other models is modeled as direct memory access operations. To our knowledge, this represents a novel approach.

3.2   Translator

Each instruction set architecture that we want to support has to provide a disassembler and a translator to our intermediate representation. The disassembler tokenizes the instructions, fetches the implicit or explicit opcode arguments, and dispatches this information for translation. Our translator interface consists of only two functions: `translate(mmu, addr, ir)`; `syscall(env, mmu, opcode)`. The first translates block at address `addr` using the current memory contents as reflected by the `mmu` and returns the intermediate representation `ir`. For each opcode we have a translating function (or a handler) that receives the opcode arguments and writes out the equivalent functionality in IR opcodes

A typical x86 opcode translation will look like `gen_opcode(dst, src, aux, mod)` where the first three represent operands that can have various types like register, memory, immediate value. The last argument, `mod`, represents the instruction modifier that can dictate a switch to a different addressing mode (e.g. 16-bit) or a special request (e.g. repeating the instruction multiple times, locking etc.). The function call will generate a stream of equivalent XIR instructions.

```
gen_add(dst, src, aux, mod)
  if (dst->type == OP_MEM && src->type == OP_IMM)
    reg_t tmp = alloc_reg();

    ld(dst->width, tmp, dst->r, dst->imm);
    add(dst->width, tmp, 0, src->imm);
    st(dst->width, dst->r, tmp, dst->imm);

    free_reg(tmp);
```

In the above we depict the x86 ADD translation where the destination is the memory address of an integer to which we have to add an immediate value. This translates to three XIR operations: we load the integer value from memory to a temporary register (`ld`), then we perform the addition (`add`), and store back the result (`st`). Notice that we used the destination width to dictate the addressing mode. This makes the code portable and adaptable to word size changes.

As earlier discussed, `syscall` provides instruction emulation for particular instruction subsets. The registers and memory layout are prepared by the translator before calling out to the compiler to solve the specifics of the `opcode` given the current execution environment. Thus, when encountering a special instruction the emulator will pause and exit translation, emulate (part of) the instruction on the real CPU, write the results in translation state registers re-enter and resume translation. Here is a quick example for the x86 FABS instruction

```
gen_fabs()                  emu_fabs()
  sys(UD_Ifabs, 0, 0);        double fpdata = FPU_ST(0);
                              if (!isnan(fpdata))}
                                FPU_ST(0) = fabs(fpdata);
```

Once the disassembler, udis86 in this case [23], decodes the instruction it calls gen_fabs from the translator in order to obtain IR. This being a special FPU (or x87) instruction, the event is marked through a syscall with the appropriate opcode id that the complier will handle. The IR is thus a single syscall instruction. When the compiler reaches this instruction, it ties it via the identifier to the special complier function emu_fabs that will know how to handle the special opcode via x87 specific instructions as can be seen above. Through similar syscall mechanisms, the tool can also handle kernel (ring-0) sample emulation.

A special mention is required in regards to the handling of flags. The flags register does not have a special status. It is manipulated as any other register and it is modeled in an architecture specific way by each translator. Internal changes and checks can be protected by fsave and frestore guards. Post translation, the compilers are in charge of keeping the flags sound. In particular, the XIR virtual machine mimics the flag behavior of x86.

3.3   Compiler

Once everything is translated, the XIR instructions can be executed via interpretation, compilation, or a mixture of the two (also called tiered compilation). Interpretation is done through the XIR virtual machine (XIRVM). The implementation is straight forward: for each IR function (see ADD example translated above) we execute each XIR instruction in the emulator's own process space. The sample is isolated in a memory mapped region where all XIRVM operations perform their tasks. Note that we only need to implement a few VM instructions; the ones listed in Table 1.

```
exec_st(mmu, env, pc, dst, src, imm, flags)
  b = flags & BITS_MASK;
  addr = env->regs[dst] + imm;
  val = read_reg(env, b, src);
  size = 1 << b;

  set_word_le(&val, val);

  page = mmu->pte[addr >> PAGE_BITS]
  offset = addr & (PAGESZ - 1);
  if (page != 0 && offset + size <= PAGESZ)
    memcpy((uint8_t *) page + offset, &val, size);
  else
    mmu->write_memory(addr, &val, size))
```

In the above example we depict the XIR store (st) virtual machine interpretation. The first instructions fetch the addressing mode in b, the memory address from the destination operand, and the value to be written from the source operand. Based on the size b we store the read value in proper endianess and alignment according to the target architecture. Here we assume it is word sized, but it can be any subdivision or multiple of it. Next, the memory address is translated into a page and offset within the virtual machine memory management unit. If the page is already mapped, we perform a simple memory copy instruction. Otherwise we call out to the MMU to perform the write, which also implies a page mapping operation beforehand.

Compilation is performed via just-in-time (JIT) compilation strategies. Similar to the interpreter, each IR function is compiled and executed natively on the host machine. Implementation is also straight forward due to the reduced number of instructions in the XIR ISA. We tested with several JITs for both 32-bit and 64-bit targets. For x86 we used AsmJIT [13].

```
gen_mv(dst, src, imm, flags)
  b = flags & BITS_MASK;

  switch (b)
  case B32:
    if (src)
      as.mov(eax, XIR_REG32(src));
      if (imm)
        as.lea(eax, dword_ptr(eax, imm));
      as.mov(XIR_REG32(dst), eax);
    else
      as.mov(XIR_REG32(dst), imm);
    break;
```

In the above example we depict the XIR move (mv) JIT compilation. The first instructions fetch the addressing mode in b and in the displayed operations we assume it is 32-bit, but it can obviously be any other mode. If the source operand is defined, we have to emit a register-register move instruction. If only the immediate value imm is defined, then we move it to the destination register and we are done. If both the source and the immediate operands are defined, then we treat it as imm as an offset from src.

As with other systems, the interpreter is generally slower than the compiler. But often we found that when a XIR function is not repeatedly called, the effort of compiling the code outruns the gain in running native code. Thus in these cases it might be better to just use the interpreter. To handle this scenario we implemented tiered compilation [3,9], where the IR is compiled only if its usage passed a certain threshold. In order to improve the performance of the translate-compile cycle, we added caching for IR functions such that already codeblocks that have already been processed can go straight to execution.

3.4 Memory Management Unit

Earlier we saw memory store operations, What happens when any of the following needs to be emulated: MOV EAX, [1000]; JMP [EDX]; STOS DWORD PTR ES:[EDI]. The instructions alone can not describe the entire system state, we need to keep track of memory writes and reads. This involves having an initial memory state before starting the emulation process. This initial state is operating system (OS) dependent. The stack state is also partially dictated by the OS in general, and by its C library implementation and by its format for executables. Thus doing writes and reads forces us to set and maintain an internally stored memory map.

To address these issues, we designed a transparent platform-agnostic memory management unit (MMU). Its contents is data without any semantics or logic tied to it. We choose to represent it as a flat 4096-bytes paging system such that memory access can be done with $O(1)$ complexity. The memory is allocated contiguously and grouped into memory regions. These are automatically managed by the MMU when memory is allocated or freed by the emulator. A caching mechanism is set in place in order to take a big load off of the translator and the compiler resulting in big speed-ups. Overall this makes it a performant and clean memory representation.

```
read_memory(va, buffer, size);        pmap(sz, perf_va, actual_va, flags, min_va, max_va);
write_memory(va, buffer, size);       pmap_lookup(count, pref_va, min_va, max_va);
void dump(dmp_dir);                   pmap_remove(start_va, end_va);
```

The interface is simple and similar to what system programmers are used to encounter when dealing with memory. The first functions map pages into memory; `pmap` wires the required pages for a `sz` sized buffer with optional constraints such as virtual address (`va`) interval or forcing a fixed mapping via `pref_va` and `flags`. Calls to the read and write memory operations were presented earlier in the compiler section; the functions require a virtual address, the buffer and its size. Finally, `dump` is a very useful function to be called at various emulation points in order to inspect the memory layout and its contents. It can be used for malware analysis, information retrieval or debugging tasks.

3.5   File System

With an MMU, we still have to address other memory problems during execution. Consider the following sequence that can appear in our emulated sample

```
01002E8D PUSH ESI
01002E8E LEA EAX, [EBP-0x8]
01002E91 PUSH EAX
01002E92 CALL DWORD [0x1001074]
7DD85AB0 CALL DWORD 0x7dd85ab5
```

representing an API call to `kernel32.dll!GetSystemTimeAsFileTime`; a function implementation inside a shared system library. These are usually stored as imports inside a special section of the sample's executable in respect to the executable format of the underlying operating system. Almost all executables have at least a few such imports in order to function properly.

The same issue arises when the sample wants to access the file system for common input-output (IO) operations such as creating, reading, or writing to files and directories. In Windows operating systems it might even call out to manipulate registry entries, or similarly on Linux touch and modify `/proc` entries. While we can emulate or get around some of these issues, most calls do not have a clean solution and thus require the presence of a file system.

We address this issue by creating a virtual file system (VFS) that stores created or modified files throughout the emulation process. In addition it provides a minimal file system environment resembling the expected OS and it also takes care of special features such as registry and mimics special files such as the ones found in `/proc` and `/dev`. Thus VFS provides an interface for creating and managing file system containers that are platform specific and that are generated before the emulation process through an archiving like tool.

```
init(container);                unlink(path);
fd = open(path, mode);          stat(path, size, attributes, mode, base);
close(fd);                      seek(fd, pos);
read(fd, buffer, size);         chmod(path, attributes);
write(fd, buffer, size );       rename(from, to);
```

After loading the container with init, the VFS interface follows the UNIX system call conventions for handling files.

3.6   Executable Loader

With the system memory and file system present, the final missing puzzle is the executable loader. Without it the API call problem still exists: a connection between the sample and the library needs to be made and that link is present in the sample file. Each executable follows an executable format depending on the operating system. The executable format dictates how the file is partitioned into sections. The sections contain information about external dependencies, including libraries and the functions therein used by the current sample. Thus, a loader should setup the virtual address space, including the stack, for the sample and resolve links to external libraries.

For popular platforms such as Linux, BSD or Mac that use the ELF format [15, 22], open-source implementations exist that can be integrated in the emulator. Windows uses a similar but different format called portable executable (PE) [21] that is mostly undocumented and depends on the kernel version. Given the wide impact of malware and other malicious software on the Windows platform, we also designed and implemented a PE loader. Our PE loader mimics as close as possible the NT kernel, passes all non-conforming but loading samples we found in the wild, and passes all tests on the Corkami dataset [1].

When providing the actual library implementations, existing solutions either emulate the real functions and run them outside emulation or use external binaries, perhaps the exact platform library binaries, and run them inside the emulator. Because of the delicate subject of distributing external binaries, but also the man-hour impact of rewriting the existing ones, we chose to provide both options. The emulator will try the native implementation and, if it can not find the function, it will try to find the binary in the VFS and load it. Of course, for internal laboratory use it is enough to create a file system container with the original libraries which is completely possible via the VFS functionality.

Writing your own native implementations does come with advantages such as the fact that you trust the code (since you wrote it) and can thus gain extra performance by running it outside emulation. Also, in general, the implementations are simpler and smaller in size. The down sides are the fact that running it outside of emulation means that if it crashes it brings the entire process to a halt and it is also harder to debug.

Using external libraries wrapped in a VFS container has the advantage of having each library call going through the emulation layer and thus gaining better control and insight on the whole process. Also, crashing does not affect the emulator. The down sides are increased complexity due to emulation and running through abstractions that might not be needed for the task at hand. A windows library has to account for many use-cases and inter-connections and comes with no redistribution rights.

3.7 Instrumentation and Information Retrieval

Dtrace is a modern dynamic tracing tool [16] used in most modern operating systems [8] for debugging, accounting, logging and other information retrieval tasks such as reverse engineering [2]. Unlike most tools, dtrace has the advantage of having zero cost when disabled, a feat accomplished through machine dependent tricks. This allowed for the spread and setup of multiple instrumentation points (or probes) at no cost. When needed, these information points can be enabled and executed (or fired up).

In our emulator we followed the dtrace model and implemented a similar functionality across all modules. The probes have no cost when setup and can be fired at any time during emulation. Once implemented, this enabled us to quickly gain useful features such as feedback at any point during emulation, peaking at mapped memory, registers, stack, executable sections, and the file system. The instrumentation framework has no performance impact on the emulation.

```
probe_enable(probe_id);        probe_create(probe_id, name, provider, enabler);
probe_disable(probe_id);       probe_register(probe_id, consumer, consumer_id);
                               probe_cb_consumers(probe_id, context);
```

We defined the probe interface is as follows. A probe has a provider and multiple consumers. Once a provider creates a probe, a consumer can register using the probe unique identification number or the probe name. Registered consumers are walked through when a probe is fired either from the probed function itself or through a generic consumers callback. If the probe has a broadcast-like functionality, the later is preferred. If a certain list of conditions need to be fulfilled for a consumer trigger to be pulled, then the former is the way to go.

4 Results

Information Retrieval. Through the use of the instrumentation probes, we built a flexible configuration framework that, during emulation, allows us to change (with immediate effect) all the emulation options, tweak the interpreter, compiler and the tiered compilation threshold, and also switch caching algorithms. Through the same configuration interface we support multiple level logging for all of the emulator's modules that can be turned on, off or switched to a different verbosity at any time.

```
010029E3 push ebx ----------------+ ST32 [r165-0x4], r164
010029E3                          - MV32 r165, r165-0x4
010029E4 push edi ----------------+ ST32 [r165-0x4], r168
010029E4                          - MV32 r165, r165-0x4
```

```
010029E5 call dword [0x1001058] --+ MV32 r165, r165-0x4
010029E5                          + MV32 r32, 0x10029EB
010029E5                          + ST32 [r165], r32
010029E5                          + LD32 r32, [0x01001058]
010029E5                          - RET r32
```

In this example we turned on IR debugging to see how the translator turned x86 machine code (left hand side) into XIR instructions (right hand side).

We also have a probe interface that can stop the emulation process and feed memory regions through the MMU to static analysis tools for further insight. Based on these results, the external tools can change the behaviour or control flow of the analyzed sample before resuming emulation.

Command Line Debugger. We put together multiple probes to create a command line tool for inspecting, controlling and changing the emulation process. This tool includes debugger functionality like setting breakpoints, watchpoints and more sophisticated conditional stopping points all through the use of probes. This tool can also produce on-demand MMU dumps during emulation for signature inspection.

```
> break 0x7DE9FA40
> ping.exe
EMULATING ping.exe
Breakpoint 0 at 0x7DE9FA40
> probe x86_step_mode
> set log:ir 1
> next
DEBUG - debug_code.cpp:301 - ir:
Source -> IR:
7DE9FA90 mov dword [ebp-0x10], 0xffffffff + MV32 r32, 0xFFFFFFFF
7DE9FA90                                  + ST32 [r166-0x10], r32
7DE9FA90                                  - RET 0x7DE9FA97
Breakpoint 1 at 0x7DE9FA90
```

Above is an example inside the debugger. First we set breakpoint at an address inside the Windows `ping` executable and then proceed to run the sample. The debugger stops when the address is reached. Then we set fire the stepping mode probe that turns every codeblock into a single instruction, enable the logging level for the IR translation and proceed to the next instruction.

Stopping. We provide deterministic stopping that is agnostic to the host hardware. The goal is to be able to stop the emulation process around the same instruction no matter if we run on an Intel Xeon or a small ARM device. To do that we started an ample analysis where we marked the important nodes in the dynamic analyzer, added counters in these key positions, ran the emulator through large corpus of varied data samples and at the end stored the execution time and the final counter values. The corpus consisted of m samples with n counters each such that $m \gg n$. Thus a given sample has an execution time $t = \begin{pmatrix} c_1 & c_2 & c_3 & \ldots & c_n \end{pmatrix} \begin{pmatrix} w_1 & w_2 & w_3 & \ldots & w_n \end{pmatrix}^T$. Let $T \in \mathbb{R}^m$ be the vector consisting of all sample execution times, $C \in \mathbb{R}^{m \times n}$ the counters matrix and $w \in \mathbb{R}^n$ the weights. These measurements lead to a simple least-squares problem [7] $T = Cw$ whose solution are the associated weights w.

This model leads to some nice practical properties. We can start with a small set of counters which leads us to a fair approximation thus gaining a fast start-up. This starting point can be continuously adjusted and improved through counter addition and elimination but also through the addition of new sample information. This can also be seen as a profiling tool.

We name the weight values metrics. The speed of a platform is measured as metrics per second. We can now build a deterministic threshold by computing only once an average platform speed, and setting a metric threshold based on that. If a process was stopped we know exactly where. As a side effect, we also get an implicit time threshold for free. For example, if we have an average platform speed of 50 metrics per second, we can set the threshold to 150 metrics which results in a 3 s maximum emulation time per sample.

Production. The tool has been integrated and used successfully in an anti-malware engine environment (acting as a generic unpacker and memory inspection tool and doubling the product detection rate), as a bulk scanning tool for malware and clean sets, and also as a debugger-like reverse-engineering tool for sample analysis. Three applications that seamlessly integrated the library with success. This lead to a few nice properties, software wise. The emulator is reentrant and has built-in exception and fault protection for POSIX and Windows operating systems. Through continuous integration, it is tested weekly on $1,000,000+$ samples with support for multiple debugging and quality assurance tools such as OProfile and Electric Fence.

The emulator is highly portable. For example the bulk scanning tool runs on Linux, OpenBSD and Windows with 32-bit and 64-bit Intel-derivate CPUs. Also quick nightly scans are conducted on a wide range of system configurations, both big endian and little endian, with hardware platforms such as Intel 32-bit and 64-bit, ARMv5 and ARMv7, MIPS-64, PowerPC, Sparc, Sparc64, HP-PA, and on operating systems such as Windows (versions from Windows XP up to Windows 10), OS X, Linux, FreeBSD, OpenBSD, NetBSD, Solaris, IllumOS, Darwin and others. The solution is compiled with all mainline compilers: Visual Studio, GCC, and CLang.

5   Conclusion and Future Work

In this paper we presented a reverse engineering tool that can be used for information retrieval and anti-malware techniques. Our main contribution has been the design and implementation of an instrumentation framework created to provide insight on the emulation process that is achieved via the translation to an intermediate representation and then compilation of the studied sample. In the results section we show-cased its application to multiple tasks such as information retrieval tool, debugger and its ability to integrate in an anti-malware production environment. Due to the reduced number of instructions in the XIR

ISA, adding translators and JITs is not a difficult task which makes us consider adding an LLVM translator in the near future.

References

1. Alberitin, A.: Corkami PE files corpus (2015). https://code.google.com/archive/p/corkami/wikis/PE.wiki.   https://github.com/corkami/pocs/tree/master/PE. Accessed 17 Apr 2020
2. Beauchamp, T., Weston, D.: Dtrace: the reverse engineer's unexpected swiss army knife. Blackhat Europe (2008)
3. Bebenita, M., Chang, M., Wagner, G., Gal, A., Wimmer, C., Franz, M.: Trace-based compilation in execution environments without interpreters. In: Proceedings of the 8th International Conference on the Principles and Practice of Programming in Java, pp. 59–68 (2010)
4. Bellard, F.: Qemu, a fast and portable dynamic translator. In: USENIX Annual Technical Conference, FREENIX Track, vol. 41, p. 46 (2005)
5. Blaauw, G.A., Brooks Jr, F.P.: Computer Architecture: Concepts and Evolution. Addison-Wesley Longman Publishing Co., Inc. (1997)
6. Cifuentes, C., Van Emmerik, M.: UQBT: adaptable binary translation at low cost. Computer 33(3), 60–66 (2000)
7. Golub, G.H., Van Loan, C.F.: Matrix Computations, vol. 3. JHU Press, Baltimore (2012)
8. Gregg, B., Mauro, J.: DTrace: Dynamic Tracing in Oracle Solaris, Mac OS X, and FreeBSD. Prentice Hall Professional (2011)
9. Hartmann, T., Noll, A., Gross, T.: Efficient code management for dynamic multi-tiered compilation systems. In: Proceedings of the 2014 International Conference on Principles and Practices of Programming on the Java Platform: Virtual machines, Languages, and Tools, pp. 51–62 (2014)
10. Henderson, A., et al.: Make it work, make it right, make it fast: building a platform-neutral whole-system dynamic binary analysis platform. In: Proceedings of the 2014 International Symposium on Software Testing and Analysis, pp. 248–258 (2014)
11. Intel: Intel® 64 and IA-32 architectures software developer's manual. Intel (2019)
12. Jamil, T.: RISC versus CISC. IEEE Potentials 14(3), 13–16 (1995)
13. Kobalicek, P.: asmjit-complete x86/x64 JIT assembler for C++ language (2011)
14. Lawton, K.P.: Bochs: a portable PC emulator for Unix/X. Linux J. 1996(29es), 7 (1996)
15. Lu, H.: ELF: from the programmer's perspective (1995)
16. McDougall, R., Mauro, J., Gregg, B.: Solaris Performance and Tools: DTrace and MDB Techniques for Solaris 10 and OpenSolaris. Prentice Hall, Hoboken (2006)
17. Nethercote, N.: Dynamic binary analysis and instrumentation. Technical report, University of Cambridge, Computer Laboratory (2004)
18. Nethercote, N., Seward, J.: Valgrind: a framework for heavyweight dynamic binary instrumentation. ACM SIGPLAN Not. 42(6), 89–100 (2007)
19. Null, L., Lobur, J.: The Essentials of Computer Organization and Architecture. Jones & Bartlett Publishers, Burlington (2014)
20. O'Callahan, R., Jones, C., Froyd, N., Huey, K., Noll, A., Partush, N.: Engineering record and replay for deployability. In: 2017 USENIX Annual Technical Conference (USENIX ATC 2017), pp. 377–389 (2017)

21. Pietrek, M.: Peering inside the PE: a tour of the Win32 (R) portable executable file format. Microsoft Syst. J.-US Edition **9**(3), 15–38 (1994)
22. Shapiro, R., Bratus, S., Smith, S.W.: "Weird machines" in ELF: a spotlight on the underappreciated metadata. In: Presented as part of the 7th USENIX Workshop on Offensive Technologies (2013)
23. Thampi, V.: Udis86: disassembler library for x86 and x86-64 (2009)
24. Troger, J., Cifuentes, C.: Analysis of virtual method invocation for binary translation. In: Ninth Working Conference on Reverse Engineering, 2002 Proceedings, pp. 65–74. IEEE (2002)
25. Ung, D., Cifuentes, C.: Dynamic binary translation using run-time feedbacks. Sci. Comput. Program. **60**(2), 189–204 (2006)

M-Sel: A Message Selection Functional Encryption from Simple Tools

Ahmad Khoureich Ka$^{(\boxtimes)}$ [iD]

Université Alioune Diop de Bambey, Bambey, Senegal
ahmadkhoureich.ka@uadb.edu.sn

Abstract. In this paper, we put forward a new practical application of Inner-Product Functional Encryption (IPFE) that we call *Message Selection functional encryption* (M-Sel) which allows users to decrypt selected portions of a ciphertext. In a message selection functional encryption scheme, the plaintext is partitioned into a set of messages $M = \{m_1, \ldots, m_t\}$. The encryption of M consists in encrypting each of its elements using distinct encryption keys. A user with a functional decryption key sk_x derived from a selection vector x can access a subset of M from the encryption thereof and nothing more. Our construction is generic and combines a symmetric encryption scheme and an inner product functional encryption scheme, therefore, its security is tied to theirs. By instantiating our generic construction from a DDH-based IPFE we obtain a message selection FE with constant-size decryption keys suitable for key storage in lightweight devices in the context of Internet of Things (IoT).

Keywords: Functional Encryption · Inner-Product Functional Encryption · Adaptive Security

1 Introduction

1.1 Functional Encryption

Unlike traditional Public-Key Encryption ($\mathcal{PE}$), which allows a user with a decryption key to uncover the entire encrypted data, Functional Encryption ($\mathcal{FE}$) allows a finer control over the amount of information accessible to each user from the ciphertext. For a more meaningful formulation, let $c = \mathsf{Encrypt}(m)$ be a ciphertext and sk_f a secret key derived from a function f, the decryption of c using sk_f reveals nothing more than $f(m)$. The key sk_f is also called functional decryption key.

Functional encryption first appeared in the forms of Identity-Based Encryption [14,19,32], Searchable Encryption [1,13], Attribute-Based Encryption [11,24,31] and Predicate Encryption [26,29]. But the formal study of functional encryption giving its definitions and various security notions was done later by Boneh, Sahai and Waters [15] and O'Neill [30]. The first $\mathcal{FE}$ schemes for less

© The Author(s), under exclusive license to Springer Nature Switzerland AG 2024
M. Manulis et al. (Eds.): SecITC 2023, LNCS 14534, pp. 79–96, 2024.
https://doi.org/10.1007/978-3-031-52947-4_7

general functionality was proposed by Abdalla *et al.* [4]. Their schemes allow the evaluation of the inner product $\langle x, y \rangle$ of two vectors (x encrypted and y associated with a decryption key sk_y). Therefore, these schemes are called Inner-Product Functional Encryption (IPFE) schemes. The publication of Abdalla *et al.* [4] has aroused a lot of interest among researchers [7,8,10] as application fields are diverse and varied.

Although it is not required that the function associated with the decryption key be hidden, function hiding is very important since its guarantees that sensitive information on the plaintext do not leak. If f is known, information on the plaintext m can be gained from $f(m)$. Therefore, the inner-product functionality with function hiding is investigated in [12,20,21].

The single input inner-product functionality is extended to the multi-user setting [2,5,6,17,18,22,28]. The latter setting refers to Multi-Input Functional Encryption (MIFE) and Multi-Client Functional Encryption (MCFE). MIFE introduced in [23] is designed for scenarios where input data $m_1, \ldots, m_n$ come from different sources. Each functional decryption key sk_f is derived from a multi-input function f that allows computation of $f(m_1, \ldots, m_n)$ from encrypted data $\mathsf{Encrypt}(m_1), \ldots, \mathsf{Encrypt}(m_n)$. Also, the requirement that nothing beyond $f(m_1, \ldots, m_n)$ is revealed applies. MCFE allows the same computation as MIFE but for input data coming from clients $1, \ldots, n$ who do not trust each other. Each client i using a secret encryption key generates a ciphertext $c_i = \mathsf{Encrypt}(m_i, t, i)$ for a plaintext m_i associated with a tag t and an index i. However, MCFE is more restrictive than MIFE on decryption since a decryption key allows the computation of $f(m_1, \ldots, m_n)$ only if the corresponding ciphertexts $c_1, \ldots, c_n$ are labeled with the same tag t.

1.2   This Work

This work introduces a new type of functional encryption scheme that we call *Message Selection functional encryption* (M-Sel), which has several attractive real-life applications. For example:

Classified Documents. The document owner identifies the elements of information that must be classified and establishes the level of classification for each such element. A document $M = \{m_1, \ldots, m_t\} \in 2^{\{0,1\}^*}$ is considered as a set of messages which can be words, phrases, paragraphs, images, etc. To encrypt M, one computes $C = \{\mathsf{Encrypt}(sk_1, m_1), \ldots, \mathsf{Encrypt}(sk_t, m_t)\}$ where each $m_{i, i \in [1..t]}$ is encrypted using a secret key sk_i. Decrypting C using a functional key sk_x derived from a selection vector $x \in \mathbb{Z}_2^\ell$ yields a subset of M.

Image Sharing. A cloud server hosts images consisting of set of encrypted layers (e.g., map layers in Geographic Information System (GIS)). With their functional decryption key each user accesses a new image obtained by flattening a subset of layers.

Chat room. Participants produce encrypted message flows and each of them can only view message flows associated to their functional decryption key.

M-Sel uses a symmetric encryption scheme $\mathcal{SE}$, an inner-product functional encryption scheme IPFE and hashing. Our construction can succinctly be presented as follows: the plaintext is partitioned into a set of plaintexts $M = \{m_1, \ldots, m_t\} \in 2^{\{0,1\}^*}$. For each $m_i \in M$ we pick a random $s_i \in \mathbb{Z}_p^*$, derive a bit string $\sigma_i \leftarrow H(s_i)$ and compute $u_i = \mathcal{SE}.\mathsf{Encrypt}(\sigma_i, m_i)$. Then, a vector $\boldsymbol{y}_i$ in the canonical basis of $\mathbb{Z}_2^\ell$ is chosen and s_i is hidden by computing $v_i = \mathsf{IPFE}.\mathsf{Encrypt}(mpk, s_i \cdot \boldsymbol{y}_i)$. Therefore, the encryption of m_i is (u_i, v_i). A user with a functional decryption key $sk_{\boldsymbol{x}}$ derived from a selection vector $\boldsymbol{x} \in \mathbb{Z}_2^\ell$ accesses m_i if $\mathsf{IPFE}.\mathsf{Decrypt}(sk_{\boldsymbol{x}}, v_i) = s_i$. For more details, please refer to the Sect. 3 of the paper.

We prove that our message selection functional encryption scheme have indistinguishable encryptions under a chosen-plaintext attack (IND-CPA) if the underlying $\mathcal{SE}$ and IPFE schemes are IND-CPA secure.

1.3 Related Work

Abdalla, Bourse, De Caro and Pointcheval [4] are the first to propose a functional encryption scheme for the inner product functionality. They provided two simple and efficient constructions for IPFE, one based on the Decision Diffie-Hellman assumption (DDH) and the other based on the Learning-With-Errors assumption (LWE). However, the IPFE schemes in [4] are only proven secure in the selective security model where the adversary is asked to declare its challenge messages before the setup of the security game. Subsequently, Agrawal *et al.* [8] proposed an improvement to attain full security under the DDH, LWE, and Decision Composite Residuosity (DCR) assumptions. Chosen ciphertext secure IPFE schemes are first obtained by Benhamouda *et al.* [10]. Their construction is based on projective hash functions with homomorphic properties. These proposals are of great theoretical interest but are not sufficiently efficient for practical applications. Since either they require that the inner product $\langle \boldsymbol{x}, \boldsymbol{y} \rangle$ be small enough for the decryption to work or their parameters sizes are impractical. Finally, Castagnos *et al.* [16] provided IPFE schemes which are efficient for the evaluation of unbounded inner products modulo a prime p. The efficiency of their constructions is obtained by relying on a cyclic group where the DDH assumption holds containing a subgroup where the discrete logarithm problem is easy.

The message selection functionality can be tackled in the naive way with traditional Hybrid Public-key Encryption $\mathcal{HPE}$ which is capable of encrypting arbitrary bit strings. Hybrid public-key encryption combines a symmetric encryption scheme $\mathcal{SE}$ and a public-key encryption scheme. In this context, the public-key encryption scheme is called key-encapsulation mechanism $\mathsf{KEM} = (\mathsf{Gen}, \mathsf{Encaps}, \mathsf{Decaps})$.

The naive scheme is the following. For a plaintext $M = \{m_1, \ldots, m_\ell\} \in 2^{\{0,1\}^*}$, generate ℓ independent key pairs $\{sk_i, pk_i\}_{i=1}^\ell$, set $mpk = \{pk_1, \ldots, pk_\ell\}$ and $msk = \{sk_1, \ldots, sk_\ell\}$. Apply the encryption algorithm of $\mathcal{HPE}$ to mpk and M to obtain $C \leftarrow \{\mathcal{HPE}.\mathsf{Encrypt}(pk_i, m_i)\}_{i=1}^\ell = \{(c_i, c_i')\}_{i=1}^\ell$ where $(c_i, s_i) \leftarrow \mathsf{KEM}.\mathsf{Encaps}(1^\lambda, pk_i)$ and $c_i' = \mathcal{SE}.\mathsf{Encrypt}(s_i, m_i)$. A user who wants to access a subset of M from C is given the secret keys sk_i corresponding to the indices of the selected elements of M.

In Table 1 we summarize the comparison between our approach (M-Sel) based on functional encryption and the naive one based on traditional hybrid public-key encryption in terms of key size and ciphertext size. For this comparison, we consider the instantiation M-Sel$_{DDH}$ of M-Sel from the DDH-based IPFE scheme of [8]. M-Sel$_{DDH}$ is described in Sect. 5. Without loss of generality, we assume that the secret keys sk_i are randomly picked from $\mathbb{Z}_p$ and the corresponding public keys pk_i are picked from a cyclic group $\mathbb{G}$ of prime order p.

Table 1. Comparing M-Sel and the naive approach based on $\mathcal{HPE}$. $|M| = \sum_{i=1}^{\ell} |m_i|$.

	mpk	msk	Ciphertext	Decryption key
The naive scheme	$\ell \log p$	$\ell \log p$	$\ell \log p + |M|$	$\mathcal{O}(\ell \log p)$
M-Sel$_{DDH}$	$\ell \log p$	$2\ell \log p$	$\ell(\ell + 2) \log p + |M|$	$2 \log p$

We note that the size of the ciphertext in M-Sel is quadratic in ℓ whereas it is linear in ℓ in the naive solution. However, it is important to note that the advantage of our scheme over the naive one is its short and constant size decryption key which is significantly smaller than that of the naive scheme (which consists of a set of $\mathcal{O}(\ell)$ secret keys). This makes M-Sel interesting for key storage in lightweight devices in the context of Internet of Things (IoT).

1.4   Organization

The remainder of this paper is organized as follows. Section 2 is devoted to primitives used as components in M-Sel and various settings of encryption. In Sect. 3 we describe the construction of our message selection functional encryption scheme. The security analysis of M-Sel is done in Sect. 4. We show an instantiation of M-Sel from the DDH-based IPFE scheme of [8] in Sect. 5. Section 6 concludes this work.

2   Basic Tools

In this section, we recall the syntax of symmetric encryption and of inner-product functional encryption. We also discuss the setting of multi-recipient encryption and the setting of multiple encryptions.

2.1   Symmetric Encryption

Definition 1 (Symmetric Encryption Scheme). *A symmetric encryption scheme* $\mathcal{SE} = $ (KeyGen, Encrypt, Decrypt) *consists of 3 polynomial-time algorithms:*

1. KeyGen(1^λ) *takes as input a security parameter λ and returns a key sk.*
2. Encrypt(sk, m) *takes as input a key sk and a plaintext message $m \in \{0,1\}^*$ and returns a ciphertext $c \leftarrow$ Encrypt($sk, m; r$) $\in \{0,1\}^*$ where r is randomly picked from the coins set associated to $\mathcal{SE}$. We consider r to be a part of the ciphertext.*
3. Decrypt(sk, c) *takes as input a key sk and a ciphertext c and returns a message m or an error denoted by the symbol $\perp$.*

For correctness it is required that Decrypt(sk, Encrypt(sk, m)) $= m$ *for all $m \in \{0,1\}^*$.*

A symmetric encryption scheme can be used in the multi-recipient setting with randomness re-use. We define multi-recipient encryption as follow:

Multi-recipient Encryption Schemes and Randomness Re-use. Let $\mathcal{SE} = $ (KeyGen, Encrypt, Decrypt) be a standard symmetric encryption scheme. Consider n receivers, numbered $1, \ldots, n$ each of which has its secret key sk_i. A sender picks random coins $r_1, \ldots, r_n$ from the coins set associated to $\mathcal{SE}$ and uses the symmetric encryption scheme $\overline{\mathcal{SE}} = $ (KeyGen, $\overline{\text{Encrypt}}$, Decrypt) to compute $C \leftarrow \overline{\mathcal{SE}}.\overline{\text{Encrypt}}((sk_1, \ldots, sk_n), (m_1, \ldots, m_n); (r_1, \ldots, r_n)) = (c_1, \ldots, c_n)$, where $c_i \leftarrow \mathcal{SE}.\text{Encrypt}(sk_i, m_i; r_i)$. Each receiver i recovers the plaintext $m_i = \mathcal{SE}.\text{Decrypt}(sk_i, c_i)$. The symmetric encryption scheme $\overline{\mathcal{SE}}$ is termed the Multi-Recipient Encryption Scheme (MRES) associated to $\mathcal{SE}$. When all the coins r_i are equal ($r_i = r$ for $i \in [1 .. n]$) that is $c_i \leftarrow \mathcal{SE}.\text{Encrypt}(sk_i, m_i; r)$, $\overline{\mathcal{SE}}$ is termed the Randomness Re-using MRES (RR-MRES) associated to the underlying standard encryption scheme $\mathcal{SE}$.

The definition of security for multi-recipient encryption schemes first appeared in [27] and was later refined in [9]. Following [9], we define hereunder indistinguishable encryptions under a chosen-plaintext attack (IND-CPA) experiment for RR-MRES. Let $\overline{\mathcal{SE}} = $ (KeyGen, $\overline{\text{Encrypt}}$, Decrypt) be a randomness re-using symmetric multi-recipient encryption scheme, let $\mathcal{A}$ be an adversary and λ be the security parameter. $\mathcal{A}$ has access to an oracle which takes a vector of $n \in \text{poly}(\lambda)$ messages and outputs a ciphertext vector.

Experiment. $\text{Exp}_{\overline{\mathcal{SE}}, \mathcal{A}}^{\text{IND-RR-CPA}}(\lambda)$

$(t, sk_{t+1}, \ldots, sk_n) \leftarrow \mathcal{A}(1^\lambda)$ such that $1 \leq t \leq n \in \text{poly}(\lambda)$
For each $i \in [1 .. t]$ do $sk_i \leftarrow \overline{\mathcal{SE}}.\text{KeyGen}(1^\lambda)$ EndFor
$SK \leftarrow (sk_1, \ldots, sk_n)$
$(m_0^1, \ldots, m_0^t; m_1^1, \ldots, m_1^t; m_{t+1}, \ldots, m_n) \leftarrow \mathcal{A}^{\overline{\mathcal{SE}}(SK, \cdot)}$
$b \xleftarrow{R} \{0,1\}$
$M \leftarrow (m_b^1, \ldots, m_b^t, m_{t+1}, \ldots, m_n)$
$r \xleftarrow{R}$ Coins
$C \leftarrow \overline{\mathcal{SE}}.\overline{\text{Encrypt}}(SK, M; r)$

$$b' \leftarrow \mathcal{A}^{\overline{\mathcal{SE}}(SK,\cdot)}(C)$$
Return 1 if $b' = b$, 0 otherwise

It is mandated that $|m_0^i| = |m_1^i|$ for all $i \in [1 .. t]$. Coins is the coins set associated to $\mathcal{SE}$. Notice that when given the security parameter adversary $\mathcal{A}$ outputs $n - t$ secret keys and in the challenge phase in addition to messages $m_0^1, \ldots, m_0^t$ and $m_1^1, \ldots, m_1^t$ it provides $n - t$ other messages. As indicated in [9], this solves the problem of insider attacks ($\mathcal{A}$ has successfully corrupted $n - t$ users).

Definition 2 (IND-CPA security of RR-MRES). *The advantage of any poly (λ)-time adversary $\mathcal{A}$ in the experiment $\text{Exp}_{\mathcal{SE},\mathcal{A}}^{\text{IND-RR-CPA}}(\lambda)$ is defined as follow:*

$$\text{Adv}_{\overline{\mathcal{SE}},\mathcal{A}}^{\text{IND-RR-CPA}}(\lambda) = 2 \cdot \Pr\left[\text{Exp}_{\overline{\mathcal{SE}},\mathcal{A}}^{\text{IND-RR-CPA}}(\lambda) = 1\right] - 1.$$

A randomness re-using symmetric multi-recipient encryption scheme $\overline{\mathcal{SE}}$ is IND-CPA secure, if the function $\text{Adv}_{\overline{\mathcal{SE}},\mathcal{A}}^{\text{IND-RR-CPA}}(\cdot)$ is negligible.

Theorem 1 (RR-MRES security [9]). *Fix a symmetric-key encryption scheme $\mathcal{SE} = (\text{KeyGen}, \text{Encrypt}, \text{Decrypt})$ and a polynomial n. Let $\overline{\mathcal{SE}} = (\text{KeyGen}, \overline{\text{Encrypt}}, \text{Decrypt})$ be the corresponding RR-MRES. If $\mathcal{SE}$ is reproducible then for any polynomial-time adversary $\mathcal{B}$, there exists a polynomial-time adversary $\mathcal{A}$, such that:*

$$\text{Adv}_{\overline{\mathcal{SE}},\mathcal{B}}^{\text{IND-RR-CPA}}(\lambda) \leq n(\lambda) \cdot \text{Adv}_{\mathcal{SE},\mathcal{A}}^{\text{IND-CPA}}(\lambda)$$

Also, [9] states that if $\mathcal{F}$ is a pseudorandom function family then the symmetric encryption scheme $\text{CBC}[\mathcal{F}]$ that operates in CBC mode is reproducible. For the remainder of the paper, we consider $\mathcal{SE}$ to be a symmetric encryption scheme that operates in CBC mode.

2.2   Functional Encryption

Functional Encryption is formalized by Boneh, Sahai and Waters in [15]. It is related to the notion of functionality. Inner product functional encryption [4] is a special case of functional encryption and was first provided by Abdalla, Bourse, De Caro and Pointcheval.

Definition 3 (Functionality) *A functionality F defined over $(\mathcal{K}, \mathcal{M})$ is a function $F : \mathcal{K} \times \mathcal{M} \to \Sigma \cup \{\bot\}$, where $\mathcal{K}$ is a key space, $\mathcal{M}$ is a message space and Σ is an output space.*

Definition 4 (Inner-Product Functional Encryption). *Inner-product functional encryption is designed for the functionality $F : \mathcal{R}^\ell \times \mathcal{R}^\ell \to \mathcal{R} \cup \{\bot\}$ such that $F(\boldsymbol{x}, \boldsymbol{y}) = \langle \boldsymbol{x}, \boldsymbol{y} \rangle$ for some ring $\mathcal{R}$ and a natural number ℓ. An inner product functional encryption scheme $\text{IPFE} = (\text{Setup}, \text{KeyDer}, \text{Encrypt}, \text{Decrypt})$ consists of 4 polynomial-time algorithms:*

1. $\mathsf{Setup}(1^\lambda, 1^\ell)$ *takes as input a security parameter* λ *and a functionality parameter* ℓ *and returns a master public key mpk and a master secret key msk.*
2. $\mathsf{KeyDer}(msk, \boldsymbol{x})$ *takes as input the master secret key msk and a key* $\boldsymbol{x} \in \mathcal{R}^\ell$ *and derives a secret key* $sk_{\boldsymbol{x}}$.
3. $\mathsf{Encrypt}(mpk, \boldsymbol{y})$ *takes as input the master public key mpk and a plaintext* $\boldsymbol{y} \in \mathcal{R}^\ell$ *and returns a ciphertext* $c_{\boldsymbol{y}}$.
4. $\mathsf{Decrypt}(mpk, sk_{\boldsymbol{x}}, c_{\boldsymbol{y}})$ *takes as input the master public key mpk, a secret key* $sk_{\boldsymbol{x}}$ *and a ciphertext* $c_{\boldsymbol{y}}$ *and returns* $\langle \boldsymbol{x}, \boldsymbol{y} \rangle$.

For correctness, it is required that for all $\boldsymbol{x} \in \mathcal{R}^\ell$ *and all* $\boldsymbol{y} \in \mathcal{R}^\ell$, *we have* $\mathsf{Decrypt}(mpk, sk_{\boldsymbol{x}}, \mathsf{Encrypt}(mpk, \boldsymbol{y})) = \langle \boldsymbol{x}, \boldsymbol{y} \rangle$ *or* $\bot$ *with negligible probability.*

The ring $\mathcal{R}$ is either $\mathbb{Z}$ or $\mathbb{Z}_p$ for some prime number p. When the inner product is computed in $\mathbb{Z}_p$, the KeyDer algorithm must monitor secret key requests to avoid giving an adversary decryption keys associated with linearly independent vectors. Indeed, an adversary can request secret keys associated to vectors which are linearly dependent in $\mathbb{Z}_p$ but linearly independent in $\mathbb{Z}$. Such linearly independent secret keys can lead to a solvable system of linear equations where the unknowns are the components of the master secret key. Therefore, the KeyDer algorithm must be stateful [8]. Meaning that the adversary obtains redundant information when trying to collect more than $\ell - 1$ linearly independent secret keys since the KeyDer algorithm will return a linear combination of the previous secret keys.

The definition of security for IPFE in the sense of indistinguishable encryptions under a chosen-plaintext attack (IND-CPA) is given via the following experiment. Let $\mathcal{A}$ be an adversary.

Experiment $\mathsf{Exp}^{\mathsf{IND\text{-}CPA}}_{\mathsf{IPFE}, \mathcal{A}}(\lambda)$

> Let $1 \le q_1 \le q \in \mathsf{poly}(\lambda)$; $\ell \in \mathsf{poly}(\lambda)$; $S \leftarrow \emptyset$; $S_{\boldsymbol{x}} \leftarrow \emptyset$
> $(mpk, msk) \leftarrow \mathsf{Setup}(1^\lambda, 1^\ell)$
> For each $i \in [1 \mathrel{..} q_1]$ do
> $\quad \boldsymbol{x}_i \leftarrow \mathcal{A}(mpk, S)$
> $\quad sk_{\boldsymbol{x}_i} \leftarrow \mathsf{KeyDer}(msk, \boldsymbol{x}_i)$
> $\quad S \leftarrow S \cup sk_{\boldsymbol{x}_i}$ $\triangleright$ First phase of secret key queries, $\boldsymbol{x}_i \in \mathcal{R}^\ell$.
> $\quad S_{\boldsymbol{x}} \leftarrow S_{\boldsymbol{x}} \cup \boldsymbol{x}_i$
> EndFor
> $(\boldsymbol{y}_0, \boldsymbol{y}_1) \leftarrow \mathcal{A}(mpk, S)$ $\triangleright$ Challenge phase.
> $b \xleftarrow{R} \{0, 1\}$
> $C \leftarrow \mathsf{Encrypt}(mpk, \boldsymbol{y}_b)$
> For each $i \in [q_1 \mathrel{..} q]$ do
> $\quad \boldsymbol{x}_i \leftarrow \mathcal{A}(mpk, S, C)$
> $\quad sk_{\boldsymbol{x}_i} \leftarrow \mathsf{KeyDer}(msk, \boldsymbol{x}_i)$
> $\quad S \leftarrow S \cup sk_{\boldsymbol{x}_i}$ $\triangleright$ Second phase of secret key queries.
> $\quad S_{\boldsymbol{x}} \leftarrow S_{\boldsymbol{x}} \cup \boldsymbol{x}_i$
> EndFor

$b' \leftarrow \mathcal{A}(mpk, S, C)$
Return 1 if $b' = b$, 0 otherwise

It is mandated in the challenge phase and in the second phase of secret key queries that $\langle \boldsymbol{x}_i, \boldsymbol{y}_0 \rangle = \langle \boldsymbol{x}_i, \boldsymbol{y}_1 \rangle$ for all $\boldsymbol{x}_i \in S_{\boldsymbol{x}}$.

Definition 5 (IND-CPA security of IPFE). *The advantage of any* $\mathrm{poly}(\lambda)$*-time adversary* $\mathcal{A}$ *in the experiment* $\mathsf{Exp}_{\mathsf{IPFE},\mathcal{A}}^{\mathsf{IND\text{-}CPA}}(\lambda)$ *is defined as follow:*

$$\mathsf{Adv}_{\mathsf{IPFE},\mathcal{A}}^{\mathsf{IND\text{-}CPA}}(\lambda) = 2 \cdot \Pr\left[\mathsf{Exp}_{\mathsf{IPFE},\mathcal{A}}^{\mathsf{IND\text{-}CPA}}(\lambda) = 1\right] - 1.$$

An inner-product functional encryption scheme IPFE *has indistinguishable encryptions under a chosen-plaintext attack, if the function* $\mathsf{Adv}_{\mathsf{IPFE},\mathcal{A}}^{\mathsf{IND\text{-}CPA}}(\cdot)$ *is negligible.*

Multiple Encryptions. Using the same master public key to encrypt multiple messages is termed Multiple Encryptions (ME). The security of ME is related to that of the based encryption scheme. Hereunder, we define indistinguishable encryptions under a chosen-plaintext attack (IND-CPA) experiment for multiple encryptions. Let $\mathcal{FE} = (\mathsf{Setup}, \mathsf{KeyDer}, \mathsf{Encrypt}, \mathsf{Decrypt})$ be a functional encryption scheme for the functionality F, let $\mathcal{K}$ be the key space, let $\mathcal{M}$ be the message space, let $\mathcal{A}$ be an adversary and λ be the security parameter.

Experiment $\mathsf{Exp}_{\mathcal{FE},\mathcal{A}}^{\mathsf{IND\text{-}ME\text{-}CPA}}(\lambda)$

Let $1 \leq q_1 \leq q \in \mathrm{poly}(\lambda)$; $t \in \mathrm{poly}(\lambda)$; $S \leftarrow \emptyset$; $S_k \leftarrow \emptyset$
$(mpk, msk) \leftarrow \mathsf{Setup}(1^\lambda)$

First phase of secret key queries $\quad \triangleright$ Syntactically identical to that of $\mathsf{Exp}_{\mathsf{IPFE},\mathcal{A}}^{\mathsf{IND\text{-}CPA}}(\lambda)$.

$(m_0^1, \ldots, m_0^t; m_1^1, \ldots, m_1^t) \leftarrow \mathcal{A}(mpk, S) \quad \triangleright$ Challenge phase.
$b \xleftarrow{R} \{0, 1\}$
$C \leftarrow (\mathsf{Encrypt}(mpk, m_b^1), \ldots, \mathsf{Encrypt}(mpk, m_b^t))$

Second phase of secret key queries $\quad \triangleright$ Syntactically identical to that of $\mathsf{Exp}_{\mathsf{IPFE},\mathcal{A}}^{\mathsf{IND\text{-}CPA}}(\lambda)$.

$b' \leftarrow \mathcal{A}(mpk, S, C)$
Return 1 if $b' = b$, 0 otherwise

It is mandated in the challenge phase and in the second phase of secret key queries that $F(k_i, m_0^j) = F(k_i, m_1^j)$ for all $k_i \in S_k \subset \mathcal{K}$ and $|m_0^j| = |m_1^j|, m_0^j, m_1^j \in \mathcal{M}$ for $j \in [1 .. t]$.

Definition 6 (IND-CPA security of ME). *The advantage of any* $\text{poly}(\lambda)$*-time adversary* $\mathcal{A}$ *in the experiment* $\text{Exp}_{\mathcal{FE},\mathcal{A}}^{\text{IND-ME-CPA}}(\lambda)$ *is defined as follow:*

$$\text{Adv}_{\mathcal{FE},\mathcal{A}}^{\text{IND-ME-CPA}}(\lambda) = 2 \cdot \Pr\left[\text{Exp}_{\mathcal{FE},\mathcal{A}}^{\text{IND-ME-CPA}}(\lambda) = 1\right] - 1.$$

A functional encryption scheme $\mathcal{FE}$ *has indistinguishable multiple encryptions under a chosen-plaintext attack, if the function* $\text{Adv}_{\mathcal{FE},\mathcal{A}}^{\text{IND-ME-CPA}}(\cdot)$ *is negligible.*

Theorem 2 (Multiple encryptions security [25]). *If a public-key encryption scheme* $\mathcal{PE}$ *is* CPA*-secure, then it also has indistinguishable multiple encryptions.*

3 Our Message Selection FE Scheme

In this section, we describe our functional encryption scheme for the message selection functionality.

Definition 7 (Message Selection Functionality). *Let* $\mathscr{S}$ *be the set containing finite sets of messages such that for every* $M \in \mathscr{S}$, $2^M \subset \mathscr{S}$. *Consider* $2^M = \{M_w\}_{w \in \{0,1\}^{|M|}}$ *as an indexed family of sets. The message selection functionality is the function* $F : \{0,1\}^n \times \mathscr{S} \to \mathscr{S} \cup \{\bot\}$ *such that* $F(w, M) = M_w$ *where* n *is a natural number.*

Let $\mathcal{SE} = (\text{KeyGen}, \text{Encrypt}, \text{Decrypt})$ be a symmetric encryption scheme operating in CBC mode with key length κ. Let $\text{IPFE} = (\text{Setup}, \text{KeyDer}, \text{Encrypt}, \text{Decrypt})$ be an inner-product functional encryption scheme. The construction of M-Sel is as follow:

Setup$(1^\lambda, 1^\ell)$. This algorithm performs the following steps:

1. Choose a cryptographic hash function $H : \mathbb{Z}_p \to \{0,1\}^\kappa$ for some prime number $p > 2^\lambda$.
2. Call IPFE.Setup$(1^\lambda, 1^\ell)$ to obtain a master secret key msk and a master public key mpk.

KeyDer(msk, x) derives from $x \in \mathbb{Z}_2^\ell$ a functional key $sk_x \leftarrow$ IPFE. KeyDer(msk, x).

Encrypt(mpk, M). To encrypt a plaintext $M = \{m_1, m_2, \ldots, m_t\} \in 2^{\{0,1\}^*}$ this algorithm performs the following steps:

1. Let $S \leftarrow \emptyset$.
2. Let $\mathbb{B}_\ell$ be the canonical basis of $\mathbb{Z}_2^\ell$.
3. Pick a random coins r from the coins set associated to $\mathcal{SE}$.

4. For each $i \in [1 .. t]$ do:
  4.1 Pick a random number $s_i \in \mathbb{Z}_p^* \backslash S$; $S \leftarrow S \cup s_i$.
  4.2 Compute $u_i \leftarrow \mathcal{SE}.\mathsf{Encrypt}(H(s_i), m_i; r)$.
  4.3 Choose $\boldsymbol{y}_i \in \mathbb{B}_\ell$ and compute $v_i \leftarrow \mathsf{IPFE}.\mathsf{Encrypt}(mpk, s_i \cdot \boldsymbol{y}_i)$.
5. Return the ciphertext $C = (r, u_1, v_1, \ldots, u_t, v_t)$.

Decrypt$(sk_{\boldsymbol{x}}, C)$. Using $sk_{\boldsymbol{x}}$ to decrypt the ciphertext $C = (r, u_1, v_1, \ldots, u_t, v_t)$, this algorithm performs the following steps:

1. Let $M_{\boldsymbol{x}} = \emptyset$.
2. For each $i \in [1 .. t]$ do:
  2.1 Compute $\rho_i = \mathsf{IPFE}.\mathsf{Decrypt}(sk_{\boldsymbol{x}}, v_i)$. Note that $\rho_i = \langle \boldsymbol{x}, s_i \cdot \boldsymbol{y}_i \rangle$ is either equal to 0 or s_i.
  2.2 If $\rho_i = 0$ then return to step 2.1. for the next value of i. Otherwise, compute $m_i = \mathcal{SE}.\mathsf{Decrypt}(H(\rho_i), u_i; r)$.
  2.3 If $m_i = \bot$ then return to step 2.1. for the next value of i. Otherwise, Set $M_{\boldsymbol{x}} \leftarrow M_{\boldsymbol{x}} \cup m_i$
3. Return the plaintext $M_{\boldsymbol{x}}$.

Correctness. For each $i \in [1 .. t]$, we have that

$$\mathcal{SE}.\mathsf{Decrypt}\Big[H\big[\mathsf{IPFE}.\mathsf{Decrypt}(sk_{\boldsymbol{x}}, v_i)\big], u_i; r\Big] = \mathcal{SE}.\mathsf{Decrypt}\Big[H\big[\langle \boldsymbol{x}, s_i \cdot \boldsymbol{y}_i \rangle\big], u_i; r\Big]$$

$$= \begin{cases} \mathcal{SE}.\mathsf{Decrypt}\big(H(0), u_i; r\big) \\ \text{or} \\ \mathcal{SE}.\mathsf{Decrypt}\big(H(s_i), u_i; r\big) \end{cases}$$

$$= \begin{cases} \bot \\ \text{or} \\ m_i \end{cases}$$

Therefore, $\mathsf{Decrypt}(sk_{\boldsymbol{x}}, C) \in 2^M$.

4   Security Against Chosen-Plaintext Attack

Here, we prove that M-Sel has indistinguishable encryptions under a chosen-plaintext attack assuming the underlying symmetric CBC encryption scheme $\mathcal{SE}$ and inner product functional encryption scheme IPFE are IND-CPA secure.

The experiment $\mathsf{Exp}_{\mathsf{M\text{-}Sel},\mathcal{A}}^{\mathsf{IND\text{-}CPA}}(\lambda)$ by which we define IND-CPA security for M-Sel is syntactically identical to the experiment $\mathsf{Exp}_{\mathcal{FE},\mathcal{A}}^{\mathsf{IND\text{-}ME\text{-}CPA}}(\lambda)$ given in Sect. 2.2 except for some slight differences presented below:

1. The key space is $\mathbb{Z}_2^\ell$.
2. F is the message selection functionality.
3. In the challenge phase, adversary $\mathcal{A}$ chooses two distinct sets of messages $M_0 \leftarrow \{m_0^1, \ldots, m_0^t\}$, $M_1 \leftarrow \{m_1^1, \ldots, m_1^t\} \in 2^{\{0,1\}^*}$ subject to the restriction that, $F(\boldsymbol{x}_i, M_0) = F(\boldsymbol{x}_i, M_1)$ for all $\boldsymbol{x}_i \in S_{\boldsymbol{x}} \subset \mathbb{Z}_2^\ell$.

Theorem 3. *If the underlying $\mathcal{SE}$ and* IPFE *schemes are* IND-CPA *secure, then* M-Sel *is* IND-CPA *secure.*

We recall the definition of perfect secrecy.

Definition 8. (*Perfectly Secret* [25]). *An encryption scheme* $\mathcal{E} =$ (KeyGen, Encrypt, Decrypt) *with message space* $\mathcal{M}$ *is* perfectly secret *if for every probability distribution over* $\mathcal{M}$ *every message* $m \in \mathcal{M}$, *and every ciphertext* $c \in \mathcal{C}$ *for which* $\Pr[C = c] > 0$:

$$\Pr[M = m | C = c] = \Pr[M = m].$$

(The requirement that $\Pr[C = c] > 0$ *is a technical one needed to prevent conditioning on a zero-probability event.)*

Proof (of Theorem 3). Let $\mathcal{A}$ be an IND-CPA adversary that has advantage $\epsilon(\lambda)$ against M-Sel by making $q \in \text{poly}(\lambda)$ secret key queries. Since M-Sel uses $\mathcal{SE}$ and IPFE, we consider the following extreme cases:

- Case 1: the underlying IPFE seems perfectly secret. Therefore, the security of the RR-MRES based on the underlying $\mathcal{SE}$ reduces to the security of M-Sel. We present an adversary $\mathcal{B}$ that interacts with $\mathcal{A}$ to break the $\mathcal{SE}$-based RR-MRES.
- Case 2: the underlying $\mathcal{SE}$ primitive seems perfectly secret. Therefore, the security of the ME based on the underlying IPFE reduces to the security of M-Sel. We present an adversary $\mathcal{C}$ that interacts with $\mathcal{A}$ to break the IPFE multiple encryptions.

Let F be the message selection functionality.

Case 1. Let $\overline{\mathcal{SE}} = $ (KeyGen, $\overline{\text{Encrypt}}$, Decrypt) be the RR-MRES associated to $\mathcal{SE}$. Adversary $\mathcal{B}$ challenges the IND-CPA security of $\overline{\mathcal{SE}}$. Let λ be the security parameter and ℓ be the functionality parameter of the underlying IPFE. Consider the following interactions between $\mathcal{B}$ and $\mathcal{A}$:

$(t, sk_{t+1}, \ldots, sk_n) \leftarrow \mathcal{B}(1^\lambda)$ such that $1 \leq t \leq n \in \text{poly}(\lambda)$

For each $j \in [1 .. t]$ do: $sk_j \xleftarrow{R} \overline{\mathcal{SE}}.\text{KeyGen}(1^\lambda)$ EndFor ❶
$SK \leftarrow (sk_1, \ldots, sk_n)$
$(mpk, msk) \leftarrow$ M-Sel.Setup$(1^\lambda, 1^\ell)$ ❷
Let $1 \leq q_1 \leq q \in \text{poly}(\lambda)$; $S \leftarrow \emptyset; S_x \leftarrow \emptyset$
For each $i \in [1 .. q_1]$ do
$\quad x_i \leftarrow \mathcal{A}(mpk, S)$
$\quad sk_{x_i} \leftarrow$ M-Sel.KeyDer(msk, x_i) ▷ | First phase of secret
$\quad S \leftarrow S \cup sk_{x_i}$ | key queries. $x_i \in \mathbb{Z}_2^\ell$.
$\quad S_x \leftarrow S_x \cup x_i$
EndFor
$(\{m_0^1, \ldots, m_0^t\}, \{m_1^1, \ldots, m_1^t\}) \leftarrow \mathcal{A}(mpk, S)$ ▷ | Challenge phase.
$M_0 \leftarrow \{m_0^1, \ldots, m_0^t\}$

$$M_1 \leftarrow \{m_1^1, \ldots, m_1^t\}$$
$$(m_0^1, \ldots, m_0^t; m_1^1, \ldots, m_1^t; m_{t+1}, \ldots, m_n) \leftarrow \mathcal{B}^{\overline{\mathcal{SE}}(SK, \cdot)}(M_0, M_1) \; ❸$$
$$b \xleftarrow{R} \{0, 1\}$$
$$M \leftarrow (m_b^1, \ldots, m_b^t, m_{t+1}, \ldots, m_n)$$
$$r \xleftarrow{R} \mathbb{Z}_p^*$$
$$(r, u_1, \ldots, u_t, u_{t+1}, \ldots, u_n) \leftarrow \overline{\mathcal{SE}}.\mathsf{Encrypt}(SK, M; r) \; ❹$$
$$C \leftarrow (r, u_1, \ldots, u_t, u_{t+1}, \ldots, u_n)$$

Let $\mathbb{B}_\ell$ be the canonical basis of $\mathbb{Z}_2^\ell$

```
For each j ∈ [1 .. t] do
```
$$\quad s_j \xleftarrow{R} \mathbb{Z}_p^*; \; \boldsymbol{y}_j \xleftarrow{R} \mathbb{B}_\ell$$
$$\quad v_j \leftarrow \mathsf{M\text{-}Sel.IPFE.Encrypt}(mpk, s_j \cdot \boldsymbol{y}_j)$$
```
EndFor
```
$$(r, u_1, v_1, \ldots, u_t, v_t) \leftarrow \mathcal{B}^{\overline{\mathcal{SE}}(SK, \cdot)}(M_0, M_1, C)$$
```
For each i ∈ [q₁ .. q] do
```
$$\quad \boldsymbol{x}_i \leftarrow \mathcal{A}(mpk, S, (r, u_1, v_1, \ldots, u_t, v_t))$$
$$\quad sk_{\boldsymbol{x}_i} \leftarrow \mathsf{M\text{-}Sel.KeyDer}(msk, \boldsymbol{x}_i)$$
$$\quad S \leftarrow S \cup sk_{\boldsymbol{x}_i}$$ ▷ Second phase of secret key queries.
$$\quad S_{\boldsymbol{x}} \leftarrow S_{\boldsymbol{x}} \cup \boldsymbol{x}_i$$
```
EndFor
```
$$b' \leftarrow \mathcal{A}(mpk, S, (r, u_1, v_1, \ldots, u_t, v_t))$$
$$b' \leftarrow \mathcal{B}^{\overline{\mathcal{SE}}(SK, \cdot)}(M_0, M_1, C, b')$$

❶ The challenger sets up the IND-RR-CPA security game for $\mathcal{B}$.

❷ $\mathcal{B}$ sets up the IND-CPA security game of M-Sel and gets ready to answer to secret keys queries from $\mathcal{A}$.

❸ $\mathcal{B}$ outputs its challenge messages.

❹ The challenger outputs the challenge ciphertext for $\mathcal{B}$ who also prepares the challenge ciphertext for $\mathcal{A}$.

It is mandated in the challenge phase and in the second phase of secret key queries that $F(\boldsymbol{x}_i, M_0) = F(\boldsymbol{x}_i, M_1)$ for all $\boldsymbol{x}_i \in S_{\boldsymbol{x}}$ and $M_0, M_1 \in 2^{\{0,1\}^*}$.

Assuming that the underlying IPFE primitive seems perfectly secret, we see that adversary $\mathcal{B}$ interacts with $\mathcal{A}$ as the latter would interact with the challenger during a chosen plaintext attack against M-Sel. Therefore, we have:

$$\mathsf{Adv}_{\overline{\mathcal{SE}}, \mathcal{B}}^{\mathsf{IND\text{-}RR\text{-}CPA}}(\lambda) = \mathsf{Adv}_{\mathsf{M\text{-}Sel}, \mathcal{A}}^{\mathsf{IND\text{-}CPA}}(\lambda) \tag{1}$$

Case 2. Let $\mathsf{IPFE} = (\mathsf{Setup}, \mathsf{KeyDer}, \mathsf{Encrypt}, \mathsf{Decrypt})$ be an inner-product functional encryption scheme. Adversary $\mathcal{C}$ challenges the IND-CPA multiple encryptions security of IPFE. Let λ be the security parameter and ℓ be the functionality parameter of the underlying IPFE. Consider the following interactions between $\mathcal{C}$ and $\mathcal{A}$:

Let $1 \le q_1 \le q \in \mathsf{poly}(\lambda);\ t \in \mathsf{poly}(\lambda);\ S \leftarrow \emptyset; S_x \leftarrow \emptyset$
$(mpk, msk) \leftarrow \mathsf{IPFE.Setup}(1^\lambda, 1^\ell)$ ❶
For each $i \in [1\ ..\ q_1]$ do
$\quad x_i \leftarrow \mathcal{A}(mpk, S)$
$\quad sk_{x_i} \leftarrow \mathsf{IPFE.KeyDer}(msk, x_i)$ ▷ $\begin{vmatrix} \text{First phase of secret} \\ \text{key queries. } x_i \in \mathbb{Z}_2^\ell. \end{vmatrix}$
$\quad S \leftarrow S \cup sk_{x_i}$
$\quad S_x \leftarrow S_x \cup x_i$
EndFor
$(\{m_0^1, \ldots, m_0^t\}, \{m_1^1, \ldots, m_1^t\}) \leftarrow \mathcal{A}(mpk, S)$ ▷ $\begin{vmatrix} \text{Challenge phase.} \end{vmatrix}$
$M_0 \leftarrow \{m_0^1, \ldots, m_0^t\}$
$M_1 \leftarrow \{m_1^1, \ldots, m_1^t\}$
Let $\mathbb{B}_\ell$ be the canonical basis of $\mathbb{Z}_2^\ell$ ❷
$r \xleftarrow{R} \mathbb{Z}_p^*$
For each $j \in [1\ ..\ t]$ do
$\quad y_j \xleftarrow{R} \mathbb{B}_\ell$
$\quad s_0^j \xleftarrow{R} \mathbb{Z}_p^*;\ e_0^j \leftarrow s_0^j \cdot y_j$
$\quad s_1^j \xleftarrow{R} \mathbb{Z}_p^*;\ e_1^j \leftarrow s_1^j \cdot y_j$
$\quad u_i \leftarrow \mathsf{M\text{-}Sel.}\mathcal{SE}.\mathsf{Encrypt}(H(s_0^j), m_0^j; r)$
EndFor
$(e_0^1, \ldots, e_0^t; e_1^1, \ldots, e_1^t) \leftarrow \mathcal{C}(mpk, M_0, M_1)$ ▷ $\begin{vmatrix} \langle x_i, e_0^i \rangle = \langle x_i, e_1^i \rangle \\ \text{for all } x_i \in S_x. \end{vmatrix}$
$b \xleftarrow{R} \{0, 1\}$
$(v_1, \ldots, v_t) \leftarrow (\mathsf{IPFE.Encrypt}(mpk, e_b^1), \ldots, \mathsf{IPFE.Encrypt}(mpk, e_b^t))$ ❸
$C \leftarrow (v_1, \ldots, v_t)$
$(u_1, v_1, \ldots, u_t, v_t) \leftarrow \mathcal{C}(mpk, M_0, M_1, C)$ ❹
For each $i \in [q_1\ ..\ q]$ do
$\quad x_i \leftarrow \mathcal{A}(mpk, S, (u_1, v_1, \ldots, u_t, v_t))$
$\quad sk_{x_i} \leftarrow \mathsf{IPFE.KeyDer}(msk, x_i)$ ▷ $\begin{vmatrix} \text{Second phase of secret} \\ \text{key queries.} \end{vmatrix}$
$\quad S \leftarrow S \cup sk_{x_i}$
$\quad S_x \leftarrow S_x \cup x_i$
EndFor
$b' \leftarrow \mathcal{A}(mpk, S, (u_1, v_1, \ldots, u_t, v_t))$
$b' \leftarrow \mathcal{C}(mpk, M_0, M_1, C, b')$

❶ The challenger sets up the IND-ME-CPA security game and gets ready to answer to secret keys queries from $\mathcal{C}$ who itself gets those secret key queries from $\mathcal{A}$.
❷ $\mathcal{C}$ prepares the challenge ciphertext for $\mathcal{A}$.
❸ The challenger outputs the challenge ciphertext for $\mathcal{C}$.
❹ $\mathcal{C}$ outputs the challenge ciphertext for $\mathcal{A}$.

It is mandated in the challenge phase and in the second phase of secret key queries that $F(x_i, M_0) = F(x_i, M_1)$ for all $x_i \in S_x$ and $M_0, M_1 \in 2^{\{0,1\}^*}$.

Assuming that the underlying $\mathcal{SE}$ primitive seems perfectly secret, we see that adversary $\mathcal{C}$ interacts with $\mathcal{A}$ as the latter would interact with the challenger during a chosen plaintext attack against M-Sel. Therefore, we have:

$$\mathsf{Adv}^{\mathsf{IND\text{-}ME\text{-}CPA}}_{\mathsf{IPFE},\mathcal{C}}(\lambda) = \mathsf{Adv}^{\mathsf{IND\text{-}CPA}}_{\mathsf{M\text{-}Sel},\mathcal{A}}(\lambda) \tag{2}$$

By summing up Eqs. 1 and 2, we obtain:

$$\mathsf{Adv}^{\mathsf{IND\text{-}CPA}}_{\mathsf{M\text{-}Sel},\mathcal{A}}(\lambda) = \frac{1}{2} \cdot \mathsf{Adv}^{\mathsf{IND\text{-}RR\text{-}CPA}}_{\mathcal{SE},\mathcal{B}}(\lambda) + \frac{1}{2} \cdot \mathsf{Adv}^{\mathsf{IND\text{-}ME\text{-}CPA}}_{\mathsf{IPFE},\mathcal{C}}(\lambda)$$

From Theorem 1, we know that if a symmetric encryption scheme operates in CBC mode and is IND-CPA secure then the corresponding RR-MRES is also IND-CPA secure. Therefore, $\mathsf{Adv}^{\mathsf{IND\text{-}RR\text{-}CPA}}_{\mathcal{SE},\mathcal{B}}(\lambda)$ is negligible. From Theorem 2, we also have $\mathsf{Adv}^{\mathsf{IND\text{-}ME\text{-}CPA}}_{\mathsf{IPFE},\mathcal{C}}(\lambda)$ is negligible. Thus, $\mathsf{Adv}^{\mathsf{IND\text{-}CPA}}_{\mathsf{M\text{-}Sel},\mathcal{A}}(\lambda)$ is negligible and we conclude that M-Sel is IND-CPA secure. □

5   Instantiation from a DDH-Based IPFE Scheme

Instantiation of M-Sel from IPFE schemes of [16] which compute efficiently the inner product is straightforward. Therefore, we give here an instantiation from the DDH-based IPFE scheme of [8] for which the inner product is hard to compute. That DDH-based IPFE scheme (see Fig. 1) can give short ciphertexts and keys using elliptic curves [3].

Algorithm $\mathsf{Setup}(1^\lambda, 1^\ell)$

1. Choose a cyclic group $\mathbb{G}$ of prime order $p > 2^\lambda$ with generators g, h
2. $\boldsymbol{s} = (s_1, \dots, s_\ell) \overset{R}{\leftarrow} \mathbb{Z}_p^\ell$
3. $\boldsymbol{t} = (t_1, \dots, t_\ell) \overset{R}{\leftarrow} \mathbb{Z}_p^\ell$
4. For each $i \in [1 .. \ell]$
   compute $h_i = g^{s_i} \cdot h^{t_i}$
5. Return
   $msk = (\boldsymbol{s}, \boldsymbol{t})$,
   $mpk = (\mathbb{G}, g, h, \{h_i\}_{i=1}^\ell)$

Algorithm $\mathsf{Encrypt}(mpk, \boldsymbol{y})$
$\boldsymbol{y} = (y_1, \dots, y_\ell) \in \mathbb{Z}_p^\ell$

1. Pick $r \overset{R}{\leftarrow} \mathbb{Z}_p^*$
2. Compute $C = g^r, D = h^r$
3. Compute $\{E_i = g^{y_i} \cdot h_i^r\}_{i=1}^\ell$
4. Return $C_{\boldsymbol{y}} = (C, D, E_1, \dots, E_\ell)$

Algorithm $\mathsf{KeyDer}(msk, \boldsymbol{x})$
$\boldsymbol{x} = (x_1, \dots, x_\ell) \in \mathbb{Z}_p^\ell$

1. Compute $\alpha = \sum_{i=1}^\ell s_i \cdot x_i$
2. Compute $\beta = \sum_{i=1}^\ell t_i \cdot x_i$
3. Return $sk_{\boldsymbol{x}} = (\alpha, \beta)$

Algorithm $\mathsf{Decrypt}(mpk, sk_{\boldsymbol{x}}, C_{\boldsymbol{y}})$
$sk_{\boldsymbol{x}} = (\alpha, \beta)$

1. Compute
   $E_{\boldsymbol{x}} = (\prod_{i=1}^\ell E_i^{x_i})/(C^\alpha \cdot D^\beta)$
2. Return $\langle \boldsymbol{x}, \boldsymbol{y} \rangle = \log_g(E_{\boldsymbol{x}})$

Fig. 1. DDH-based IPFE scheme of Agrawal *et al.* [8].

To suit our M-Sel scheme, we customize the decryption algorithm so that it does not compute the actual value of $\langle \boldsymbol{x}, \boldsymbol{y} \rangle$ but returns $E_{\boldsymbol{x}} = g^{\langle \boldsymbol{x}, \boldsymbol{y} \rangle}$. In the remainder of the paper, to avoid confusion, we denote Decrypt* this customization of Decrypt. This immunizes M-Sel against the main drawback of DDH-based IPFE schemes that is the inner product $\langle \boldsymbol{x}, \boldsymbol{y} \rangle$ must be small enough for the decryption to work.

DDH-Based M-Sel. In the description hereunder of M-Sel$_{DDH}$, we only show steps in our generic construction (in Sect. 3) that change.

Let $\mathcal{SE} = (\mathsf{KeyGen}, \mathsf{Encrypt}, \mathsf{Decrypt})$ be a symmetric encryption scheme operating in CBC mode with key length κ. Let IPFE$_{DDH} = (\mathsf{Setup}, \mathsf{KeyDer}, \mathsf{Encrypt}, \mathsf{Decrypt})$ be the DDH-based IPFE scheme of [8]. Let $\mathbb{G}$ be a cyclic group of prime order $p > 2^{\lambda}$ with generators g, h.

Setup$(1^{\lambda}, 1^{\ell})$.

1. Choose a cryptographic hash function $H : \mathbb{G} \to \{0, 1\}^{\kappa}$.

KeyDer$(msk, \boldsymbol{x})$. *No changes.*

Encrypt(mpk, M). $M = \{m_1, m_2, \ldots, m_t\} \in 2^{\{0,1\}^*}$.

4.2. Compute $u_i \leftarrow \mathcal{SE}.\mathsf{Encrypt}(H(g^{s_i}), m_i; r)$.

Decrypt$(sk_{\boldsymbol{x}}, C)$. $C = (r, u_1, v_1, \ldots, u_t, v_t)$.

2.1. Compute $\rho_i = \text{IPFE}_{DDH}.\mathsf{Decrypt}^{\star}(sk_{\boldsymbol{x}}, v_i)$. Note that $\rho_i = g^{\langle \boldsymbol{x}, s_i \cdot \boldsymbol{y}_i \rangle}$ is either equal to the identity element $1_{\mathbb{G}}$ or g^{s_i}.

2.2. If $\rho_i = 1_{\mathbb{G}}$ then return to step 2.1. for the next value of i. Otherwise, compute $m_i = \mathcal{SE}.\mathsf{Decrypt}(H(\rho_i), u_i; r)$.

6 Conclusion

We proposed a generic construction for the message selection functionality called M-Sel that achieves security against adaptive adversaries. M-Sel can be efficient an practical when instantiated with an efficient inner-product functional encryption (IPFE) scheme. An instantiation of M-Sel from a DDH-based IPFE was also presented. The latter instantiation has short and constant size decryption key thus, suitable for key storage in lightweight devices in the context of Internet of Things (IoT).

Acknowledgements. We would like to thank the anonymous reviewers for providing helpful comments and suggestions about this work.

References

1. Abdalla, M., Bellare, M., Catalano, D., Kiltz, E., Kohno, T., Lange, T., Malone-Lee, J., Neven, G., Paillier, P., Shi, H.: Searchable encryption revisited: consistency properties, relation to anonymous IBE, and extensions. In: Shoup, V. (ed.) CRYPTO 2005. LNCS, vol. 3621, pp. 205–222. Springer, Heidelberg (2005). https://doi.org/10.1007/11535218_13
2. Abdalla, M., Benhamouda, F., Gay, R.: From single-input to multi-client inner-product functional encryption. In: Galbraith, S.D., Moriai, S. (eds.) ASIACRYPT 2019. LNCS, vol. 11923, pp. 552–582. Springer, Cham (2019). https://doi.org/10.1007/978-3-030-34618-8_19
3. Abdalla, M., Bourse, F., Caro, A.D., Pointcheval, D.: Better security for functional encryption for inner product evaluations. Cryptology ePrint Archive, Paper 2016/011 (2016). https://eprint.iacr.org/2016/011
4. Abdalla, M., Bourse, F., De Caro, A., Pointcheval, D.: Simple functional encryption schemes for inner products. In: Katz, J. (ed.) PKC 2015. LNCS, vol. 9020, pp. 733–751. Springer, Heidelberg (2015). https://doi.org/10.1007/978-3-662-46447-2_33
5. Abdalla, M., Bourse, F., Marival, H., Pointcheval, D., Soleimanian, A., Waldner, H.: Multi-client inner-product functional encryption in the random-oracle model. In: Galdi, C., Kolesnikov, V. (eds.) SCN 2020. LNCS, vol. 12238, pp. 525–545. Springer, Cham (2020). https://doi.org/10.1007/978-3-030-57990-6_26
6. Abdalla, M., Catalano, D., Fiore, D., Gay, R., Ursu, B.: Multi-input functional encryption for inner products: function-hiding realizations and constructions without pairings. In: Shacham, H., Boldyreva, A. (eds.) CRYPTO 2018. LNCS, vol. 10991, pp. 597–627. Springer, Cham (2018). https://doi.org/10.1007/978-3-319-96884-1_20
7. Abdalla, M., Catalano, D., Gay, R., Ursu, B.: Inner-product functional encryption with fine-grained access control. In: Moriai, S., Wang, H. (eds.) ASIACRYPT 2020. LNCS, vol. 12493, pp. 467–497. Springer, Cham (2020). https://doi.org/10.1007/978-3-030-64840-4_16
8. Agrawal, S., Libert, B., Stehlé, D.: Fully secure functional encryption for inner products, from standard assumptions. In: Robshaw, M., Katz, J. (eds.) CRYPTO 2016. LNCS, vol. 9816, pp. 333–362. Springer, Heidelberg (2016). https://doi.org/10.1007/978-3-662-53015-3_12
9. Bellare, M., Boldyreva, A., Staddon, J.: Randomness re-use in multi-recipient encryption schemeas. In: Desmedt, Y.G. (ed.) PKC 2003. LNCS, vol. 2567, pp. 85–99. Springer, Heidelberg (2003). https://doi.org/10.1007/3-540-36288-6_7
10. Benhamouda, F., Bourse, F., Lipmaa, H.: CCA-secure inner-product functional encryption from projective hash functions. In: Fehr, S. (ed.) PKC 2017. LNCS, vol. 10175, pp. 36–66. Springer, Heidelberg (2017). https://doi.org/10.1007/978-3-662-54388-7_2
11. Bethencourt, J., Sahai, A., Waters, B.: Ciphertext-policy attribute-based encryption. In: 2007 IEEE Symposium on Security and Privacy (SP '07), pp. 321–334 (2007). https://doi.org/10.1109/SP.2007.11
12. Kim, S., Lewi, K., Mandal, A., Montgomery, H., Roy, A., Wu, D.J.: Function-hiding inner product encryption is practical. In: Catalano, D., De Prisco, R. (eds.) SCN 2018. LNCS, vol. 11035, pp. 544–562. Springer, Cham (2018). https://doi.org/10.1007/978-3-319-98113-0_29

13. Boneh, D., Di Crescenzo, G., Ostrovsky, R., Persiano, G.: Public key encryption with keyword search. In: Cachin, C., Camenisch, J.L. (eds.) EUROCRYPT 2004. LNCS, vol. 3027, pp. 506–522. Springer, Heidelberg (2004). https://doi.org/10.1007/978-3-540-24676-3_30
14. Boneh, D., Franklin, M.: Identity-Based Encryption from the Weil Pairing. In: Kilian, J. (ed.) CRYPTO 2001. LNCS, vol. 2139, pp. 213–229. Springer, Heidelberg (2001). https://doi.org/10.1007/3-540-44647-8_13
15. Boneh, D., Sahai, A., Waters, B.: Functional encryption: definitions and challenges. In: Ishai, Y. (ed.) TCC 2011. LNCS, vol. 6597, pp. 253–273. Springer, Heidelberg (2011). https://doi.org/10.1007/978-3-642-19571-6_16
16. Castagnos, G., Laguillaumie, F., Tucker, I.: Practical fully secure unrestricted inner product functional encryption modulo p. In: Peyrin, T., Galbraith, S. (eds.) ASIACRYPT 2018. LNCS, vol. 11273, pp. 733–764. Springer, Cham (2018). https://doi.org/10.1007/978-3-030-03329-3_25
17. Chotard, J., Dufour Sans, E., Gay, R., Phan, D.H., Pointcheval, D.: Decentralized multi-client functional encryption for inner product. In: Peyrin, T., Galbraith, S. (eds.) ASIACRYPT 2018. LNCS, vol. 11273, pp. 703–732. Springer, Cham (2018). https://doi.org/10.1007/978-3-030-03329-3_24
18. Chotard, J., Dufour-Sans, E., Gay, R., Phan, D.H., Pointcheval, D.: Multi-client functional encryption with repetition for inner product. Cryptology ePrint Archive, Paper 2018/1021 (2018). https://eprint.iacr.org/2018/1021
19. Cocks, C.: An identity based encryption scheme based on quadratic residues. In: Honary, B. (ed.) Cryptography and Coding 2001. LNCS, vol. 2260, pp. 360–363. Springer, Heidelberg (2001). https://doi.org/10.1007/3-540-45325-3_32
20. Datta, P., Dutta, R., Mukhopadhyay, S.: Functional encryption for inner product with full function privacy. In: Cheng, C.-M., Chung, K.-M., Persiano, G., Yang, B.-Y. (eds.) PKC 2016. LNCS, vol. 9614, pp. 164–195. Springer, Heidelberg (2016). https://doi.org/10.1007/978-3-662-49384-7_7
21. Datta, P., Dutta, R., Mukhopadhyay, S.: Strongly full-hiding inner product encryption. Theoret. Comput. Sci. **667**, 16–50 (2017). https://doi.org/10.1016/j.tcs.2016.12.024
22. Datta, P., Okamoto, T., Tomida, J.: Full-hiding (unbounded) multi-input inner product functional encryption from the k-Linear Assumption. In: Abdalla, M., Dahab, R. (eds.) PKC 2018. LNCS, vol. 10770, pp. 245–277. Springer, Cham (2018). https://doi.org/10.1007/978-3-319-76581-5_9
23. Goldwasser, S., Gordon, S.D., Goyal, V., Jain, A., Katz, J., Liu, F.-H., Sahai, A., Shi, E., Zhou, H.-S.: Multi-input functional encryption. In: Nguyen, P.Q., Oswald, E. (eds.) EUROCRYPT 2014. LNCS, vol. 8441, pp. 578–602. Springer, Heidelberg (2014). https://doi.org/10.1007/978-3-642-55220-5_32
24. Goyal, V., Pandey, O., Sahai, A., Waters, B.: Attribute-based encryption for fine-grained access control of encrypted data. In: Proceedings of the 13th ACM Conference on Computer and Communications Security, CCS '06, pp. 89–98. Association for Computing Machinery, New York (2006). https://doi.org/10.1145/1180405.1180418
25. Katz, J., Lindell, Y.: Introduction to Modern Cryptography, Second Edition. Chapman & Hall/CRC, New York (2014). https://doi.org/10.1201/b17668
26. Katz, J., Sahai, A., Waters, B.: Predicate encryption supporting disjunctions, polynomial equations, and inner products. In: Smart, N. (ed.) EUROCRYPT 2008. LNCS, vol. 4965, pp. 146–162. Springer, Heidelberg (2008). https://doi.org/10.1007/978-3-540-78967-3_9

27. Kurosawa, K.: Multi-recipient public-key encryption with shortened ciphertext. In: Naccache, D., Paillier, P. (eds.) PKC 2002. LNCS, vol. 2274, pp. 48–63. Springer, Heidelberg (2002). https://doi.org/10.1007/3-540-45664-3_4

28. Nguyen, K., Pointcheval, D., Schädlich, R.: Function-hiding dynamic decentralized functional encryption for inner products. Cryptology ePrint Archive, Paper 2022/1532 (2022). https://eprint.iacr.org/2022/1532

29. Okamoto, T., Takashima, K.: Fully secure functional encryption with general relations from the decisional linear assumption. In: Rabin, T. (ed.) CRYPTO 2010. LNCS, vol. 6223, pp. 191–208. Springer, Heidelberg (2010). https://doi.org/10.1007/978-3-642-14623-7_11

30. O'Neill, A.: Definitional issues in functional encryption. Cryptology ePrint Archive, Paper 2010/556 (2010). https://eprint.iacr.org/2010/556

31. Sahai, A., Waters, B.: Fuzzy identity-based encryption. In: Cramer, R. (ed.) EUROCRYPT 2005. LNCS, vol. 3494, pp. 457–473. Springer, Heidelberg (2005). https://doi.org/10.1007/11426639_27

32. Shamir, A.: Identity-based cryptosystems and signature schemes. In: Blakley, G.R., Chaum, D. (eds.) CRYPTO 1984. LNCS, vol. 196, pp. 47–53. Springer, Heidelberg (1985). https://doi.org/10.1007/3-540-39568-7_5

Deniable Public-Key Authenticated Quantum Key Exchange

Jeroen van Wier[1]([✉])[iD], Arash Atashpendar[1,2,3][iD], and Peter Roenne[1][iD]

[1] SnT, University of Luxembourg, Esch-sur-Alzette, Luxembourg
{jeroen.vanwier,peter.roenne}@uni.lu
[2] itrust consulting, Niederanven, Luxembourg
[3] itrust Abstractions Lab, Leudelange, Luxembourg
arash@abstractionslab.lu

Abstract. In this work, we explore the notion of deniability in public-key authenticated quantum key exchange (QKE), which allows two parties to establish a shared secret key without leaving any evidence that would bind a session to either party. The deniability property is expressed in terms of being able to simulate the transcripts of a protocol. The ability to deny a message or an action has applications ranging from secure messaging to secure e-voting and whistle-blowing. While quite well-established in classical cryptography, it remains largely unexplored in the quantum setting. Here, we first present a natural extension of classical definitions in the simulation paradigm to the setting of quantum computation and formalize the requirements for a deniable QKE scheme. We then prove that the BB84 variant of QKE, when authenticated using a strong designated verifier signature scheme, satisfies deniability and, finally, propose a concrete instantiation.

Keywords: Public-key Cryptography · Deniability · Quantum Cryptography · Post-Quantum Cryptography · Quantum Key Distribution · Authenticated Quantum Key Exchange · Designated-Verifier Signatures

1 Introduction

Among the wide variety of anticipated cybersecurity challenges, the possibility of the emergence of scalable quantum computers poses a serious threat to our current information security infrastructure and has been receiving increasingly more attention from the information security community over the past few decades. While quantum computing would have its advantages, Shor's algorithm [16] for efficiently computing discrete logarithms and performing integer factorization showed that quantum computing is a double-edged sword as it can be equally damaging when used for the purpose of compromising public-key (PK) cryptosystems that guarantee the security of today's modern communication systems.

These concerns are perhaps best exemplified by recent advances that have prompted calls by the National Security Agency (NSA) for transitioning to post-quantum (PQ) secure cryptosystems and the call for PQ secure proposals, initiated by the National Institute of Standards and Technology (NIST) as part of a standardization process for post-quantum algorithms [17].

M. Manulis et al. (Eds.): SecITC 2023, LNCS 14534, pp. 97–112, 2024.
https://doi.org/10.1007/978-3-031-52947-4_8

On the other hand, Quantum Key Exchange (QKE), provides security without relying on computational assumptions as in PQ key exchange protocols, but at the cost of developing new infrastructure to support quantum channels. Whereas such quantum communication infrastructures for a long time were mostly of academic interest, both terrestrial and satellite networks are now being deployed in practice and planned at large scale, see e.g. [7,10].

Deniability constitutes a subtle and fundamental concept in cryptography that has many applications ranging from secure messaging (e.g., the Signal protocol) to coercion-resistance in secure e-voting to deniable transmission and storage in the context of data breaches. On a more fundamental and theoretical level, deniability shares an intimate connection with incoercible secure multi-party computation [5]. Yet, it has received very little attention in the quantum setting and thus presents a wealth of open questions.

Attempts at providing security against quantum adversaries can be broken down into two classes, namely those that largely rely on classical constructions that are conjectured to be quantum-secure, often classified as post-quantum cryptography, e.g., lattice-based cryptography, and those that make use of quantum information processing and thus fall in the realm of quantum cryptography, such as quantum key exchange. In both cases, and perhaps more surprisingly in the context of quantum cryptography, the notion of deniability has been largely neglected to the extent that there exist only a few works on this topic in the literature [1–3].

In this work, we focus on deniability in public-key authenticated QKE in the simulation paradigm wherein a scheme is considered to be deniable if its transcripts can be simulated. This becomes relevant in a setting with two parties A and B, in which one of the parties is dishonest (i.e., the adversary $\mathcal{M}$) and the goal is to prevent either one from proving to a judge that they exchanged a key with a specific party in a given session. Now, if the transcript obtained by $\mathcal{M}$ could have been simulated without having access to the honest party's secret key, the resulting evidence cannot convincingly associate a specific party with a given session. Note that in the case of deniable key exchange, not only the communication but also the resulting session secret should be simulatable [8].

The particular choice of considering public-key authentication for QKE is motivated by the following observations. As already pointed out in the seminal work of Di Raimondo et al. [8] on deniable authenticated key exchange for classical schemes, deniability for symmetric key exchange protocols in the simulation paradigm is trivially satisfied. Secondly, to cope with the criticism that unconditionally secure QKE requires pre-shared symmetric keys for authentication, a problem that scales quadratically with the number of connected users, the idea of using public-key authentication algorithms for performing QKE with everlasting security had been considered for quite a while until its security was formally proved by Mosca et al. in [13]. For a detailed analysis of PK-authenticated QKE, we refer the reader to [11].

While PK-authenticated QKE solves the problem of pre-shared keys, the signatures also introduce non-repudiation. In this paper, we demonstrate how a deniable QKE can be constructed in the PK setting, in order to regain the deniability from the symmetric setting, by authenticating via quantum-safe strong designated verifier signatures (SDVS), e.g. obtained from lattices as in [14], thus being potentially quantum secure. This implies that the resulting deniable QKE scheme would provide everlasting security, i.e., unless the adversary breaks the authentication during a limited window of attack, the derived shared secret key retains information theoretic security. Note that due to a unique property of QKE, namely that of non-attributability [11] (i.e., the final secret key being completely independent of the classical communication and the initial pre-shared key), the simulatability of the classical communication and that of the secret key itself can be considered separately. The latter follows from the inherent properties of QKE and, to establish the deniability of our solution, it thus suffices to show that the transcript of the authentication can be simulated, i.e., the authentication is deniable.

Related Work. Compared to classical cryptography, deniability remains largely unexplored in the context of quantum and post-quantum cryptography. More specifically, in a paper by Beaver [3] focusing on a setting motivated by an earlier work by Canetti et al. [6] on deniable encryption, it is mainly argued that QKE protocols are not necessarily deniable. In a related work [2], Atashpendar et al. revisit Beaver's analysis and formalize the problem of coercer-deniability in terms of the indistinguishability of coercer views, which considers a scenario wherein the adversary can demand that the honest parties reveal their private randomness in order to verify whether or not their revealed secret key is real or fake. They also establish a link between covert quantum communication and deniability, as well as a relation between entanglement distillation and information theoretic deniability.

However, [2] concludes with a number of open questions, including an analysis of public-key authenticated QKE in the simulation paradigm, which is the focus of our work.

The work of Canetti et al. [6] led to a long series of works on deniability for various cryptographic primitives, including a formalization of deniability for authenticated key exchange in the simulation paradigm by Di Raimondo et al. [8], which in turn was an extension of the definitional work of Dwork et al. [9] on deniable authentication in the context of zero-knowledge proofs. We refer the reader to [1,2] and references therein for more details on deniability in cryptography.

Contributions. We adopt the security framework for authenticated QKE given in [13] and adapt the classical definition of deniable AKEs [8] to the quantum setting for public-key authenticated QKE and formulate it in terms of the simulatability of protocol transcripts in a game-based setting.

We prove in Theorem 1 that a public-key authenticated QKE protocol satisfies deniability when authenticated using an SDVS with non-transferability against quantum adversaries. We also propose the first concrete instance of a deniable PK-authenticated QKE, which is a BB84 variant whose deniability follows as a corollary of Theorem 1.

2 Preliminaries

Notation. We write $y \leftarrow A(x)$ to denote that algorithm A outputs y on input x and use $\perp \leftarrow A$ to denote that A produced an error. We write $\boldsymbol{v}$ to denote a vector of values and v_i to denote the i-th value of this vector. We use $\kappa \in \mathbb{N}$ to denote the security parameter, and implicitly assume it is passed to all algorithms of schemes in unary, i.e. in the form 1^κ. Lastly, we use $f(n) \leq \mathrm{negl}(n)$ to denote that a function f is *negligible*, which means that $f(n)^{-1}$ is superpolynomial. We use $[n]$ to denote the set $\{0, \ldots, n\}$.

While we deal with notions from quantum computing, their understanding is not critical to the work and thus we refer to [19] for an overview of quantum computing. We adopt the standard bra-ket notation from quantum computing. We denote pure states with $|\cdot\rangle$ and mixed states with ρ. We use $(+)$ to denote the $\{|0\rangle, |1\rangle\}$ basis and $(\times)$ to denote the $\{|+\rangle, |-\rangle\}$ basis. We denote the class of quantum polynomial-time algorithms as QPT (the quantum equivalent of PPT) and use $\mathcal{D}_1 \approx_q \mathcal{D}_2$ to denote that two probability distributions cannot be distinguished with more than negligible probability by any QPT distinguisher.

Strong Designated Verifier Signatures (SDVS). The classical communication in authenticated QKE poses a challenge for deniability because a receiver must be able to verify that a message came from the correct sender, but this task must be impossible for any eavesdropper. Note that we focus explicitly on the setting of public-key authentication, which presents the problem that a standard signature, verifiable by anyone with the signer's public key, would prove the involvement of the signer. In the symmetric-key setting, this problem would be trivially solved, as any signature can only be verified by the signer and the intended recipient, and either party can create the same signatures. To achieve these same properties in the public-key setting, we make use of strong designated verifier signatures.

Definition 1. *A* designated verifier signature scheme (DVS scheme) *is a tuple* (Setup, KeyGen, Sign, Verify, Simulate) *of* PPT *algorithms such that:*

- Setup*: Produces the public parameters of a scheme,* params*. It is implicitly assumed that these parameters are passed to the following algorithms.*
- KeyGen*: Produces a keypair* (pk, sk).
- $\mathsf{Sign}_{S \to V}(m) := \mathsf{Sign}(\mathsf{sk}_S, \mathsf{pk}_S, \mathsf{pk}_V, m)$*: Upon input of a sender's keypair, a verifier's public key, and a message* m*, produces a signature* σ.
- $\mathsf{Verify}_{S \to V}(m, \sigma) := \mathsf{Verify}(\mathsf{sk}_V, \mathsf{pk}_V, \mathsf{pk}_S, m, \sigma)$*: Upon input of a verifier's keypair, a sender's public key, a message* m*, and a signature* σ*, outputs the validity of* σ *(a boolean value).*
- $\mathsf{Simulate}_{S \to V}(m) := \mathsf{Simulate}(\mathsf{sk}_V, \mathsf{pk}_V, \mathsf{pk}_S, m)$*: Upon input of a verifier's keypair, a sender's public key, and a message* m*, produces a signature* σ'.

We list some relevant properties of DVS schemes, but refer to [12,15] for more details. *Correctness* of a DVS means that for any valid signature $\sigma \leftarrow \mathsf{Sign}_{S \to V}(m)$, $\mathsf{Verify}_{S \to V}(m, \sigma)$ outputs 1 with overwhelming probability. *Unforgeability* of a DVS means that only the signer and the verifier can create a valid signature between them. *Non-transferability* of a DVS ensures that no party can distinguish between valid signatures and their simulations. Lastly, *sender-privacy* of an SDVS guarantees that only the signer and the verifier know the signer's identity and differentiates strong designated verifier schemes from normal designated verifier schemes. Since these last two properties will be used in this work, we give the formal definition in a game-based setting.

Definition 2. *A DVS scheme $\Pi = (\mathsf{KeyGen}, \mathsf{Sign}, \mathsf{Verify}, \mathsf{Simulate})$ is computationally non-transferable if for any adversary $\mathcal{A}$,*

$$\mathsf{Adv}^{\mathsf{NT}}_{\Pi,\mathcal{A}}(\kappa) := \Pr_{b \in \{0,1\}} \left[\mathsf{G}^{\mathsf{NT}}_{\Pi,\mathcal{A}}(\kappa, b) = b \right] - \frac{1}{2} \leq \mathrm{negl}(\kappa),$$

where the game $\mathsf{G}^{\mathsf{NT}}_{\Pi,\mathcal{A}}$ is defined as follows:

Algorithm 1: $\mathsf{G}^{\mathsf{NT}}_{\Pi,\mathcal{A}}(\kappa, b)$

---

1 params ← Setup
2 $(\mathsf{pk}_S, \mathsf{sk}_S) \leftarrow \mathsf{KeyGen}$
3 $(\mathsf{pk}_V, \mathsf{sk}_V) \leftarrow \mathsf{KeyGen}$
4 $(m^*, \mathsf{state}) \leftarrow \mathcal{A}(1, \mathsf{params}, \mathsf{pk}_S, \mathsf{sk}_S, \mathsf{pk}_V, \mathsf{sk}_V)$
5 **if** $b = 0$ **then**
6    $\sigma^* = \mathsf{Sign}_{S \to V}(m^*)$
7 **else**
8    $\sigma^* = \mathsf{Simulate}_{S \to V}(m^*)$
9 $b' \leftarrow \mathcal{A}(2, \mathsf{state}, \sigma^*)$
10 Output b'

For sender-privacy, we explicitly choose a definition that has been adapted to work in the $n + 1$-party setting. For the interested reader we refer to [20] for more information on this choice.

Definition 3 ([20]). *A DVS scheme Π is sender-private, if for any adversary $\mathcal{A}$ and any n,*

$$\mathsf{Adv}^{\mathsf{SendPriv}}_{\Pi,\mathcal{A}}(\kappa, n) := \Pr_{c \leftarrow \{0,1\}} \left[\mathsf{G}^{\mathsf{SendPriv}}_{\Pi,\mathcal{A}}(\kappa, n, c) = c \right] - \frac{1}{2} \leq \mathrm{negl}(\kappa),$$

where $\mathsf{G}^{\mathsf{SendPriv}}_{\Pi,\mathcal{A}}$ is defined as in Algorithm 2, using the oracles defined right below the algorithm.

Algorithm 2: $G_{\Pi,\mathcal{A}}^{\mathsf{SendPriv}}(\kappa, n, c)$

---

1 params ← Setup
2 $(\mathsf{pk}_{P_0}, \mathsf{sk}_{P_0})$ ← KeyGen; ... ; $(\mathsf{pk}_{P_n}, \mathsf{sk}_{P_n})$ ← KeyGen
3 (m^*, state) ← $\mathcal{A}^{\mathcal{O}_{sign}, \mathcal{O}_{veri}^{(1)}, \mathcal{O}_{sim}}(1, \mathsf{params}, \mathsf{pk}_{P_0}, \ldots, \mathsf{pk}_{P_n})$
4 $\sigma^* = \mathsf{Sign}_{P_c \to P_n}(m^*)$
5 c' ← $\mathcal{A}^{\mathcal{O}_{sign}, \mathcal{O}_{veri}^{(2)}, \mathcal{O}_{sim}}(2, \mathsf{state}, \sigma^*)$
6 Output c'

- $\mathcal{O}_{sign}$: *On input* (m_i, s, v) *returns* $\sigma_i := \mathsf{Sign}_{P_s \to P_v}(m_i)$ *if* $s, v \in [n]$ *and* $\bot$ *otherwise.*
- $\mathcal{O}_{sim}$: *On input* (m_i, s, v) *returns* $\sigma_i := \mathsf{Simulate}_{P_s \to P_v}(m_i)$ *if* $s, v \in [n]$ *and* $\bot$ *otherwise.*
- $\mathcal{O}_{veri}^{(1)}$: *On input* (m_i, σ_i, s, v) *returns* $\mathsf{Verify}_{P_s \to P_v}(m_i, \sigma_i)$ *if* $s, v \in [n]$ *and* $\bot$ *otherwise.*
- $\mathcal{O}_{veri}^{(2)}$: *On input* (m_i, σ_i, s, v) *returns* $\mathsf{Verify}_{P_s \to P_v}(m_i, \sigma_i)$ *if* $s, v \in [n]$ *and* $\sigma_i \neq \sigma^*$, *and* $\bot$ *otherwise.*

In this paper, we will make use of the SDVS scheme proposed in [14], called SUSDVS, which satisfies the above properties when assuming some properties of lattices explained in Sect. 3.

BB84. In order to give a specific instantiation of a deniable QKE algorithm, we will use the *BB84* protocol [4]. In Algorithm 3, we describe the protocol abstractly, to give an intuition. The exact implementation of the protocol in our chosen model can be found in Appendix A. For both privacy amplification and information reconciliation, we will use 2-universal hash functions, as described in [13].

3 Framework

Security Model. We use the QKD model from [13] to model the combination of classical and quantum communication, for which we provide a brief overview here. Each *party* in this model has access to both a classical and a quantum Turing machine, connected by a private tape. Furthermore, the classical machine has access to a private randomness tape and both machines can communicate to other parties over public tapes. Two or more parties may execute a *protocol*, which is specified as a series of subroutines. Each subroutine is triggered by an *activation* over one of the tapes. In Appendix A, we present an overview of the exact activations that can be performed.

Modeling the Adversary. In our work, the main objective of the adversary is to prove the involvement of a party in a key exchange protocol, e.g. to prove

---

Algorithm 3: BB84 with protection against a δ error rate

---

1 Alice generates two random bit strings $a, b \in \{0,1\}^{n_1}$, encodes a_i into $|\psi_i\rangle$ in basis $(+)$ if $b_i = 0$ and in $(\times)$ otherwise, and $\forall i \in [1, |a|]$ sends $|\psi_i\rangle$ to Bob.

2 Bob generates a random bit string $b' \in \{0,1\}^{n_1}$ and upon receiving the qubits, measures $|\psi_i\rangle$ in $(+)$ or $(\times)$ according to b'_i to obtain a'_i.

3 Bob announces b', Alice announces b, and both discard a'_i where $b_i \neq b'_i$, ending up with n_2 bits.

4 Alice picks a set of check bits at random from a by uniformly including or excluding each bit and announces it. Let k_A be the non-check bits of a and k_B be the non-check bits of a'.

5 Alice and Bob compare their check bits and abort if the error exceeds a predefined threshold δ.

6 Alice constructs a 2-universal hash functions F and computes $F' = F(k_A)$.

7 Alice constructs a 2-universal hash functions G and a random permutation P and announces F, F', P, and G.

8 Bob uses F and F' to correct k_B to k'_B.

9 Alice and Bob use $G(P(k_A))$ and $G(P(k'_B))$ respectively as their final secret key.

---

that A talked to B. The model, as presented in [13], was mainly used for an eavesdropping adversary, but in our case, we will consider the adversary to always be the initiator (A) or responder (B) in a protocol. The reason for this is that if no adversary $\mathcal{M}$ can prove that A talked to $\mathcal{M}$, then surely $\mathcal{M}$ can also not prove that A talked to B. This argument is also made in [8], although we provide some alternate views on this in the discussion.

Concretely, this means we model the adversary as a quantum and classical Turing machine, who can perform the QKE protocol with any number of *honest* parties P_i. The adversary can be the initiator or responder in any of these interactions. For any adversary $\mathcal{M}$, we write $\text{View}_{\mathcal{M}}$ to mean the complete contents of $\mathcal{M}$'s memory at the end of execution, including all keys that were established with the other parties.

Security Assumptions. The security and deniability of the particular scheme we present rely on several assumptions regarding the quantum safeness of lattice problems, inherited from the SDVS scheme used. In particular, these are the SIS and ISIS problems, which are thought to be quantum secure. In Appendix B we present the exact parameters needed.

4 Deniability

We first provide a natural extension of the classical definition of deniability given in [8] to the quantum setting, by making both the adversary and the distinguisher a QPT algorithm. In the following definition, the adversary $\mathcal{M}$ is given access to the public keys of an arbitrary number of honest parties, with whom $\mathcal{M}$ can interact. $\mathcal{M}$ is also given an auxiliary input from the set AUX. The simulator is given all the same inputs as $\mathcal{M}$, including the same classical randomness, but cannot interact with the honest parties.

Definition 4. *A QKE scheme* $(\mathsf{AKG}, \Sigma_I, \Sigma_R)$ *is deniable w.r.t. AUX if for any QPT adversary* $\mathcal{M}$ *there exists a QPT simulator* $\mathsf{SIM}_\mathcal{M}$ *s.t.*

$$\forall \kappa \in \mathbb{N}, aux \in \mathsf{AUX} : \mathcal{R}eal(\kappa, aux) \approx_q \mathcal{S}im(\kappa, aux),$$

where

$$\mathcal{R}eal(\kappa, aux) = [(\mathsf{sk}_i, \mathsf{pk}_i) \leftarrow \mathsf{AKG}(1^\kappa); (aux, \mathbf{pk}, \mathsf{View}_\mathcal{M}(\mathbf{pk}, aux))]$$
$$\mathcal{S}im(\kappa, aux) = [(\mathsf{sk}_i, \mathsf{pk}_i) \leftarrow \mathsf{AKG}(1^\kappa); (aux, \mathbf{pk}, \mathsf{SIM}_\mathcal{M}(\mathbf{pk}, aux))].$$

Definition 5. *Given a public-key signature scheme* $(\mathsf{AKG}, \mathsf{Sign}, \mathsf{Verify})$*, we define the QKE scheme* $\mathsf{AuthBB} := (\mathsf{AKG}, \Sigma_I, \Sigma_R)$ *(authenticated BB84), where* Σ_I *and* Σ_R *are as in Algorithm 5 and Algorithm 6 respectively, which can be found in Appendix A. This is the implementation of BB84 as described before, in the above-presented model and using the public-key signature scheme for the classical authentication.*

We restate the definition of deniability, in order to relate deniability to the properties of SDVS, which are presented in a game-based setting.

Definition 6 (Restatement of Definition 4 with AUX = {0}). *A QKE scheme* $\Pi = (\mathsf{AKG}, \Sigma_I, \Sigma_R)$ *is deniable if for any QPT adversary* $\mathcal{M}$ *there exists a QPT simulator* $\mathsf{SIM}_\mathcal{M}$ *that does not interact with any party s.t. no QPT distinguisher* $\mathcal{F}$ *can achieve non-negligible advantage* $\mathsf{Adv}^{\mathsf{Den}}_{\Pi, \mathcal{F}, \mathcal{M}, \mathsf{SIM}_\mathcal{M}}(\kappa, n)$*, which is the advantage in winning the game* $\mathsf{G}^{\mathsf{Den}}_{\Pi, \mathcal{F}, \mathcal{M}, \mathsf{SIM}_\mathcal{M}}$ *as defined in Algorithm 4.*

Algorithm 4: $\mathsf{G}^{\mathsf{Den}}_{\Pi, \mathcal{F}, \mathcal{M}, \mathsf{SIM}_\mathcal{M}}(\kappa, n, b)$

1 $(\mathsf{pk}_{P_0}, \mathsf{sk}_{P_0}) \leftarrow \mathsf{AKG}; \ldots; (\mathsf{pk}_{P_{n-1}}, \mathsf{sk}_{P_{n-1}}) \leftarrow \mathsf{AKG}$
2 Let $\mathbf{pk} = \mathsf{pk}_{P_0} \ldots \mathsf{pk}_{P_{n-1}}$
3 **if** $b = 0$ **then**
4 $\quad \lfloor \ b' \leftarrow \mathcal{F}(\mathsf{View}_\mathcal{M}(\mathbf{pk}), \mathbf{pk})$
5 **else**
6 $\quad \lfloor \ b' \leftarrow \mathcal{F}(\mathsf{SIM}_\mathcal{M}(\mathbf{pk}), \mathbf{pk})$
7 Output b'

The advantage of $\mathcal{F}$ *in this game is defined as:*

$$\mathsf{Adv}^{\mathsf{Den}}_{\Pi, \mathcal{F}, \mathcal{M}, \mathsf{SIM}_\mathcal{M}}(\kappa, n) := \Pr_{b \leftarrow \{0,1\}} \left[\mathsf{G}^{\mathsf{Den}}_{\Pi, \mathcal{F}, \mathcal{M}, \mathsf{SIM}_\mathcal{M}}(\kappa, n, b) = b \right] - \frac{1}{2}$$

4.1   Deniable PK-Authenticated BB84

In the following theorem, we provide a concrete scheme that satisfies our version of deniability, however we emphasize that the precise schemes chosen for this (in particular SUSDVS) are simply examples and not critical to the satisfiability of the definition, another possibility could be the scheme presented in [18].

Theorem 1. AuthBB *with authentication scheme* Π_{SDVS} *is deniable if* Π_{SDVS} *is an* SDVS *with non-transferability and sender-privacy against quantum adversaries.*

Proof. Fix an arbitrary $\mathcal{M}$. This adversary $\mathcal{M}$ can generate many different key-pairs to perform protocol sessions with the honest parties, or even use public keys for which they do not know the private key. However, it is not the goal of the adversary to impersonate or trick any of the honest parties, but simply to convince a third-party that they interacted with one of the honest parties. Thus, w.l.o.g. we assume that, for each session, the adversary either uses a keypair $(\mathsf{pk}_{\mathcal{M}}, \mathsf{sk}_{\mathcal{M}})$ for which $\mathcal{M}$ knows the secret key or uses $\mathsf{pk}'_{\mathcal{M}}$ for which $\mathcal{M}$ does not know the private key. $\mathsf{SIM}_{\mathcal{M}}$ simulates $\mathcal{M}$ and all P_i, except:

(*) For each P_i, generate a keypair $(\mathsf{pk}'_{P_i}, \mathsf{sk}'_{P_i})$.
(1) Each call of $\mathsf{Sign}_{P_i \to \mathcal{M}}$ is replaced with $\mathsf{Simulate}_{P_i \to \mathcal{M}}$.
(2) Each call of $\mathsf{Sign}(\mathsf{sk}_{P_i}, \mathsf{pk}_{P_i}, \mathsf{pk}'_{\mathcal{M}}, x)$ is replaced with $\mathsf{Sign}(\mathsf{sk}'_{P_i}, \mathsf{pk}'_{P_i}, \mathsf{pk}'_{\mathcal{M}}, x)$.
(3) Each call of Verify is replaced with $\top$.

By definition, each P_i performs only honest executions of the protocol, thus only uses its private key in Sign and Verify. Furthermore, each Sign using sk_{P_i} is replaced with either a Sign using sk'_{P_i} or a $\mathsf{Simulate}$, which does not make use of sk_{P_i}. Each Verify is replaced with a static $\top$, which also does not use sk_{P_i}. This means $\mathsf{SIM}_{\mathcal{M}}$ can run on input $\mathbf{pk}$, i.e. simulate each party P_i without the knowledge of sk_{P_i}.

First we show that change (1) is undetectable by an adversary. Define $P_i^{(1)}$ to be the simulation of P_i after modification (1) and $\mathsf{SIM}_{\mathcal{M}}^{(1)}$ to be the simulation of $\mathcal{M}$ interacting with $P_i^{(1)}$ instead of P_i. Let Π be AuthBB using Π_{SDVS}. For any fixed distinguisher $\mathcal{F}$, let $\mathcal{H}_{start}$ be the $b = 0$ instance of $\mathsf{G}^{\mathsf{Den}}_{\Pi, \mathcal{F}, \mathcal{M}, \mathsf{SIM}_{\mathcal{M}}^{(1)}}$ and $\mathcal{H}_{end}$ be the $b = 1$ instance. Let $\mathcal{H}_0, \ldots, \mathcal{H}_m$ be a series of hybrids such that $\mathcal{H}_0 = \mathcal{H}_{start}$, $\mathcal{H}_m = \mathcal{H}_{end}$ and each step $\mathcal{H}_k \to \mathcal{H}_{k+1}$ replaces one $\mathsf{Sign}_{P_i \to \mathcal{M}}(x)$ with $\mathsf{Simulate}_{P_i \to \mathcal{M}}(x)$.

Suppose, for some fixed k, there exists a QPT distinguisher $\mathcal{D}$ that can distinguish between $\mathcal{H}_k$ and $\mathcal{H}_{k+1}$, where one $\mathsf{Sign}_{P_i \to \mathcal{M}}(x)$ is replaced in the step $\mathcal{H}_k \to \mathcal{H}_{k+1}$. We use this distinguisher to build an adversary $\mathcal{A}$ that breaks the non-transferability of Π_{SDVS}, as follows:

– $\mathcal{A}$ receives $(1, \mathsf{params}, \mathsf{pk}_S, \mathsf{sk}_S, \mathsf{pk}_V, \mathsf{sk}_V)$.
– $\mathcal{A}$ runs $\mathcal{H}_k$, but replaces $(\mathsf{pk}_{P_i}, \mathsf{sk}_{P_i}, \mathsf{pk}_{\mathcal{M}}, \mathsf{sk}_{\mathcal{M}})$ with $(\mathsf{pk}_S, \mathsf{sk}_S, \mathsf{pk}_V, \mathsf{sk}_V)$ before running $\mathcal{F}$.

- $\mathcal{A}$ stops $\mathcal{H}_k$ before the replaced $\mathsf{Sign}_{P_i \to \mathcal{M}}(x)$ call and outputs (x, state), where state is the state of $\mathcal{A}$ at this point.
- $\mathcal{A}$ receives $(2, \mathsf{state}, \sigma^*)$ and restores from state.
- $\mathcal{A}$ replaces $\mathsf{Sign}_{P_i \to \mathcal{M}}(x)$ with σ^* and continues running $\mathcal{H}_k$.
- $\mathcal{A}$ runs $\mathcal{D}$ and outputs what $\mathcal{D}$ outputs.

Observe that in the $b = 0$ case of $\mathsf{G}^{\mathsf{NT}}_{\Pi_{\mathsf{SDVS}}, \mathcal{A}}$, the Sign is replaced by $\mathsf{Sign}_{S \to V}(x)$ and in the $b = 1$ case it is replaced by $\mathsf{Simulate}_{S \to V}(x)$. Furthermore, observe that the insertion of the $(\mathsf{pk}_S, \mathsf{sk}_S, \mathsf{pk}_V, \mathsf{sk}_V)$ keypairs is only a relabeling of the keypairs, but ensures that the $b = 0$ case of $\mathsf{G}^{\mathsf{NT}}_{\Pi_{\mathsf{SDVS}}, \mathcal{A}}$ is equal to $\mathcal{H}_k$ and the $b = 1$ case equal to $\mathcal{H}_{k+1}$, thus the distinguishing probability of $\mathcal{D}$ is the same as the winning probability of $\mathcal{A}$ in the $\mathsf{G}^{\mathsf{NT}}_{\Pi_{\mathsf{SDVS}}, \mathcal{A}}$ game, which would imply that $\mathsf{Adv}^{\mathsf{NT}}_{\Pi_{\mathsf{SDVS}}, \mathcal{A}}$ is non-negligible. Since this is a contradiction, it must be the case that no such $\mathcal{D}$ exists.

For modification (2), the argument is similar. Suppose, in a chain of hybrids similar to the one above, there are two hybrids $\mathcal{H}$ and $\mathcal{H}'$, where $\mathcal{H}'$ is the result of replacing one call of $\mathsf{Sign}(\mathsf{sk}_{P_i}, \mathsf{pk}_{P_i}, \mathsf{pk}'_{\mathcal{M}}, x)$ with $\mathsf{Sign}(\mathsf{sk}'_{P_i}, \mathsf{pk}'_{P_i}, \mathsf{pk}'_{\mathcal{M}}, x)$ in $\mathcal{H}$ and some QPT distinguisher $\mathcal{D}$ can distinguish between them. We use this distinguisher to build an adversary $\mathcal{B}$ that breaks the $n + 2$-party sender-privacy of Π_{SDVS}, as follows:

- $\mathcal{B}$ receives $(1, \mathsf{params}, \mathsf{pk}_0, \ldots, \mathsf{pk}_{n+1})$.
- $\mathcal{B}$ runs $\mathcal{H}$, but replaces $(\mathsf{pk}_{P_i}, \mathsf{pk}'_{P_i}, \mathsf{pk}_{P_0}, \ldots, \mathsf{pk}_{P_{i-1}}, \mathsf{pk}_{P_{i+1}}, \ldots, \mathsf{pk}_{P_{n-1}}, \mathsf{pk}'_{\mathcal{M}})$ with $(\mathsf{pk}_0, \ldots, \mathsf{pk}_{n+1})$ before running $\mathcal{F}$. All Sign, Simulate and Verify calls involving some P_j are performed by oracle calls.
- $\mathcal{B}$ stops $\mathcal{H}$ before the $\mathsf{Sign}(\mathsf{sk}_{P_i}, \mathsf{pk}_{P_i}, \mathsf{pk}'_{\mathcal{M}}, x)$ call that will be replaced in $\mathcal{H}'$ and outputs (x, state), where state is the state of $\mathcal{A}$ at this point.
- $\mathcal{B}$ receives $(2, \mathsf{state}, \sigma^*)$ and restores from state.
- $\mathcal{B}$ replaces $\mathsf{Sign}(\mathsf{sk}_{P_i}, \mathsf{pk}_{P_i}, \mathsf{pk}'_{\mathcal{M}}, x)$ with σ^* and continues running $\mathcal{H}$.
- $\mathcal{B}$ runs $\mathcal{D}$ and outputs what $\mathcal{D}$ outputs.

Observe that in the $b = 0$ case of $\mathsf{G}^{\mathsf{SendPriv}}_{\Pi_{\mathsf{SDVS}}, \mathcal{B}}$, Sign is replaced by $\mathsf{Sign}(\mathsf{sk}_{P_i}, \mathsf{pk}_{P_i}, \mathsf{pk}'_{\mathcal{M}}, x)$ and in the $b = 1$ case it is replaced by $\mathsf{Sign}(\mathsf{sk}'_{P_i}, \mathsf{pk}'_{P_i}, \mathsf{pk}'_{\mathcal{M}}, x)$. Furthermore, observe that the replacement of the public keys for all honest parties and pk'_{P_i} is simply a relabeling, since they were all honestly generated. The only public key that is not honestly generated was $\mathsf{pk}'_{\mathcal{M}}$, however since the adversary, by definition, does not know the corresponding private key the replacement is undetectable to the adversary. The replacements of the keys ensures that the $b = 0$ case of $\mathsf{G}^{\mathsf{SendPriv}}_{\Pi_{\mathsf{SDVS}}, \mathcal{B}}$ is equal to $\mathcal{H}$ and the $b = 1$ case equal to $\mathcal{H}'$, thus the distinguishing probability of $\mathcal{D}$ is the same as the winning probability of $\mathcal{B}$ in the $\mathsf{G}^{\mathsf{SendPriv}}_{\Pi_{\mathsf{SDVS}}, \mathcal{B}}$ game, which would imply that $\mathsf{Adv}^{\mathsf{SendPriv}}_{\Pi_{\mathsf{SDVS}}, \mathcal{B}}$ is non-negligible. Since this is a contradiction, it must be the case that no such $\mathcal{D}$ exists.

For modification (3), observe that both the initiator and the responder perform their verification after having done all their communication. This means that it is impossible for $\mathcal{M}$ to prove to a third party whether the key exchange was accepted or rejected by P_i. Any communication between $\mathcal{M}$ and P_i after the protocol using the newly established key can be simulated, as the simulator would also have the key. Modification (3) ensures that, for the simulator, even invalid signatures are accepted by the simulated honest parties, but this change cannot alter the behaviour of the simulated adversary as the adversary cannot detect this change. In fact, for each session the simulated honest party could stop their execution after the last message is sent since the rest of the execution is private and does not influence future sessions.

□

Corollary 1. *Under Assumptions B1 and B2 defined in Appendix B,* SUSDVS *(from [14]) is an* SDVS *with non-transferability against quantum adversaries, thus* AuthBB *using* SUSDVS *is deniable in the standard model.*

4.2   Eavesdropping on Interactions Between Honest Parties

In Theorem 1 we assume that the honest parties only perform QKE sessions with the adversary, arguing that the adversary has no more power as a third-party observer than she has as one of the participants. This assumption was also made in [8] and we consider it fundamentally sound. However, one can consider what happens if we relax it and give the adversary the ability to force two honest parties to perform a QKE session. The reason that this setting is interesting, is that the simulator is no longer able to create a signature between two honest parties, as doing so requires the private key of either of the honest parties. E.g. if two-party ring signatures were used for authentication, then when Alice and Bob communicate the adversary can prove that at least one of them was present, which would defy deniability.

To solve this problem, one can use the sender-privacy property of an SDVS scheme. The simulator simply generates a keypair for each simulated honest party and uses this to sign any messages, still designating the verifier by their original public key. Since all eavesdropped sessions are between honest parties, the simulator can skip the verification of these signatures. The sender-privacy property ensures that no third party can distinguish between these incorrect signatures and any correct ones the adversary might have collected.

5   Discussion and Future Work

While the work presented here provides a firm basis for deniability in the quantum setting, some obvious open problems remain. Firstly, our protocol delays all authentication until the end. This is done to stop the adversary from intentionally sending an invalid signature to cause an abort, as the simulator would not be able to perform the verification when simulating the honest parties. However, this intentional abort can only be caused by the behaviour of the adversary, which the simulator knows. Thus, intuitively deniability should be achievable without this modification.

Furthermore, in the case of QKE, there is inherent independence between the classical communication and the established key, meaning that the classical part of the transcript contains no information about the established key [13]. This leads us to conjecture that using any deniable public-key authentication might be enough to create a deniable QKE protocol.

Finally, we limit ourselves to the case where AUX = {0} for simplicity, however we conjecture that this restriction is not necessary and that the provided proof extends to any AUX.

Acknowledgements. This work was supported by the Luxembourg National Research Fund (FNR), under the joint CORE project Q-CoDe (CORE17/IS/11689058/Q-CoDe/Ryan) and the CORE project EquiVox (C19/IS/13643617/EquiVox/Ryan), as well as the LUX4QCI Luxembourg Experimental Network for Quantum Communication Infrastructure project, co-funded by the Digital Europe Programme under the Grant Agreement No. 101091508.

A   Appendix: The [13] Model

In this appendix we elaborate on the [13] model. The classical Turing machine can receive the following activations:

- SendC(Ψ, msg): The Turing machine resumes the *session* with identifier Ψ using msg as input. Ψ may also be a vector of session identifiers, where it is clear from context which one belongs to the receiving party and which to other parties.
- SendC(params, pid): When SendC is received without a session identifier it indicates the start of a new protocol execution with public parameters params.
- Q2C(msg): This activation indicates a classical output of the quantum Turing machine and activates the classical Turing machine with the most recent session.

The quantum Turing machine has the following activations:

- SendQ(ρ): The quantum Turing machine activates with as input the state ρ.
- C2Q(msg): The quantum Turing machine is activated by the classical Turing machine with message msg.

We use Ψ to denote *ephemeral* variables, which are variables that are bound to a session. After each activation, the Turing machines may send activations over their respective public channel and the private channel between them. At the end of a session, the classical Turing machine of both parties outputs four values:

- sk, the shared secret key established during this session, or $\bot$ if execution failed.
- pid, the identifier of the other party involved in this session.
- A vector $v = (v_0, \dots)$, where each v_i is a vector of labels of values.
- A vector $u = (u_0, \dots)$, where each u_i is a vector of labels of values.

A protocol is *correct* if, when all messages are delivered without changes or reordering, both parties output the same key sk and the same vector v. Each classical value Ψ_d has a label $\ell(\Psi_d)$ and an adversary can partner a value by issuing Partner$(\ell(\Psi_d))$ to learn the value corresponding to the label. An adversary can also partner a session Ψ, learning the value sk if it has been output. Note that if an adversary learns a value without partnering (through public communication, for example), this value remains *unpartnered*. A session Ψ is *fresh* as long as every v_i contains at least (the label of) one value that the adversary has not partnered and the adversary has not partnered Ψ or any session Ψ' with the same v and sk and, *at the time of output*, there is least one value in each u_i with which the adversary has not partnered. This signifies the main difference between v and u: values in u pose no security risk if revealed after the key has been established, but values in v do.

A.1 BB84 in This Model

In Algorithms 5 and 6 we present, respectively, the initiator and responder roles in the [4] QKD protocol, following the [13] model.

B Appendix: Lattice Hardness Problems Needed for [14]

In this appendix, we briefly present the following assumptions, which are conjectured to hold in the presence of quantum computers, but refer to [14] for their precise statements. We use the following (simplified) parameters:

- $|\mathsf{msg}|$ is the length of the message being signed,
- κ is the security parameter,
- $h = O(\log \kappa)$
- $m = O(\kappa h)$,
- $q = \mathsf{poly}(\kappa)$ is a sufficiently large number,
- $l \leq (p-1)\kappa$, where p is the smallest prime dividing q, and
- $s = O(\sqrt{\kappa l h}) \cdot \omega(\sqrt{\log \kappa})^2$ a sufficiently large parameter.

Definition 7 ([14]). *Given a uniformly random matrix $A \in \mathbb{Z}_q^{n \times m}$ and a syndrome $u \in \mathbb{Z}_q^n$, the $\mathsf{ISIS}_{q,m,\beta}$ problem is to find a nonzero vector $v \in \mathbb{Z}^m$ such that $Av = u \pmod{q}$ and $\|v\| \leq \beta$.*

The $\mathsf{SIS}_{q,m,\beta}$ problem is the $\mathsf{ISIS}_{q,m,\beta}$ problem for $u = 0$.

Assumption B1. *The $\mathsf{SIS}_{q,m,\beta}$ problem is hard for sufficiently large $q = \sqrt{(|\mathsf{msg}| + 4ms^2)\kappa} + \omega(\sqrt{\log \kappa})$ and $\beta = \sqrt{|\mathsf{msg}| + 4ms^2}$. The $\mathsf{SIS}_{q,m,\beta}$ problem and $\mathsf{ISIS}_{q,m,\beta}$ problem are hard for sufficiently large $q = O(l^{3/2}\kappa^3 \log^{5/2} \kappa) \cdot \omega(\sqrt{\log \kappa})^6$, $m = O(\kappa \log q)$, and $\beta = s\sqrt{2m}O(l\kappa^{3/2}k^{3/2}) \cdot \omega(\sqrt{\log \kappa})^3$.*

Furthermore, we have the following assumption on the hardness of distinguishing lattices, where q is prime. Here $\mathcal{D}_{\Lambda_w^\perp(A),s}$ denotes the distribution of sampling from $\{z \in \mathbb{Z}^\kappa \mid Az = w(\mod q)\}$ according to a Gaussian distribution.

Algorithm 5: Σ_I

Upon Activation: SendC(start, initiator, R)

1.1 Create a new session Ψ^I with responder identifier R

1.2 Read n_1 random bits Ψ^I_{dIR}

1.3 Read n_1 random bits Ψ^I_{bI}

1.4 Send activation C2Q($\Psi^I_{dIR}, \Psi^I_{bI}, R$)

1.5 Send activation SendC(Ψ^I, start, responder, I) to R

Upon Activation: C2Q($\Psi^I_{dIR}, \Psi^I_{bI}, R$)

2.1 Prepare ρ to be the bitwise encoding of Ψ^I_{dIR} in the $(+)$ or $(\times)$ basis if the corresponding bit of Ψ^I_{bI} is 0 or 1 respectively

2.2 Send activation SendQ(ρ) to R

Upon Activation: SendC($\Psi^I, \Psi^R, \Psi^R_{bR}$)

3.1 Discard all bit positions from Ψ^I_{dIR} for which Ψ^I_{bI} is not equal to Ψ^R_{bR}; Let n_2 denote the amount of bits left in Ψ^I_{dIR}

3.2 Read n_2 random bits Ψ^I_{indIR}; Let Ψ^I_{chkIR} be the substring of Ψ^I_{dIR} for which the bits of Ψ^I_{indIR} are 1 and Ψ^I_{kIR} the substring for which they are 0; Let n_3 be the length of Ψ^I_{kIR}

3.3 Send activation SendC($\Psi^I, \Psi^R, \Psi^I_{bI}, \Psi^I_{indIR}, \Psi^I_{chkIR}$) to R

Upon Activation: SendC($\Psi^I, \Psi^R, \varepsilon, \sigma_R$)

4.1 Read random bits Ψ^I_F to construct a 2-universal hash function F and compute $F' \leftarrow F(\Psi^I_{kIR})$

4.2 Read random bits $\Psi^I_{P,G}$ to construct a 2-universal hash function G and a random permutation P and compute $\Psi^I_{skIR} \leftarrow G(P(\Psi^I_{kIR}))$

4.3 Compute $\sigma_I \leftarrow \text{Sign}(\Psi_I, \Psi_R, \Psi^I_{bI}, \Psi^I_{indIR}, \Psi^I_{chkIR}, F, F', P, G, I)$

4.4 Send activation SendC($\Psi^I, \Psi^R, F, F', P, G, \sigma_I$) to R

4.5 Abort if Verify($\sigma_R, (\Psi^I, \Psi^R, \Psi^R_{bR}, \varepsilon, R)$) fails

4.6 Output $(\text{sk} = \Psi^I_{skIR}, pid = R, v = (\ell(\Psi^I_{dIR}), \ell(\Psi^R_{dIR}), \ell(\Psi^I_{bI}), \ell(\Psi^R_{bR}), \ell(\Psi^I_F), \ell(\Psi^I_{P,G})), u = (\text{sk}_I))$

Assumption B2 (Assumption 2.1 in [14]). *Let* $m_1, m_2 = O(\kappa \log q)$, A, R *uniform random matrices from* $\mathbb{Z}_q^{\kappa \times m_1}$, $C_0, \ldots, C_l$ *uniform random matrices from* $\mathbb{Z}_q^{\kappa \times m_2}$, $\boldsymbol{w}$ *a fixed vector from* $\mathbb{Z}_q^\kappa$, $\mu \in \{0,1\}^l$ *a secret bitstring, and* $C_\mu = C_0 + \sum_{j=1}^l \mu_j C_j$, *then it is hard to distinguish between* $\mathcal{D}_{\Lambda_{\boldsymbol{w}}^\perp (A|C_\mu),s}$ *and* $\mathcal{D}_{\Lambda_{\boldsymbol{w}}^\perp (R|C_\mu),s}$ *without any information on* μ.

Algorithm 6: Σ_R

Upon Activation: SendC(Ψ^I, start, responder, R)

1.1 Create a new session Ψ^R with initiator identifier I

1.2 Read n_1 random bits Ψ^R_{bR}

1.3 Send activation C2Q(Ψ^R_{bR})

Upon Activation: C2Q(Ψ^R_{bR}) combined with SendQ(ρ)

2.1 Set Ψ^R_{dIR} to be the qubit-wise measurement of ρ in the $(+)$ or $(\times)$ basis if the corresponding bit of Ψ^R_{bR} is 0 or 1 respectively

2.2 Send activation Q2C(Ψ^R_{dIR})

Upon Activation: Q2C(Ψ^R_{dIR})

3.1 Send activation SendC(Ψ^I, Ψ^R, Ψ^R_{bR}) to I

Upon Activation: SendC(Ψ^I, Ψ^R, Ψ^I_{bI}, Ψ^I_{indIR}, Ψ^I_{chkIR})

4.1 Discard all bit positions from Ψ^R_{dIR} for which Ψ^I_{bI} is not equal to Ψ^R_{bR}

4.2 Let Ψ^R_{chkIR} be the substring of Ψ^R_{dIR} for which the bits of Ψ^I_{indIR} are 1 and Ψ^R_{kIR} the substring for which they are 0

4.3 Let ε be the proportion of bits of Ψ^I_{chkIR} that do not match Ψ^R_{chkIR}; abort if $\varepsilon > \delta$, where δ is the error rate parameter.

4.4 Compute $\sigma_R \leftarrow$ Sign(Ψ^I, Ψ^R, Ψ^R_{bR}, ε, R)

4.5 Send activation SendC(Ψ^I, Ψ^R, ε, σ_R) to I

Upon Activation: SendC(Ψ^I, Ψ^R, F, F', P, G, σ_I)

5.1 Abort if Verify(σ_I, (Ψ_I, Ψ_R, Ψ^I_{bI}, Ψ^I_{indIR}, Ψ^I_{chkIR}, F, F', P, G, I)) fails

5.2 Use F and F' to correct Ψ^R_{kIR} to $\Psi^R_{kIR'}$

5.3 Compute $\Psi^R_{skIR} \leftarrow G(P(\Psi^R_{kIR'}))$

5.4 Output (sk $= \Psi^R_{skIR}$, $pid = I$, $v =$ $(\ell(\Psi^I_{dIR}), \ell(\Psi^R_{dIR}), \ell(\Psi^I_{bI}), \ell(\Psi^R_{bR}), \ell(\Psi^I_F), \ell(\Psi^I_{P,G}))$, $u = (sk_R)$)

References

1. Atashpendar, A.: From information theory puzzles in deletion channels to deniability in quantum cryptography. Ph.D. thesis, University of Luxembourg, Luxembourg (2019). https://arxiv.org/pdf/2003.11663.pdf

2. Atashpendar, A., Policharla, G.V., Rønne, P.B., Ryan, P.Y.A.: Revisiting deniability in quantum key exchange. In: Gruschka, N. (ed.) NordSec 2018. LNCS, vol. 11252, pp. 104–120. Springer, Cham (2018). https://doi.org/10.1007/978-3-030-03638-6_7

3. Beaver, D.: On deniability in quantum key exchange. In: Knudsen, L.R. (ed.) EUROCRYPT 2002. LNCS, vol. 2332, pp. 352–367. Springer, Heidelberg (2002). https://doi.org/10.1007/3-540-46035-7_23

4. Bennett, C.H., Brassard, G.: Quantum cryptography: public key distribution and coin tossing. In: International Conference on Computers, Systems and Signal Processing (India, December 1984), pp. 175–9 (1984)

5. Canetti, R., Gennaro, R.: Incoercible multiparty computation. In: Proceedings of 37th Conference on Foundations of Computer Science, pp. 504–513 (1996). https://doi.org/10.1109/SFCS.1996.548509

6. Canetti, R., Dwork, C., Naor, M., Ostrovsky, R.: Deniable encryption. In: Kaliski, B.S. (ed.) CRYPTO 1997. LNCS, vol. 1294, pp. 90–104. Springer, Heidelberg (1997). https://doi.org/10.1007/BFb0052229
7. Chen, Y.-A., et al.: An integrated space-to-ground quantum communication network over 4,600 kilometres. Nature **589**(7841), 214–219 (2021)
8. Di Raimondo, M., Gennaro, R., Krawczyk, H.: Deniable authentication and key exchange. In: Proceedings of the 13th ACM Conference on Computer and Communications Security. CCS '06, pp. 400–409. ACM, Alexandria, Virginia, USA (2006). https://doi.org/10.1145/1180405.1180454
9. Dwork, C., Naor, M., Sahai, A.: Concurrent Zero-knowledge. J. ACM **51**(6), 851–898 (2004). https://doi.org/10.1145/1039488.1039489
10. European Quantum Communication Infrastructure (EuroQCI) — Shaping Europe's digital future. https://digital-strategy.ec.europa.eu/en/policies/european-quantum-communication-infrastructure-euroqci. Accessed 09 July 2021
11. Ioannou, L.M., Mosca, M.: A new spin on quantum cryptography: avoiding trapdoors and embracing public keys. In: Yang, B.-Y. (ed.) PQCrypto 2011. LNCS, vol. 7071, pp. 255–274. Springer, Heidelberg (2011). https://doi.org/10.1007/978-3-642-25405-5_17
12. Jakobsson, M., Sako, K., Impagliazzo, R.: Designated verifier proofs and their applications. In: Maurer, U. (ed.) EUROCRYPT 1996. LNCS, vol. 1070, pp. 143–154. Springer, Heidelberg (1996). https://doi.org/10.1007/3-540-68339-9_13
13. Mosca, M., Stebila, D., Ustaoğlu, B.: Quantum key distribution in the classical authenticated key exchange framework. In: Gaborit, P. (ed.) PQCrypto 2013. LNCS, vol. 7932, pp. 136–154. Springer, Heidelberg (2013). https://doi.org/10.1007/978-3-642-38616-9_9
14. Noh, G., Jeong, I.R.: Strong designated verifier signature scheme from lattices in the standard model. Secur. Commun. Netw. **9**(18), 6202–6214 (2016)
15. Saeednia, S., Kremer, S., Markowitch, O.: An efficient strong designated verifier signature scheme. In: Lim, J.-I., Lee, D.-H. (eds.) ICISC 2003. LNCS, vol. 2971, pp. 40–54. Springer, Heidelberg (2004). https://doi.org/10.1007/978-3-540-24691-6_4
16. Shor, P.W.: Algorithms for quantum computation: discrete logarithms and factoring. In: Proceedings 35th Annual Symposium on Foundations of Computer Science, pp. 124–134 (1994). https://doi.org/10.1109/SFCS.1994.365700
17. of Standards, N.I., (NIST), T.: Post-Quantum Cryptography Standardization (2017). https://csrc.nist.gov/projects/post-quantum-cryptography/post-quantum-cryptography-standardization. Accessed 22 July 2019
18. Sun, X., Tian, H., Wang, Y.: Toward quantum-resistant strong designated verifier signature from isogenies. In: 2012 Fourth International Conference on Intelligent Networking and Collaborative Systems, pp. 292–296 (2012). https://doi.org/10.1109/iNCoS.2012.70
19. Watrous, J.: The Theory of Quantum Information. Cambridge University Press, Cambridge (2018)
20. van Wier, J.: On SDVS sender privacy in the multi-party setting. CoRR abs/2107.06119 (2021). arXiv: 2107.06119. https://arxiv.org/abs/2107.06119

Towards a Secure and Transparent Blockchain-Based System for e-Commerce Deliveries

Anastasia Theodouli[✉][iD], Evdoxia Manganopoulou, Athanasios Kalfoutzos,
Athanasios Tzikas, Christos Tsislianis, Dimosthenis Ioannidis[iD],
Konstantinos Votis[iD], and Dimitrios Tzovaras[iD]

Information Technologies Institute, Centre for Research and Technology Hellas,
6th km Harilaou, 57001 Thermi, Thessaloniki, Greece
anastath@iti.gr

Abstract. National and cross-border e-commerce deliveries require cooperation between several parties as it involves, in addition to the transport of products, complex procedures and financial transactions. In this context, several issues need to be tackled such as personalization of the delivery, product information traceability (track and trace), logging and auditing of important actions to avoid disputes between stakeholders, and workflow automation as regards frequently repeated processes. The unique features of Blockchain technology allowed the usage of Blockchain for increasing transparency and accountability in the supply chain and e-commerce sector. In this paper, we present a blockchain-based system that attempts to deal with the aforementioned issues that arise in national and cross-border e-commerce deliveries thus boosting transparency, traceability, accountability and overall security in such contexts.

Keywords: blockchain · e-commerce · transparency · security · smart contracts · IoT

1 Introduction

The need for security and transparency in the transportation of products is growing more and more nowadays. The transport of packages through courier companies requires cooperation between their stakeholders as it involves except for product transfer, complex processes, and financial transactions. The complexities are even more prominent in cross-border transportations. There are plenty of cases in that packages have been lost or damaged especially in cross-border transports where a lot of intermediate links are involved, without finding the real culprit. Moreover, it is often the delivery of the packages to be dramatically delayed or their packaging be damaged. It is also frequent that recipients in critical deliveries cannot be authenticated in an indisputable manner with current authentication mechanisms such as hand-written signatures or usage of

M. Manulis et al. (Eds.): SecITC 2023, LNCS 14534, pp. 113–125, 2024.
https://doi.org/10.1007/978-3-031-52947-4_9

Personal Identification Number (PIN). Another common issue is the distortion of temperature-sensitive packages due to their increase in temperature during their transport. Non automated frequently repeated processes increase the workload of employees in courier companies, increase paper usage thus having bad ecological impact, and do not allow efficient management of transportation resources (e.g. tracks that may not contain enough load). The reasons mentioned above have led to customer dissatisfaction, the tension between stakeholders, and the inefficient management of resources in courier companies. The specific features of Blockchain technology render it suitable for applications in supply chain management and e-commerce as it can solve many of the aforementioned problems. Firstly, it allows all the companies that participate in cross-border transport of products to share a common view of data since each block in the blockchain includes a set of transactions, and when a new transaction is added to a block, a record of the transaction is added to the ledger of every participant that participates in the Blockchain network. As such, complex processes are more easily tracked since there is no need to view/update common information in each and every individual information system of the companies involved. Moreover, Blockchain is a distributed ledger technology that supports recording information in an immutable way. As such, by logging critical actions to the blockchain it can be used as a source of truth when there are disputes between stakeholders and ensure accountability. The logging in the Blockchain system can include, as the most important actions, such as the delivery, the receipt, and the return of a product. Besides, logging the checkpoints and the corresponding time through which the package passes ensures transparency and traceability during the product transportation. Furthermore, in the case of temperature-sensitive packages, the temperature exceedance (if any) as well as the id of the IoT thermal device performing the measurement, can be recorded in the system. This will have as an outcome the control of the product at all times and the reduction of lost or damaged packages. What is more, Blockchain can provide the public key infrastructure and digital signature through which authenticity of the data signed can be verified. Using the Blockchain Public key infrastructure, recipients in critical deliveries can be authenticated in an indisputable manner by submitting transactions that include their digital signatures with them. Besides, smart contracts are supported by most of the modern Blockchain Platforms. Smart contracts are scripts that can automate processes and be executed based on a predefined set of rules agreed upon by the involved stakeholders. Many of the aforementioned non automated frequently repeated processes can be automated by leveraging smart contracts. In this paper, we present our contribution, a blockchain-based system that aims to provide an entire solution regarding secure and transparent transactions in e-commerce deliveries by tackling one by one the aforementioned problems. It should be noted that the proposed system has been validated against four real business scenarios in frames of the TRANSFARENCY Epanek project:

1. Personalised Delivery: In critical deliveries, the recipient should be authenticated in an indisputable way. Current authentication mechanisms for signing the delivery of a product such as hand-written signatures or usage of Personal

Identification Number (PIN) are not so efficient. Blockchain uses Public Key Infrastructure (PKI) in order to allow all clients to sign the transactions that they submit to the Blockchain network with their cryptographic credentials. Submitting a signed transaction upon the receipt of a product solves the problem of the personalization of a delivery in an efficient way. In the case that the Recipient cannot receive the product on their own, they can change the name and the address of the Recipient and let the new Recipient sign in the same way using Blockchain.

2. Track and trace the progress of a product transportation: The customer will have the chance to monitor the package when passing through checkpoints to reduce the chance of being lost or damaged. The passage of checkpoints and the time that it takes place will be recorded in the blockchain platform to ensure transparency and traceability.

3. Logging and auditing of critical actions in terms of security: The critical actions like delivery, receipt and return of a product will be logged in the blockchain network so as to allow the resolution of conflicts between stake-holders and to ensure accountability.

4. Workflow automation: The automation of repetitive actions in transportation companies has several benefits such as, reduction of transportation time, fewer mistakes, and overall better resources management of the courier companies. Moreover, it will have positive ecological impact by reducing paper consumption. The proposed system leverages smart contracts in order to support automation as regards the following processes:

   (a) The automatic billing of the recipient in cases of non-return of defective products within the agreed period of time

   (b) The assurance of payment of the intermediate companies involved in the cross-border transportations by ensuring the Proof Of Delivery of the product to all intermediate courier companies using Blockchain

   (c) The coordination of the courier companies involved in cross-border transportations in order to reduce the means of transport traveling without (sufficient) load at the cross-border level, so as to reduce the required time of transport procedures.

   (d) The Control of temperature-sensitive packets using IoT devices: There are packages whose temperature must be within certain limits throughout the shipment. For this reason, thermal IoT devices will be placed inside the packages to measure the temperature at any time. In case the temperature exceeds the permissible limits, the recipient and the sender will be automatically notified so that they can take informed decisions (e.g. the recipient may not be willing to receive the product), the system will automatically issue a suggestion to the courier company as to whether the recipient should be charged or not, and the exceedance of temperature will be regarded as a critical action and as such it will be recorded in the blockchain platform.

The remainder of this paper is structured as follows. In Sect. 2 we present similar works that have been implemented in the fields of our business cases. In

Sect. 3 we present the design of the proposed blockchain-based system including business scenarios, users involved, and system architecture, while in Sect. 4 we present the implementation details with focus on the description of the smart contracts. Finally, Sect. 5 concludes the paper.

2 Related Work

This section describes previous works related to the business scenarios against which our system was validated, namely: a) track and trace b) logging and auditing c) workflow automation. To the authors' knowledge, there are no papers in personalised delivery using Blockchain and this constitutes a novelty of this work.

2.1 Track and Trace Using Blockchain

1. S. Terzi et al. [1] describe how Blockchain technology can be implemented in the logging and tracing of the ingredients from the time they were shipped to the time they were purchased by the customers. This will prevent the falsification of many products such as medicines and electronics while it provides the possibility of monitoring them in a short time. Furthermore, it describes how authentication works for users who maintain an identity on the Blockchain network. Undoubtedly, Blockchain can guarantee insurance, uprightness, and responsibility in the supply chain, logistics, and multi-level agile manufacturing systems.
2. Khaled Salah et al. [2] present a solution for monitoring and detecting soybeans throughout the agricultural supply chain. The basis of the implementation is the Ethereum Blockchain platform and smart contracts which contribute to the management and control of all interactions and transactions between involved participants in the supply chain ecosystem. All transactions are recorded and stored in the Blockchain immutable ledger and then linked to a decentralized file system (IPFS) for transparency, security, and reliability.

2.2 Logging and Auditing Using Blockchain

1. Konstantinos Moschou et al. [3] present a methodology focusing on the evaluation of the performance of transactions by two different processors for the same use case and for the same type of transaction developed using the Hyperledger Sawtooth platform. In addition, the methodology was tested and the outcomes, that can be considered useful for the future design of Blockchain solutions, were depicted.
2. Benedikt Putz et al. [4] analyze a new system for maintaining the integrity of records, which is based on Blockchain technology and unreliable proof of existence is stored from generated records. It guarantees secure recording and is independent of trusted third parties, specific material, and possible modifications to the records.

3. Nicholas D. Pattengale and Corey M. Hudson [5] implemented a technique for the unchanging recording of actions and the ability of queries to the Blockchain network for a cross-site genomic dataset access audit trail. The main goal is an efficient structure of time and space in order to store and regain access to the gene data logs. The implementation is based on the MultiChain platform which supports effective queries of data for single clause constraints and heuristic and binary search techniques for queries containing conjunctions of clause limits, and various timestamp queries.

2.3 Workflow Automation Using Blockchain

1. Kristen N. Griggs et al. [6] propose a blockchain-based smart contract system monitors the patients in real-time and supports medical interventions. It also, sends notifications both to patients and doctors and records all activities on a blockchain network. This would significantly improve remote patient monitoring, contribute to automated information to the involved parties and protect the health information that origin from IoT devices. The implementation is based on the Ethereum protocol. More specifically, there is communication between the system and sensor, and all events are recorded on a blockchain network.
2. Haya R. Hasan and Khaled Salah [7] propose a blockchain-based system that ensures Proof Of Delivery (PoD) of digital assets and automatic settlement of payments when the asset is transported using a single or multiple intermediate transporters. Authors use Ethereum Smart Contracts to let all intermediate transporters to verify a key that is stored within a Smart Contract deployed in the Ethereum network, they also use a chain of Smart Contracts to propagate a payment settlement function in all intermediate transporters if the key verification is done successfully in all intermediate transporters.

3 Proposed Blockchain-Based System

In this section, we present our a blockchain-based system that aims to provide an entire solution regarding secure and transparent transactions in e-commerce deliveries.

3.1 Business Scenarios

The proposed system was validated against four business cases that are prominent in the national and cross-border e-commerce field. The four business scenarios are the following, (i) Personalised Delivery, (ii) Track and trace the progress of a product transportation, (iii) Logging and auditing of critical actions in terms of security, and (iv) Workflow automation. More details about each scenario and how blockchain is used to enhance several security aspects in frames of each of the business scenarios is provided in Sect. 1 above.

3.2   Users

Corporate Senders. The senders of the parcels are responsible for delivering the package to the courier company employees. Additionally, they need to provide information about the recipient and indicate if it is a critical shipment. In the case of a sensitive package, they are required to declare the acceptable temperature range in which the package can be kept unchanged. Through the proposed system, they have the ability to track the progress of the shipment and the arrival of the package at various checkpoints in real-time. Moreover, through automated flows (smart contracts), automated updates to the recipient regarding environmental conditions throughout the transportation of the product can be made if it is temperature-sensitive. Additionally, the sender can be automatically charged for the specific shipment in cases where the accepted value limit is exceeded.

Recipients. Recipients are responsible for receiving the parcels from courier company employees. Through the proposed system, they have the ability to track the progress and location of the expected product, at specific checkpoints. In the case where a shipment is declared as critical by the sender, recipients digitally sign using Blockchain Public Key Infrastructure the delivery of the parcel upon receipt. Recipients also have the ability, through their dedicated web application, to transfer their rights to another recipient when they are not available to receive the product, as well as to change the delivery address if they cannot receive it at the initially declared address. Additionally, they can monitor the most significant actions taken during the product's shipment as the system records the most important and critical actions. If a package is declared as temperature-sensitive, they can receive automated updates if the temperature exceeds a specific allowable range.

Employees of the First Courier Company. This category includes distributors, drivers, and employees who interact with the proposed system in frames of the four business scenarios against which the system is being validated. Distributors are responsible for transporting the product from the company store to the recipient. Distributors are required to verify the identity of the recipient in the case of a critical shipment and inform the system about the delivery or return of the product. Distributors do not directly interact with the proposed system for the needs of the scenarios. The company's drivers determine the weight and volume of the package to calculate the load in the coordination of the courier companies involved in cross-border transportations in order to reduce the means of transport traveling without (sufficient) load which is a sub-scenario of workflow automation as it has been mentioned in Sect. 1 above. Company employees are responsible for collecting the parcels and initiating the entire shipment process. Additionally, they are responsible for placing the IoT device on sensitive packages to support certain automated workflows of the project. Finally, in the scenario of payment to intermediate companies involved in cross-border transportation once the transportation is completed, it is within their responsibilities to handle the payment processes.

Employees of the Second Courier Company. These users are the same as the users of the first company, but belong to the second courier company. The second courier company is a mock company used for the purposes of the following two sub-scenarios that are examined at a cross-border level and belong to the workflow automation scenario, (i) Payment of intermediary companies involved in the transportation of the product at the cross-border level, provided that the transportation has been successfully completed, and (ii) Coordination of the involved organizations/companies in order to reduce the transportation means that travel without (sufficient) load at the cross-border level. In Particular, the drivers of the second courier company have their own web applications and participate in the aforementioned sub-scenarios.

3.3   System Architecture

The system architecture has been designed by using the "4+1 Architectural View Model (AVM)" [8]. It describes the system's architecture based on various simultaneous views. 4+1 Architectural View Model (AVM) is an open architecture description framework consisting of four primary viewpoints, namely a) Logical view b) Process View c) Development View d) Physical View. In this paper, we concentrate on the Development View, by describing the system components as well as their interfaces and technical specifications. Each component is described in detail by analyzing its subcomponents and technologies used to implement it.

– Transfarency applications. These are web interfaces that allow the Users, i.e. corporate senders, recipients, and employees of courier companies to interact with the Blockchain network through the Middleware API in order for the them to issue queries to the Blockchain, view the results of the queries and submit transactions relevant with the four business scenarios against which the TRANSFARENCY system was validated. Transfarency applications were implemented using React.js v17.0.2[1], Bootstrap v2.1.2[2] and Socket.io v4.5.4[3] and communicate with the Middleware API using API calls over https and also using the Websocket API for interactive two-way communication that allows the implementation of notifications.
– Middleware API. The Middleware API serves as the communication gateway between the information systems of the courier companies and the transfarency applications with the Blockchain network. It is responsible for issuing transactions and connecting end users to the Blockchain network as it includes all the libraries that facilitate the connection to the Blockchain network. The middleware API uses a node.js server v10.24.1[4] and contains the following

---

[1] https://react.dev/.
[2] https://getbootstrap.com/.
[3] https://socket.io/.
[4] https://nodejs.org/en.

packages: express, body parser, cors, socket.io and uses specific modules and classes from the Hyperledger Fabric SDK for node.js v2.2 to interact with the Blockchain network, i.e. fabric-ca-client version 2.2.4 and fabric-network version 2.2.4 [9].

- Permissioned Blockchain network. This is a peer to peer network run by multiple organisations who form a consortium. In this work, the organisations that run the network nodes are the two courier companies that participate in the cross-border scenarios. The permissions of each organisation are defined by a set of policies. Smart contracts which are deployed to the nodes of the network are used to generate transactions which change the world state of the ledger which holds the data of the business objects. The network is built using Hyperledger Fabric v2.2.4 [9] and the smart contracts, also termed as chaincode in Hyperledger Fabric, are written in JavaScript. The Blockchain network communicates with the Middleware API using gRPC calls [10] and exchange messages using Protocol Buffers. The choice of Hyperledger Fabric is made because its permissioned nature fits our business scenarios, it does not contain any transaction fees, and it is scalable due to its low-cost consensus algorithms.

- Identity Management System. Users that access TRANSFARENCY applications and external information system software clients are registered with the Authorisation server and upon successful registration, they are enrolled with the Hyperledger Fabric CA by the Courier company administrator. This process creates the certificate and private key which is used in order to sign the transactions that they issue to the Blockchain network (e.g. when the Recipient signs a personalised delivery). When they want to access Blockchain network resources, they first issue an authentication request to the Authorisation Server which authenticates them and upon successful authentication they are given access to the Blockchain network resources based on the permissions that have been granted. Authorisation server is implemented with keycloak [11] technology that uses OAuth 2.0 and OpenID Connect (OIDC) protocols. This is a component that has been developed in frames of H2020 FEVER project [12,13], and it was properly integrated in the TRANS-FARENCY architecture. External information systems of courier companies can be connected with the TRANSFARENCY system by communicating with the Middleware RestFul API over https after being properly authenticated and authorised by the Identity Management System. In the case of cross-border scenarios, each courier company should own its own Authorisation Server and Hyperledger Fabric CA and its own administrator who should revoke client certificates when necessary. There is no further credential validation e.g. cross-validation with external authorities and this is a limitation of the system. The system architecture is depicted in Figure 1 below. External Systems, identity management system and internal components of the TRANSPARENCY architecture are shown with different colours as it appears in the included legend.

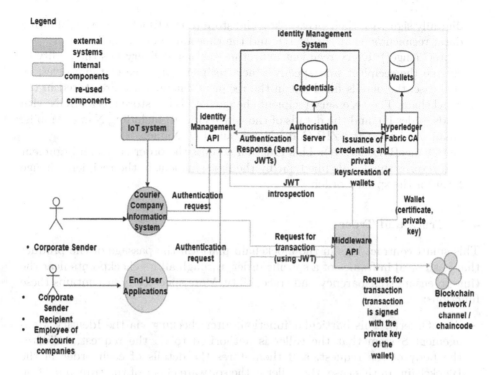

Fig. 1. System Architecture of our proposed system

4   Smart Contracts

As it has been mentioned in Sect. 3.3 above, within the Blockchain network, there are deployed the Smart contracts that hold the business logic that changes the world state of the ledger which holds the data of the business objects. In this section, we will describe the Smart Contracts that were designed, developed, and deployed to the Blockchain network to meet the requirements of the four business case scenarios that have been described in Sect. 3.1 above.

4.1   Personalised Delivery

This smart contract contains functions that allow recipients to sign the Delivery of a product using their private key during critical deliveries in which the recipient need to be authenticated in an indisputable way. It also contains functions that allow the define a new recipient for a specific delivery by logging the change in the blockchain. More specifically, the contract has the function:

- StoreSignature(): When the package reaches the recipient, the recipient receives a notification and is required to sign for the specific delivery. This function, following the authorization of the request via the Identity Management System and validation of the request body, allows the Recipient to

digitally sign with their private key and store to the Blockchain the following
data: recipient's email, order ID, and the timestamp of the delivery.
- StoreChange(): Every recipient expecting package delivery has the ability to
change the recipient and specify a new recipient in place of themselves. In
this case, the details filled out in the recipient change form are stored in the
Blockchain. The necessary recipient change details are stored as a JSON with
fields: order ID, and the details of the new recipient, including Name, Mobile,
email, Address, City, ZIP Code, Notes, and Bell Name.
- GetChangeByOrderID(): This function accepts the order ID as an argument
and returns the details filled out by the first recipient in the recipient change
form for the specific order.

4.2   Track and Trace

This smart contract logs in the blockchain platform the passage of the product
that is shipped in frames of a specific order, through all its checkpoints near the
time to ensure transparency and traceability. More specifically, it contains these
functions:

- StoreOrder(): This particular function, after checking via the Identity Management System that the caller is authorised to do the request, validates
the body of the request, and then stores the details of each order in the
Blockchain. In this case, the caller is the software client of the transportation
company. This function changes the state of the ledger.
- StoreCheckpoint(): This particular function, after checking via the Identity
Management System that the caller is authorised to do the request, validates
the body of the request and stores in the Blockchain the details of each
checkpoint which correspond to a specific order. In this case, the caller is
the software client of the transportation company. This function changes the
state of the ledger.
- GetAllCheckpoints(): This is a getter function that accepts the order ID as
an argument and returns all the checkpoints from which this specific order
has passed through.

4.3   Logging and Auditing

As mentioned above, apart from the need to track and trace each product, there
are some critical events (delivery, receipt and return of a product) that need
to be logged in the blockchain as a digital evidence to resolve future conflicts
between stakeholders. The functions of the smart contract are the same as the
ones described in Sect. 4.2, during the storage of the checkpoint there is a specific
field that marks the checkpoint as critical or not. Back in the web interfaces of
the transfarency apps, there are specific filters that allow the user to filter the
checkpoints by their criticality to easily sort out the ones that can be used as a
digital evidence.

4.4   Workflow Automation

This smart contract contains functions that automate repetitive processes that are described as sub-scenarios of the workflow automation scenario in Sect. 1 above. To achieve automation, the functions of this smart contract first apply the business logic of each sub-scenario and then they use Contract Events in order to send notifications to the listeners of the middleware API for specific critical actions depending on each sub-scenario. These notifications are then propagated from the middleware API to the web interfaces of the users using socket.io.

- NotifyRecepientCharged(): This specific function is called by the middleware API after the expiration of a countdown timer, which signifies the end of the specified return period for a product and the consequent release of the charge to the recipient. The function accepts three arguments from the middleware API: the calculated expiration date (expirationDate), the order code (orderID), and the charge amount (amount). After verifying that the expiration date has indeed passed, it triggers/emits a contract event that is listened to by the middleware API. Subsequently, it notifies the recipient with a notification that their charge for the particular order has been activated, providing relevant information such as the order number and the charge amount. Additionally, the function records the timestamp of the event, along with the order ID and the recipient's charge amount, in the blockchain. A composite key is also generated based on the order ID and amount to facilitate data retrieval and access. The listener responsible for receiving and processing the event is located in the chaincode, which resides in the middleware API. This listener connects to the Blockchain network and communicates with the chaincode connected to the Gateway. Finally, to complete the scenario, the notification emitted by the smart contract and subsequently received by the listener is delivered to the end user via socket.io.
- DriverNotification(): In the case of a cross-border shipment, this function sends a notification through the Blockchain to the delivery driver, urging them to apply for availability with another transportation company in order to deliver the package.
- DeclareAvailability(): When a driver from another transportation company applies for availability, a notification is sent to the driver of the second transportation company, inviting them to accept or reject the package delivery based on the availability of their transportation vehicle. After receiving the response, a notification is sent back to the driver of the first transportation company, informing them of the acceptance or rejection of the package.
- DeclareArrival(): If the driver of the second transportation company accepts the package for delivery, the driver of the first transportation company is informed through a notification and is prompted to make a declaration of arrival when they reach the delivery location.
- StoreHash(): In the case of cross-border shipments, this function generates a unique hash with the shipment number as an argument and stores it on the

Blockchain. This is done to enable future comparison of keys. The generated hash serves as a reference point for ensuring the authenticity and integrity of the shipment information.

- ProofofDelivery(): This function is called when the driver of the second transportation company presses the "Confirmation of Shipment Key" button via the web interface of their application with the goal of ensuring transparency through the Blockchain. Subsequently, a comparison of the encoded keys is performed. In case of a match, both the driver of the first transportation company and the sender are notified of the successful delivery of the package to the second company. A similar process is followed when the recipient presses the "Confirmation of Shipment Key" button at the time of receiving the package. The stored hash is compared with the hash generated in the middleware. If they match, the drivers of both transportation companies are informed that the package has reached its destination and payment can be processed.
- IotReport(): In the case of shipping sensitive packages with temperature monitoring through IoT devices, recorded temperature data is transmitted. If the duration of temperature deviation exceeds or equals 10% of the total recording time, a notification is sent to both the sender and the recipient. This notification informs them of the temperature deviation.

5   Conclusions and Future Work

In this work, we proposed a blockchain-based system that attempts to solve well known problems that arise in national and cross-border e-commerce deliveries. The system leverages the blockchain technology to boost transparency, traceability, accountability and overall security in such contexts. The proposed system was validated against four business scenarios that are prominent in the national and cross-border e-commerce field. The four business scenarios are the following, (i) Personalised Delivery, (ii) Track and trace the progress of a product transportation, (iii) Logging and auditing of critical actions in terms of security, and (iv) Workflow automation. As a future step, we propose to perform an extensive performance and storage scalability analysis and adjustment of the system in accordance with the findings (e.g. usage of hashes of orders and checkpoints and references of the orders and checkpoints to the external information systems of the transportation companies, instead of storing on-chain the data per se). Moreover, the legal aspects of users' credential verification may be explored. Finally, the system may be compared with similar platforms in terms of privacy, confidentiality, performance, and scalability such as the one developed in frames of the H2020 EFPF project [14].

Acknowledgements. Authors acknowledge support from the Research-Innovate-Create project funded by the Greek state (Epanek) project TRANSFARENCY (T2E DK-04541).

References

1. Terzi, S., et al.: Transforming the supply-chain management and industry logistics with blockchain smart contracts. In: Proceedings of the 23rd Pan-Hellenic Conference on Informatics, pp. 9–14 (2019)
2. Salah, K., et al.: Blockchain-based soybean traceability in agricultural supply chain. IEEE Access **7**, 73295–73305 (2019)
3. Moschou, K., et al.: Performance Evaluation of different Hyperledger Sawtooth transaction processors for Blockchain log storage with varying workloads. In: 2020 IEEE International Conference on Blockchain (Blockchain), pp. 476–481. IEEE (2020)
4. Putz, B., Menges, F., Pernul, G.: A secure and auditable logging infrastructure based on a permissioned blockchain. Comput. Secur. **87**, 101602 (2019)
5. Pattengale, N.D., Hudson, C.M.: Decentralized genomics audit logging via permissioned blockchain ledgering. BMC Med. Genomics **13**(7), 1–9 (2020)
6. Griggs, K.N., et al.: Healthcare blockchain system using smart contracts for secure automated remote patient monitoring. J. Med. Syst. **42**(7), 1–7 (2018)
7. Hasan, H.R., Salah, K.: Blockchain-based proof of delivery of physical assets with single and multiple transporters. IEEE Access **6**, 46781–46793 (2018). https://doi.org/10.1109/ACCESS.2018.2866512
8. Kruchten, P.B.: The 4+1 view model of architecture. IEEE Softw. **12**(6), 42–50 (1995)
9. A Blockchain Platform for the Enterprise. https://hyperledger-fabric.readthedocs.io/en/release-2.2/index.html. Accessed 15 July 2023
10. Fabric-common: How to set gRPC settings. https://hyperledger.github.io/fabric-sdk-node/release-2.2/tutorial-grpc-settings.html. Accessed 15 July 2023
11. Open Source Identity and Access Management. https://www.keycloak.org/. Accessed 15 July 2023
12. Flexible Energy Production, Demand and Storage-based Virtual Power Plants for Electricity Markets and Resilient DSO Operation. https://fever-h2020.eu. Accessed 15 July 2023
13. Černe, G., et al.: Organizing the flexible energy market for bridging smart energy communities. In: 2022 18th International Conference on the European Energy Market (EEM), Ljubljana, Slovenia, pp. 1–5 (2022). https://doi.org/10.1109/EEM54602.2022.9920991
14. Mastos, T.D., et al.: Introducing an application of an industry 4.0 solution for circular supply chain management. J. Cleaner Prod. **300**, 126886 (2021)

Attacking Secure-Element-Hardened MCUboot Using a Low-Cost Fault Injection Toolkit

Mario Noseda[ID] and Simon Künzli[✉]

Institute of Embedded Systems, Zurich University of Applied Sciences,
Winterthur, Switzerland
{mario.noseda,simon.kuenzli}@zhaw.ch
https://www.zhaw.ch/ines

Abstract. The bootloader is a critical part of a device's secure startup, and its interactions with firmware images require cryptographic operations. Instead of storing keys for authentication and encryption in the bootloader, one can harden the system by offloading the key storage and all cryptographic operations to a secure element. This paper analyzes the susceptibility of MCUboot used in conjunction with a secure element to voltage fault injection during firmware image verification. We designed and built a low-cost voltage fault injection tool using a Cortex-M7 MCU and an analog switch, which can achieve a timing resolution of 6.67 ns. We found vulnerable instructions in the glue code between the bootloader and the secure element library. By targeting these vulnerable instructions, we showed how an attacker could bypass a signature verification performed by a secure element by faulting a Nordic nRF52840 host MCU. While secure elements are still suited for securely storing keys and other sensitive data, a holistic approach is required to secure a device against fault injection. Otherwise, the threat of fault injection could diminish the benefits of secure bootloaders and secure elements.

Keywords: Fault injection · Voltage glitching · MCUboot · Secure elements · Ethical hacking · Hardware implant · Embedded systems

1 Introduction

The bootloader is one of the most critical pieces of software in a device for multiple reasons (e.g., security, safety, dependability, IP theft, and brand reputation). Specifically, it is a security concern as the bootloader runs with the highest privileges and initializes the root of trust (RoT) and all the cryptographic hardware. Justifiably, Morel and Couroussé [1] declared the bootloader to be the Achilles' heel of an IoT system. Attackers can target the bootloader with fault injection (FI) attacks for executing unauthenticated code by either faulting functions that check the authenticity of the code or directly gaining code execution with elevated privileges by re-enabling debug or testing interfaces [2].

M. Manulis et al. (Eds.): SecITC 2023, LNCS 14534, pp. 126–143, 2024.
https://doi.org/10.1007/978-3-031-52947-4_10

Also, scenarios where attackers induced multiple consecutive faults for breaching a target have been documented [3]. Moreover, extracting the firmware images of the target device allows for searching them for software vulnerabilities (e.g., buffer overflow), which attackers can use for conventional exploits. This approach is especially interesting for threat actors as software exploitations generally scale much better [4].

Instead of executing unauthenticated code, it might be even more valuable for an attacker to compromise the bootloader itself. Modifying the bootloader through some vulnerability allows the attacker to completely negate any cryptographic security measures as the boot process runs with the highest privileges. In order to prevent such malicious modification, first-stage bootloaders are generally immutable to serve as an RoT. Unfortunately, vulnerabilities in immutable bootloaders are highly problematic as manufacturers cannot patch them afterward, making it impossible to fix affected devices. Further, extracting the bootloader code might reveal sensitive data, such as the symmetric keys some bootloaders use for decrypting and authenticating images. This information effectively grants an attacker complete control over a device and all its future upgrades, even over other devices if keys have been reused. In such a case, the attacker can easily decrypt firmware updates and search them for vulnerabilities [1].

Compromised IoT devices can subsequently be used as a vehicle for larger attacks like breaching other hosts on the same network [5] or launching a botnet [6]. Ronen et al. [7] created a native and autonomously self-spreading ZigBee worm for the Philips Hue light system by extracting the symmetric encryption and authentication keys from the bootloader.

Offloading cryptographic operations and keys to a secure element might be advantageous, as their tamper-resistant memory protects keys and other sensitive data from modification or extraction. Depending on the use case, they can offer higher performance and reduced energy consumption compared to executing the cryptographic algorithms on the MCU [8]. However, adding a secure element might give developers a false sense of security, as it does not necessarily increase the overall protection of the device against fault injection threats. In this paper, we advise that the threat analysis should not just focus on where sensitive data is stored or processed. Instead, a holistic approach to viewing a device's security is required by considering side-channel threats.

Our contribution consists of analyzing an application that uses MCUboot [9] as the bootloader and an externally connected secure element for all cryptographic operations (e.g., firmware image authentication). We present (1) the code section vulnerable to fault injection attacks and (2) how we managed to boot malicious firmware with a voltage fault injection attack by bypassing the firmware image verification offloaded onto the secure element. Furthermore, we (3) developed our own voltage fault injection tool constructed from inexpensive off-the-shelf parts. We discuss fault injection countermeasures to protect devices from such attacks in Sect. 3, but applying them is out of scope for this paper. Our work increases the security of IoT devices by providing developers with information on how comparably little effort and cost attackers need to spend to bypass sophisticated countermeasures like secure elements.

This paper is structured accordingly: Sect. 2 explains the basic concepts of voltage FI attacks needed to understand the subsequent attack. Section 3 lists various mitigations for impeding or preventing FI attacks. Section 4 introduces a secure-element-hardened MCUboot implementation we used as this project's target. Section 5 describes how we bypassed the secure element's firmware image verification using FI attacks. Section 6 discusses the applicability of such attacks and their required effort. Finally, we draw appropriate conclusions in Sect. 7 and describe future work related to the findings of this study.

2 Voltage Fault Injection

FI using voltage transients (colloquially known as "voltage glitching") has been studied extensively for quite some time [10–12]. Injecting transient voltage glitches over some physical interface into a target (e.g., supply pins) results in electrical transients at the circuit level. These transients might manifest as faulty bits at the micro-architectural level if they managed to be captured by a logic gate, memory cell, or flip-flop. Finally, these faulty bits propagate to the application level as faulty instructions or data [13, 14].

Various fault models exist for predicting the consequences of such attacks. Kazemi et al. [15] categorize the high-level fault consequences into two main groups: control flow corruption (disrupting the execution or order of instructions, branches, and statements) and data flow corruption (compromising the integrity or confidentiality of data). Timmers et al. [16] assume in their fault model that the fault flips a variable amount of bits in the current instruction, thus modifying it into any other valid instruction supported by the architecture. Their model then classifies the subsequent outcome as either instruction corruption or instruction skipping. The former occurs if the faulty instruction changes the behavior or state of the device, like modifying a used register or branching to an arbitrary address. The latter occurs whenever the faulty instruction has no impact on the state and execution flow at all, like modifying an unused register or adding zero to a register.

Attackers can craft simple exploits with such faults, like skipping a (conditional) branch instruction or changing the value read from a configuration register. It is important to note that many of these exploits can happen on all levels, i.e., the functions above and below on the call stack of the targeted function, because faults can propagate through parameters and return values. However, some attackers do not limit themselves to such simple exploits and create significantly more complex attacks. For example, glitching the size argument of a memcpy() command might result in a buffer overflow that the attacker can exploit using shellcode injection [17].

We have to agree with Bittner et al. [2], which state that various manufacturers seemingly ignore the threat of FI, even though smartcard manufacturers have been equipping their products with FI mitigations for the last 20 years.

3   Fault Injection Mitigations

Timmers et al. [16] propose three principles for mitigating FI. Firstly, deflecting attacks by decreasing the probability of a successful FI attack. Introducing randomness into the execution order or adding delays makes the target significantly less predictable. Secondly, if fault injections can be detected quickly enough, the target might be able to halt before any real damage (like exfiltrating sensitive information) has taken place. Lastly, reacting to FI attacks after they have been detected by imposing penalties (like timeouts or erasing the device) can make them impractically slow.

In order to follow these principles, software and hardware mitigations can be utilized. Belleville et al. [18] propose an automated software countermeasure that protects vulnerable software components with run-time code polymorphism. Lalande et al. [19] propose a non-compiler-based software mitigation that ensures control flow integrity (CFI) with incrementing and decrementing counters on function calls. This mitigation comes at a high cost, as their experiments with hardening an Advanced Encryption Standard (AES) implementation resulted in a 400% execution time and 272% size overhead on an ARM Cortex-M3 MCU.

Generally, hardware mitigations are less costly regarding execution time and memory footprint. However, they might require further development or manufacturing steps, increasing the production cost. For example, developers can use heat- and solvent-resistant epoxy to protect decoupling capacitors and voltage rails, embed planes in multi-layer printed circuit boards (PCBs) that act as decoupling capacitors, or redesign the device with an MCU that has fully integrated voltage regulators [2]. Moreover, various proposals for (micro-) architecture extensions exist, like entering secure trap handlers when faults have been detected [20], CFI based on computing message authentication codes (MAC) over executed instructions and comparing them against expected MACs [21], or CFI based on cryptographic sponges [22]. De Clercq et al. [23] analyzed and summarized many hardware-based solutions in their survey.

MCUboot allows the developer to set the software-based fault injection hardening (FIH) to one of four levels: *off*, *low* (simple CFI with global counter inc/dec on function call/return, and a failure loop hardened against loop escaping), *medium* (all FIH low features, constants with large hamming distance, and redundant variables and checks), and *high* (all FIH medium features, random delays between redundant variable checks) [24]. Atilano et al. [25] analyzed the effectiveness of the mitigations using simulation and provided feedback containing several issues to the MCUboot developers. In addition, the mitigations stop as soon as MCUboot calls into either MbedTLS or TinyCrypt (depending on the algorithm used), as all publicly available information indicates that neither is hardened against FI attacks. In the case of this project, it makes no significant difference whether MCUboot calls into an unhardened crypto library or an unhardened secure element software development kit (SDK). In both cases, the target probably contains more than enough code vulnerable to FI attacks for the attacker to exploit. Even if a secure element SDK contains some form of FIH, these mitigations might not be compatible with those used in the bootloader, requiring some potentially vulnerable glue code to translate between the mitigations. For example, one form of FIH consists of encoding a single return value into two separate but logically-coupled variables (e.g., value and its 1 s-complement). Comparing this hardened return value against a constant requires two if statements (and thus two compare instructions). This hardening forces the attacker to inject multiple faults when attempting to tamper with the comparison result, significantly decreasing the chance of a successful attack. However, the bootloader and the secure element SDK might not encode such a hardened value in the same way, and the required translation might result in a single point of failure. This inconsistency could result in a high probability of success for the attackers despite FIH. In general, discrepancies in the implementation of FIH create weak points at all junctions between the bootloader and secure element SDK.

We agree with Witteman et al. [26] that both soft- and hardware mitigations are necessary for adequate FI protection. It is exceedingly important to consider FI protections already during development, as FI can severely undermine the effectiveness of other countermeasures. Secure elements contain the necessary protections against FI, and bypassing some of the secure element's functionality (like the firmware image verification bypass presented in this project) will not threaten the confidentiality of its keys. However, it still might be enough to reach a given attack goal, like booting malicious firmware images.

4   Device Hardening with Secure Elements

Securely booting firmware images requires the bootloader to verify the firmware image signature with the public key embedded in the bootloader code. This signature verification (key material and procedure) must be hardened against tampering. Using a secure element for both immutably storing the public key and executing the verification reduces the attack surface significantly. MCUboot can be modified to use an externally connected secure element for key storage and executing the signature verification [27]. Figure 1 illustrates MCUboot's boot procedure — both off-the-shelf and with such modifications. In the default

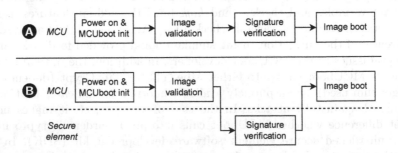

Fig. 1. Basic boot procedure when using MCUboot off-the-shelf **A** and after modifying it to use a secure element for verifying the signature **B** .

MCUboot procedure **Ⓐ**, the bootloader executes its initialization before validating the firmware image (checking for errors and faulty configuration). Then, the bootloader checks the signature with the public key embedded in the bootloader code and boots the image if the checks are successful. In contrast, procedure **Ⓑ** shows MCUboot offloading the signature verification and booting the image depending on the secure element's response. MCUboot's boot procedure contains more steps (like swapping images after a firmware upgrade and downgrade prevention), which have been omitted here for conciseness.

In order to prove the feasibility of this concept, the authors of [27] used a Nordic nRF52840 development kit (DK), ran a simple application built with the Zephyr real-time operating system (RTOS), and used the modified MCUboot as the bootloader, representing a straightforward way to incorporate a secure element into MCUboot.

5 Fault Injection in Practice

We used the work in [27] as the target for our attack setup. In our attack scenario, we bypassed the signature verification performed by the secure element, resulting in the target booting a malicious firmware image. Our work demonstrates how even low-cost FI tools can circumvent sophisticated countermeasures like secure elements.

5.1 Code Section Vulnerable to Fault Injection

As described in Sect. 3, MCUboot contains a fault injection hardening (FIH) module for preventing FI attacks. Unfortunately, FIH is turned off by default[1] when using MCUboot in a Zephyr version 3.1.0 application. This opposes the "secure by default" principle, as it leaves room for human error. For example, forgetting to enable the protection, accidentally disabling it, or not enabling it due to obliviousness. However, even enabling the highest level of FIH would not protect the following code section from being attacked to bypass the secure element's signature verification. This is because the FIH is only applied internally and stops when calling functions outside MCUboot.

Listing 1 shows MCUboot's `bootutil_verify_sig()` function as modified by the authors of [27]. Instead of MbedTLS, the function now invokes the secure element's SDK at **Ⓐ** for the signature verification. Dictated by the function signature, the if statement at **Ⓑ** converts the return value from the secure element SDK to either a zero (success) or non-zero (failure) value.

Listing 2 demonstrates the resulting assembly instructions. A compare branch on zero (`cbz`) instruction branches to the specified address if the value in the tested register is zero. If the signature verification fails, `R3` contains zero, and the `cbz` instruction at address `8e6` branches to address `930`. Thus, an FI attack

---

[1] https://github.com/zephyrproject-rtos/mcuboot/blob/
e58ea98aec6e5539c5f872a98059e461d0155bbb/boot/zephyr/Kconfig#L343.

Listing 1. Modified firmware image verification function for executing the ECDSA verify on the secure element **A** and converting the return value from the secure element SDK **B** .

```
int bootutil_verify_sig(uint8_t *hash, uint32_t hashlen,
                        uint8_t *sig, size_t siglen,
                        uint8_t key_id)
{
    /* Code snipped for conciseness */
    status = sec_elem_ecdsa_verify(hash, hashlen, sig,  A
                                   siglen, &success);

    if (status != SEC_ELEM_OK) {
        /* Code snipped for conciseness */
        return -EIO;
    }

    if (success) {  B
        LOG_INF("Image verification successful");
        return 0;
    } else {
        LOG_ERR("Image verification unsuccessful");
        return -EFAULT;
    }
}
```

Listing 2. Vulnerable assembly instructions resulting from `bootutil_verify_sig()`.

```
       878: add      sp, #28                        Clean up stack
       87a: ldmia.w  sp!, {r4, r5, r6, r7, r8, r9, pc}    Return
       ...
       8e2: ldrb.w   r3, [sp, #23]         Load "success" in R3
 if    8e6: cbz      r3, 930                    Branch if R3 == 0
 !=0   8e8: movs     r1, #73                     LOG_INF parameter
       8ea: ldr      r0, [pc, #108]              LOG_INF parameter
       8ec: bl       d256 <log_printk>             Print LOG_INF
       8f0: movs     r0, #0                  Set return value "0"
       8f2: b.n      878             Branch to function epilogue
       ...
 ==0   930: movs     r1, #69                     LOG_ERR parameter
       932: ldr      r0, [pc, #56]               LOG_ERR parameter
       934: bl       d256 <log_printk>             Print LOG_ERR
       938: mvn.w    r0, #13         Set return value "-EFAULT"
       93c: b.n      878             Branch to function epilogue
```

resulting in skipping this `cbz` instruction boots an invalid image. Alternatively, the attack might also be successful if it modifies the `cbz` instruction instead of skipping it, as long as it does not branch anywhere or corrupt any currently used registers.

5.2   Attack Setup

Figure 2 contains the attack setup consisting of three main components and the corresponding data flow. The *glitcher* for generating a voltage glitch with a configurable width and offset in relation to the trigger signal, the *target* under attack, and the *Raspberry Pi* for coordinating the automatic glitching process by configuring the glitcher, setting up the target, and starting the glitching process.

Regarding the data flow, the glitcher needs two connections to the target: one for picking up a trigger signal and one for injecting the glitch. The Pi needs bidirectional communication with the glitcher to configure the next glitching parameters (useful for sweeping through various configurations). Furthermore, the Pi sets up the target (and provides further stimuli if needed) to get the target to execute the previously determined vulnerable code. Lastly, the Pi needs feedback from the target (e.g., GPIOs, communication protocol, or power consumption through side-channel power analysis) to determine if the glitch succeeded.

We developed our glitcher using a Teensy 4.0 development board [28] and a Maxim MAX4619 analog switch. The Teensy generates the glitch signal for controlling the analog switch, which drives the target to the desired voltage levels. Figure 3 illustrates the basic structure of the glitcher. V_{Target} needs to be connected to the target, and depending on the glitch signal of the Teensy, the analog switch either connects V_{Normal} or V_{Glitch} to the target pin. A power

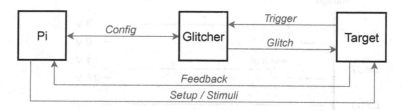

Fig. 2. Main components of the attack setup with their corresponding data flow.

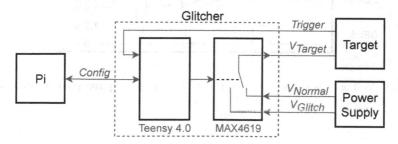

Fig. 3. Basic structure of the glitcher. Connections between Pi and target have been removed for clarity.

supply supplies the desired normal and glitch voltages. Running the Teensy's NXP i.MX RT1062 at its maximum frequency of 600 MHz resulted in a timer clock frequency of 150 MHz due to the fixed prescaler of 4. Thus, we achieved a glitch width and offset resolution of 6.67 ns.

5.3   Target Modifications

Most targets must be modified to increase the probability of a successful FI attack. According to the datasheet, the power supply circuitry of the nRF52840 consists of low-dropout regulators (LDOs) and DC/DC regulators, which output the 1.3 V system power. Additionally, it has six decoupling pins (*DEC1-6*) to ensure the stability of the internal power regulation circuitry (LDO, DC/DC). According to the reference circuitry in the datasheet, hardware designers need to connect specific capacitors to these pins. However, Nordic has not published any further information, for example, which decoupling pin is attached to the core voltage rail. According to this Nordic DevZone thread[2], they even seem reluctant about specifying voltage tolerances. We determined a suitable pin for injecting glitches by measuring the voltage traces during boot and making an educated guess on which pin might be attached to the core voltage rail. Figure 4 contains the measured traces, and only *DEC1* and *DEC4/6* have stable voltages near the declared 1.3 V system power. We assume that *DEC4/6* are connected to the output of the last DC/DC regulator because of the ripple, and *DEC1* is the core voltage rail at 1.1 V.

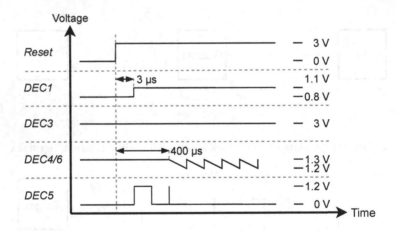

Fig. 4. Voltage traces measured on the nRF52840 decoupling pins during boot.

---

[2] https://devzone.nordicsemi.com/f/nordic-q-a/60633/the-tolerance-of-voltage-of-dec-pins-of-52840.

Thus, we decided to inject glitches on pin *DEC1*. In order to increase the probability of a successful glitch, we tried to remove as many capacitors as possible using trial and error while still checking that the target boots successfully. In our case, we could only remove the capacitor on *DEC3*, as any other removed capacitor resulted in the target not booting anymore. Figure 5 shows the wire connected to the capacitor on *DEC1*, where the glitcher will inject voltage glitches.

There is a possibility that the remaining decoupling capacitors still protect the MCU too well from glitches. Thus, the methods described in the following Sect. 5.4 would not be able to find any suitable glitching parameters. In this case, reducing the capacitance instead of removing the capacitors could make the MCU more susceptible to glitches while maintaining the target's ability to boot.

5.4 Determining Suitable Glitching Parameters

The search space would grow enormously if we had to guess all parameters for the attack. Fortunately, finding suitable parameters can be split into independent processes. Figure 6 illustrates that the attacker must determine the glitch width and voltage level **A** first. Subsequently, the attacker must find the correct offset between the trigger and the glitch **B** to hit the vulnerable instruction. We will explain step **A** in this section and step **B** in Sect. 5.5.

Determining the glitch width and voltage levels uses a straightforward technique with only a minor limitation. For this approach, we must erase and flash the target with a different application, likely requiring a second target

Fig. 5. Wire connected to capacitor on pin DEC1 of nRF52840 DK for injecting glitches.

hardware because it cannot be erased, reprogrammed, or because we cannot flash the original bootloader and firmware back afterward.

Generally, a single glitch results in one of the following three outcomes. If the glitch width and voltage levels are just right, the induced fault manifests as corrupted control or data flow. Deviating from this sweet spot either causes a reset or halt (usually called "mute" as the target does not respond either way) or does not impact the target. As FI is a stochastic attack method, any given set of glitching parameters is not guaranteed to always result in the same outcome. Thus, repeated testing of various glitching configurations helps to determine the one with the highest probability of inducing a fault.

An application providing direct feedback after injecting a glitch expedites the search for suitable glitching parameters significantly. Flashing the target with the code in Listing 3 instructs it to increment the `count` variable continuously and print the computed value over a serial connection afterward. While

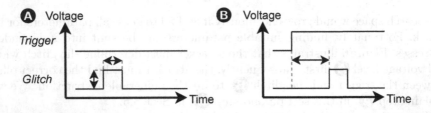

Fig. 6. Determining the glitch width and the glitch voltage level **A** and finding a suitable offset to hit the vulnerable instruction **B** .

Listing 3. Test application for finding suitable glitch width by incrementing a counter in a loop and printing the computed value afterward.

```
void main(void)
{
    volatile uint32_t i,count,iteration;
    iteration = 0;

    while (1) {
        count = 0;

        gpio_pin_set(TRIGGER_PIN, 1);
        for (i=0; i<I_LOOP; i++) {
            count++;
        }
        gpio_pin_set(TRIGGER_PIN, 0);
        print("Iteration %u: %u %u", iteration, i, count);
        iteration++;
    }
}
```

incrementing `count`, the application sets a GPIO high, which functions as a trigger signal. The Pi then instructs the glitcher to generate glitches continuously while the trigger GPIO is high and subsequently checks the output of the target for irregular behavior. The Pi automatically configures the glitcher with different glitch widths during multiple iterations and finally prints the accumulated results. Changing the glitching voltage might be required if the glitch width resolution is too coarse for a given target [29]. In such a case, some width always results in normal target behavior, and the next possible width always results in a mute target. However, this technique is not required as our glitcher's width resolution is high enough for the target at hand.

Figure 7 illustrates the detailed attack setup with all the required interconnections. As explained in Sect. 5.2, the V_{Target} pin of the glitcher is the pole of a single-pole double-throw analog switch. The *DEC1* pin previously determined where the glitcher will inject voltage transients into the nRF52840 does not have to be supplied with any power during normal operation. Thus, the normally closed throw of the glitcher is left floating. The normally open throw is

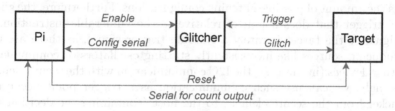

Fig. 7. Attack setup for determining a suitable glitching width.

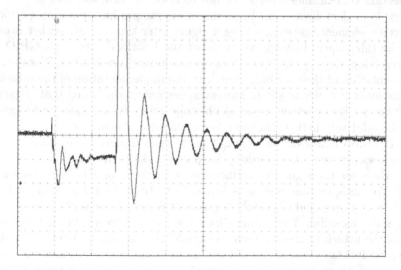

Fig. 8. Voltage trace measured on the *DEC1* pin while being pulled to ground for 170 ns including the subsequent ringing when releasing the pin again (500 mV & 100 ns per div.).

connected to ground, resulting in the *DEC1* pin being pulled low during a glitch. Figure 8 shows the voltage trace at *DEC1* while being pulled to ground during a 170 ns glitch. Significant ringing (regarding time and voltage) occurred after releasing the pin. It is unclear which part of the recorded behavior is responsible for the fault injection. However, this information is optional as the attacker determines the injection timing empirically, as will be explained in Sect. 5.5.

It turns out that the best glitch width slightly changes ($\pm$ 20 ns) during the day, probably due to temperature and other environmental changes. However, having a script on the Pi that automatically checks for the current best glitch width instead of doing it by hand is very beneficial as we can rerun it before executing the actual attack.

5.5 Executing the Actual Attack

In order to maximize the probability of a successful FI attack, the attacker needs to control as many unknown variables as possible. If something is not fully controllable, narrowing it down to a small range is crucial, as this significantly reduces the amount of possible glitching configurations. Furthermore, the glitcher needs a trigger that does not jitter relative to the vulnerable instruction. The reset signal of the target is rarely a suitable trigger signal, as there are many jitter-inducing sources like inconsistently starting oscillators or communication with other devices (in this case, the I2C communication with the secure element). Interestingly, we can use such communication as a trigger point because the last packet from the secure element to the host (containing the decision if the signature is valid) always has the same time offset in relation to the vulnerable code section that decides whether or not to boot the firmware image.

As this project focuses on bypassing a cryptographic operation performed by a secure element, creating a trigger signal after the nth I2C packet is out of scope for this paper. Instead, we modified the bootloader to set a GPIO high after receiving the last I2C packet of the signature verification. Notably, this instrumentation of the code only expedites the implementation of the attack but does not make it easier to glitch. Moreover, designing something that triggers on the nth I2C packet or setting up an oscilloscope with advanced protocol triggering would be relatively little extra work for a determined attacker.

As the coordinator of the attack, the Pi needs to determine whether or not an attack was successful. Regarding this project, the bootloader blinks the DK's LED1 whenever the signature verification fails, thus signaling an unsuccessful attack. We designed our malicious firmware to blink LED2 as soon as it gets booted to indicate that the fault bypassed the signature verification and the attack was successful. This setup allows the glitcher to quickly determine the result of the attack by monitoring two GPIOs. Having observable GPIO outputs is also plausible for a real-world scenario, as there are usually various signals that we can tap. Otherwise, side-channel attacks like power analysis usually have no trouble identifying when a target enters an infinite loop, like the one it enters when the firmware image verification fails.

Figure 9 shows the final attack setup. The only difference between this setup and the one used for determining a suitable glitch width is that the serial connection used to output the count values has been replaced with the two GPIOs that signal either an aborted boot (signature verification detected a malicious firmware image) or a successful glitch (malicious firmware image booted). Like the automated glitch width detection from Sect. 5.4, a script running on the Pi automatically tries a range of offsets relative to the trigger signal until it succeeds and the malicious firmware image is booted.

Figure 10 shows a photo of the final attack setup. Various parts on the glitcher's prototyping board are only needed for development purposes. Everything can easily fit on a PCB smaller than the Teensy by only including the required parts and using an SMD package of the analog switch. Furthermore, we used a secure element add-on board to attach the secure element to the nRF52840 DK.

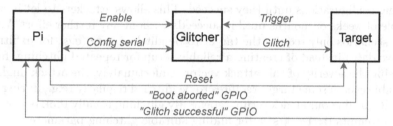

Fig. 9. Attack setup for attacking the actual target and bypassing the firmware image verification.

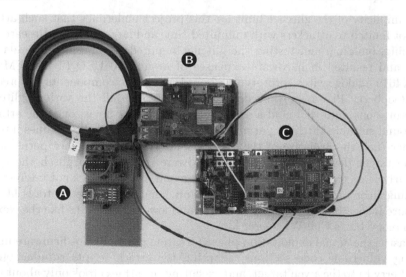

Fig. 10. Photo of the final attack setup, consisting of the glitcher **A** , Raspberry Pi **B** , and target **C** .

Using the described methods, tools, and setup, we successfully bypassed the signature verification performed by the secure element, resulting in the target booting a malicious firmware image.

6   Discussion

Voltage FI is an entirely non-deterministic process, which makes it exceedingly hard to quantify the required time to find suitable glitching parameters (i.e., voltage, width, and offset). The lack of knowledge about what really happens inside the MCU during a glitch only exacerbates the problem, and insights from manufacturers would be necessary to investigate this in more detail. Adapting an attack setup to a new target (picking up a trigger signal, finding the best pin to inject the glitch, removing as many capacitors as possible, customizing attack scripts) might take a couple of person-days of work. However, most attack setups do not require any further attention afterward and continuously try various glitching configurations until they succeed. This allows attackers to let it run for a couple of weeks or months until it succeeds without any further effort. Various attack scenarios only require the target to be glitched once (e.g., for exfiltrating sensitive data) instead of creating a reliable setup for repeated glitching, further increasing the severity of this attack vector. Unfortunately, the attack might still be feasible even if some target requires to be glitched regularly (e.g., during every boot). Regarding our attack setup, repeatedly glitching usually took between one to 100 attempts ($\approx$ 1–100 s) after finding suitable glitching parameters.

6.1   Required Effort

The simplicity of the glitcher built for this project underlines that such attacks are not limited to attackers with unlimited time and large budgets. Researching, planning, building, and testing the glitcher required around 40 person-days of work and resulted in hardware expenses of around 30 USD (Teensy, Maxim MAX4619 analog switch, prototyping board, and basic components). Moreover, the Raspberry Pi was only needed to sweep through all the various glitching configurations until we found a successful combination. Thus, once the attacker has found suitable glitching parameters, they can program these values into the glitcher (i.e., the firmware of the Teensy) and attach the glitcher permanently to the target device. This so-called "hardware implant" can glitch the target regularly (e.g., during every boot) or on-demand. For attackers not interested in building their own glitchers, there are commercially available FI tools like the "Riscure Inspector FI" [30] or open-source and low-cost solutions like the NewAE Technology Inc.'s ChipWhisperer [31].

Lastly, the actual exploitation phase (creating the malicious firmware image, finding vulnerable code sections, adapting the attack scripts running on the Raspberry Pi to the given target, and executing the attack) took only about three person-days. This high affordability (regarding time and cost), combined with setups that repeatedly attack targets, results in an attack vector that seriously threatens a device's security.

6.2   Fault Injection Applicability

In this project, we reached our attack goal of bypassing the firmware image verification by skipping a "compare branch on zero" instruction and thus changing the control flow. Many other exploits are feasible because virtually any change in control and data flow is possible. However, the odds of success for such attacks depend on two main factors: First, the target hardware must be susceptible to fault injection. We observe that many products contain components (e.g., microcontrollers) with little to no hardware protection, allowing injected faults to manifest themselves on the application level. Other types of FI (e.g., electromagnetic, optical, clock) require different mitigations, further exacerbating the problem. Second, the target's application must offer sufficient possibilities (i.e., vulnerable instructions) to reach a desired attack goal through changes to the control and data flow. Thus, applying software mitigations lowers the probability of a successful attack significantly by reducing the amount of vulnerable instruction. As discussed in Sect. 3, such software-based mitigations can be quite costly regarding execution time and memory footprint. This project demonstrates that even a comparatively small amount of unprotected glue code leaves a device vulnerable to FI.

7   Conclusion and Further Research

Fault injection poses a significant threat to a device's security by corrupting the control or data flow, allowing various attacks like extracting sensitive data or tampering with the execution flow to reach a given attack goal. Our attack did not threaten the confidentiality or integrity of the keys stored in the tamper-resistant memory of the secure element. We bypassed the signature verification performed by the secure element by targeting vulnerable instructions executed in the host MCU instead of the secure element itself — effectively circumventing the secure element completely. This attack demonstrates that glue code between hardened pieces of software can leave the device vulnerable to fault injection, thus requiring a holistic approach to secure a device against fault injection.

Regarding our specific attack scenario, we demonstrate that an attacker can bypass the firmware image verification on a secure element by targeting the code between MCUboot and the secure element SDK with voltage glitching. Furthermore, this attack can conceivably be carried out by anyone as it is not cost prohibitive. Moreover, the used hardware for glitching is so inexpensive and readily available that one can use it as a hardware implant, which can glitch the target regularly or on-demand instead of a single time (e.g., for exfiltrating sensitive data).

Further research on protecting glue code between hardened pieces of software from FI attacks is necessary — for example, applying mitigations and analyzing their effectiveness against FI attacks. Additionally, their impact on cost, computational performance, memory footprint, energy consumption, and other important metrics must be evaluated.

References

1. Morel, L., Couroussé, D.: Idols with feet of clay: on the security of bootloaders and firmware updaters for the IoT. In: 2019 17th IEEE International New Circuits and Systems Conference (NEWCAS), pp. 1–4 (2019)
2. Bittner, O., Krachenfels, T., Galauner, A., Seifert, J.P.: The forgotten threat of voltage glitching: a case study on Nvidia Tegra X2 SoCs. In: 2021 Workshop on Fault Detection and Tolerance in Cryptography (FDTC), pp. 86–97 (2021)
3. van den Herrewegen, J., Oswald, D., Garcia, F.D., Temeiza, Q.: Fill your boots: enhanced embedded bootloader exploits via fault injection and binary analysis. IACR Trans. Cryptographic Hardware Embedded Syst. **2021**(1), 56–81 (2020)
4. Milburn, A., Timmers, N., Wiersma, N., Pareja, R., Cordoba, S.: There will be glitches: Extracting and analyzing automotive firmware efficiently (2018). https://www.riscure.com/publication/extracting-and-analyzing-automotive-firmware-efficiently/ (Accessed 13 March 2023), Black Hat USA 2018
5. Cui, A., Costello, M., Stolfo, S.J.: When firmware modifications attack: a case study of embedded exploitation. In: 2013 20th Annual Network & Distributed System Security Symposium (2013)
6. Shwartz, O., Mathov, Y., Bohadana, M., Elovici, Y., Oren, Y.: Reverse engineering IoT devices: effective techniques and methods. IEEE Internet Things J. **5**(6), 4965–4976 (2018)
7. Ronen, E., Shamir, A., Weingarten, A.O., O'Flynn, C.: IoT goes nuclear: creating a zigbee chain reaction. In: 2017 IEEE Symposium on Security and Privacy (SP), pp. 195–212 (2017)
8. Noseda, M., Zimmerli, L., Schläpfer, T., Rüst, A.: Performance analysis of secure elements for iot. IoT **3**(1), 1–28 (2021)
9. MCUboot. https://www.mcuboot.com/, (Accessed 09 April 2023)
10. Bar-El, H., Choukri, H., Naccache, D., Tunstall, M., Whelan, C.: The sorcerer's apprentice guide to fault attacks. Proc. IEEE **94**(2), 370–382 (2006)
11. Boneh, D., DeMillo, R.A., Lipton, R.J.: On the importance of checking cryptographic protocols for faults. In: Fumy, W. (ed.) Advances in Cryptology – EUROCRYPT '97, pp. 37–51. Springer, Berlin (1997). https://doi.org/10.1007/3-540-69053-0_4
12. Kömmerling, O., Kuhn, M.G.: Design principles for tamper-resistant smartcard processors. In: USENIX Workshop on Smartcard Technology (Smartcard 99). USENIX Association, Chicago, Illinois (1999)
13. Kazemi, Z., Norollah, A., Kchaou, A., Fazeli, M., Hely, D., Beroulle, V.: An in-depth vulnerability analysis of RISC-V micro-architecture against fault injection attack. In: 2021 IEEE International Symposium on Defect and Fault Tolerance in VLSI and Nanotechnology Systems (DFT), pp. 1–6 (2021)
14. Yuce, B., Schaumont, P., Witteman, M.: Fault attacks on secure embedded software: threats, design, and evaluation. J. Hardware Syst. Sec. **2**(2), 111–130 (2018)
15. Kazemi, Z., Fazeli, M., Hely, D., Beroulle, V.: Hardware security vulnerability assessment to identify the potential risks in a critical embedded application. In: 2020 IEEE 26th International Symposium on On-Line Testing and Robust System Design (IOLTS), pp. 1–6 (2020)
16. Timmers, N., Spruyt, A., Witteman, M.: Controlling PC on ARM using fault injection. In: 2016 Workshop on Fault Diagnosis and Tolerance in Cryptography (FDTC), pp. 25–35 (2016)

17. Timmers, N., Spruyt, A.: Bypassing secure boot using fault injection (2016). https://www.riscure.com/publication/bypassing-secure-boot-using-fault-injection/ (Accessed 24 July 2023), Black Hat Europe 2016

18. Belleville, N., Couroussé, D., Heydemann, K., Charles, H.P.: Automated software protection for the masses against side-channel attacks. ACM Trans. Architec. Code Optimiz. (TACO) 15(4), 1–27 (2018)

19. Lalande, J.-F., Heydemann, K., Berthomé, P.: Software countermeasures for control flow integrity of smart card C codes. In: Kutyłowski, M., Vaidya, J. (eds.) ESORICS 2014. LNCS, vol. 8713, pp. 200–218. Springer, Cham (2014). https://doi.org/10.1007/978-3-319-11212-1_12

20. Yuce, B., Deshpande, C., Ghodrati, M., Bendre, A., Nazhandali, L., Schaumont, P.: A secure exception mode for fault-attack-resistant processing. IEEE Trans. Dependable Secure Comput. 16(3), 388–401 (2019)

21. De Clercq, Ret ak.: SOFIA: software and control flow integrity architecture. In: 2016 Design, Automation & Test in Europe Conference & Exhibition (DATE), pp. 1172–1177 (2016)

22. Werner, M., Unterluggauer, T., Schaffenrath, D., Mangard, S.: Sponge-based control-flow protection for IoT devices. In: 2018 IEEE European Symposium on Security and Privacy (EuroS&P), pp. 214–226 (2018)

23. De Clercq, R., Verbauwhede, I.: A survey of hardware-based control flow integrity (CFI). arXiv preprint arXiv:1706.07257 (2017)

24. Ban, T.: HW fault injection mitigation. https://www.trustedfirmware.org/docs/ TF-M_fault_injection_mitigation.pdf, (Accessed 03 March 2023)

25. Atilano, E., De Grandmaison, A., Heydemann, K., Bouffard, G.: Assessing the effectiveness of MCUboot protections against fault injection attacks. https://resources.linaro.org/en/resource/ibFLwRzhpZjBfvY5jhPypJ,   (Accessed   10 November 2023)

26. Witteman, M.: Secure application programming in the presence of side channel attacks. https://www.riscure.com/publication/secure-application-programming-presence-side-channel-attacks/, (Accessed 01 March 2023)

27. Eugster, L., Stuck, S.: Secure Firmware Updates für IoT. Bachelor's thesis, ZHAW Zurich University of Applied Sciences (2022)

28. Teensy 4.0. https://www.pjrc.com/store/teensy40.html, (Accessed 01 March 2023)

29. van Woudenberg, J., O'Flynn, C.: The Hardware Hacking Handbook. No Starch Press, San Francisco, CA (May 2021)

30. Riscure Inspector FI. https://www.riscure.com/security-tools/inspector-fi/, (Accessed 01 March 2023)

31. NewAE Technology Inc., ChipWhisperer. https://www.newae.com/chipwhisperer, (Accessed 01 March 2023)

OpenBSD Formal Driver Verification with SeL4

Adriana Nicolae[1], Paul Irofti[1,2(✉)], and Ioana Leuştean[1]

[1] LOS-CS-FMI, University of Bucharest, Bucharest, Romania
adriana.stancu@unibuc.ro, ioana@fmi.unibuc.ro
[2] Institute for Logic and Data Science, Bucharest, Romania
paul@irofti.net

Abstract. The seL4 microkernel is currently the only kernel that has been fully formally verified. In general, the increased interest in ensuring the security of a kernel's code results from its important role in the entire operating system. One of the basic features of an operating system is that it abstracts the handling of devices. This abstraction is represented by device drivers - the software that manages the hardware. A proper verification of the software component could ensure that the device would work properly unless there is a hardware failure. In this paper, we choose to model the behavior of a device driver and build the proof that the code implementation matches the expected behavior. The proof was written in Isabelle/HOL, the code translation from C to Isabelle was done automatically by the use of the C-to-Isabelle Parser and AutoCorres tools. We choose Isabelle theorem prover because its efficiency was already shown through the verification of seL4 microkernel.

Keywords: formal verification · operating systems · secure systems

1 Introduction

The kernel is a crucial component of the system, and direct access to hardware resources leads to an increased risk if a malfunction occurs. In our case, seL4 was designed as a microkernel in order to reduce the impact of software problems to the system's functionalities.

The main topic of interest in the analysis of the seL4 microkernel is the way to prove the functional correctness through the Isabelle/HOL theorem prover. The methods applied in system verification are more powerful and accurate than automated verification techniques such as model checking, static analysis, or deploying the entire kernel in a type-safe language. This method of proving in Isabelle all the critical properties of the systems allows the analysis of specific aspects such as exploring the branches of execution of safe scenarios (safe execution), but also a set of specifications and proofs of kernel behavior reaching the analysis of implementation in C of the kernel for the ARM platform.

In this paper we investigate the process of adapting and applying the seL4 verification process for verify parts of another operating system and present a

M. Manulis et al. (Eds.): SecITC 2023, LNCS 14534, pp. 144–156, 2024.
https://doi.org/10.1007/978-3-031-52947-4_11

concrete case for the `octrng(4)` driver for the Octeon/MIPS64 platform provided by the OpenBSD operating system.

Outline. In Sect. 2 we introduce the necessary seL4 concepts which, together with the methodology from Sect. 3 regarding the translation of C code to Isabelle theorem prover, allow us to present the verification of the OpenBSD driver in Sect. 4. In Sect. 5 we conclude with limitations and future research.

2 SeL4 Verification Structure

SeL4 [9] is part of the L4 family - along with other implementations that share the same L4 interface: Pistachio [11], Fiasco [10] or Hazelnut [3]. The proofs that underlie the verification of seL4 system are in the form of Hoare structures that have in their center a code component or whole functions. The difficulty of verifying the seL4 micro-kernel lies in formulating pre-conditions and post-conditions that accurately represent security properties that it must meet. At the same time, the formal representation must be as close as possible to the structure and functionalities implemented in the source code. Although work to implement its proofs was started in 2009 formal proofs of the kernel are still maintained up to date with publicly available source code.

A key aspect of the design of a microkernel and the properties of the C code in relation to the form of their verification is the separation of kernel functions calls in two phases [8]: verification and execution. The verification phase can be understood as a stage of validation of the preconditions: the input data and the permissions on the actions to be performed are verified. The execution consists in the actual running of the system function, benefiting from its verification because the preconditions have already been verified in the previous phase.

Note that in the verification phase the system status is not changed otherwise this separation would no longer be relevant. This brings a valuable advantage in the verification process because it simplifies the system call proof: execution will not return an error if the verification phase has been completed successfully.

2.1 SeL4 Memory Management

SeL4 kernel memory allocation model transfers allocation control from kernel space to applications that have this permission. Memory management permission is represented by having a structure called capability [6]. As a consequence the kernel heap memory can be precisely partitioned between applications: each application has that part of the heap for which it has a capability that gives it that authority. Separating heap memory is especially important for expressing and demonstrating security properties (integrity and confidentiality).

The basic features of the kernel memory allocation model are as follows [8]: allocation is explicit and is performed only when assigning a type (retype) to an untyped memory area, allocation is strictly delimited by the specified free memory kernel objects are not shared or reused.

This memory management model leaves the responsibility for verifying security policies outside the kernel. All that is left is to verify the correctness of the memory allocation algorithm in the kernel. The properties of interest being that allocated objects are within the corresponding areas of free memory and that memory regions allocated to objects do not overlap.

Memory allocation capabilities can be transferred between the kernel components. Transfers are represented as a tree in which the capabilities are the nodes of the tree. Freeing memory is done in two steps that invalidate all references to that region: search for all the capabilities for which access rights are granted on the memory object and then delete all these capabilities and mark the memory region as free. For the first stage, the capability transfer tree is used to find and invalidate all capabilities that allow permissions on the memory region. In the second stage, it is verified through the same tree that there are no references in other objects or global references to the area to be released.

2.2 Memory Access Verification

Memory access is an interesting topic in order to model as accurately as possible the behavior of a C program. In Isabelle pointers are represented as a new type of data, `datatype a ptr = Ptr word32`, which means that the pointer is represented only by the 32-bit address it contains. Using this representation one can reason about heap memory.

Here an important problem is raised when we pass from one pointer type to another. For example, if we have two `float` and `int` pointers to the same address, after we use one to change the value from the address to which it points, we cannot be sure that the other has not been changed. To ensure that pointers of different types point to different addresses, the Burstall-Bornat model is used as a solution [2] where heap memory is separated into types. Thus each data type has its own function that maps pointers to their values:

```
record state =
   heap_int :: word32 → int
   heap_float :: word32 → float
   heap_intptr :: word32 → addr...
```

While this solves the issues mentioned above, it also renders type casts unusable. A memory area, once allocated, remains defined in the corresponding heap memory section until it is released.

3   Methodology: C to Isabelle Conversion

A key component of the formal check in seL4 is the bridge between C language and the proofs in Isabelle [13]. This is also the most complex part of the proofs because the semantics of the C language must be taken into account such as the ones mentioned in the previous section but also data structures storage, pointer arithmetic and others. In Isabelle memory addressing is represented by a function defined on the address space without information about the type of data to which the address refers. The way different types of data are stored is treated separately [12]. Abstracting how memory access, data alignment, and how different data types are modeled removed the need for higher-level proofs to employ repetitive checks, such that a pointer is not null before being accessed, instead these checks are already defined as constraints.

The correctness of the C language semantics is not, however, treated as critical to the proofs of the whole system because it adds an additional verification level: the validation of the correspondence between the formal model and the result obtained after compilation. The proof technique used to ensure the correspondence between the abstract specifications, the formal model of the source code, and the model resulting from the analysis of the binary file is called a refinement. A refinement is defined in [8] as: "Program C is a refinement of program A, if the set of behaviors of program C is a subset of the behaviors described by program A". Here a behavior means a sequence of steps given by a change of system state and the transition between these states. The state of the system consists of the state of its components (memory, processes, resources) belonging to the user space and to the kernel space.

3.1 Isabelle/HOL Theorem Prover

Isabelle is an interactive theorem prover that supports several types of formal logic systems. Isabelle/HOL is Isabelle's specialization of Higher Order Logic (HOL). HOL is a type-based logic whose system resembles the one from functional programming languages [1]. Existing types can be classified [9] into:

- basic types, e.g. bool(boolean), nat($\mathbb{N}$) or int($\mathbb{Z}$)
- type constructors, e.g. list and set types. Type constructors are written postfix, that is, after their arguments. For example, nat list is the type of lists whose elements are natural numbers.
- types of functions are denoted by "$\Rightarrow$";
- types of variables are denoted by $'a, 'b$, etc.

Terms are represented like in functional programming: by applying functions to certain types of arguments. If we have f a function of type $\tau_1 \Rightarrow \tau_2$ and t is a term of type τ_1 then ft is a term of type τ_2. In Isabelle the notation $t::\tau$ is used to represent that the term t is of type τ. Isabelle's proofs are structured in theories. A theory is a collection of types, functions and theorems, just like a module in a programming language. A theory has the following format

```
theory T
imports B1 ... Bn
begin
  statements, definitions, proofs
end
```

where B1 ... Bn are the names of the existing theories on which the T theory is based. Each T theory must be in a file called T.thy. HOL contains a Main theory, which contains all predefined basic theories, such as arithmetic, lists, or sets. A theory can include a list of more .thy files. In practice, to have all theories needed for parsing and basic proofs we have to include `AutoCorres.AutoCorres`. Proofs can take the form of theorems or lemmas, both can be used inside other proofs. There are specific keywords for applying these in order to reach our goal [13], for example the most common keywords used in our proofs are: `unfolding x` - which applies the definition of x on the current goal and `apply x` - which refers to other theorems or set of rules to be used.

3.2   Parsing C to Isabelle

Approaching the C language from the perspective of obtaining a semantic model on which valid reasoning be built is an important contribution of the seL4 system and deserves to be studied in detail. Several steps are taken to translate the C code from seL4 into Isabelle [4], steps that we will also need to take for the OpenBSD driver:

1. each C source file is parsed by an external preprocessor, which extends `#include` formulas and macro commands and other directives
2. the result is translated into Simpl by the C-to-Isabelle analyzer [12]
3. each structure in the program is represented by a record in Isabelle
4. local and global variables are analyzed to generate two new types: a global variables record `globals` and "a myvars" record for locals
5. functions are translated in equivalent Simpl language representation;
6. proofs are performed on the generated functions to specify which global variables modify them

The post-translation steps in Simpl are embedded in the AutoCorres tool [4]. Because this tool uses the result of the C-to-Isabelle parser as input, AutoCorres supports the same subset of the C language. Programs that use loops, function calls, cast between various types, pointer arithmetic, structures, and recursion are supported, but references to local variables, "goto" and "switch" expressions, unions, floating point arithmetic operations or the use of pointers to functions are not supported. The example in [4] shows how one can go from the implementation in C of a simple function to the C-to-Isabelle parser output (with which it is quite difficult to work) and then to the final form after running the AutoCorres tool. In essence, the purpose of the AutoCorres tool is to abstract the low-level representation from the C-to-Isabelle parser into a high-level one by:

- performing the conversion between the deeply embedded representation to the shallowly embedded one (as described below)
- abstracting the arithmetic operations at 32-bit machine word level into operations on the whole set of integers and natural numbers
- abstracting the heap memory at byte level into separate data-type areas using the Burstall-Bornat model [2]
- simplifying the code and translating the variable types from the Simpl representation into a form that is easy to reason in Isabelle.

Deeply vs Shallowly Embedded Representations. Before we can begin to formally reason about a program, we must first translate it into the logic used by our theorem demonstrator. To bring the C code into Isabelle, it is necessary to decide which aspects of the code will be translated into the demonstrator logic. If the emphasis is on the C program structure and its preservation in Isabelle, we say that deeply embedded representation is used. If the semantics of the program are important in the translation process, then we have a shallowly embedded representation of the source code in Isabelle logic. AutoCorres has the role of conversion between the structural representation of the C language given by the C-to-Isabelle parser into the semantic representation on which reasoning will be performed.

An example from [4] tries to explain the difference between the two forms of code representation starting from: $2 + 2 = 4$. If we want to prove that the left side is equal to the right side, we perform the addition (treating the expression as shallowly embedded) and state that the proposition is true. If we look at the structure of the equation (deeply embedded), on the left we have 3 characters and on the right only one. Thus we can say that the two parts are not equal because we did not give any semantics to the assembly operation and its terms. Structural treatment is not helpful if we want to prove certain statements about a program. For this reason, the semantic representation of the C code is an important contribution in the verification of the seL4 kernel, and this is done through the AutoCorres tool.

The semantic representation obtained with AutoCorres aims to capture the behavior of C programs where the representation in Isabelle can show that the program might change the overall state of the system, might contain loops which may not end, might have exceptions or other errors and so on. These requirements are covered by the extensive use of existing monads in Simpl (Skip, Basic, Cond, Guard, etc.) and the addition of new constructs such as `gets`, `return`, `whileLoop`. The later provides a great similarity between the imperative language of the source and the functional one in which it is modeled.

3.3 C Subset Limitations

In our work we needed to tackle the C-language constraints mentioned above, so we used only a subset of the C99 standard specifications [7]. The most relevant restriction is that pointers to functions are not supported. Pointer data types are defined as functions that return data stored at those addresses. If the pointers refer to the address of a function, there is no guarantee that the reference cannot be circular and that the address of the function must also be resolved. Other issues that we ran into include control flow sequences such as code jumps using "goto" or "switch" which are not supported and compiler optimization for data positioning in memory when dealing with unions or bit fields.

Calling Function Pointers. The limitation of not being able to call functions that were set via their address to a function pointer was a major drawback

in the integration of the OpenBSD driver because we needed to address pro-
grammable tasks to be executed in the future. The tasks may come from the
device driver, the timer or other sources. The main loop can only call the corresponding function that was set via its pointer. Below we depict a simplified
program to showcase the issue where the C-to-Isabelle parser fails to translate
the last function because the call to foo() is done via the function pointer p_fun.

```
static int counter;
void foo(void) { counter++; }
void (*p_fun)(void);
void set_function(void) { p_fun = foo; }
void call_function(void) {
    if(p_fun) p_fun();
}
```

Workarounds cannot provide the full proof, they only skip certain parts of
the program or proofs in order to provide a translation avoiding the part were
the function pointer is used. We list here a few options:

- skip parsing call_function by adding the DONT_TRANSLATE annotation, we used
  this in the proof because the other translations were not affected, we only had
  to avoid proving annotations the function pointer;
- add the following annotations before parsing the C file, this will assert those
  theorems as axioms rather than try to prove them:

```
declare [[quick_and_dirty = true]]
declare [[sorry_modifies_proofs = true]]
```

- add annotations before parsing the C file, this will not try to prove the theorem that involves function pointers

```
[[calculate_modifies_proofs = false]]
```

4   Driver Verification

Drivers are pieces of software that are part of a monolithic kernel (but can also
run is userspace), whose purpose is to interact with hardware devices or buses
and to provide a interface between the kernel and those components. We choose
to verify drivers as a further development of seL4 verification because drivers
are independent enough from the kernel structure, thus the verification process
does not need to take into consideration the particularities of the kernel where
the driver came from.

The main objective of driver modeling in Isabelle is to generalize the verification of kernel drivers and make it OS-agnostic. We started from an OpenBSD
driver which suffered adaptations meant to decouple its dependency on the kernel mid-layer. This simulation comes at a cost, we have to assume that the
rest of the system works correctly because the verification will cover only the
driver functionality. We applied this assumption to hardware related components
like bus communication and reading/writing form device registers. We assume

that the bus works correctly and the register behavior matches the datasheet specifications. In general, this separation between the software driver and the hardware components is helpful for identifying the source of defective device behavior. Theorems, code and data are available at https://gitlab.com/system.verification

4.1 OpenBSD Octrng Driver

The driver used for prototyping seL4 verification is a hardware random number generator for Octeon boards. We choose this driver because it has a small configuration sequence and it is pretty isolated from the OpenBSD kernel (there are no major dependencies from other drivers or kernel components). The driver structure is very simple, it has two important functions. First the driver initialization routine, `octrng_attach` whose purpose is to configure the hardware in order to start generating random values. To do this it maps the registers of the device in the main address space and sets bits 62 and 63 (`OCTRNG_ENABLE_OUTPUT, OCTRNG_ENABLE_ENTROPY`) of register 0×1180040000000 (`OCTRNG_CONTROL_ADDR`). The device starts generating random values. Afterwards, `octrng_rnd`, the second function, is called periodically to retrieve the random value generated by the device from register 0×1400000000000 (`OCTEON_RNG_BASE + OCTRNG_ENTROPY_REG`). The random value is be added to the entropy pool on each call.

4.2 Mid-Layer Decoupling

Before parsing the C driver implementation into Isabelle, some OpenBSD kernel mid-layer particularities had to be decoupled and implemented separately so that the driver can stand on its own. We mimicked:

Bus Communication. The original driver accesses the bus via `bus_space_x()` functions, where `x` can refer to register mapping, reading or writing on the bus. In our case, we replace the bus access with simple reading or writing to local memory. This way, bus behavior is copied for read/write commands except for the timing (a bus write may need more time than writing to a local variable). In our case timing is not relevant because all actions are done sequentially.

Device Registers. Because the bus communication is simulated, we implement and express register behavior using local memory with a static structure containing only the required fields from the registers. For octrng driver, we only need the control register, so we had a static structure `rng_regs` with only one member `control_addr` which will be the absolute address of the control register.

Reading and writing the device register is done by mapping the physical registers in memory. This involves communication with the device via the bus on which it is located. For our model however, the device is just a representation of the actual one, so there are no physical registers and our bus transfers are simply read-write operations from the device register structure.

Our model resembles as much as possible the internal register behavior. For the octrng driver, only some registers are important and so we have to cover only these cases: enabling the output bit, the entropy bit and reading the control value. We implement this with two helper functions set_register and get_register. The first function modifies the required register with a given value while the second one reads the control register or returns the value of the current timer if both output and entropy flags are set.

Global Timer. In our model the timer serves two purposes. The first is inherited from the original driver: scheduling a call to the random function every 10 milliseconds. The other has been added for verification purposes and is not present on the actual hardware device: mimicking the random value by returning the timer value instead of the random value from the device register. Note that because we do not have access to an actual timer, we will simply use a global variable that will be incremented by the idle() function each time the main loop schedules a task (see below).

Task Scheduling. The initialization call to the attach function of the driver is done from a separate file whose purpose is to simulate a very simple scheduler. The scheduler is a loop guarded by a timeout where we check for tasks waiting to be scheduled during each iteration. This loop also calls the idle function to increase the global timer. Tasks are stored into a static structure array whose members are the timeout, the start (or arrival) time and the timeout_fun callback. Scheduling a task to run function foo() after 3 time units in the future implies adding a new task in the task queue with timeout set to 3, start set to the current time value and timeout_fun pointing to the foo() function. The task queue is a circular buffer, each task addition increments the index of the newest task added. Tasks are removed from the buffer after completion.

4.3   Proving Driver Function Correctness in Isabelle

We translate our driver model into Isabelle/HOL by applying successively the C-to-Isabelle parser and then the AutoCorres tool. A limitation of these tools is that we can only parse one .c file at a time and provide one corresponding .thy file. In seL4, some of the .c files have produced isolated theory files and these theories are then included where needed. However, there is a starting point to parse all the other files and this is the kernel_C preprocessor output file. We used the same approach by including the octrng driver and the timer implementation inside the .c file containing the main loop. The theory file contains the import statements that include AutoCorres theories and all the helper theories. The C-to-Isabelle parser is applied by declaring the input preprocessed file. After this step we have all the C functions translated into Simpl theorems. In order to obtain the final representation of these theorems, the AutoCorres tool is applied on the target file. Inside the main context of this theory we can start defining new terms, functions or proving new lemmas about the translated C functions.

After the translation into Isabelle, we can access the functions from C as theorems in Isabelle. For example, C function `foo` is represented as a theorem named `foo'_def`. All additional functions implemented in all the included files will be translated. We analyze only the two functions related to the `octrng` driver: `octrng_attach` and `octrng_rnd`. Any constants need to be redefined if we want to use the same names through the new theorems or lemmas. The C constants have been translated directly into their values, but we can give a name to the same values as Isabelle definitions (for example the enable output flag will be defined in Isabelle as `definition "OCTRNG_ENABLE_OUTPUT` $\equiv (1 << 1)::$ `word32"`).

The Attach Function. This is where the device configuration takes place and also the task of periodically checking the value is programmed. The resulting Isabelle translation of the associated modeled driver C code is:

```
Original:
    void octrng_attach(void) {
      unsigned long control_reg;

      control_reg = get_register(OCTRNG_CONTROL_ADDR);
      control_reg |= OCTRNG_ENABLE_OUTPUT;
      control_reg |= OCTRNG_ENABLE_ENTROPY;
      set_register(OCTRNG_CONTROL_ADDR,control_reg);

      add_task(octrng_rnd, 5);
    }
Isabelle:
    do ret' ← get_register' 0x0001180040000000;
      set_register' 0x0001180040000000 (ret' || 3);
      add_task' (PTR(unit) (symbol_table ''octrng_rnd'')) 5
    od
```

We now want to verify that after the execution of `octrng_attach` the device state is ready for generating random values, i.e. the control register is set correctly. We model this inside a lemma in the form of a Hoare triple $\{P\}C\{Q\}$, where P and Q are the precondition and respectively the postcondition, C is the executed program. In our case, we want to verify that running the *octrng_attach* program function in any program state, will result in the control register having set to 1 the enable output and entropy flags. So the precondition is always *True* because there are no requirements and in the postcondition we check the bits of the flags.

```
lemma octrng_attach : "{| λs. True |}
  octrng_attach'
{| λ_s.
    control_addr_C (rng_regs_'' s) && OCTRNG_ENABLE_OUTPUT ≠ 0 ∧
    control_addr_C (rng_regs_'' s) && OCTRNG_ENABLE_ENTROPY ≠ 0 |} "
```

This proof is straightforward, we only need to use **unfolding** to apply all the functions and definitions needed. The weakest precondition tool (**wp** command) computes the necessary precondition that we have to prove further. All the provided goals can be derived automatically from the function definition. Except for the bit operations where we need to explicitly apply the word_bitwise theorems.

The Periodic RNG Function. This function should constantly retrieve the "random" value and add it to the pool. Because we only have the driver part and not the rest of the OpenBSD kernel, this value will be the timer value and the randomness pool will be just a global variable which will be updated by calling this function. The modeled C implementation just reads the value from the output register and saves it into the rand_value global variable, then it schedules another function execution after 10 time units. The Isabelle representation matches the same behavior, the only difference is that all the global variables from the C program are now represented as Isabelle terms, for example the integer rand_value is translated in Isabelle as rand_value_'' a term of type sword32 (signed word on 32 bits).

```
Original:
void octrng_rnd(void) {
  unsigned int value;
  rand_value = get_register(OCTRNG_ENTROPY_REG);
  add_task(octrng_rnd, 10);
}
Isabelle:
do ret' ← get_register' 0;
  modify (rand_value_''_update (λa. ret'));
  add_task' (PTR(unit) (symbol_table ''octrng_rnd'')) 10
od
```

The verification lemma for octrng_rnd has a few more preconditions than the initialization function because we have to first make sure that the function can be executed (the task queue is not full) and then that the driver is configured properly (the output and entropy flags are set).

```
lemma octrng_rnd:
  "{| λs. timer_" s = a ∧ running_tasks_" s < MAX_QUEUE ∧
    current_tasks_" s < MAX_QUEUE ∧
    control_addr_C (rng_regs_" s) && OCTRNG_ENABLE_OUTPUT ≠ 0 ∧
    control_addr_C (rng_regs_" s) && OCTRNG_ENABLE_ENTROPY ≠ 0 |}
 octrng_rnd'
    {| λ_s. rand_value_" s=a |}! "
```

The additional clause λ s. timer_" s = a represents that in any given state s the global timer variable may have a label a for its value. What we want to prove is that the same value will be set to the global rand_value and this is the precondition λ_s. rand_value_" s = a. The verification will be done using the same proofs as for the previous lemma: first we apply the definition of all functions used and then apply the weakest precondition tool. The goals obtained this way are easy to prove by applying the auto method.

This lemma could be improved by adding other specifications like checking that the same function will be called after 10 time units or that the function will be always called in time. The proofs that involve task scheduling were avoided because the translation of the function that runs the actual task is not parsed due to the issues described in the C subset limitation section.

Main Loop and Other Lemmas. The driver functions are bound together inside a small program that simulates a simple scheduler. The main loop does the initialization of the environment including the call of the `octrng_attach` function, then the main loop checks for each time unit if there are tasks whose timeout expired so their function has to be run. We can add lemmas for those additional functions mainly because some of them might be useful in proving other properties. For example, a simple function `idle` increases the global timer after each iteration of the main loop. The lemma for this function can verify that the timer is modified exactly by 1 after its execution in any program state.

```
lemma idle_increases [simp]:
 "{| s. timer_" s = a |}
 idle'
 {| λ_s. timer_" s = a + 1 |}! "
lemma main_function:
 "{| λs. timer_" s = 0 ∧ running_tasks_'' s = 0 |}
 main'
 {| λ_s. timer_" s = TIMEOUT |}!"
```

Its proof is obvious, we only have to apply the weakest precondition tool and then the **auto** method for applying the simplifications. A proof that is more interesting is the one that states the main loop runs until a timeout occurs. This is done by limiting the timer with a maximum value, if this value is reached no other task will be called. The difference between this lemma's proof and the other is that here we have loops so we have to first provide a proof that those loops ends. Because the function that actually runs the task is not parsed, we will only prove the main loop, the one that increases the timer via the `idle` function and continuously run until timeout. This aspect is specified in the `main_function` lemma: if we call the main function from a state where the timer is not started and there are no running tasks, then at the end the timer will have reached the timeout value. In order to prove this loop we have to specify and invariant and a measure.

The invariant is a property that has to be true before, during and after the main loop ends - because we want to prove something about the timer value, the invariant specifies that at any state of the loop, the timer will have a value between 0 and the timeout limit. The measure is a value that has to decrease at each iteration - following the same model, the measure in our case is the distance between the timer and the timeout limit.

```
definition
 timer_limits_inv :: "word32 ⇒ 's lifted_globals_scheme ⇒ bool"
where
 "timer_limits_inv a s ≡ a = timer_" s ∧ 0 ≤timer_" s ∧
 timer_" s ≤ TIMEOUT "
definition
 timer_limits_measure :: " 'a ⇒ 's lifted_globals_scheme ⇒ word32"
where
 "timer_limits_measure a s ≡ a = TIMEOUT - timer_" s "
```

We can apply these two definitions via the `whileLoop_add_inv` monad and obtain a proof goal that can be further broken into smaller goals using the weakest precondition tool.

5   Conclusions

In this paper we adapted and made use of the seL4 verification framework to show that we can use the theorems and proofs of a micro-kernel operating system to successfully verify the octrng driver of the monolithic OpenBSD kernel. Besides that, we also provided a proof of concept regarding the verification of other mid-layer kernel components such as the scheduler. While this is just a small part of the large OpenBSD code base, our efforts lead to an encouraging conclusion: that the automatic abstraction of the source code using the AutoCorres tool reduces the complexity of the effort to demonstrate [5] the properties of any system outside seL4.

We hope that in the future this direction could facilitate the inclusion of verification as an important step in the development of system critical software.

References

1. Bird, R.S., Wadler, P.: Introduction to functional programming. In: Prentice Hall International series in computer science (1988)
2. Burstall, R.M.: Some techniques for proving correctness of programs which alter data structures. Machine Intell. **7**(23–50), 3 (1972)
3. Dannowski, U.: L4Ka Hazelnut. https://github.com/l4ka/hazelnut. Accessed 01 July 2021
4. Greenaway, D.: Automated proof-producing abstraction of C code, Ph.D. thesis, UNSW Sydney (2014)
5. Greenaway, D., Lim, J., Andronick, J., Klein, G.: Don't sweat the small stuff: formal verification of c code without the pain. In: Proceedings of the 35th ACM SIGPLAN Conference on Programming Language Design and Implementation (2014)
6. Heiser, G.: The seL4 microkernel-an introduction. The seL4 Foundation 1 (2020)
7. International Standard Organization: International standard ISO/IEC 9899 programming languages C - reference number ISO/IEC 9899:1999(E), second edition 1999–12-01. American National Standards Institute, New York, NY (1999)
8. Klein, G., et al.: Comprehensive formal verification of an OS microkernel. ACM Trans. Comput. Syst. **32**, 1–70 (2014)
9. Klein, G., et al.: seL4: formal verification of an OS kernel. In: Symposium on Operating Systems Principles (2009)
10. L4Re Operating System Framework: L4Re Fiasco. https://l4re.org/fiasco/build.html. Accessed 01 July 2021
11. System Architecture Group, DiSy Group: L4Ka Pistachio. https://www.l4ka.org/65.php. Accessed 01 July 2021
12. Tuch, H., Klein, G., Norrish, M.: Types, bytes, and separation logic. In: ACM-SIGACT Symposium on Principles of Programming Languages (2007)
13. University of Cambridge, Technische Universität München: Isabelle homepage. https://isabelle.in.tum.de/. Accessed 01 July 2021

An Efficient Small Modulus Test and Its Applications to Delegated Computation Without Preprocessing

Matluba Khodjaeva[1]($\boxtimes$) and Giovanni di Crescenzo[2]

[1] CUNY John Jay College of Criminal Justice, New York, NY, USA
mkhodjaeva@jjay.cuny.edu
[2] Peraton Labs Inc., Basking Ridge, NJ, USA
gdicrescenzo@peratonlabs.com

Abstract. Delegation of operations used in cryptographic schemes from a computationally weaker client to a computationally stronger server has been advocated to expand the applicability of cryptosystems to computing with resource-constrained devices. Classical results for the verification of integer and polynomial products are based on a test due to Pippenger, Yao and Kaminski which verifies these operations modulo a small prime. In this paper we describe and prove an efficient small integer modulus test and show its application to single-server delegated computation of operations of interest in cryptosystems. In particular, we show single-server delegated computation protocols, *without any preprocessing*, for the following operations:

1. modular multiplication of two public group values,
2. modular inverse of a public group value,
3. modular inverse of a private group value, and
4. exponentiation of a public base to a small public exponent in the RSA group.

Our protocols satisfy result correctness, input privacy (unless the input is public), result security and client efficiency. Previous work satisfied only a subset of these properties, or required preprocessing, or satisfied lower client efficiency.

Keywords: Small Modulus Test · Applied Cryptography · Secure Delegation · Group Theory

1 Introduction

Server-aided cryptography (starting with, e.g., [1,11,22]) addresses the problem of resource-constrained clients, such as IoT devices, delegating or outsourcing cryptographic computations to computationally more powerful servers. Currently, this area is seeing a renewed interest because of the increasing popularity of various computing trends (i.e., computing over IoT devices' data, cloud/edge/fog computing, etc.), and the need to efficiently implement cryptographic schemes and their sometimes relatively expensive operations on them.

© The Author(s), under exclusive license to Springer Nature Switzerland AG 2024
M. Manulis et al. (Eds.): SecITC 2023, LNCS 14534, pp. 157–177, 2024.
https://doi.org/10.1007/978-3-031-52947-4_12

The ubiquitous deployment of resource-constraint devices makes the security designer's life harder, in that the task of guaranteeing the security of these devices becomes less and less manageable. The natural approach of running a preprocessing phase where cryptographic keys and credentials are stored on these devices and then allowing them to participate in state-of-the-art cryptography protocols based on this stored information, may not always succeed, since sometimes these devices are deployed in use cases where physical security (specifically, confidentiality and/or integrity) of any stored secret keys or data cannot be guaranteed.

This motivated the problem studied in this paper: is it possible for a resource-constrained client to efficiently, privately and securely delegate to a server the computation of operations used in currently applied cryptography schemes, *without need for a preprocessing phase*? A solution to this problem needs to make computation for the client more efficient than in a non-delegated computation, but also needs to withstand server's attacks in learning any new information about the input to the computation (when input privacy is desired), or in disrupting the computation and fooling the client into accepting an incorrect computation result. All of the above needs to be achieved *without* a preprocessing phase storing data on the client's memory.

More generally, we require a solution to the delegation of a function F to be a 2-party protocol between client C and server S, where C and S have a brief message exchange (typically, a message from C to S followed by one from S to C; see Fig. 1), and where the following requirements are satisfied (see also Appendix A for more formal definitions):

1. δ_c-*result correctness*: if C and S honestly run the protocol, at the end of the protocol C returns $F(x)$ with some high probability δ_c;
2. ϵ_p-*input privacy*: except for some small probability ϵ_p, no new information about input x is revealed to S;
3. ϵ_s-*result security*: S should not be able, except possibly with some small probability ϵ_s, to convince C to return a result different than $F(x)$ at the end of the protocol; and
4. (t_F, t_S, t_C, cc, mc)-*efficiency*:
   - *client runtime efficiency*: C's runtime, denoted as t_C, should be significantly smaller than the runtime, denoted as t_F, of computing $F(x)$ without delegation;
   - small S's runtime t_S (i.e., a small constant times t_F);
   - small online phase communication complexity cc (i.e., ideally a small constant times input and output sizes);
   - small number of online phase messages mc (i.e., ideally, ≤ 2).

Our Contribution and Comparison with Previous Work. We show single-server protocols, *without preprocessing*, for the delegation of

1. modular multiplication of two public group values,
2. modular inverse of a public group value,
3. modular inverse of a private group value, and

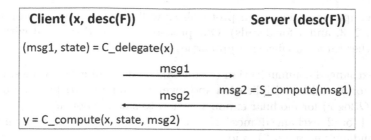

Fig. 1. Delegated computation of $y = F(x)$ without preprocessing

4. exponentiation of a public base to a small public exponent in the RSA group.

All of our protocols satisfy the following 4 properties:

- δ_c-result correctness, for $\delta_c = 1$;
- ϵ_p-input privacy (unless the input is public), for $\epsilon_p = 0$;
- ϵ_s-result security, for $\epsilon_s = 2^{-\lambda}$, where λ is a configurable statistical parameter which in applications can be set, for instance, as $= 50$); and
- client runtime efficiency, with a software implementation that achieves ratio t_F/t_C significantly larger than 1, when $\lambda = 50$ and when the value range of input length σ is consistent with the use of these operations in applied cryptography.

In the case of modular multiplication of two public values, we are not aware of any previous work satisfying these 4 properties without preprocessing. The closest results we know of are: (a) the protocol in [7], which satisfies these 4 properties with preprocessing, and (b) a protocol obtained by a direct adaptation to modular multiplication of the integer multiplication verification test [15,32], which at best achieves client efficiency in an asymptotic sense.

In the case of modular inverses, previous work (see, e.g., [5]) did achieve an efficient delegation protocol without preprocessing, even in the case where the input needs to remain private. The protocols in this paper have improved client efficiency, since the client only performs a few modular reductions with a small modulus, while in [5] the client performed a few modular multiplications.

In the case of modular exponentiation of a public base to a small public exponent in the RSA group [25], we are not aware of any previous work satisfying this set of 4 properties without any preprocessing. The closest results we are aware of are a protocol that satisfies these 4 properties but requires preprocessing [8], and the following protocols without preprocessing for large public exponents: (a) delegation of a batch of exponentiations where the client does compute a single exponentiation [9], and (c) delegation of a single exponentiation which only provably satisfies result correctness and client efficiency [24,28,33]. We note that exponentiation to a small exponent is of much interest since many library implementations of RSA encryption use small exponents, for efficiency reasons.

We show the client runtime efficiency property of our protocols in two ways: with analytical runtime expressions, and by performance measurements for a software implementation of our protocols as well as some previous protocols (see Tables 1, 2, 3, and 4 for details). Our protocols also perform well with respect to the other targeted efficiency properties; specifically:

- low exchanged communication (a constant number of group values; i.e., $cc = O(1)$ for modular multiplication and inverses, and a logarithmic number; i.e., $cc = O(\log x)$ for modular exponentiation to small exponent x),
- only 1 or 2 exchanged messages (client delegating to server, and server responding; i.e., $mc \leq 2$), and
- low server runtime (only lower order computations in addition to the delegated function).

Our main technical contribution consists of a 2-parameter generalization of Pippenger's probabilistic test [15,32] on efficiently verifying integer equations. Given an integer equation $y = a \cdot b$, this test consisted of checking whether this identity holds modulo a small random prime. We generalize this test in two ways: by using a small random integer instead of a small random prime, and by optimizing the length of this random integer as a function of the desired error probability for the test. We also give a self-contained proof of the lemma proving the effectiveness of this test.

More Related Work. Almost all past work showing proved guarantees in delegation of operations used in cryptography protocols (starting with, e.g., [14] for exponentiation and [30] for pairings), made critical use of preprocessing, as follows. The delegation protocol was divided into an offline phase and an online phase, and the client was assumed to have time resource constraints only in the online phase. While this assumption may be reasonable in many practical scenarios, it may also not be so in scenarios where we cannot guarantee the integrity and/or confidentiality of the data stored on the client's memory at the offline phase or even cached across multiple protocol executions. Thus, delegation without preprocessing of operations used in cryptography schemes, although much harder to achieve, seems to be an important capability to have for applications with resource-constrained devices.

We are only aware of the following few exceptions (i.e., single-server delegation protocols proved to satisfy the above 4 properties, without requiring any preprocessing): a protocol to delegate an inverse in a group (see, e.g., [5]), and a recent protocol to delegate any single pairing computation with public inputs [19]. With respect to batch computations, we are aware of the following solutions proved to satisfy the above 4 properties, without preprocessing: 2 protocols to delegate a batch of public-base, public-exponent, exponentiations in prime-order or RSA groups, where the client does perform a single exponentiation computation [9], and protocols to delegate a batch of public-input pairings, where the client does perform one or some pairing computations [10,23,30]. We note that in these latter protocols the client does cache some values across the batch delegation, and stress that if cached for a long time, the confidentiality and integrity of these values is also at risk (similarly as discussed for values stored during any preprocessing).

In the case of no-preprocessing delegation of a single large-exponent exponentiation modulo a composite integer, previous attempts satisfied result correctness and client efficiency [24,28,33] but were later showed to satisfy neither input privacy nor result security [4,24]. Similarly for the case of no-preprocessing delegation of a single pairing: the scheme in [13] satisfies result correctness, input privacy and client efficiency but does not target result security, and protocol 1 in [20] satisfies result correctness and client efficiency but was showed to satisfy neither input privacy nor result security in [19]. Some literature papers achieved delegation without preprocessing in the presence of 2 or more non-colluding servers; see, for instance, [29] for the delegation of pairings.

There is also much other work on delegation for operations in a different domain than what studied here, for which we refer to reader to the survey in [27] for other operations beyond cryptography and the survey in [2] for computation of arbitrary functions, with clients more powerful than considered here.

Preliminary Definitions. Let $(G, \cdot)$ denote a group, where we refer to operation $\cdot$ as multiplication, and let 1 denote G's identity element. For any $a \in G$, let $b = a^{-1}$ denote the multiplicative inverse of a; i.e., the value b such that $a \cdot b = 1$. We consider the following functions:

- $F_{mul} : G \times G \to G$, mapping any $a, b \in G$ to their multiplication $a \cdot b$.
- $F_{inv} : G \to G$, mapping any value $x \in G$ to its multiplicative inverse x^{-1}.
- $F_{exp,c} : G \times \{0,1\}^c \to G$, mapping any values $x \in G$ and any c-bit exponent e to the exponentiation x^e.

In the rest of the paper, we will consider these functions over the group $(\mathbb{Z}_m^*, \cdot \mod m)$, for an arbitrary integer m. In particular, when m is a positive integer of one of the following two forms: (1) m is a prime; (2) m is the product of two same-length primes p, q. Note that these definitions capture groups where the discrete logarithm problem or RSA/factoring problems are conjectured to be hard.

For *asymptotic efficiency* evaluation of our protocols, we will use the following definitions:

- $a(\ell)$: runtime for modular addition/subtraction of ℓ-bit values
- $m(\ell)$: runtime for modular multiplication of ℓ-bit values
- $d(\ell)$: runtime for modular inversion of an ℓ-bit value
- $m_r(\ell)$: runtime for modular reduction to an ℓ-bit modulus
- $p(\ell)$: runtime for a random generation of an ℓ-bit prime number
- $i(\ell)$: runtime for a random generation of an ℓ-bit integer
- $\eta_1 = \lceil \lambda + \log_2 \lambda + \log_2(\pi(2\sigma)) \rceil$, where $\pi(z)$ is the number of primes $\leq z$
- $\eta_2 = \lceil \lambda + \log_2 \sigma \rceil$.

For *practical runtime* evaluation, we have produced a software implementation, in Python 3.8 using the gmpy2 package, of our protocols on a macOS Big Sur Version 11.4 laptop with a 3.2 GHz Apple M1 processor with 8 cores (4 performance cores and 4 efficiency cores at 1/10th of the power) and 16 GB RAM.

2   An Identity Verification Test Modulo Small Integers

We show a 2-parameter generalization of Pippenger's probabilistic test [15,32]. Given an integer equation $y = a \cdot b$, this test consisted of randomly choosing a small prime q, and checking whether $y \bmod q = (a \bmod q) \cdot (b \bmod q)$. We generalize this test in two ways: by using a small random integer s instead of the small random prime q, and by setting the length of s as a function of the desired error probability for the test. We now show the key lemma proving the effectiveness of this test (stated in terms of zero testing since verifying the integer equation $y = a \cdot b$ is equivalent to verifying that $y - a \cdot b = 0$).

Lemma 1. Let λ, σ be integers such that $\lambda \geq 2$ and $7 \leq \sigma \leq 10^8$. Also, let N_η be the set of positive integers $\leq 2^\eta$ and > 1. For any integer x such that $1 \leq x \leq 2^\sigma$, if $\eta = \lceil \lambda + \log_2 \sigma \rceil$, it holds that

$$\mathrm{Prob}\left[q \leftarrow N_\eta : x = 0 \mod q\right] \leq 2^{-\lambda}.$$

We start the proof of Lemma 1 by providing some definitions and facts. Our goal is to compute an upper bound on the probability, denoted as $p_{\eta,\lambda,x}$, in the lemma statement; i.e., the probability that after randomly choosing an integer $q \leq 2^\eta$ and > 1, it holds that $x = 0 \mod q$. To compute an upper bound on $p_{\eta,\lambda,x}$, we first elaborate on known bounds on the product of prime numbers.

Theorem 18 in [26] states that for any integer $u < 10^8$, the product of all prime integers $\leq u$ is $> e^t$, for $t = u - 2.05282\sqrt{u}$, which is $> 2^u$ for all integers $u \geq 49$. By direct calculation, one can see that the product of all prime integers $\leq u$ is $> 2^u$ for all $7 \leq u \leq 49$. This implies the following

Fact 1. For any integer u such that $7 \leq u \leq 10^8$, the product of all prime integers $\leq u$ is $> 2^u$.

We now need a result almost identical to Corollary 1 in [18].

Fact 2. For any integers σ, x such that $7 \leq \sigma \leq 10^8$ and $x < 2^\sigma$, the number of positive integers that divide x is $\leq \sigma - 1$.

To show why Fact 2 holds, we see that by assuming that there are $b > \sigma - 1$ distinct positive integers $q_1, \ldots, q_b$ which divide x, one reaches the contradiction

$$
\begin{aligned}
2^\sigma &> x \\
&\geq \mathrm{lcm}(q_1, \ldots, q_b) \\
&\geq \mathrm{lcm}(\text{smallest } b \text{ positive integers}) \\
&\geq \text{product of all primes} \leq b \\
&> 2^\sigma
\end{aligned}
$$

where the last inequality follows from Fact 1, after setting $u = \sigma$.

Using the above facts, we can now compute the desired upper bound on probability $p_{\eta,\lambda,x}$ as follows.

$$p_{\eta,\lambda,x} \leq \frac{\text{number of positive integers dividing } x}{\text{number of integers } \leq 2^\eta \text{ and } > 1}$$

$$\leq \frac{\sigma - 1}{2^\eta - 1} \leq \frac{\sigma}{2^\eta} \leq \frac{\sigma}{2^{\lambda + \log_2 \sigma}} \leq \frac{1}{2^\lambda},$$

where the first inequality follows by the definition of $p_{\eta,\lambda,x}$, the second inequality follows from Fact 2, the fourth inequality follows from the definition of η in the lemma statement, and the third and fifth inequalities follow by algebraic simplifications.   □

3 No-Preprocessing Delegation of Group Multiplication

In this section we show the first single-server delegation protocols for group multiplication, without any preprocessing. Formally, we obtain the following

Theorem 1. Let σ be computational security parameter, let m be a σ-bit integer, and let λ be a statistical security parameter. There exist (constructively) a single-server protocol $\mathcal{P}^{mul}$ without preprocessing for delegating computation of function F_{mul} in group $(\mathbb{Z}_m^*, \cdot \mod m)$, satisfying the properties of 1-correctness, $2^{-\lambda}$-security, and (t_F, t_S, t_C, mc, cc)-efficiency, where, for $\eta = \lceil \lambda + \log_2 \sigma \rceil$,

- $t_C = 5$ η-bit-modulus reductions of σ-bit integers

    $+ 2$ η-bit-values multiplications $+ 1$ η-bit-value addition;
- $t_S = 1$ multiplication $+ 1$ division mod m,
- $mc = 1$, $cc = 2$

We also remark that the asymptotic expression of t_C is $O(m_r(\eta) + m(\eta) + a(\eta))$, which improves over non-delegated computation runtime $t_F = m(\sigma)$ of ring multiplication for a large region of the (λ, σ) parameter space, including values of highest practical interest, when using the most recommended algorithms in applied cryptography (i.e., Karatsuba's algorithm, Toom-Cook's algorithm and the grade-school algorithm).

In the rest of this section we show the proof of Theorem 1.

Informal Description of $\mathcal{P}^{mul}$. Our starting point is the delegation protocol, *with* preprocessing, for multiplication modulo primes from [7], here denoted as $\mathcal{P}_{pre}^{mul}$. In this latter protocol, the online input to C and S consists of two integers a, b and a prime modulus p, and its online phase starts with S computing the product $w = a \cdot b$ over the integers and sending to C the decomposition of w modulo p (i.e., the quotient w_0 and the remainder w_1 of the division of w by p). After that, C verifies the equation $a \cdot b = w_0 \cdot p + w_1$ modulo a small random prime q, which was chosen in the offline phase. Protocol $\mathcal{P}_{pre}^{mul}$ uses a verification test which extended a well-known test for probabilistic verification of multiplication over the integers, mentioned by Yao [32] and Kaminski [15], and credited in both papers to Pippenger (see, e.g., example 2 in [15] for a description of the protocol). The extension consists in a configurable choice of the size of the small prime modulus q, based on the desired error probability for the test.

As the offline of $\mathcal{P}_{pre}^{mul}$ essentially only consists of randomly choosing a small prime and storing it on C's memory, a natural approach to obtain a delegation protocol *without* preprocessing consists of moving this step into C's program in the online phase. We denote the resulting protocol as $\mathcal{P}_{opm}^{mul}$. As detailed in Table 1, when implementing $\mathcal{P}_{opm}^{mul}$ for practical parameter values, C's runtime is significantly slower than a non-delegated computation. After we realized that this is due mainly to the random choice and testing of the small prime, we considered using a version of this probabilistic verification test based on arbitrary small integers as moduli (instead of primes), as in Sect. 2, for which the random modulus choice is very efficient and no primality testing of the modulus is needed. Our Lemma 1 shows that this approach is sound, and the size of this integer is not much different (in fact, slightly smaller) than the size of the prime integer chosen in [7]. As a consequence, in the resulting delegation protocol, denoted as $\mathcal{P}^{mul}$, C's runtime is smaller than non-delegated computation, even if no preprocessing is used.

Formal Description of $\mathcal{P}^{mul}$. Consider the group $(\mathbb{Z}_m^*, \cdot \mod m)$, for some positive integer m. We now formally describe a 1-server protocol $\mathcal{P}^{mul} = (C, S)$ for the delegation of multiplication of public online group values a and b in $\mathbb{Z}_m^*$, where $|a| = |b| = \sigma$, and with statistical parameter λ.

Online Input to C and S: $1^\sigma, 1^\lambda$, integer $m \in \{0,1\}^\sigma$, $a, b \in \mathbb{Z}_m^*$

Online Phase Instructions:

1. S computes $w := a \cdot b$ (i.e., the product, over $\mathbb{Z}$, of integers a and b)
   S computes w_0, w_1 such that $w = w_0 \cdot m + w_1$ (over $\mathbb{Z}$), where $0 \le w_1 < m$
   S sends w_0, w_1 to C
2. C randomly chooses an integer $s < 2^\eta$, where $\eta = \lceil \lambda + \log_2 \sigma \rceil$
   C computes $w_0' := w_0 \mod s$ and $w_1' := w_1 \mod s$
   C computes $a' := a \mod s$, $b' := b \mod s$ and $m' := m \mod s$
   If $a' \cdot b' \ne w_0' \cdot m' + w_1' \mod s$ then
       C returns: $\perp$ and the protocol halts
   C returns: $y := w_1$

Properties of $\mathcal{P}^{mul}$: The proofs for the result correctness and result security of $\mathcal{P}^{mul}$, the latter using Lemma 1, can be found in Appendix B.

The *efficiency* property follows by protocol inspection. In particular, S computes one multiplication of two σ-bit values over $\mathbb{Z}$, and one reduction of a σ-bit integer modulo m, and C computes five reductions modulo the η-bit integer s of integers of size at most σ and one verification check which requires one addition and two multiplications modulo the η-bit integer s.

In Table 1 we report on the practical efficiency of the scheme, based on our software implementation of the scheme, one main takeaway being that C's runtime t_C is smaller than non-delegated computation t_F (i.e., the delegation improvement ratio t_F/t_C is > 1) for all values of most interest of parameters λ, σ; specifically, $\lambda = 50$ and $\sigma \in \{1024, 2048, 3072\}$. We also report the ratio t_F/t_C for two related protocols: protocol $\mathcal{P}_{pre}^{mul}$ from [7] with preprocessing, and the protocol $\mathcal{P}_{opm}^{mul}$ which has no preprocessing, where C chooses a prime modulus s in the online phase. The takeaways there are that, for such practical parameter values: (1) delegation would not improve C's runtime in $\mathcal{P}_{opm}^{mul}$; (2) delegation does improve C's runtime in $\mathcal{P}^{mul}$ by a multiplicative factor between 1.7 and 4 depending on the modulus size; and (3) the delegation improvement ratio for $\mathcal{P}^{mul}$, not using preprocessing, is about half the ratio of $\mathcal{P}_{pre}^{mul}$, which does use preprocessing, or larger.

Table 1. Performance results for the delegation of $F_{mul}(a, b) = a \cdot b \mod m$ in $\mathbb{Z}_m^*$, where $|m| = \sigma$, $\lambda = 50$, $t_{Cm}(\eta) \leq 5m_r(\eta) + 2m(\eta) + a(\eta)$ and $t_F = 1.19\text{E-}05\,\text{s}$.

Protocol/Pre-processing		t_C	t_F/t_C			$\sigma = 3072$	
			$\sigma = 2048$	$\sigma = 3072$	$\sigma = 4096$	t_P	t_C
m is a prime integer							
$\mathcal{P}_{pre}^{mul}$	Yes	$t_{Cm}(\eta_1)$	3.479	4.852	6.578	5.78E-05	2.44E-06
$\mathcal{P}_{opm}^{mul}$	No	$t_{Cm}(\eta_1) + p(\eta_1)$	0.108	0.185	0.314	0	6.43E-05
$\mathcal{P}^{mul}$	No	$t_{Cm}(\eta_2) + i(\eta_2)$	1.694	2.716	3.973	0	4.43E-06
m is the product of 2 same-length primes							
$\mathcal{P}_{pre}^{mul}$	Yes	$t_{Cm}(\eta_1)$	3.538	4.728	6.501	6.46E-05	2.53E-06
$\mathcal{P}_{opm}^{mul}$	No	$t_{Cm}(\eta_1) + p(\eta_1)$	0.122	0.198	0.306	0	6.06E-05
$\mathcal{P}^{mul}$	No	$t_{Cm}(\eta_2) + i(\eta_2)$	1.731	2.701	3.999	0	4.34E-06

4   No-Preprocessing Delegation for Group Inverses

In this section we present single-server protocols for delegated computation of group inverses which have improved client efficiency over previous work. Our protocols build on the multiplication delegation protocol in Sect. 3. Formally, our result is the following

Theorem 2. Let σ be computational security parameter, let m be a σ-bit integer, and let λ be a statistical security parameter. There exist (constructively) two single-server protocols $\mathcal{P}_1^{inv}$, for input scenario 'x public online', and $\mathcal{P}_2^{inv}$, for input scenario 'x private online', for delegating computation of function F_{inv}, in group $(\mathbb{Z}_m^*, \cdot \mod m)$, satisfying the properties of 1-result-correctness, $2^{-\lambda}$-result-security, and (t_F, t_S, t_C, mc, cc)-efficiency, where, for $\eta = \lceil \lambda + \log_2 \sigma \rceil$,

– for $\mathcal{P}_1^{inv}$: $\epsilon_s = 2^{-\lambda}$, $t_F = 1$ inversion,
  $t_C = 5$ η-bit-modulus reductions $+ 2$ η-bit-values multiplications
    $+ 1$ η-bit-value addition,
  $t_S = 1$ inversion $+ 1$ multiplication $+ 1$ division mod m,
  $mc = 1$, $cc = 3$

- for $\mathcal{P}_2^{inv}$ (also satisfying input-privacy): $\epsilon_s = 2^{-\lambda}$, $t_F = 1$ inversion,
  $t_C = 2$ group multiplications + 5 η-bit-modulus reductions
      + 2 η-bit-values multiplications + 1 η-bit-value addition,
  $t_S = 1$ inversion + 1 multiplication + 1 division mod m,
  $mc = 2$, $cc = 4$.

In the rest of this section we prove Theorem 2, by describing the two claimed protocols in the two different input scenarios and their properties. Specifically, we describe delegation of inversion $F_{inv}(x) = x^{-1} \mod m$ in group $(\mathbb{Z}_m^*, \cdot \mod m)$, using a protocol $\mathcal{P}^{mul}$ for delegation of multiplication $F_{mul}(a, b) = a \cdot b \mod m$, such as the protocol from Sect. 3, where inputs a and b are public online.

4.1   The "x Public Input" Scenario

Our first protocol consists of a single message by the server including the inverse value $x^{-1} \mod m$ of the input x and the client delegating the computation of the product $x \cdot x^{-1} \mod m$, using protocol $\mathcal{P}^{mul}$ from Sect. 3, and checking that the result obtained at the end of this protocol execution is equal to 1.

Formal Description of Protocol $\mathcal{P}_1^{inv}$.

Input Scenario: x public online

Online Input to C and S: σ, λ, $desc(F_{inv})$, x

Online Phase Instructions:

1. S computes $w := x^{-1} \mod m$ and sends w to C
2. C and S use protocol $\mathcal{P}^{mul}$, for $a = x$ and $b = w$, and parameters σ, λ,
      resulting in C obtaining z;
3. If $z \neq 1$ then C **returns** $\perp$ and the protocol halts
4. C **returns** $y := w$ and halts.

Properties of $\mathcal{P}_1^{inv}$: The proofs for the result correctness and result security properties, the latter using Lemma 1, can be found in Appendix C.

The *efficiency* properties follow directly by protocol inspection and the same properties of $\mathcal{P}^{mul}$. In particular, we note that if $\mathcal{P}^{mul}$ consists of a single message from S to C, as the protocol in Sect. 3, then so does $\mathcal{P}_1^{inv}$.

In Table 2 we report on the practical efficiency of the scheme, based on our software implementation of $\mathcal{P}_1^{inv}$, one main takeaway being that C's runtime t_C is smaller than non-delegated computation t_F (i.e., the delegation improvement ratio t_F/t_C is > 1) for all values of most interest of parameters λ, σ; specifically, $\lambda = 50$ and $\sigma \in \{2048, 3072, 4096\}$. We also report the ratio t_F/t_C for two related protocols: protocol $\mathcal{P}_{1,pre}^{inv}$ with preprocessing (using the multiplication protocol with preprocessing from [7]), and the protocol $\mathcal{P}_{1,opm}^{inv}$ which has no preprocessing, where C chooses a prime modulus s in the online phase. The takeaways there are that, for such practical parameter values: (1) delegation would not improve C's runtime in $\mathcal{P}_{1,opm}^{inv}$; (2) delegation does improve C's runtime in $\mathcal{P}_1^{inv}$ by a multiplicative factor between 4.8 and 8.1 depending on the modulus size; and (3) the delegation improvement ratio for $\mathcal{P}_1^{inv}$, not using preprocessing, is about half the ratio of $\mathcal{P}_{1,pre}^{inv}$, which does use preprocessing, or larger.

Table 2. Performance results for the delegation of $F(x) = x^{-1} \mod m$ in $\mathbb{Z}_m^*$, where x is public, m is a σ-bit prime, $\lambda = 50$, $t_{Cm}(\eta) \leq 5m_r(\eta) + 2m(\eta) + a(\eta)$ and $t_F = 3.19\text{E-}05\,\text{s}$.

Protocol/Pre-processing		t_C	t_F/t_C			$\sigma = 3072$	
			$\sigma = 2048$	$\sigma = 3072$	$\sigma = 4096$	t_P	t_C
$\mathcal{P}_{1,pre}^{inv}$	Yes	$t_{Cm}(\eta_1)$	10.008	13.394	16.235	6.30E-05	2.35E-06
$\mathcal{P}_{1,opm}^{inv}$	No	$t_{Cm}(\eta_1) + p(\eta_1)$	0.359	0.488	0.816	0	6.73E-05
$\mathcal{P}_1^{inv}$	No	$t_{Cm}(\eta_2) + i(\eta_2)$	4.782	6.543	8.111	0	4.79E-06

4.2 The "x Private Input" Scenario

Our second protocol $\mathcal{P}_2^{inv}$ starts with the client sending a randomized version of the input to the server. Then it continues with the client delegating the computation of the inverse of the randomized input, using our first protocol $\mathcal{P}_1^{inv}$. Finally, the client derives the result by removing the randomizer. Input masking techniques have already been used in many delegation protocols in the literature. In the case of inverse delegation, it is interesting to note that it does not require the client to store any preprocessing values.

Formal Description of Protocol $\mathcal{P}_2^{inv}$.

Input Scenario: x private online

Online Input to C σ, $desc(F_{inv})$, x
Online Input to C σ, $desc(F_{inv})$

Online Phase Instructions:

1. C randomly chooses $r \in G$, computes $z := x \cdot r \mod m$, and sends z to S;
2. S computes $w := z^{-1}$ and sends w to C
3. C and S use protocol $\mathcal{P}^{mul}$ for $a = z$ and $b = w$, and parameters σ, λ, resulting in C obtaining v;
4. If $v \neq 1$ then C **returns** $\bot$ and the protocol halts
5. C **returns** $y := r \cdot w \mod m$ and halts.

Properties of $\mathcal{P}_2^{inv}$: The proofs for the result correctness, input privacy and result security properties, the latter using Lemma 1, can be found in Appendix D.

The *efficiency* properties of $\mathcal{P}_2^{inv}$ follow directly by protocol inspection and the same properties of $\mathcal{P}_1^{inv}$ and $\mathcal{P}^{mul}$. In particular, note that t_C only increases by $2 \cdot m(\sigma)$ with respect to protocol $\mathcal{P}_1^{inv}$.

In Table 3 we report on the practical efficiency of the scheme, based on our software implementation of $\mathcal{P}_2^{inv}$, where we reach analogue conclusions as for $\mathcal{P}_1^{inv}$ on the effectiveness of delegation.

5 No-Preprocessing Delegation for Small-Exponent Exponentiation in RSA Groups

We discuss the first protocol to delegate small-exponent exponentiation in the RSA group $\mathbb{Z}_n^*$, in the input case where both the base and the exponent are

Table 3. Performance results for the delegation of $F(x) = x^{-1} \mod m$ in $\mathbb{Z}_m^*$, where x is private, m is a σ-bit prime, $\lambda = 50$, and $t_F = 3.11\text{E-05}\,\text{s}$

Protocol/Pre-processing		t_F/t_C			$\sigma = 3072$	
		$\sigma = 2048$	$\sigma = 3072$	$\sigma = 4096$	t_P	t_C
$\mathcal{P}_{2,pre}^{inv}$	Yes	2.977	3.110	2.858	6.70E-05	1.00E-05
$\mathcal{P}_{2,opm}^{inv}$	No	0.606	0.791	1.013	0	3.93E-05
$\mathcal{P}_2^{inv}$	No	2.504	2.832	2.653	0	1.09E-05

public, without preprocessing. This is obtained by carefully combining a specific variant of the square-and-multiply algorithm with the delegation protocol $\mathcal{P}^{mul}$ for multiplication from Sect. 3. Formally, we obtain the following

Theorem 3. Let σ be computational security parameter, let m be a σ-bit integer, let λ be a statistical security parameter, and let e be a $c - bit$ integer, where c is constant with respect to σ and λ. There exist (constructively) a single-server protocols $\mathcal{P}^{exp}$, for input scenario 'x and e public', for delegating computation of function F_{exp}, in group $(\mathbb{Z}_m^*, \cdot \mod m)$, satisfying the properties of 1-result-correctness, $2^{-\lambda}$-result-security, and (t_F, t_S, t_C, mc, cc)-efficiency, where, for $\eta = \lceil \lambda + \log_2 \sigma \rceil$,

- $\epsilon_s = 2^{-\lambda}$, $t_F = 1$ exponentiation to a c-bit exponent,
- $t_C = O(c)$ η-bit-modulus reductions of σ-bit integers

$$+ O(c) \; \eta\text{-bit-values multiplications}$$
- $t_S = O(c)$ multiplications and divisions mod m,
- $mc = 1$, $cc \leq 8c$.

Informal Description of $\mathcal{P}^{exp}$. Our protocol $\mathcal{P}^{exp}$ can be seen as an optimized simulation of the (iterative) square and multiply algorithm for modular exponentiation, while using a multiplication delegation subprotocol, such as protocol $\mathcal{P}^{mul}$ in Sect. 3, to compute squares and multiplications modulo n in this algorithm. A similar approach has already been taken in [8], where, however, both protocols for multiplication and exponentiation did need a preprocessing phase including the generation and storage of the small prime modulus.

The natural approach to remove the preprocessing phase would be similar as for the results in Sects. 2 and 3: replacing the small prime modulus with a small integer modulus, and letting C generate the small modulus during the protocol (as opposed to doing that in some preprocessing phase). It turns out that this is not yet sufficient to achieve effective delegation (i.e., for the delegation improvement ratio t_F/t_C to be > 1), and further optimizations are needed. Thus, we consider the iterative protocol structure of the square and multiply algorithm, and try to let the client run as many operations as possible only once instead of once for each multiplication, as it would happen on a direct simulation of the algorithm, with calls to protocol $\mathcal{P}^{mul}$ from Sect. 3. In particular, we apply the following 3 optimizations:

1. C only chooses the small integer modulus s once;
2. C only compute the reduction of m modulo the small modulus s once.
3. The protocol uses the version of the square and multiply algorithm where the exponent is expressed in binary and the 'multiply' part of the algorithm only multiplies the value computed until then by a fixed number (i.e., the input base); accordingly, C only computes the reduction of the input base modulo the small integer s once, instead of once for each multiplication operation carried out for each exponent bit $= 1$.

Formal Description and Properties of $\mathcal{P}^{exp}$. A formal description of $\mathcal{P}^{exp}$ is very similar as the construction in [8] and is detailed in Appendix E.

The result correctness and result security properties of $\mathcal{P}^{exp}$, the latter using Lemma 1, follow from the above informal description.

In Table 4 we report on the practical efficiency of the scheme, based on our software implementation of $\mathcal{P}^{exp}$, where we reach analogue conclusions as for our previous protocols, on the effectiveness of delegation.

Table 4. Performance results for the delegation of $F(x) = x^e \mod n$, when x and e are public, m is a σ-bit product of 2 same-length primes, e is a c-bit integer, and $\lambda = 50$.

Protocol/Pre-processing		t_F/t_C			
		$c = 8$		$c = 32$	
		$\sigma = 2048$	$\sigma = 3072$	$\sigma = 2048$	$\sigma = 3072$
$\mathcal{P}^{exp}_{pre}$	Yes	1.543	2.652	1.157	2.240
$\mathcal{P}^{exp}_{opm}$	No	0.288	0.571	0.500	0.782
$\mathcal{P}^{exp}$	No	1.448	2.716	1.532	2.586

6 Conclusions

We showed single-server protocols, without preprocessing, for the single-server delegation of the following operations, used in several cryptosystems:

1. modular multiplication of two public group values,
2. modular inverse of a public group value,
3. modular inverse of a private group value, and
4. exponentiation of a public base to a small public exponent in the RSA group.

Our protocols satisfy result-correctness, input-privacy (unless the input is public), result-security, and client-efficiency (with respect to non-delegated computation) for parameter values of interest in cryptography applications. To the best of our knowledge, the only other single-server protocols in the literature satisfying these properties were presented for the delegation of:

1. a pairing, with both inputs being public, and
2. a batch of public-base and public-exponent exponentiation operations in discrete-log and RSA groups.

Several open problems remain in this area of single-server delegation without preprocessing, especially with respect to operations where input privacy is required, and our results should be interpreted as a step in this direction.

Acknowledgements. Work by Matluba Khodjaeva was supported by the NSF CNS - CISE MSI Research Expansion grant N2131182 and PSC CUNY Cycle 53. Work by Giovanni Di Crescenzo, was supported by the Defense Advanced Research Projects Agency (DARPA), contract n. HR001120C0156. Approved for Public Release, Distribution Unlimited. The U.S. Government is authorized to reproduce and distribute reprints for Governmental purposes notwithstanding any copyright annotation hereon. Disclaimer: The views and conclusions contained herein are those of the authors and should not be interpreted as necessarily representing the official policies or endorsements, either expressed or implied, of DARPA, or the U.S. Government.

A   Formal Definitions

In this section we recall the formal definition (based on [12,14]), of delegation protocols and their correctness, privacy, security, and efficiency requirements.

Basic Notations. The expression $z \leftarrow T$ denotes randomly and independently choosing z from set T. By $y \leftarrow A(x_1, x_2, \ldots)$ we denote running the algorithm A on input $x_1, x_2, \ldots$ and any random coins, and returning y as output. By $(y, tr) \leftarrow (A(u_1, u_2, \ldots), B(v_1, v_2, \ldots))$ we denote running the interactive protocol between A, with input $u_1, u_2, \ldots$ and any random coins, and B, with input $v_1, v_2, \ldots$ and any random coins, where tr denotes A's and B's messages in this execution, and y is A's final output.

System Scenario: Entities and Protocol. We consider a system with a single client, denoted by C, and a single server, denoted by S, who are connected by an authenticated channel, and therefore do not consider any integrity or replay attacks on this channel. Differently than much of previous work in the area, we consider a delegation protocol without *offline phase* or *preprocessing* client computations, typically storing extra values in client's memory, and only consider client computations in what is also called *online phase* in the literature, where C has time constraints.

Let σ denote the computational security parameter (derived from hardness considerations of the underlying computational problem), and let λ denote the statistical security parameter (defined so that statistical test failure events with probability $2^{-\lambda}$ are extremely rare). Both parameters are expressed in unary notation (i.e., $1^\sigma, 1^\lambda$). We think of σ as being asymptotically much larger than λ. Let F denote a function and $desc(F)$ denote F's description. Assuming $1^\sigma, 1^\lambda, desc(F)$ are known to both C and S, we define a *client-server protocol for the delegated (n-instance) computation of F* as the execution: $\{(y, tr) \leftarrow (C(x), S)\}$, where both parties are assume to be aware of inputs

$(1^\sigma, 1^\lambda, desc(F))$, which we will ofter omit for brevity, and tr is the transcript of the communication exchanged between C and S.

Correctness Requirement. Informally, the correctness requirement states that if both parties follow the protocol, C obtains some output at the end of the protocol, and this output is, with high probability, equal to the value obtained by evaluating function F on C's input. Formally, we say that a no-preprocessing client-server protocol (C, S) for the delegated computation of F satisfies δ_c-*correctness* if for any x in $Dom(F)$,

$$\text{Prob}\left[\,out \leftarrow \text{CorrExp}_F : out = 1\right] \geq \delta_c,$$

for some δ_c close to 1, where experiment CorrExp is:

1. $(y, tr) \leftarrow (C(x), S)$
2. if $y = F(x)$, then **return:** 1 else **return:** 0

Privacy Requirement. Informally, the privacy requirement should guarantee the following: if C follows the protocol, a malicious adversary corrupting S cannot obtain any information about C's input x from a protocol execution. This is formalized by extending the indistinguishability-based approach typically used in definitions for encryption schemes. Let (C, S) be a no-preprocessing client-server protocol for the delegated computation of F. We say that (C, S) satisfies ϵ_p-*privacy (in the sense of indistinguishability) against a malicious adversary* if for any algorithm A, it holds that

$$\text{Prob}\left[\,out \leftarrow \text{PrivExp}_{F,A} : out = 1\right] \leq 1/2 + \epsilon_p,$$

for some ϵ_p close to 0, where experiment PrivExp is:

1. $(x_0, x_1, aux) \leftarrow A(desc(F))$
2. $b \leftarrow \{0, 1\}$
3. $(y, tr) \leftarrow (C(x_b), A(aux))$
4. $d \leftarrow A(tr, aux)$
5. if $b = d$ then **return:** 1 else **return:** 0.

Security Requirement. Informally, the security requirement states that for any efficient and malicious adversary corrupting S and even choosing C's input tuple x, at the end of the protocol, C cannot be convinced to obtain some output tuple z containing a value $z \neq F(x)$ Formally, we say that the client-server protocol (C, S) for the delegated n-instance computation of F satisfies ϵ_s-*security against a malicious adversary* if for any algorithm A,

$$\text{Prob}\left[\,out \leftarrow \text{SecExp}_{F,A} : out = 1\right] \leq \epsilon_s,$$

for some ϵ_s close to 0, where experiment SecExp is:

1. $(\vec{x}, aux) \leftarrow A(desc(F))$

2. $(\vec{z}, tr) \leftarrow (C(x), A(aux))$
3. if $z \in \{\perp, F(x)\}$ then **return:** 0 else **return:** 1.

We consider different input scenarios, where the input x may be *private* or *public*. The above definition considered the "x private" input scenario. The definition for the "x public" input scenario is obtained by the following slight modifications: (1) S is also given x as input; (2) no input privacy is required.

B   Properties of $\mathcal{P}^{mul}$

The *correctness* property follows by observing that if C and S follow the protocol, then S computes w_0, w_1 as $w = a \cdot b = w_0 \cdot m + w_1$ and the equation $a \cdot b = w_0 \cdot m + w_1$ is satisfied over $\mathbb{Z}$ and is therefore satisfied also modulo the small prime s. This prevents C to return $\perp$, and allows C to return the correct output value $w_1 = w \mod m = a \cdot b \mod m$.

To prove the *security* property against any malicious S we need to compute an upper bound ϵ_s on the security probability that an adversary corrupting S convinces C to output a y such that $y \neq a \cdot b \mod m$.

We continue the proof of the unbounded security property by defining the following events:

- $e_{y,\neq}$, defined as "C outputs y such that $y \neq a \cdot b \mod m$"
- e_t, defined as "S's message contains w_0, w_1 such that $a \cdot b \neq w_0 \cdot m + w_1 \mod m$".

We now compute an upper bound on the probability of event $e_{y,\neq}$, conditioned on event e_t. We observe that, when event e_t is true, it holds that $a \cdot b \mod m \neq w_1$. In this scenario, for event $e_{y,\neq}$ to happen, it needs to hold that

$$(a \mod s)(b \mod s) = (w_0 \mod s)(m \mod s) + w_1 \mod s.$$

This happens when

$$(a \cdot b - w_0 \cdot m - w_1) = 0 \mod s.$$

By setting $x = a \cdot b - w_0 \cdot m - w_1$, and applying Lemma 1 for this value of x, we obtain that the probability that $x = 0 \mod s$ is at most $2^{-\lambda}$, which implies the following

Fact 3. $\mathrm{Prob}\left[e_{y,\neq} \mid e_t\right] \leq 2^{-\lambda}$

We then observe that when event e_t is false, then the message from S follows the protocol and therefore $e_{y,\neq}$ is also false. This implies the following

Fact 4. $\mathrm{Prob}\left[e_{y,\neq} \mid \neg e_t\right] = 0$

We can now compute an upper bound on the probability of event $e_{y,\neq}$. We have that $\text{Prob}\,[\,e_{y,\neq}\,]$ is

$$
\begin{aligned}
&= \text{Prob}\,[\,e_t\,]\,\text{Prob}\,[\,e_{y,\neq}|e_t\,] + \text{Prob}\,[\,\neg\,e_t\,]\,\text{Prob}\,[\,e_{y,\neq}|\neg\,e_t\,]\\
&\leq \text{Prob}\,[\,e_{y,\neq}|\neg\,e_t\,] + \text{Prob}\,[\,e_{y,\neq}|\neg\,e_t\,]\\
&\leq \text{Prob}\,[\,e_{y,\neq}|\neg\,e_t\,] \;\leq\; 2^{-\lambda},
\end{aligned}
$$

where the first equality and the first inequality follow from basic probability facts; the second inequality follows by applying Fact 4, and the last inequality follows by applying Fact 3.

C   Properties of $\mathcal{P}_1^{inv}$

The *result correctness* property follows directly by observing that if C and S follow the protocol, the same property of $\mathcal{P}^{mul}$ implies that

$$
z = a \cdot b \quad \bmod m = x \cdot w \quad \bmod m = x \cdot (x^{-1}) \quad \bmod m = 1,
$$

after which C returns $y = w = x^{-1} \bmod m$.

To prove the *result security* property against any malicious S we need to compute an upper bound ϵ_s on the security probability that an adversary corrupting S convinces C to output a y such that $y \neq x^{-1} \bmod m$. Assume this adversary sends w' to C and runs $\mathcal{P}^{mul}$ with C, resulting in C obtaining z'. Now, because C checks whether $z' \neq 1$, the only possible cheating strategy for the adversary is that of convincing C to accept that $z' = 1$ and z' is the product of x and w', even when w' is not the inverse of x. By the result security property of $\mathcal{P}^{mul}$, this can only happen with probability at most $2^{-\lambda}$.

D   Properties of $\mathcal{P}_2^{inv}$

The *result correctness* property follows directly by observing that if C and S follow the protocol, the same property of $\mathcal{P}^{mul}$ implies that

$$
v = z \cdot w \quad \bmod m = (x \cdot r) \cdot z^{-1} \quad \bmod m = (x \cdot r) \cdot (x \cdot r)^{-1} \quad \bmod m = 1,
$$

after which C returns $y = r \cdot w = r \cdot (x \cdot r)^{-1} = r \cdot r^{-1} \cdot x^{-1} = x^{-1} \bmod m$.

The *input privacy* follows by observing that C only sends a random group value to S.

To prove the *result security* property against any malicious S we need to compute an upper bound ϵ_s on the security probability that an adversary corrupting S convinces C to output a y such that $y \neq x^{-1} \bmod m$. Assume this adversary, after receiving z from c, sends w' to C and runs $\mathcal{P}^{mul}$ with C, resulting in C obtaining v'. Now, because C checks whether $v' \neq 1$, the only possible cheating strategy for the adversary is that of convincing C to accept that $v' = 1$ and v' is the product of z and w', even when w' is not the inverse of z. By the result security property of $\mathcal{P}^{mul}$, this can only happen with probability $\leq 2^{-\lambda}$.

E   Protocol $\mathcal{P}^{exp}$

To formally define protocol $\mathcal{P}^{exp} = (C, S)$ for the delegated computation of x^e mod m, we use definitions and algorithms from protocol $\mathcal{P}^{mul}$ as well as an optimized version of it, as mentioned in Sect. 5 and further discussed below.

First, by $\mathcal{P}^{mul} = (S_m, C_m)$ we denote a protocol for the delegation of function F_{mul} with statistical parameter λ_m, for public inputs a and b, such as the protocol in Sect. 3. In particular, the notation $(q, r) \leftarrow S_m(a, b)$ refers to an execution of the $\mathcal{P}^{mul}$ server's algorithm with inputs a, b, returning message (q, r) for C, such that $a \cdot b = q \cdot m + r$, where $0 \leq r < m$. Similarly, the notation $d \leftarrow C_m(a, b, q, r)$ refers to an execution of the $\mathcal{P}^{mul}$ client's algorithm with inputs a, b, and server's message (q, r), and returning decision bit d where $d = 1/0$ depending on whether C_m accepts/does not accept the statement $r = a \cdot b \mod n$.

While algorithm S will run S^m, algorithm C will run an optimized version of C^m, which reuses the same modulus s, and the same values $m' = m \mod s$ and $x' = x \mod s$, whenever possible across the multiple uses of multiplication delegation within exponentiation delegation, as we now define. Given a randomly chosen η-bit integer s, and values $m' = m \mod s$ and $x' = x \mod s$, we define the notation $d \leftarrow C'_m(a, b, q, r, s, m', x')$ to refer to a variant of algorithm C_m, where the computation of s and m' are replaced by the use of its arguments s, m', and the use of x as a product factor in correspondence of a bit of exponent e being $= 1$ is replaced by the use of its argument x'. Here, by using C'_m, the client only computes the values s, m', x' once, while by using C_m, it would have recomputed each of these values either $\log e$ or about $(\log e)/2$ times.

We now formally describe protocol $\mathcal{P}^{exp}$ to delegate small-exponent exponentiation function $F_{exp,c}$, which maps $x \in \mathbb{Z}_m^*$ to $x^e \mod m$. in a group $\mathbb{Z}_m^*$, where x and e are public, and e has c bits.

Online Input to C and S: $1^\sigma, 1^\lambda, 1^c, m \in \{0,1\}^\sigma, x \in \mathbb{Z}_m^*, e \in \{0,1\}^c$

Online Phase of $\mathcal{P}^{exp}$:

1. S sets $z = x$, $y = 1$ and $i = 1$
2. While $e > 1$ do
   S computes $(q_{1i}, r_{1i}) = S_m(z, z)$ and sets $z = r_{i1}$
   if e is even then
      S sets $q_{2i} = r_{2i} = 0$, $i = i + 1$ and $e = e/2$
   if e is odd then
      S computes $(q_{2i}, r_{2i}) = S_m(z, x)$ and sets
      S sets $z = r_{i2}$, $i = i + 1$ and $e = (e - 1)/2$
3. S sends $((q_{11}, r_{11}, q_{21}, r_{21}), \ldots, (q_{1c}, r_{1c}, q_{2c}, r_{2c}))$ to C
4. C sets $i = 1$ and $z = x$
5. C randomly chooses an η-bit integer s, where $\eta = \lceil \lambda + \log_2 \sigma \rceil$
   C computes $m' = m \mod s$ and $x' = x \mod s$
6. While $e > 1$ do
      if e is even then
         C computes $d_{1i} = C_m(z, z, q_{1i}, r_{1i}, s, m', x')$

if $d_{1i} = 0$ then C halts
    else C sets $z = r_{1i}$, $i = i + 1$ and $e = e/2$ if e is odd then
C computes $d_{1i} = C_m(z, z, q_{1i}, r_{1i}, s, m', x')$ and sets $z = r_{1i}$
C computes $d_{2i} = C_m(z, x', q_{2i}, r_{2i}, s, m', x')$ and sets $z = r_{2i}$
if $d_{1i} = 0$ or $d_{2i} = 0$ then C halts
    else C sets $i = i + 1$ and $e = (e - 1)/2$
7. C **returns:** $y = r_{2i}$ and halts

References

1. Abadi, M., Feigenbaum, J., Kilian, J.: On hiding information from an oracle. J. Comput. Syst. Sci. **39**(1), 21–50 (1989)
2. Ahmad, H., et al.: Primitives towards verifiable computation: a survey. Front. Comput. Sci. **12**(3), 451–478 (2018)
3. Bellare, M., Garay, J.A., Rabin, T.: Fast batch verification for modular exponentiation and digital signatures. In: Nyberg, K. (eds.) EUROCRYPT 1998. LNCS, vol. 1403, pp. 236–250. Springer, Heidelberg (1998). https://doi.org/10.1007/BFb0054130
4. Bouillaguet, C., Martinez, F., Vergnaud, D.: Cryptanalysis of modular exponentiation outsourcing protocols. Comput. J. **65**(9), 2299–2314 (2022)
5. Cavallo, B., Di Crescenzo, G., Kahrobaei, D., Shpilrain, V.: Efficient and secure delegation of group exponentiation to a single server. In: Mangard, S., Schaumont, P. (eds.) Radio Frequency Identification. Security and Privacy Issues, pp. 156–173. Springer, Cham (2015). https://doi.org/10.1007/978-3-319-24837-0_10
6. Crandall, R., Pomerance, C.: Prime Numbers: A Computational Perspective, 2nd edn. Springer, New York (2005). https://doi.org/10.1007/0-387-28979-8
7. Di Crescenzo, G., Khodjaeva, M., Shpilrain, V., Kahrobaei, D., Krishnan, R.: Single-server delegation of ring multiplications from quasilinear-time clients. In: Proceedings of SINCONF 2021, pp. 1–8 (2021)
8. Di Crescenzo, G., et al.: On single-server delegation of RSA. In: Bella, G., Doinea, M., Janicke, H. (eds.) SecITC 2022. LNCS, vol. 13809, pp. 81–101. Springer, Cham (2023). https://doi.org/10.1007/978-3-031-32636-3_5
9. Di Crescenzo, G., Khodjaeva, M., Kahrobaei, D., Shpilrain, V.: Computing multiple exponentiations in discrete log and RSA groups: from batch verification to batch delegation. In: Proceedings of CNS 2017, pp. 531–539 (2017)
10. Di Crescenzo, G., Khodjaeva, M., Morales Caro, D.: Single-server batch delegation of variable-input pairings with unbounded client lifetime. In: Proceedings of ADIoT 2023, ESORICS 2023 Workshops, LNCS. Springer, to appear (2023)
11. Feigenbaum, J.: Encrypting problem instances. In: Williams, H.C. (eds.) CRYPTO 1985. LNCS, vol. 218, pp. 477–488. Springer, Heidelberg (1986). https://doi.org/10.1007/3-540-39799-X_38
12. Gennaro, R., Gentry, C., Parno, B.: Non-interactive verifiable computing: outsourcing computation to untrusted workers. In: Rabin, T. (eds.). CRYPTO 2010. LNCS, vol. 6223, pp. 465–488. Springer, Heidelberg (2010). https://doi.org/10.1007/978-3-642-14623-7_25
13. Girault, M., Lefranc, D.: Server-aided verification: theory and practice. In: Roy, B. (eds.). ASIACRYPT 2005. LNCS, vol. 3788, pp. 605–623. Springer, Heidelberg (2005). https://doi.org/10.1007/11593447_33

14. Hohenberger, S., Lysyanskaya, A.: How to securely outsource cryptographic computations. In: Kilian, J. (eds.). TCC 2005. LNCS, vol. 3378, pp. 264–282. Springer, Heidelberg (2005). https://doi.org/10.1007/978-3-540-30576-7_15

15. Kaminski, M.: A note on probabilistically verifying integer and polynomial products. J. ACM **36**(1), 142–149 (1989)

16. Karatsuba, A., Ofman, Y.: Multiplication of many-digital numbers by automatic computers. Proc. USSR Acad. Sci. **145**, 293–294 (1963). Translation in Physics-Doklady **7**, 595–596 (1963)

17. Karatsuba, A.A.: The complexity of computations. Proc. Steklov Inst. Math. **211**, 169–183 (1995). Translation from Trudy Mat. Inst. Steklova **211**, 186–202 (1995)

18. Karp, R.M., Rabin, M.O.: Efficient randomized pattern-matching algorithms. In: Rep. TR-31-81. Harvard Univ. Center for Research in Computing Technology, Cambridge (1981)

19. Khodjaeva, M., Di Crescenzo, G.: On single-server delegation without precomputation. In: Proceedings of 20th International Conference on Security and Cryptography, SECRYPT 2023, ScitePress, pp. 540–547 (2023)

20. Kalkar, O., Sertkaya, I., Tutdere, S.: On the batch outsourcing of pairing computations. Comput. J. **66**(10), 2437–2446 (2022)

21. Liu, J.K., Au, M.H., Susilo, W.: Self-generated-certificate public-key cryptography and certificateless signature/encryption scheme in the standard model. In: Proceedings of the ACM Symposium on Information, Computer and Communications Security. ACM Press (2007)

22. Matsumoto, T., Kato, K., Imai, H.: Speeding up secret computations with insecure auxiliary devices. In: Goldwasser, S. (eds.). CRYPTO 1988. LNCS, vol. 403, pp. 497–506. Springer, New York (1990). https://doi.org/10.1007/0-387-34799-2_35

23. Mefenza, T., Vergnaud, D.: Verifiable outsourcing of pairing computations. Technical report (2018)

24. Rangasamy, J., Kuppusamy, L.: Revisiting single-server algorithms for outsourcing modular exponentiation. In: Chakraborty, D., Iwata, T. (eds.). INDOCRYPT 2018. LNCS, vol. 11356, pp. 3–20. Springer, Cham (2018). https://doi.org/10.1007/978-3-030-05378-9_1

25. Rivest, R., Shamir, A., Adleman, L.: A method for obtaining digital signatures and public-key cryptosystems. Commun. ACM **21**(2), 120–126 (1978)

26. Rosser, J., Schoenfeldl, L.: Approximate formulas for some functions of prime numbers. Ill. J. Math. **6**, 64–94 (1962)

27. Shan, Z., Ren, K., Blanton, M., Wang, C.: Practical secure computation outsourcing: a survey. ACM Comput. Surv. **51**(2), 31:1–31:40 (2018)

28. Su, Q., Zhang, R., Xue, R.: Secure outsourcing algorithms for composite modular exponentiation based on single untrusted cloud. Comput. J. **63**, 1271 (2020)

29. Tong, L., Yu, J., Zhang, H.: Secure outsourcing algorithm for bilinear pairings without pre-computation. In: Proceedings of IEEE DSC (2019)

30. Tsang, P.P., Chow, S.S.M., Smith, S.W.: Batch pairing delegation. In: Miyaji, A., Kikuchi, H., Rannenberg, K. (eds.) Advances in Information and Computer Security. LNCS, vol. 4752, pp. 74–90. Springer, Heidelberg (2007). https://doi.org/10.1007/978-3-540-75651-4_6

31. Wasserman, H., Blum, M.: Software reliability via run-time result-checking. J. ACM **44**(6), 826–849 (1997). Proc. IEEE FOCS 94

32. Yao, A.: A lower bound to palindrome recognition by probabilistic turing machines. In: Tech. Rep. STAN-CS-77-647 (1977)
33. Zhou, K., Afifi, M., Ren, J.: ExpSOS: secure and verifiable outsourcing of exponentiation operations for mobile cloud computing. IEEE Trans. Inf. Forens. Secur. **12**(11), 2518–2531 (2017)

Learning Burnside Homomorphisms with Rounding and Pseudorandom Function

Dhiraj K. Pandey$^{(\boxtimes)}$ (ID) and Antonio R. Nicolosi (ID)

Stevens Institute of Technology, Hoboken, NJ 07030, USA
{dpandey1,anicolos}@stevens.edu

Abstract. The use of *pseudorandom function* (PRF) and *weak* PRF as foundational primitives is common in a variety of cryptographic applications, including encryption, authentication, and identification. In this paper, we present a new PRF construction derived from a *weak* PRF family. Specifically, we propose a derandomization technique from a post-quantum hardness assumption known as *learning Burnside homomorphisms with noise* (B_n-LHN). Through the derandomization, a new hardness assumption arises, which we refer to as *learning Burnside homomorphisms with rounding* (B_n-LHR). We establish the security of the derandomization by demonstrating that the B_n-LHR problem is at least as hard as the B_n-LHN problem.

In the work by Naor and Reingold (NR), a PRF construction is introduced based on a *weak* PRF family, utilizing a novel cryptographic primitive called a *pseudorandom synthesizer* (PRS). However, this approach necessitates an excessively large key size to design a PRF family. To overcome this issue and produce a more efficient PRF construction, we design a length-doubling *pseudorandom generator* (PRG) from a *weak* PRF. Here, the PRG is defined using the secret-key components of a PRF. Notably, in our PRF construction, the length-doubling PRG exhibits efficiency primarily when employed as an intermediate function. We also provide insight into the B_n-LHR problem by discussing the details of the concatenation operation and error distribution in the Burnside group.

Keywords: Post Quantum Cryptography · Derandomization · (Weak) Pseudorandom Function · Burnside Group · Learning Homomorphisms with Noise/Rounding

1 Introduction

Baumslag et al. introduced a group-theoretic learning problem called *learning homomorphisms with noise* (LHN) as a generalization of the *learning parity with noise* (LPN) and *learning with errors* (LWE) problems [3,5,8,25,28–32]. In this context, the *learning Burnside homomorphisms with noise* (B_n-LHN) problem focuses on recovering the homomorphism between Burnside groups based on probabilistic polynomial sample pairs of preimage and distorted image. Several aspects

© The Author(s), under exclusive license to Springer Nature Switzerland AG 2024
M. Manulis et al. (Eds.): SecITC 2023, LNCS 14534, pp. 178–196, 2024.
https://doi.org/10.1007/978-3-031-52947-4_13

related to the security and cryptography of the B_n-LHN problem, such as random-self reducibility, error distribution, and 1-bit symmetric cryptosystem, have been extensively studied [5,11]. However, the construction of a fundamental crypto-graphic primitive, namely a *pseudorandom function* (PRF) family, based on the B_n-LHN problem remains an open question and has not been developed yet.

PRF designs can be categorized into two main approaches: (1) theory-based and (2) heuristic-based. In the theory-based approach, well-established hardness assumptions are used to construct a PRF family, while the heuristic-based app-roach relies on practical heuristics to design a PRF family [4]. Heuristic-based designs are often efficient to implement and suitable for practical applications. However, their security is not rigorously justified, as demonstrated in the design of Rijndael's AES [20]. In this paper, our objective is to construct a PRF family based on a post-quantum hardness assumption, namely the decisional B_n-LHN assumption [5].

A PRF is a mathematical function that produces output that appears to be random, even though it is generated by a deterministic algorithm. The output of a PRF is dependent on the secret-key which makes it computationally infeasible for a probabilistic polynomial time ($\mathcal{PPT}$) adversary to distinguish the output oracle from the random oracle without knowing the uniformly sampled secret-key. A distribution of a PRF should be defined in such a way that it is easy to sample a function from the distribution and it is efficient to evaluate a function. Because of the adaptive power to the $\mathcal{PPT}$ adversary, the PRF is considered hard to design. For a PRF construction, this paper uses the standard definition of the PRF from [7,13,21,23,24,36].

Consider a PRF family denoted by $F = \{F_\lambda\}$, where each function $f_k : \{0,1\}^l \rightarrow \{0,1\}^l$ in F_λ is defined by a secret-key k. For a uniformly sampled secret-key k, the function f_k is a PRF, meaning that no $\mathcal{PPT}$ adversary can distinguish the polynomially many outputs $\{f_k(a_i)\}$ from truly random outputs. The adversary is allowed to make adaptive queries to the inputs $\{a_i\}$. Similarly, in a weak PRF family denoted by $Z = \{Z_\lambda\}$, a randomly selected function $\zeta_k : \{0,1\}^l \rightarrow \{0,1\}^l$ from Z_λ exhibits the property that it is computationally infeasible for any $\mathcal{PPT}$ adversary to distinguish polynomially many samples $\{a_i, \zeta_k(a_i)\}$ from samples drawn from a truly random source. Here, a_i is a random string selected from $\{0,1\}^l$, and the adversary does not possess adaptive query power over the inputs $\{a_i\}$ [26].

The concept of a PRF construction was initially explored in a seminal paper by Goldreich, Goldwasser, and Micali (GGM) [13]. GGM introduced the use of a length-doubling *pseudorandom generator* (PRG) as an intermediate component in constructing a PRF. A deterministic function $G : \{0,1\}^l \rightarrow \{0,1\}^{l'}$, with $l' > l$, is considered a PRG if no efficient adversary can distinguish the polynomial outputs $\{G(s_i)\}$ from truly random outputs [6,12,18].

The PRF construction proposed by GGM is defined as follows: Let $G : \{0,1\}^l \rightarrow \{0,1\}^{l'}$ be a length-doubling PRG, where $l' = 2l$. The output $G(s_i)$ is divided into two equal halves, denoted as $G^{(0)}(s_i)$ and $G^{(1)}(s_i)$, representing the left and right halves, respectively. For a given secret-key k, the function f_k in the PRF family, when applied to an input $x = x_1 \ldots x_m$, is defined as

$$f_k(x_1 \ldots x_m) = G^{(x_m)}(\ldots(G^{(x_2)}(G^{(x_1)}(k)))\ldots). \tag{1}$$

Roughly after a decade, Naor and Reingold (NR) introduced a new primitive, called a *pseudorandom synthesizer* (PRS), and designed a PRF family [26,27]. In their paper, they also presented a construction for PRS using a weak PRF family. Furthermore, in their subsequent work [27], NR proposed a constant-depth PRF construction using a set of intermediate PRGs. The construction of these intermediate PRGs relies on the decisional Diffie-Hellman (DDH) assumption, where the function is defined based on the secret-key components of a PRF. It is important to note that the security of these intermediate PRGs is inherently tied to the security of the DDH assumption.

A PRS $S : \{0,1\}^l \times \{0,1\}^l \to \{0,1\}^l$ is defined as follows: Let $C_S(U,V)$ be the t^2 sequential l-bits from $S(u_i,v_j)$ for $1 \le i,j \le t$, where $U = \{u_1,\ldots,u_t\}$ and $V = \{v_1,\ldots,v_t\}$ are the set of l-bit strings. Given the sets U and V with uniform entries, a function S is a PRS if no $\mathcal{PPT}$ adversary can distinguish the outputs $C_S(U,V)$ from the random outputs. NR defined PRS-based PRF construction as follows: Let $\{S_{k_1},\ldots,S_{k_{\log m}}\}$ be a set of functions in a PRS family. A function $f_{\tilde{k}}$ in a PRF family for an input $x = x_1 \ldots x_m$ is defined as

$$f_{\tilde{k}}(x_1 \ldots x_m) = SQ_{S_{k_{\log m}}}(\ldots(SQ_{S_{k_2}}(SQ_{S_{k_1}}(a_{1,x_1},\ldots,a_{m,x_m})))\ldots). \tag{2}$$

The secret-key for the function $f_{\tilde{k}}$ is $\tilde{k} = \langle k,a \rangle$, where $k = \langle k_1,\ldots,k_{\log m} \rangle$ and $a = \langle a_{1,0},a_{1,1},\ldots,a_{m,0},a_{m,1} \rangle$. The squeeze function $SQ_{S_k}(u_1,\ldots,u_m)$ is defined as $\{u'_1,\ldots,u'_{\lceil \frac{m}{2} \rceil}\}$ where $u'_i = S_k(u_{2i-1},u_{2i})$ for $1 \le i \le \lfloor \frac{m}{2} \rfloor$. If m is odd, then $u'_{\lceil \frac{m}{2} \rceil} = u_m$. The PRF construction in GGM utilizes a sequential approach based on *pseudorandom generators* (PRGs). It requires m invocations of the PRG to compute the output $f_k(x_1 \ldots x_m)$ as shown in Eq. (1). On the other hand, NR employs a parallel approach for the PRF construction using a PRS family, which is inherently parallel in nature. This parallel construction involves $\log m$ layers for the independent computations, as shown in Eq. (2). At each layer i, where $1 \le i \le \log m$, there are $\frac{m}{2^i}$ independent PRS invocations, resulting in a total of m PRS invocations to compute the output $f_{\tilde{k}}(x_1 \ldots x_m)$. The key advantage of NR's PRS-based PRF construction lies in its ability to leverage parallel computation at each layer. Conversely, the main advantage of GGM's PRG-based PRF construction is the utilization of a smaller key size.

Contribution. In this paper, we present a construction of a PRF from a weak PRF family using a design proposed by NR [26]. However, we observe a significant limitation in this construction, which is its large secret-key size. This limitation becomes even more critical when using a weak PRF from the B_n-LHR assumption. Moreover, we propose an alternative construction for a PRF utilizing a weak PRF family, where the secret-key size is $p+pq$, where p denotes the entropy of a word in a Burnside group B_n and q denotes the entropy of a homomorphism in a set of homomorphisms from B_n to B_r. The proposed PRF construction is developed in two steps, making use of the decisional B_n-LHN assumption, which is a post-quantum hardness assumption.

The security of the B_n-LHN problem hinges on the secrecy of the homomorphisms between Burnside groups and the presence of random errors within the problem formulation. In the first step, we introduce a derandomization process for the B_n-LHN problem, where the random errors are replaced by a deterministic rounding operation. This process establishes a novel hardness assumption termed as *learning Burnside homomorphisms with rounding* (B_n-LHR). Furthermore, we establish the equivalence in security between the B_n-LHR problem and the well-established B_n-LHN problem. Consequently, the resulting deterministic B_n-LHR assumption provides a weak PRF family.

In the second step, we proceed to design a PRF from the aforementioned weak PRF family. Specifically, we define a PRF $f_{\tilde{k}} : \{0,1\}^m \to \{0,1\}^p$, for an input $x = x_1 \ldots x_m$ and secret-key $\tilde{k} = \langle k, a_0 \rangle$, as follows:

$$f_{\tilde{k}}(x_1 \ldots x_m) = G_{\zeta_k(a_m)}^{(x_m)}(\ldots (G_{\zeta_k(a_2)}^{(x_2)}(G_{\zeta_k(a_1)}^{(x_1)}(a_0)))\ldots). \tag{3}$$

Above, the secret-key component k in a secret-key $\tilde{k} = \langle k, a_0 \rangle$ defines a weak PRF $\zeta_k : \{0,1\}^p \to \{0,1\}^p$ and a_0 is an initial secret for the first function $G_{\zeta_k(a_1)}$. A set $\{a_1, \ldots, a_m\}$ is public, where a_i is sampled uniformly from the Burnside group B_n. The function $G_{\zeta_k(a_j)} : \{0,1\}^p \to \{0,1\}^{2p}$ is defined in Construction 3. Finally, we establish the security of a PRF construction by demonstrating that a length-doubling function $G_{\zeta_k(a_i)}$ acts as a PRG with the Theorem 3.

Outline. Section 2 provides an introduction to the fundamental concepts of a relatively free group, specifically focusing on a Burnside group. It further delves into the elucidation of error distribution, a crucial element for establishing a post-quantum hardness assumption known as B_n-LHN.

In Sect. 3, a derandomization technique for the B_n-LHN assumption is presented. The chapter explores the establishment of the hardness equivalence between two key assumptions: B_n-LHN and B_n-LHR. Additionally, the chapter presents a construction that defines a length-preserving weak *pseudorandom function* (PRF) based on the B_n-LHR assumption.

Section 4 explores two distinct approaches to constructing a *pseudorandom function* (PRF) from a weak PRF family. Within this context, the chapter introduces two fundamental primitives: *pseudorandom synthesizer* (PRS) and *pseudorandom generator* (PRG). Notably, the PRG-based design offers a significant reduction in the secret-key size compared to alternative methods.

2 Background

2.1 Notation

Throughout our discussions, λ denotes the security parameter and $\mathbb{N}$ denotes the set of natural numbers. We utilize log to refer to the binary logarithm. For a set S, $a \xleftarrow{\$} S$ denotes an element a sampled uniformly from S. Similarly, for a distribution D over a set S, $a \xleftarrow{D} S$ represents an element a in a set S sampled according to a distribution D. A bit-string $\langle w_1, \ldots, w_m \rangle$ denotes the concatenation of strings $w_1, \ldots, w_m$ that may be of different lengths. However, in an algebraic context, $G = \langle X \rangle$ denotes a (relatively) free group G generated by a generating set X. For some polynomial function $poly()$, $\{a_i\}$ denotes a set $\{a_1, \ldots, a_{poly(\lambda)}\}$, and a_i denotes an ith element in a set $\{a_i\}$ for $1 \leq i \leq poly(\lambda)$.

2.2 Free Group

Let $X = \{x_1, \ldots, x_n\}$ denote an arbitrary set of symbols, where $n \in \mathbb{N}$. Within X, each element x and its inverse x^{-1} (or equivalently, x^2) are referred to as literals. A word w represents a finite sequence of literals from X, as defined in Eq. (4). A word w is considered reduced if all instances of sub-words $x\,x^{-1}$ or $x^{-1}\,x$ are eliminated. The length of a reduced word w is determined by the number of positions occupied by literals and is denoted as $|w|$. The empty word is denoted as 1, and its length is represented as $|1| = 0$.

$$w = x_{i_1}^{\alpha_1} \ldots x_{i_k}^{\alpha_k}, \qquad x_{i_j} \in X, \alpha_j \in \{1, 2\}, k \in \mathbb{N}. \tag{4}$$

A group G is called a free group with a generating set X, denoted by $G = \langle X \rangle$, if every nontrivial element in G is a reduced word in X. In this definition, X is called a free basis of G, and G is said to be a free group on X [15,17,33]. For a free group $G = \langle X \rangle$, following universal property holds: for every mapping $\phi : X \to H$, for some group H, there exist a unique homomorphism $\varphi : G \to H$, so the following diagram commutes (Fig. 1).

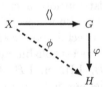

Fig. 1. Universal property of a free group $G = \langle X \rangle$.

2.3 Relatively Free Group: Burnside Groups

If N is a normal subgroup of a free group G, then the factor group G/N is called relatively free if N is fully invariant. That is, $\phi(N) \subseteq N$ for any endomorphism ϕ of G. A Burnside group B_n is a (relatively) free group with a generating set $X = \{x_1, \ldots, x_n\}$ where the order of all the words in B_n is 3 [15–17,19]. The concatenation operation (.) between words $w_1, w_2 \in B_n$ is to write w_1 and w_2 side by side and generate the reduced word in B_n. It is denoted by $w = w_1.w_2$

for any $w_1, w_2 \in B_n$. Since the order of B_n is 3, $w.w.w = 1$ for all $w \in B_n$. The *empty word* is the identity in B_n and represented by 1. Each word in $B_n = \langle X \rangle$ can also be represented in normal form as in Eq. (5). More details are explained in [1,2,9,10,16,17,34]. In the normal representation of a word w in B_n, α_i, $\beta_{i,j}$, $\gamma_{i,j,k}$ are the exponents of generators (x_i), 2-commutators ($[x_i, x_j]$), and 3-commutators ($([x_i, x_j, x_k])$) respectively. The order of a group B_n is $|B_n| = 3^{\tilde{n}}$ where $\tilde{n} = n + \binom{n}{2} + \binom{n}{3}$.

$$w = \prod_{1 \le i \le n} x_i^{\alpha_i} \prod_{1 \le i < j \le n} [x_i, x_j]^{\beta_{i,j}} \prod_{1 \le i < j < k \le n} [x_i, x_j, x_k]^{\gamma_{i,j,k}}. \tag{5}$$

The concatenation operation is the most primitive operation in B_n. Let $\alpha_i^{(1)}$, $\beta_{i,j}^{(1)}$, and $\gamma_{i,j,k}^{(1)}$ are the exponents for $w_1 \in B_n$. Similarly, let $\alpha_i^{(2)}$, $\beta_{i,j}^{(2)}$, and $\gamma_{i,j,k}^{(2)}$ are the exponents for $w_2 \in B_n$. Equation (6) shows the efficient concatenation $w = w_1.w_2$, where α_i, $\beta_{i,j}$, and $\gamma_{i,j,k}$ are the exponents in w for $1 \le i < j < k \le n$. Note: $+_3$ and $\times_3$ are addition and multiplication modulo 3 operations respectively.

$$\alpha_i \leftarrow \alpha_i^{(1)} +_3 \alpha_i^{(2)},$$
$$\beta_{i,j} \leftarrow \beta_{i,j}^{(1)} +_3 \beta_{i,j}^{(2)} +_3 (\alpha_j^{(1)} \times_3 \alpha_i^{(2)} \times_3 2),$$
$$\gamma_{i,j,k} \leftarrow \gamma_{i,j,k}^{(1)} +_3 \gamma_{i,j,k}^{(2)} +_3 (\beta_{i,j}^{(1)} \times_3 \alpha_k^{(2)})$$
$$+_3 (\beta_{j,k}^{(1)} \times_3 \alpha_i^{(2)})$$
$$+_3 (\beta_{i,k}^{(1)} \times_3 \alpha_j^{(2)} \times_3 2)$$
$$+_3 (\alpha_k^{(1)} \times_3 \alpha_i^{(2)} \times_3 \alpha_j^{(2)})$$
$$+_3 (\alpha_j^{(1)} \times_3 \alpha_i^{(2)} \times_3 \alpha_k^{(2)} \times_3 2)$$
$$+_3 (\alpha_j^{(1)} \times_3 \alpha_k^{(1)} \times_3 \alpha_i^{(2)} \times_3 2). \tag{6}$$

The abelianization operation collects all the generators and corresponding exponents in $w \in B_n$ as in Eq. (7).

$$\rho(w) = \prod_{1 \le i \le n} x_i^{\alpha_i}. \tag{7}$$

Finitely generated Burnside groups can also be construed as geometric entities through the utilization of Cayley graphs. The Cayley graph of a Burnside group B_n, defined with respect to a generator set $X = \{x_1, \ldots, x_n\}$, characterizes group words as vertices. An edge connects two vertices if and only if multiplication by a generator (or its inverse) transforms one into the other. The Cayley distance between two words is established as the shortest path length between their corresponding vertices within the Cayley graph. The Cayley norm of a word is thus defined as its distance from the identity word within the Cayley graph. Based on the implementation observations, Table 1 displays the frequency distribution at each Cayley norm layer within a Cayley graph of a Burnside group B_r for the specific case of $r = 4$.

Table 1. A frequency of words in B_r, where $r = 4$.

Cayley norm (l)	#Words at Cayley norm layer l ($|B_r^l|$)
$l = 0$	1
$l = 1$	8
$l = 2$	48
$l = 3$	264
$l = 4$	1,356
$l = 5$	6,624
$l = 6$	29,008
$l = 7$	124,416
$l = 8$	492,012
$l = 9$	1,472,032
$l = 10$	2,122,312
$l = 11$	520,560
$l = 12$	13,896
$l = 13$	384
$l = 14$	48
$|B_r| = \sum\limits_{l=0}^{14} |B_r^l|$	4,782,969

2.4   Error Distribution

As emphasized in Sect. 2.5, errors significantly contribute to the hardness of the B_n-LHN problem. In the context of the Burnside group B_r ($n \gg r \in \mathbb{N}$), the error distribution Ψ is generated by concatenating generators in random order, accompanied by random exponents. The probability mass function of errors $e \in B_r$ is precisely defined as follows [5]:

$$\forall e \in B_r, \quad \Pr_{e \xleftarrow{\Psi} E} [e] = \Pr_{\mathbf{v} \xleftarrow{\$} \mathbb{F}_3^r, \sigma \xleftarrow{\$} S_r} \left[e = \prod x_{\sigma_i}^{v_i} \right]. \tag{8}$$

In Eq. (8), v_i is the ith component of a vector $\mathbf{v} = (v_1, \ldots, v_r)$ sampled uniformly from a field $\mathbb{F}_3^r$. S_r is the set of all permutations of a set $\{1, \ldots, r\}$. The probability mass function in Eq. (8) generates $r! \times 3^r$ possible errors in B_r.

Multiset of Errors, Errors, and Abelianized Errors. Let $M = \cup M_l$, $0 \leq l \leq r$, represents a multiset of errors as defined in Eq. (8). M_l is a collection of errors with Cayley norm l. Let $E = \bigcup E_l$, where E_l is the corresponding underlying set of multiset M_l. The underlying function $f : M \to E$ is defined by simplifying an error in M by using the multiple concatenation operations in the Burnside group B_r. Let A be the set of the abelianized errors and $\rho : E \to A$ be the corresponding abelianization as defined in Eq. (7). The order of the multiset

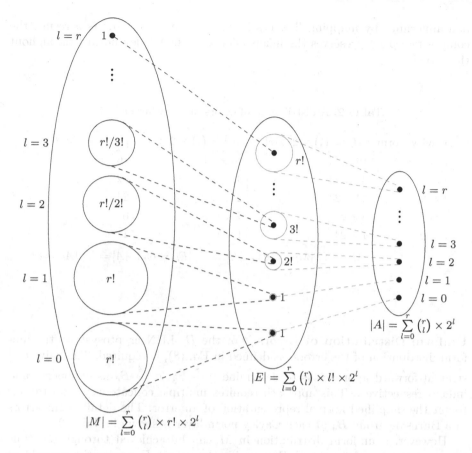

Fig. 2. Function $f : M \to E$ with $r!/l!$ pre-images of an error. Note: l is a Cayley norm of an error in B_r.

M is $r! \times 3^r$. The order of the set A is 3^r. Similarly, the order of the subsets M_l, E_l, and A_l is $r! \times 2^l \times \binom{r}{l}$, $l! \times 2^l \times \binom{r}{l}$, and $2^l \times \binom{r}{l}$ respectively.

Since the function f maps an error from M_l to E_l, M_l has exactly $r!/l!$ preimages of an error in E_l. Equivalently, exactly $r!/l!$ errors in M_l are the different representations for an error in E_l as shown in Fig. 2. If we consider $r!/l!$ (same) errors in M_l as a cluster, then there are $l! \times 2^l \times \binom{r}{l}$ such clusters in M_l.

Lemma 1. *The distribution of abelianized errors in $A \subset B_r$ is uniform if and only if the distribution of the errors in $M \subset B_r$ is uniform.*

Proof. Let $f : M \to E$ and $\rho : E \to A$ denote the functions representing simplification and abelianization, respectively. The proof is straightforward due to the fact that the composition of f and ρ ($\rho \circ f$) remains unaffected by the Cayley norm l, where $0 \le l \le r$. Specifically, the function f maps exactly $r!/l!$ errors from M_l to an error in E_l, while the function ρ compensates for non-uniformity by mapping $l!$ errors in E_l to an error in A_l. As a result, the composition $\rho \circ f$ preserves the independence of the Cayley norm l throughout the process.

Table 2. A distribution of errors in B_r, where $r = 4$.

Cayley Norm	$\|M_l\| = \binom{r}{l} \times 2^l \times r!$	$\|E_l\| = \binom{r}{l} \times 2^l \times l!$	$\|A_l\| = \binom{r}{l} \times 2^l$
$l = 4 (= r)$	16×24	16×24	16
$l = 3$	32×24	32×6	32
$l = 2$	24×24	24×2	24
$l = 1$	8×24	8×1	8
$l = 0$	1×24	1×1	1
	$\|M\| = \sum_{l=0}^{r} \|M_l\| = 1944$	$\|E\| = \sum_{l=0}^{r} \|E_l\| = 633$	$\|A\| = \sum_{l=0}^{r} \|A_l\| = 81$

Uniform Distribution of Errors. For the B_n-LHN cryptosystem, the uniform distribution of the errors, as defined in Eq. (8), is required. The naive and straight-forward approach is to determine $v \xleftarrow{\$} \mathbb{F}_3^r$, $\sigma \xleftarrow{\$} S_r$ as exponents and indices respectively. This approach requires multiple concatenation operations to get the simplified normal representation of an error. The detail of the errors in a Burnside group B_4 at each Cayley norm layer is shown in Table 2.

However, a uniform distribution in M can be achieved through one-time pre-computation of the set E. We provide the subset E_l appropriate weight so that the induced distribution in M is uniform, which is the requirement of the B_n-LHN cryptosystem. For the uniform distribution of errors in the set A, the probability of an error should be $1/3^r$. Since exactly $l!$ preimages in E_l maps to an error in A_l via function ρ, probability given to the set of errors in E_l should be $(2^l \times \binom{r}{l})/3^r$. Since the distribution in M and A are equivalent, with distribution weight to the subset E_l as $(2^l \times \binom{r}{l})/3^r$, we can achieve uniform distribution of M, that is, the distribution Ψ.

2.5   Learning Burnside Homomorphism with Noise (B_n-LHN)

The universal property of the free groups can be extended to the relatively free groups, the Burnside groups B_n and B_r with $n \gg r \in \mathbb{N}$. There exists a homomorphism $\varphi : B_n \rightarrow B_r$ for any random mapping from a generating set $X \subseteq B_n$ to a Burnside group B_r. Let Φ_n be the set of homomorphisms from B_n to B_r. For each generator in the generating set X, there are $\|B_r\| = 3^{\tilde{r}}$ possible mappings where $\tilde{r} = r + \binom{r}{2} + \binom{r}{3}$. The order of a set of all homomorphisms is $\|\Phi_n\| = \|B_r\|^n$. A few notations used in the subsequent discussions are as follows:

- Recall that the distribution Ψ represents the error distribution in the set of errors $E \subset B_r$ (Details are in Sect. 2.4).
- Let $\varphi \in \Phi_n$ be a homomorphism. The distribution A_φ^Ψ is defined as a distribution with outputs $\{a_i, w_i\}$, where a_i is randomly chosen from B_n and $w_i = \varphi(a_i).e_i$ with $e_i \xleftarrow{\Psi} E$. On the other hand, R_φ^Ψ is defined as a corresponding random distribution with outputs $\{a_i, w_i\}$, where both a_i and w_i are chosen uniformly from B_n and B_r respectively.
- $\mathcal{O}^{A_\varphi^\Psi}$ and $\mathcal{O}^{R_\varphi^\Psi}$ are the oracles with distributions A_φ^Ψ and R_φ^Ψ respectively.

The decisional B_n-LHN assumption is formally stated as follows:

Definition 1 (Decisional B_n-LHN Assumption). *For any probabilistic polynomial-time (PPT) adversary $\mathcal{A}$, there exists a negligible function negl(.) such that:*

$$\left| \Pr_{\varphi \xleftarrow{\$} \Phi_n} \left[\mathcal{A}^{\mathcal{O}^{A_\varphi^\Psi}}(1^\lambda) = 1 \right] - \Pr \left[\mathcal{A}^{\mathcal{O}^{R_\varphi^\Psi}}(1^\lambda) = 1 \right] \right| \leq negl(\lambda). \tag{9}$$

The decisional B_n-LHN problem is to distinguish the oracles $\mathcal{O}^{A_\varphi^\Psi}$ and $\mathcal{O}^{R_\varphi^\Psi}$ with a non-negligible advantage from given polynomial samples. By setting the value of n, a level of security of $n \log(|B_r|)$ bits can be achieved from the decisional B_n-LHN problem.

2.6 Minicrypt Using [SPSDOLLAR1DOLLARSPS]-LHN Assumption

A symmetric cryptosystem based on the hardness of decisional B_n-LHN problem is defined as follows [5]:

KeyGen(1^λ) - The secret-key is $\varphi \xleftarrow{\$} \Phi_n$.

Encryption - Let τ be a (public) word in B_r with Cayley norm greater than or equal to $2r$. To encrypt a message bit i, ciphertext $\langle a, w \rangle$ is generated where $a \xleftarrow{\$} B_n$ and $w = \varphi(a).e.\tau^i$ with the error sampled from a set of errors E according to the distribution Ψ.

Decryption - To decrypt a ciphertext $\langle a, w \rangle$, we compute $w' = \varphi(a)^{-1}.w$. The plaintext bit i is 0 if the Cayley norm of a word w' is less than or equal to r. Otherwise, the plaintext bit i is 1.

3 Derandomization and Weak PRF

In 1984, Goldreich, Goldwasser, and Micali (GGM) introduced the pioneering definition of a *pseudorandom function* (PRF) family and devised its construction using a length-doubling *pseudorandom generator* (PRG) [13]. A decade later, Naor and Reingold (NR) proposed an alternative primitive called a *pseudorandom synthesizer* (PRS) for constructing a PRF [26,27]. The GGM construction offers the advantage of a shorter key size, while the NR construction provides a PRF family that exhibits lower depth and allows for parallel computations.

The following section commences by introducing a derandomization technique for the B_n-LHN assumption. This technique leads to the formulation of a novel hardness assumption, termed learning Burnside homomorphisms with rounding (B_n-LHR). We subsequently delve into the exploration of the hardness equivalence between these two assumptions. Finally, we present a construction of a length-preserving weak PRF using the B_n-LHR assumption. Throughout the subsequent discussions, the following notations will be utilized:

- Recall, E is the set of errors in the Burnside group B_r.
- The definitions of the error sphere operation ($\mathcal{E}$) and core operation ($\mathcal{C}$) are given in Definitions 2 and 3, respectively.
- $B_r^{(L)}$ and $B_r^{(R)}$ are two disjoint subsets (equal in size) of a Burnside group B_r such that $|\mathcal{C}(B_r^{(L)})| = |\mathcal{C}(B_r^{(R)})|$ and $|B_r| = |B_r^{(L)}| + |B_r^{(R)}|$. Note: If the cardinality of the word set B_r is an odd number, we can selectively eliminate a randomly chosen word from B_r and subsequently partition the resultant set into the corresponding disjoint subsets, denoted as $B_r^{(L)}$ and $B_r^{(R)}$.
- For a homomorphism $\varphi \in \Phi_n$, $A_\varphi^{[]}$ represents a distribution with outputs $\{a_i, v_i\}$, where $a_i \xleftarrow{\$} B_n$ and $v_i = \lfloor \varphi(a_i) \rceil$. The rounding operator, $\lfloor \rceil$, is defined in Definition 4. As well as, $R_\varphi^{[]}$ represents a random distribution with outputs $\{a_i, v_i\}$ where $a_i \xleftarrow{\$} B_n$ and $v_i \xleftarrow{\$} \{0, 1\}$.
- $\mathcal{O}^{R_\varphi^{[]}}$ and $\mathcal{O}^{R_\varphi^{[]}}$ are the corresponding oracles with distributions $A_\varphi^{[]}$ and $R_\varphi^{[]}$ respectively.

Definition 2 (Error Sphere, $\mathcal{E}$). *The error sphere of a word w in a Burnside group B_r with a set of errors E, denoted by $\mathcal{E}(w)$, is the set of words $w.e$ for all $e \in E$. Similarly, the error sphere of a subset S in B_r is defined as:*

$$\mathcal{E}(S) = \bigcup_{w \in S} \mathcal{E}(w). \tag{10}$$

Definition 3 (Core, $\mathcal{C}$). *The core of a subset S in a Burnside group B_r with a set of errors E, denoted by $\mathcal{C}(S)$, is a subset of S with maximum size and is defined as:*

$$\mathcal{C}(S) = \{max \ S_c \mid \mathcal{E}(S_c) \subseteq S\}. \tag{11}$$

3.1 Learning Burnside Homomorphism with Rounding (B_n-LHR) Problem

The presence of random errors in the B_n-LHN problem adds an additional layer of complexity beyond the challenge of finding the pre-image of the one-way function. We introduce a method to make the B_n-LHN problem significantly harder by excluding the random errors present in the original problem. This process, known as *derandomization*, leads to an equivalent problem called B_n-LHR. The new problem is proven to be at least as hard as B_n-LHN, as discussed in Theorem 1. The decisional B_n-LHR assumption is defined in Definition 5. Similarly, the B_n-LHR problem is to distinguish the oracles $\mathcal{O}^{A_\varphi^{\lfloor\rceil}}$ over $\mathcal{O}^{R_\varphi^{\lfloor\rceil}}$ with a non-negligible advantage from given polynomial samples.

Definition 4 (Rounding Operator, $\lfloor\rceil$). *For a word $a \in B_n$ and a homomorphism $\varphi \in \Phi_n$, the rounding operator ($\lfloor\rceil$) is defined as:*

$$\lfloor\varphi(a)\rceil = \begin{cases} 0, & \text{if } \varphi(a) \in B_r^{(L)}, \\ 1, & \text{otherwise.} \end{cases} \tag{12}$$

Definition 5 (Decisional B_n-LHR Assumption). *For any probabilistic polynomial-time (PPT) adversary $\mathcal{A}$, there exists a negligible function negl(.) such that:*

$$\left| \Pr_{\varphi \xleftarrow{\$} \Phi_n} \left[\mathcal{A}^{\mathcal{O}^{A_\varphi^{\lfloor\rceil}}}(1^\lambda) = 1 \right] - \Pr\left[\mathcal{A}^{\mathcal{O}^{R_\varphi^{\lfloor\rceil}}}(1^\lambda) = 1 \right] \right| \leq negl(\lambda). \tag{13}$$

Theorem 1. *The decisional B_n-LHR assumption is as hard as the decisional B_n-LHN assumption.*

Proof. Assume, for the sake of contradiction, that there exists a PPT distinguisher $\mathcal{A}$ for the challenge oracles $\mathcal{O}^{A_\varphi^{\lfloor\rceil}}$ and $\mathcal{O}^{R_\varphi^{\lfloor\rceil}}$ with an advantage $\epsilon(\lambda)$. We will use $\mathcal{A}$ to construct a PPT distinguisher $\mathcal{B}$ for the challenge oracles $\mathcal{O}^{A_\varphi^\psi}$ and $\mathcal{O}^{R_\varphi^\psi}$.

We begin by dividing B_r into subsets $B_r^{(L)}$ and $B_r^{(R)}$, ensuring that the corresponding cores, $\mathcal{C}(B_r^{(L)})$ and $\mathcal{C}(B_r^{(R)})$, are equal. Next, let $\langle a_i, w_i \rangle$ be an input sample obtained from the challenge oracle (which can be either $\mathcal{O}^{A_\varphi^\psi}$ or $\mathcal{O}^{R_\varphi^\psi}$) to the adversary $\mathcal{B}$ for unknown $\varphi \xleftarrow{\$} \Phi_n$. The adversary $\mathcal{B}$ proceeds as follows:

- The adversary $\mathcal{B}$ rejects an input $\langle a_i, w_i \rangle$ if a word w_i is not from either $\mathcal{C}(B_r^{(L)})$ or $\mathcal{C}(B_r^{(R)})$, and requests the next sample $\langle a_{i+1}, w_{i+1} \rangle$ from the challenge oracle.
- If a word w_i in the input $\langle a_i, w_i \rangle$ belongs to $\mathcal{C}(B_r^{(L)})$, then the adversary $\mathcal{B}$ sends the pair $\langle a_i, 0 \rangle$ to the distinguisher $\mathcal{A}$.
- Similarly, for an input sample $\langle a_i, w_i \rangle$ where the word w_i is in $\mathcal{C}(B_r^{(R)})$, the adversary $\mathcal{B}$ forwards $\langle a_i, 1 \rangle$ to the adversary $\mathcal{A}$.

With polynomial input samples $\{a_i, v_i\}$ where the bit $v_i \in \{0, 1\}$, if the adversary $\mathcal{A}$ distinguishes the oracles $\mathcal{O}^{A_\varphi^{\lfloor\rceil}}$ and $\mathcal{O}^{R_\varphi^{\lfloor\rceil}}$ with advantage $\epsilon(\lambda)$ for unknown $\varphi \xleftarrow{\$} \Phi_n$, the adversary $\mathcal{B}$ distinguishes the challenge oracles $\mathcal{O}^{A_\varphi^\psi}$ and $\mathcal{O}^{R_\varphi^\psi}$ with advantage $\frac{2\sigma\epsilon(\lambda)}{|B_r|}$ where $\sigma = |\mathcal{C}(B_r^{(L)})| = |\mathcal{C}(B_r^{(R)})|$. This is based on the following observation.

For the adversary $\mathcal{B}$ with an input sample $\langle a_i, w_i \rangle$, if the challenge oracle is $\mathcal{O}^{A_\varphi^\psi}$ with $w_i = \varphi(a_i).e_i$, then $\lfloor\varphi(a_i)\rceil$ will always be 0 when w_i belongs to the core $\mathcal{C}(B_r^{(L)})$. Likewise, when the adversary $\mathcal{B}$ is provided with an input $\langle a_i, w_i \rangle$ from the challenge oracle $\mathcal{O}^{A_\varphi^\psi}$ where $w_i = \varphi(a_i).e_i$, it can be observed that $\lfloor \varphi(a_i) \rceil$ will invariably be 1 if w_i belongs to the core $\mathcal{C}(B_r^{(R)})$.

3.2 Weak PRF Construction

A weak PRF is a more constrained variant of a PRF, where the challenge oracle determines the random input values for the function as in Definition 6. In this case, the adversary lacks the adaptive capability to make queries based on the previous outputs of the function. This section initially presents the construction of a length-preserving weak PRF from a weak PRF family. Subsequently, in the following section, we explore two methods for building a PRF using a length-preserving weak PRF family. Formally, a weak PRF is defined as:

Definition 6 (Weak PRF). *Let $F = \{F_\lambda\}$ be a family of functions. For any $\mathcal{PPT}$ adversary $\mathcal{A}$, a random function $f_k : \{0,1\}^p \to \{0,1\}^q$ in F_λ is a weak PRF if the polynomial outputs $\{a_i, f_k(a_i)\}$ is computationally indistinguishable to the outputs $\{a_i, v_i\}$, where a_i and v_i are independent and sampled uniformly from $\{0,1\}^p$ and $\{0,1\}^q$ respectively.*

The decisional B_n-LHR assumption itself provides a weak PRF family where a homomorphism $\varphi \in \Phi_n$ and a rounding operator $\lfloor\rceil$ (see Definition 4) together work as a weak PRF. We construct a length-preserving weak PRF from B_n-LHR assumption as shown in Construction 1.

Construction 1 (Length-Preserving Weak PRF, ζ). *Let p be the entropy of a word in the Burnside groups B_n. A function $\zeta_k : \{0,1\}^p \to \{0,1\}^p$, with secret-key $k = \langle \varphi_1, \ldots, \varphi_p \rangle$ and input $a_i \in B_n$, is defined as:*

$$\zeta_k(a_i) = \langle \lfloor \varphi_1(a_i) \rceil, \ldots, \lfloor \varphi_p(a_i) \rceil \rangle. \tag{14}$$

Here, the secret-key components φ_i are independent and sampled uniformly from Φ_n.

We claim that the function ζ_k with a secret-key $k = \langle \varphi_1, \ldots, \varphi_p \rangle$ uniformly sampled from Φ_n^p as described in Construction 1 serves as a weak PRF. The formal proof of this claim is presented in Theorem 2 using a hybrid argument similar to the approach described in [26,27,35].

Theorem 2. *If the B_n-LHR assumption holds, it follows that the function ζ_k, where the secret-key k is uniformly sampled (as described in Construction 1), qualifies as a weak PRF.*

Proof. Let ζ_k be a function with uniformly sampled secret-key k as described in Construction 1. We consider two distributions: A_{ζ_k} and R_{ζ_k}, with output samples $\{a_i, \zeta_k(a_i)\}$ and $\{a_i, a_i'\}$, respectively, where a_i and a_i' are randomly chosen from B_n. We assume the existence of a $\mathcal{PPT}$ adversary $\mathcal{A}$ that can distinguish between the challenge oracles $\mathcal{O}^{A_{\zeta_k}}$ and $\mathcal{O}^{R_{\zeta_k}}$ with a non-negligible advantage $\epsilon(\lambda)$, for some secret-key k uniformly sampled from Φ_n^p as described in Construction 1.

By utilizing the distinguisher $\mathcal{A}$, we can construct a $\mathcal{PPT}$ distinguisher $\mathcal{B}$ for the challenge oracles $\mathcal{O}^{A_\varphi^{[]}}$ and $\mathcal{O}^{R_\varphi^{[]}}$ as follows: Recall that the challenge oracles $\mathcal{O}^{A_\varphi^{[]}}$ and $\mathcal{O}^{R_\varphi^{[]}}$ challenges the adversary $\mathcal{B}$ with polynomially many samples, either $\{a_i, \lfloor \varphi(a_i) \rceil\}$ or $\{a_i, v_i\}$ respectively, where $a_i \xleftarrow{\$} B_n$, $v_i \xleftarrow{\$} \{0,1\}$, and $\varphi \xleftarrow{\$} \Phi_n$.

We employ a hybrid argument to construct a distinguisher $\mathcal{B}$ from a distinguisher $\mathcal{A}$. For $0 \leq J \leq p$, let $\mathcal{H}^{(J)}$ denote a hybrid that outputs $\{a_i, r_i\}$, where $a_i \xleftarrow{\$} B_n$ and $r_i = \langle r_{i,1}, \ldots, r_{i,J}, \lfloor \varphi_{J+1}(a_i) \rceil, \ldots, \lfloor \varphi_p(a_i) \rceil \rangle$. Here, r_{ij} is a random bit from $\{0,1\}$ for $1 \leq j \leq J$, and φ_t is uniformly sampled for all $(J+1) \leq t \leq p$. It is evident that the hybrid $\mathcal{H}^{(0)}$ corresponds to the oracle $\mathcal{O}^{A_{\zeta_k}}$, while the hybrid $\mathcal{H}^{(p)}$ corresponds to $\mathcal{O}^{R_{\zeta_k}}$. With hybrid argument, an adversary $\mathcal{A}$ can distinguish the hybrids $\mathcal{H}^{(J)}/\mathcal{H}^{(J+1)}$ for $0 \leq J < p$ with non-negligible advantage $\frac{\epsilon(\lambda)}{p}$.

Let the distinguisher $\mathcal{B}$ receives input sample $\langle a_i, v_i \rangle$ from either of its challenge oracles $\mathcal{O}^{A_\varphi^{[]}}$ or $\mathcal{O}^{R_\varphi^{[]}}$. For a randomly selected $0 \leq J < p$ and samples $\langle a_i, v_i \rangle$, a distinguisher $\mathcal{B}$ chooses a set $\{\varphi_{J+2}, \ldots, \varphi_p\}$, where each φ_j is uniformly sampled from Φ_n for $(J+2) \leq j \leq p$. For input sample $\langle a_i, v_i \rangle$, generated either by oracles $\mathcal{O}^{A_\varphi^{[]}}$ or $\mathcal{O}^{R_\varphi^{[]}}$, the adversary $\mathcal{B}$ challenges $\mathcal{A}$ with sample $\langle a_i, r_i \rangle$ where $r_i = \langle r_{i,1}, \ldots, r_{i,J}, v_i, \lfloor \varphi_{J+2}(a_i) \rceil, \ldots, \lfloor \varphi_p(a_i) \rceil \rangle$. Here, r_{ij} is a random bit from $\{0,1\}$ for $1 \leq j \leq J$. We can easily claim that if the sample $\langle a_i, v_i \rangle$ is generated by oracle $\mathcal{O}^{A_\varphi^{[]}}$, then the adversary $\mathcal{B}$ emulates the hybrid $\mathcal{H}^{(J)}$ to the adversary $\mathcal{A}$. Otherwise, the adversary $\mathcal{B}$ turns into the hybrid $\mathcal{H}^{(J+1)}$ to the adversary $\mathcal{A}$.

Using the standard hybrid argument, we claim that if the adversary $\mathcal{A}$ can distinguish the oracles $\mathcal{H}^{(J)}/\mathcal{H}^{(J+1)}$ with a non-negligible advantage, then the distinguisher $\mathcal{B}$ can distinguish the oracles $\mathcal{O}^{A_\varphi^{[]}}$ and $\mathcal{O}^{R_\varphi^{[]}}$ with non-negligible advantage. This contradicts the assumption that the oracles $\mathcal{O}^{A_\varphi^{[]}}$ and $\mathcal{O}^{R_\varphi^{[]}}$ are indistinguishable.

4   PRF Construction from a Weak PRF Family

The weak PRF is the immediate implication of the B_n-LHR assumption. This section discusses two approaches to constructing a PRF using a collection of weak PRFs. In the first approach, we show a construction of a *pseudorandom synthesizer* (PRS) from a length-preserving weak PRF as in [26]. As the second approach, we propose a design for the length-doubling PRG using a length-preserving weak PRF family. A collection of length-doubling PRG is the basis for the GGM's PRG-based PRF construction as provided in [13].

4.1   PRS-Based PRF Construction

A few notations that are used in the subsequent discussions are as follows:

- Recall, p denotes the entropy of a word in a Burnside group B_n. Let q denotes the entropy of a homomorphism in Φ_n, which is n times the entropy of a word in a Burnside group B_r .
- A function $\zeta_k : \{0,1\}^p \to \{0,1\}^p$, where the secret-key $k = \langle \varphi_1, \ldots, \varphi_p \rangle$ is sampled uniformly from Φ_n^p, is a length-preserving weak PRF. The function is defined in Construction 1 and the corresponding proof is provided in Theorem 2.

We construct a PRS $S : \{0,1\}^{pq} \times \{0,1\}^{pq} \to \{0,1\}^{pq}$ using a length-preserving weak PRF ζ_k as in Construction 2.

Construction 2 (Pseudorandom Synthesizer, S). *For $k = \langle \varphi_1, \ldots, \varphi_p \rangle$ in Φ_n^p and $a = \langle a_1, \ldots, a_q \rangle$, where $a_i \in B_n$, a pseudorandom synthesizer $S :$ $\{0,1\}^{pq} \times \{0,1\}^{pq} \to \{0,1\}^{pq}$ is defined as*

$$S(a, k) = \langle \zeta_k(a_1), \ldots, \zeta_k(a_q) \rangle.$$

If ζ_k is a length-preserving weak PRF with a secret-key k sampled uniformly from Φ_n^p (as in Construction 1), then it is easy to visualize that a function S in Construction 2 is a *pseudorandom synthesizer* (PRS). We omit the proof but the concept is similar to [26].

PRS-Based PRF Construction. Here, we design a PRF from a PRS family $S = \{S_n\}$. Let $\{S_{k_1}, \ldots, S_{k_{\log(m)}}\}$ be a set of *pseudorandom synthesizers* in S_n, where $S_{k_i} : \{0,1\}^{pq} \times \{0,1\}^{pq} \to \{0,1\}^{pq}$ is defined as in Construction 2. Define a key $\tilde{k} = \langle a, k \rangle$ where $a = \langle a_{1,0}, a_{1,1}, \ldots, a_{m,0}, a_{m,1} \rangle$ with $a_{i,j} \in \{0,1\}^{pq}$, and $k = \langle k_1, \ldots, k_{\log(m)} \rangle$. A PRF $f_{\tilde{k}}$, for input $x = x_1 \ldots x_m$ and secret-key $\tilde{k} = \langle a, k \rangle$ is defined as

$$f_{\tilde{k}}(x_1 \ldots x_m) = SQ_{S_{k_1}}(\ldots (SQ_{S_{k_{\log(m)}}}(a_{1,x_1}, \ldots, a_{m,x_m})) \ldots). \tag{15}$$

The squeeze function $SQ_{S_{k_i}}$ is defined as

$$SQ_{S_{k_i}}(u_1, \ldots, u_{2m}) = \langle S_{k_i}(u_1, u_2), \ldots, S_{k_i}(u_{2m-1}, u_{2m}) \rangle. \tag{16}$$

Note: The disadvantage of the PRS-based PRF construction is the enormous secret-key size of a function $f_{\tilde{k}}$ in Eq. (15).

4.2   Length-Doubling PRG from a Weak PRF

The construction of a PRS-based PRF using a length-preserving weak PRF comes with an evident drawback, which is the requirement of a significantly large secret-key size. To address this, we propose an alternative approach involving a length-doubling PRG denoted as $G : \{0,1\}^p \to \{0,1\}^{2p}$, constructed using a length-preserving weak PRF $\zeta_k : \{0,1\}^p \to \{0,1\}^p$. The precise design of G can be found in Construction 3.

Initially, it may appear that utilizing the function $G_{\zeta_k(a_j)}$ with an index $\zeta_k(a_j)$ results in inefficiency due to the output being $\langle a_i, \zeta_k(a_j.a_i)\rangle$. However, the function $G_{\zeta_k(a_j)}$ becomes efficient when it serves as an intermediate PRG within a PRF construction, as demonstrated in Eq. (18). In the PRF construction outlined in Eq. (18), the components a_j for $1 \leq j \leq m$ are publicly known, while k forms a part of the secret-key. This combination ensures the effectiveness and security of the constructed PRF.

Construction 3 (Pseudorandom Generator, G) *Let $\zeta_k : \{0,1\}^p \to \{0,1\}^p$ be an efficiently computable length-preserving weak PRF as in Construction 1. A function $G_{\zeta_k(a_j)} : \{0,1\}^p \to \{0,1\}^{2p}$ is defined as*

$$G_{\zeta_k(a_j)}(a_i) = \langle G^{(0)}_{\zeta_k(a_j)}(a_i), G^{(1)}_{\zeta_k(a_j)}(a_i)\rangle$$

$$= \langle a_i, \zeta_k(a_j.a_i)\rangle. \tag{17}$$

Here, $a_i, a_j \in B_n$. Note: Dot (.) in $a_j.a_i$ is the concatenation operation in B_n.

Theorem 3. *If $Z = \{Z_\lambda\}$ is a collection of length-preserving weak PRFs and ζ_k is a function in Z_λ with secret-key k sampled uniformly as in Construction 1, then the function $G_{\zeta_k(a_j)}$ in Construction 3, for a_j sampled uniformly from B_n, is a PRG.*

Proof. In accordance with the approach presented in [35], we structure our proof based on a series of games: G_0, G_1, G_2, and G_3, all operating within the same underlying probability space. These games are constructed in a sequential manner, with each game introducing incremental modifications to the behavior of the challenge oracles. Notably, the final game (G_3) is designed in such a way that achieving the adversary's objective becomes clearly impossible. Leveraging the indistinguishability of consecutive games, we can then conclude that the adversary's advantage in the original game is negligible.

Let $A_G^{\zeta_k(a_j)}$ be a distribution whose outputs are of the form $\{a_i, \zeta_k(a_j.a_i)\}$ where $a_i \xleftarrow{\$} B_n$ and a_j is a random word in a Burnside group B_n fixed for all polynomially many samples. Furthermore, let ζ_k be a length-preserving weak PRF with a secret-key k sampled uniformly as in Construction 1. Similarly, let $R_G^{\zeta_k(a_j)}$ be a random distribution with outputs $\{a_i, a_i'\}$ where both a_i and a_i' are sampled uniformly from a Burnside group B_n.

Game G_0: On input 1^λ, the adversary $\mathcal{A}$ interacts with a challenge oracle $\mathcal{O}^{R_G^{\zeta_k(a_j)}}$ through polynomially many input samples of the form $\{a_i, a_i'\}$.

Game G_1: In game G_1, the adversary $\mathcal{A}$ interacts with polynomially many input samples of the form $\{a_i, \zeta_k(a_i)\}$ where ζ_k is a length-preserving weak PRF with a uniformly sampled secret-key k and $a_i \xleftarrow{\$} B_n$.

Game G_2: In game G_2, challenge oracle slightly modify the interacting samples. Here, the adversary $\mathcal{A}$ interacts with polynomially many input samples of the form $\{a_j^{-1}.a_i, \zeta_k(a_i)\}$ where ζ_k is a length-preserving weak PRF with a uniformly sampled secret-key k. Here, a_i is sampled uniformly from a Burnside group B_n and a_j is a random word in B_n fixed for all polynomially many samples $\{a_j^{-1}.a_i, \zeta_k(a_i)\}$.

Game G_3: In game G_3, challenge oracle re-represents the polynomially many input samples, and the adversary $\mathcal{A}$ interacts with samples $\{a_i', \zeta_k(a_j.a_i')\}$ where ζ_k is a length-preserving weak PRF with a uniformly sampled secret-key k. Here, $a_i' \xleftarrow{\$} B_n$ and a_j is a random word in B_n fixed for all polynomially many samples $\{a_i', \zeta_k(a_j.a_i')\}$.

For the games G_0 and G_1, we observe that they are computationally indistinguishable to any $\mathcal{PPT}$ adversary $\mathcal{A}$. This holds true due to the fact that ζ_k functions are a weak PRF. Moving on to the games G_1 and G_2, we find that they are statistically indistinguishable for any $\mathcal{PPT}$ adversary $\mathcal{A}$. This conclusion can be easily derived based on their construction and properties. Lastly, when considering the games G_2 and G_3, we can establish their equivalence for any $\mathcal{PPT}$ adversary $\mathcal{A}$, where the equivalence holds as a result of the transformation $a_i' = a_j^{-1}.a_i$, which ensures the indistinguishability between these games.

PRF Construction. Given $Z = \{Z_\lambda\}$ be a length-preserving weak PRF family, and let ζ_k denotes a function in Z_λ, where k is uniformly sampled from Φ_n^p (refer to Construction 1). We define $G_{\zeta_k(a_j)}$ according to Construction 3 for all publicly known a_j, $1 \leq j \leq m$, sampled uniformly from a Burnside group B_n. Now, consider a PRF $f_{\tilde{k}}$ with input $x = x_1 \ldots x_m$ and secret-key $\tilde{k} = \langle k, a_0 \rangle$, which is defined as follows:

$$f_{\tilde{k}}(x_1 \ldots x_m) = G_{\zeta_k(a_m)}^{(x_m)}(\ldots (G_{\zeta_k(a_1)}^{(x_1)}(a_0)) \ldots). \tag{18}$$

Here, $\tilde{k} = \langle k, a_0 \rangle$ is the secret-key of the function $f_{\tilde{k}}$, where a_0 is sampled uniformly from a Burnside group B_n.

5   Conclusion

In summary, this paper introduced a novel B_n-LHR assumption through the derandomization of the well-established B_n-LHN assumption. A security reduction was provided to establish the hardness of the B_n-LHR assumption. Additionally, a design for a length-preserving weak PRF from the B_n-LHR assumption was presented. Furthermore, a length-doubling *pseudorandom generator* (PRG) was devised using a collection of length-preserving weak PRFs. Importantly, this construction is of a general nature, demonstrating that any collection of weak PRFs can be utilized to construct a collection of length-doubling PRGs (as well as a PRF family using the GGM construction).

Acknowledgements. We sincerely thank the reviewers for their valuable and insightful feedback on the initial draft of this paper.

References

1. Adian, S.I.: Problema Bernsaida i tozhdestva v gruppakh. Nauka (1975)
2. Adian, S.I.: The burnside problem and related topics. Russ. Math. Surv. **65**(5), 805 (2010)
3. Ajtai, M.: Generating hard instances of lattice problems extended abstract. In: Proceedings of the Twenty-eighth Annual ACM Symposium on Theory of Computing, pp. 99–108 (1996)
4. Banerjee, A., Peikert, C., Rosen, A.: Pseudorandom functions and lattices. In: Pointcheval, D., Johansson, T. (eds.) EUROCRYPT 2012. LNCS, vol. 7237, pp. 719–737. Springer, Heidelberg (2012). https://doi.org/10.1007/978-3-642-29011-4_42
5. Baumslag, G., Fazio, N., Nicolosi, A.R., Shpilrain, V., Skeith, W.E.: Generalized learning problems and applications to non-commutative cryptography. In: Boyen, X., Chen, X. (eds.) ProvSec 2011. LNCS, vol. 6980, pp. 324–339. Springer, Heidelberg (2011). https://doi.org/10.1007/978-3-642-24316-5_23
6. Blum, M., Micali, S.: How to generate cryptographically strong sequences of pseudorandom bits. SIAM J. Comput. **13**(4), 850–864 (1984)
7. Bogdanov, A., Rosen, A.: Pseudorandom functions: three decades later. In: Tutorials on the Foundations of Cryptography. ISC, pp. 79–158. Springer, Cham (2017). https://doi.org/10.1007/978-3-319-57048-8_3
8. Brakerski, Z., Langlois, A., Peikert, C., Regev, O., Stehlé, D.: Classical hardness of learning with errors. In: Proceedings of the Forty-fifth Annual ACM Symposium on Theory of Computing, pp. 575–584 (2013)
9. Burnside, W.: On an unsettled question in the theory of discontinuous groups. Quart. J. Pure Appl. Math. **33**, 230–238 (1902)
10. Burnside, W.: The Collected Papers of William Burnside: Commentary on Burnside's Life and Work; Papers 1883–1899, vol. 1. Oxford University Press (2004)
11. Fazio, N., Iga, K., Nicolosi, A.R., Perret, L., Skeith, W.E.: Hardness of learning problems over burnside groups of exponent 3. Des. Codes Crypt. **75**(1), 59–70 (2015)
12. Goldreich, O.: A primer on Pseudorandom Generators, vol. 55. American Mathematical Society, Providence (2010)
13. Goldreich, O., Goldwasser, S., Micali, S.: How to construct random functions. J. ACM (JACM) **33**(4), 792–807 (1986)
14. Golod, E.S., Shafarevich, I.R.: On the class field tower. Izvestiya Rossiiskoi Akademii Nauk. Seriya Matematicheskaya **28**(2), 261–272 (1964)
15. Gupta, N.: On groups in which every element has finite order. Am. Math. Mon. **96**(4), 297–308 (1989)
16. Hall, M.: Solution of the burnside problem for exponent 6. Proc. Natl. Acad. Sci. U.S.A. **43**(8), 751–753 (1957)
17. Hall, M.: The Theory of Groups. Macmillan Company, New York (1959)
18. HÅstad, J., Impagliazzo, R., Levin, L.A., Luby, M.: A pseudorandom generator from any one-way function. SIAM J. Comput. **28**(4), 1364–1396 (1999). https://doi.org/10.1137/S0097539793244708
19. Ivanov, S.V.: The free burnside groups of sufficiently large exponents. Int. J. Algebra Comput. **4**, 1–308 (1994)
20. Joan, D., Vincent, R.: The design of Rijndael: AES-the advanced encryption standard. Information Security and Cryptography (2002)

21. Katz, J., Lindell, Y.: Introduction to Modern Cryptography. Chapman & Hall/CRC Cryptography and Network Security Series, CRC Press (2020). https:// books.google.com/books?id=RsoOEAAAQBAJ

22. Levi, F., van der Waerden, B.L.: Über eine besondere klasse von gruppen. Abhandlungen aus dem Mathematischen Seminar der Universität Hamburg **9**, 154–158 (1933)

23. Levin, L.A.: The tale of one-way functions. Probl. Inf. Transm. **39**(1), 92–103 (2003)

24. Luby, M.: Pseudorandomness and Cryptographic Applications, vol. 1. Princeton University Press, Princeton (1996)

25. Micciancio, D., Regev, O.: Lattice-based cryptography. Post-quantum Cryptography, pp. 147–191 (2009)

26. Naor, M., Reingold, O.: Synthesizers and their application to the parallel construction of pseudo-random functions. J. Comput. Syst. Sci. **58**(2), 336–375 (1999)

27. Naor, M., Reingold, O.: Number-theoretic constructions of efficient pseudo-random functions. J. ACM (JACM) **51**(2), 231–262 (2004)

28. Regev, O.: New lattice-based cryptographic constructions. J. ACM (JACM) **51**(6), 899–942 (2004)

29. Mihailescu, M.I., Nita, S.L.: Lattice-based cryptography. In: Pro Cryptography and Cryptanalysis, pp. 291–300. Apress, Berkeley, CA (2021). https://doi.org/10.1007/978-1-4842-6367-9_11

30. Regev, O.: On lattices, learning with errors, random linear codes, and cryptography. J. ACM (JACM) **56**(6), 1–40 (2009)

31. Regev, O.: The learning with errors problem. Invited Survey CCC **7**(30), 11 (2010)

32. Regev, O.: The learning with errors problem (invited survey). In: 2010 IEEE 25th Annual Conference on Computational Complexity, pp. 191–204. IEEE (2010)

33. Robinson, D.J.: A Course in the Theory of Groups, vol. 80. Springer, New York (2012)

34. Shanov, I.: Solution of the Burnside's problem for exponent 4. Leningrad State Univ. Ann. (Uchenye Zapiski) Mat. Ser. **10**, 166–170 (1940)

35. Shoup, V.: Sequences of games: a tool for taming complexity in security proofs. cryptology eprint archive (2004)

36. Shoup, V.: A Computational Introduction to Number Theory and Algebra. Cambridge University Press, New York (2005)

Some Results on Related Key-IV Pairs of Espresso

George Teşeleanu[1,2]([✉])[iD]

[1] Advanced Technologies Institute, 10 Dinu Vintilă, Bucharest, Romania
[2] Simion Stoilow Institute of Mathematics of the Romanian Academy,
21 Calea Grivitei, Bucharest, Romania
tgeorge@dcti.ro

Abstract. In this paper, we analyze the Espresso cipher from a related key chosen IV perspective. More precisely, we explain how one can obtain Key-IV pairs such that Espresso's keystreams either have certain identical bits or are shifted versions of each other. For the first case, we show how to obtain such pairs after 2^{32} iterations, while for the second case, we present an algorithm that produces such pairs in 2^{28} iterations. Moreover, we show that by making a minor change in the padding used during the initialization phase, it can lead to a more secure version of the cipher. Specifically, changing the padding increases the complexity of our second attack from 2^{28} to 2^{34}. Finally, we show how related IVs can accelerate brute force attacks, resulting in a faster key recovery. Although our work does not have any immediate implications for breaking the Espresso cipher, these observations are relevant in the related-key chosen IV scenario.

Keywords: Espresso · slide attacks · cryptanalysis · related keys

1 Introduction

With the growth of Internet of Things (IoT) applications, lightweight ciphers are becoming highly demanded in the IoT industry. Lightweight ciphers are required to offer users a high level of assurance, while running in resource-constrained devices. Additionally, with the rise of 5G networks, traffic volume is estimated to increase by 1000 times [11]. Hence, besides being implemented in IoT devices that usually have limited computing power and strict power constraints, lightweight ciphers should also offer low propagation delays in implementation.

Since previously cipher designs focused either on hardware size or speed, a new class of lightweight ciphers had to be introduced. Such a class was introduced in [8] and was designed to be a trade-off between hardware size and speed for a given security level. The basic idea of this new design is to combine the short propagation delays of the Galois Non-Linear Feedback Shift Registers (NFSRs) with the advantage of Fibonacci NFSRs, which are more easily analyzed from a security point of view. More precisely, the authors of [8] employ a NFSR in Gallois configuration and carry out their security analysis on a transformed NFSR

M. Manulis et al. (Eds.): SecITC 2023, LNCS 14534, pp. 197–216, 2024.
https://doi.org/10.1007/978-3-031-52947-4_14

which resembles a Fibonacci NFSR. They also provide a concrete construction, called Espresso, that is a representative of their design.

The only independent security analyses that we are aware of can be found in [13,14]. In [13], the authors propose a related key chosen IV attack on a variant of Espresso, denoted Espresso-a. Similar to [8], they transform the Galois NFSR to a Fibonacci one, however the output function is the same as that of Espresso. The authors of [14], state that the transformed NFSR studied in [8,13] are not equivalent to the original Galois NFSR, unless the output function is changed accordingly. Hence, the security analyses are not conducted on the actual cipher. To support their claim, the authors introduce a novel transformation that converts Espresso-like ciphers into LFSR filter generators. Then they provide several algebraic and fast correlation attacks that can be applied to the resulting filter generators. In light of their results, they also urge researchers to reassess Espresso's resistance against chosen IV attacks, differential attacks and weak key attacks.

Compared to previous approaches, instead of studying the equivalent Fibonacci NFSR, we propose three related key chosen IV attacks by working directly with the Galois NFSR. We will first study the differential properties of the initialization algorithm and we will show how to construct related Key-IV pairs that produce identical bits on certain positions. Our methods are influenced by the differential attacks, previously published in [4,10], designed against the Grain family. Secondly, we show a sliding property of the initialization algorithm that allows an attacker to construct related Key-IV pairs that generate shifted keystreams. Again, we were influenced by the sliding attacks devised against the Grain family (presented in [4–6,9,10]). To increase the complexity of our proposed slide attacks, we suggest a slight change to Espresso's padding. Thirdly, we propose a guess and determine attack that takes as input two or four related IV's and outputs the secret key. A similar approach[1] can be found for Grain-128a in [7] and Espresso-a in [13]. We finally note that we do not consider any of the attacks presented in this paper to be a serious threat in practice. However, they certainly expose some non-ideal behavior of the Espresso initialization algorithm.

Full version. The full version of the paper can be found here [12].

Structure of the Paper. We introduce notations and preliminaries in Sect. 2. In Sect. 3 we present differential attacks, in Sect. 4 we propose several constructions for generating related Key-IV pairs and in Sect. 5 we suggest several key recovery algorithms. We conclude in Sect. 6.

---

[1] both using only two related IV's

2   Preliminaries

Notations. Throughout the paper, the notation $\|$ denotes string concatenation, $\oplus$ denotes bitwise XOR and $|$ denotes bitwise OR. The $x \ggg i$ operator causes the bits in x to be rotated to the right by i positions. The subset $\{0, \ldots, s\} \in \mathbb{N}$ is denoted by $[0, s]$. The action of selecting a random element x from a sample space X is represented by $x \in_R X$. Hexadecimal strings are marked by the prefix 0x. We define $MID_{[\ell_1, \ell_2]}(Q) = q_{\ell_1} \| \ldots \| q_{\ell_2}$ and $LSB_{\ell_1}(Q) = MID_{0,\ell_1}(Q)$, where $Q = q_0 \| \ldots \| q_{\ell_1} \| \ldots \| q_{\ell_2} \| \ldots \| q_\ell$.

2.1   Description of Espresso

We further provide the specifications of Espresso as presented in [8]. One of the main building blocks of Espresso is a 256-bit NFSR in the Galois configuration. Let $X_i = [x_i, x_{i+1}, \ldots, x_{i+255}]$ denote the state of the NFSR at time i and let $g_j(X_i)$, where $j \in [0, 255]$, be the feedback functions of the NFSR. The nonlinear feedback functions are defined as follows

$$g_{255}(X_i) = x_i \oplus x_{i+41}x_{i+70}$$
$$g_{251}(X_i) = x_{i+252} \oplus x_{i+42}x_{i+83} \oplus x_{i+8}$$

$$g_{247}(X_i) = x_{i+248} \oplus x_{i+44}x_{i+102} \oplus x_{i+40}$$
$$g_{243}(X_i) = x_{i+244} \oplus x_{i+43}x_{i+118} \oplus x_{i+103}$$

$$g_{239}(X_i) = x_{i+240} \oplus x_{i+46}x_{i+141} \oplus x_{i+117}$$
$$g_{235}(X_i) = x_{i+236} \oplus x_{i+67}x_{i+90}x_{i+110}x_{i+137}$$

$$g_{231}(X_i) = x_{i+232} \oplus x_{i+50}x_{i+159} \oplus x_{i+189}$$
$$g_{217}(X_i) = x_{i+218} \oplus x_{i+3}x_{i+32}$$

$$g_{213}(X_i) = x_{i+214} \oplus x_{i+4}x_{i+45}$$
$$g_{209}(X_i) = x_{i+210} \oplus x_{i+6}x_{i+64}$$

$$g_{205}(X_i) = x_{i+206} \oplus x_{i+5}x_{i+80}$$
$$g_{201}(X_i) = x_{i+202} \oplus x_{i+8}x_{i+103}$$

$$g_{197}(X_i) = x_{i+198} \oplus x_{i+29}x_{i+52}x_{i+72}x_{i+99}$$
$$g_{193}(X_i) = x_{i+194} \oplus x_{i+12}x_{i+121}$$

The remaining feedback functions are of type $g_j(X_i) = x_{i+j+1}$.

Another building block of the Espresso cipher is a non-linear output function $z(X_i)$ given by

$$z(X_i) = x_{i+80} \oplus x_{i+99} \oplus x_{i+137} \oplus x_{i+227} \oplus x_{i+222} \oplus x_{i+187} \oplus x_{i+243}x_{i+217}$$
$$\oplus x_{i+247}x_{i+231} \oplus x_{i+213}x_{i+235} \oplus x_{i+255}x_{i+251} \oplus x_{i+181}x_{i+239} \oplus x_{i+174}x_{i+44}$$
$$\oplus x_{i+164}x_{i+29} \oplus x_{i+255}x_{i+247}x_{i+243}x_{i+213}x_{i+181}x_{i+174}$$

We further describe the main algorithms used by the Espresso cipher in the initialization and keystream generation phases.

Key Loading Algorithm (KLA). Espresso uses a 128-bit key K, a 96-bit initialization vector IV and a fixed 32-bit padding $P = \text{0xfffffffe}$. The key is loaded in the NFSR as follows: $X_0 = K \| IV \| P$.

Key Scheduling Algorithm (KSA). After running KLA, the output[2] $z_i = z(X_i)$ is XOR-ed to $g_{255}(X_i)$ and $g_{217}(X_i)$ update functions, *i.e.*, during one clock the update functions are updated as $g_{255}(X_i) = x_i \oplus x_{i+41}x_{i+70} \oplus z_i$ and $g_{217}(X_i) = x_{i+218} \oplus x_{i+3}x_{i+32} \oplus z_i$.

Pipeline Key Scheduling Algorithm (PKSA). Due to the pipelining of the output function some extra clocks are needed before producing the keystream. Hence, the PKSA algorithm instead of outputting(See footnote 2) z_i simply ignores it. Note that after each generated bit the NFSR's internal state is updated using the KSA routine with $g_{255}(X_i) = x_i \oplus x_{i+41}x_{i+70}$ and $g_{217}(X_i) = x_{i+218} \oplus x_{i+3}x_{i+32}$.

Pseudorandom Keystream Generation Algorithm (PRGA). After performing the KSA routine for 256 clocks and the PKSA routine for 3 clocks, bit z_i is used as the output keystream bit. After each generated bit the NFSR's internal state is updated as in the PKSA routine.

2.2   Security Model

In this paper, we will work in the *Related Key Chosen IV* security model. In this model, according to [5, Section 2.1], the adversary $\mathcal{A}$ is given access to an encryption oracle $\mathcal{O}$ that has access to the key K. Therefore, $\mathcal{A}$ can query $\mathcal{O}$ and thus obtain valid ciphertexts.

   More precisely, for each query i, the adversary first chooses the oracle's parameters: an initialization vector IV_i, a function $\mathcal{F}_i : \{0,1\}^n \to \{0,1\}^n$ and a message m_i. Then $\mathcal{O}$ encrypts m_i using the Key-IV pair $(\mathcal{F}_i(K), IV_i)$. After repeating this process several times, the adversary's task is to distinguish the keystream output from a random stream or to compute the secret key efficiently.

3   Related Key-IV Pairs

Our first goal is to construct a family of related Key-IV functions such that the adversary can distinguish the resulting keystreams from random ones with high probability. An important step to construct such pairs is the observation that the KSA and PKSA routines are invertible. More precisely, if a state X_i is obtained by applying either KSA or PKSA to X_{i-1}, we can recover X_{i-1} from X_i by rolling back one clock. We further refer to the transition functions from X_i to X_{i-1} as KSA^{-1} and PKSA^{-1}. The exact details of KSA^{-1} and PKSA^{-1} are given in the full version of the paper [12].

   We further denote by KSA$_{256}$ and KSA$_{256}^{-1}$ the KSA and KSA^{-1} routines performed for 256 clocks. Similarly, we define PKSA$_3$ and PKSA$_3^{-1}$. We also define KLA$^{-1}(X) = (LSB_{127}(X), MID_{[128,223]}(X))$ and $\Delta(X) = X \oplus \delta$, where $\delta \in \{0,1\}^{256}$. Using these routines we can obtain a pair of related Key-IVs (K, IV) and $(K, IV)_\Delta$ such that they produce almost similar initial keystreams. A high level description of the construction is provided in Fig. 1.

---
[2] during one clock

We further present an algorithm that checks which keystream positions produced by the states X_0 and $X_{0,\Delta}$ are identical. Before stating our result, we first introduce a small modification to the keystream generation algorithm. Note that this modification is only used as part of Algorithm 1 and is needed to aid us find identical positions. We also make an assumption about Espresso's keystream bits.

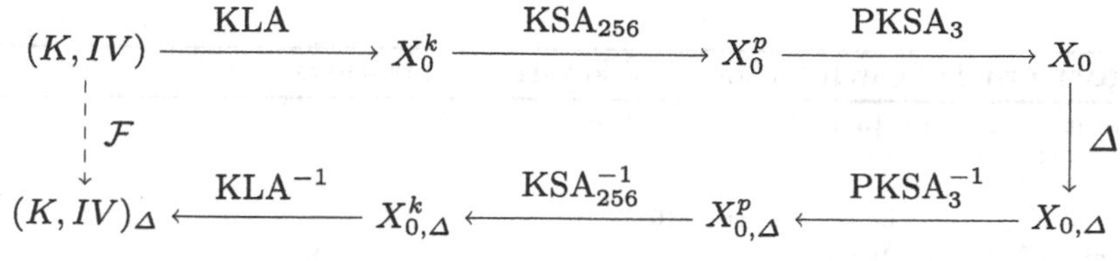

$$(K, IV) \xrightarrow{\ \ \text{KLA}\ \ } X_0^k \xrightarrow{\ \ \text{KSA}_{256}\ \ } X_0^p \xrightarrow{\ \ \text{PKSA}_3\ \ } X_0$$

$$\downarrow \mathcal{F} \qquad\qquad\qquad\qquad\qquad\qquad\qquad\qquad \downarrow \Delta$$

$$(K, IV)_\Delta \xleftarrow{\ \ \text{KLA}^{-1}\ \ } X_{0,\Delta}^k \xleftarrow{\ \ \text{KSA}_{256}^{-1}\ \ } X_{0,\Delta}^p \xleftarrow{\ \ \text{PKSA}_3^{-1}\ \ } X_{0,\Delta}$$

Fig. 1. Construction of the Related Key-IV function

Modified Pseudorandom Keystream Generation Algorithm (PRGA'). To obtain our modified PRGA we replace $\oplus$ (XOR) and $\cdot$ (AND) operations in the original PRGA with $|$ (OR) operations.

Assumption. Based on the experimental results we obtained, we further assume that the output of PRGA[3] is independently and uniformly distributed. To obtain these results 100 keystream were statistically tested using the NIST Test Suites [1,2]. During our experiments we used the default pseudorandom numbers generator implemented in the GMP library [3] to randomly generate 100 Key-IV pairs.

Theorem 1. *Let $\delta \in \{0,1\}^{256}$, q_1 the number of desired identical positions in the keystream and q_2 the maximum number of search trials. Then, Algorithm 1 finds at most q_1 identical positions in a maximum of q_2 trials.*

Proof. Let ω be the Hamming weight of δ. We note that in Algorithm 1 the bits $b_{i_1}, \ldots, b_{i_\omega}$ on position $i_1, \ldots, i_\omega$ are set. For $j \in [1, \omega]$, if bit b_{i_j} is taken into consideration while computing the output bit of PRGA then the output of PRGA' is also set due to the replacement of the original operations $\oplus$ and $\cdot$ with $|$ operations. The same argument is valid if a bit of Espresso's internal state is influenced by b_{i_j}.   □

Remark 1. Note that if we run Algorithm 1 we do not obtain all the identical positions. This is due to the fact that Algorithm 1 is prone to producing internal collisions, and thus eliminate certain positions that are identical in both keystreams. Although we do not find all the positions, our algorithm has the advantage of finding identical keystream positions automatically.

---

[3] implicitly PKSA and PKSA^{-1}

3.1   Multiple Key-IV Trials with a Fixed Differential

We further consider that the adversary is allowed to produce any related Key-IV pairs for a given fixed differential. In this case, the while loop of our proposed algorithm (Algorithm 2) has to run an expected 2^{32} times with different randomly chosen (K, IV) pairs, until $X_{0,\Delta}$ has the correct padding. Once this happens, we output a related Key-IV pair (K, IV) and (K', IV').

Algorithm 1: Search for identical keystream positions

Input: Integers $\delta \in \{0,1\}^{256}$ and $q_1, q_2 > 0$
Output: Keystream positions φ
1 Set $s \leftarrow 0$ and $\varphi \leftarrow \varnothing$
2 Let $X_0 \in \{0,1\}^{256}$ be the zero state $(0, \ldots, 0)$
3 Construct $X_{0,\Delta} = X_0 \oplus \delta$
4 **while** $|\varphi| \leq q_1$ and $s < q_2$ **do**
5 | Set $b \leftarrow \text{PRGA}'(X_{0,\Delta})$ and update state $X_{0,\Delta}$ with the current state
6 | **if** $b = 0$ **then**
7 | | Update $\varphi \leftarrow \varphi \cup \{s\}$
8 | Set $s \leftarrow s + 1$
9 **return** φ

Algorithm 2: Search for Key-IV pairs that produce almost similar initial keystreams for a given δ

Input: An integer $\delta \in \{0,1\}^{256}$
Output: Key-IV pairs (K, IV) and (K', IV')
1 Set $s \leftarrow 0$
2 **while** $s = 0$ **do**
3 | Choose $K \in_R \{0,1\}^{128}$ and $IV \in_R \{0,1\}^{96}$
4 | Run $\text{KSA}_{256}(K\|IV)$ and $\text{PKSA}_3(K\|IV)$ routines to obtain an initial state $X_0 \in \{0,1\}^{256}$
5 | Compute the state $X_{0,\Delta} = X_0 \oplus \delta$
6 | Run $\text{PKSA}_3^{-1}(X_{0,\Delta})$ and $\text{KSA}_{256}^{-1}(X_{0,\Delta})$ routines to produce state $X_{0,\Delta}^k = K'\|IV'\|P'$
7 | **if** $P' = \text{0xfffffffe}$ **then**
8 | | Set $s \leftarrow 1$
9 | | **return** (K, IV) and (K', IV')

3.2   Single Key-IV Trials with Multiple Differentials

In practice, the attacker has access to a single Key-IV pair and he has to produce a second Key-IV pair related to the one given. In this case, the attacker has to try around 2^{32} different values for δ, until Algorithm 3 outputs a pair.

In Fig. 2a we can see how cardinality of φ fluctuates depending on the iteration step i and the Hamming weight ω of δ. In [10], the authors introduce an algorithm that computes Key-IV pairs that produce similar initial Grain-128a keystreams for δ's of the form $0 \ldots 010 \ldots 0$. Our proposal (Algorithm 3) can be easily adapted to Grain-128a, and thus for comparison we also provide in Fig. 2b the evolution of $|\varphi|$ in the case of Grain-128a.

For a given Δ, let X_1 be a random state such that $X_1 \neq X_{0,\Delta}$. Note that in Algorithm 3 parameter ℓ controls the probability of obtaining identical keystream bits for states X_0 and X_1 on the positions included in φ. More precisely, the probability of obtaining a collision for X_0 and X_1 is $1/2^\ell$. In Table 1 we can see the number of δ's such that $|\varphi| \geq 16$. Hence, for $\ell = 16$ in Algorithm 3 it is sufficient to run the while loop until $j \neq 5$ since $239 \cdot 137 \cdot 110 \cdot 69 \cdot 18 \geq 2^{32}$. In the case of Grain-128a it is sufficient to run the while loop until $j \neq 4$ since $256^4 \geq 2^{32}$.

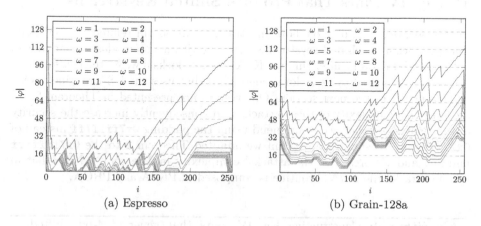

(a) Espresso   (b) Grain-128a

Fig. 2. The evolution of $|\varphi|$

Algorithm 3: Search for a Key-IV pair that produces an almost similar initial keystream with a given Key-IV pair (K, IV)

Input: A Key-IV pair (K, IV) and an integer $\ell > 0$
Output: A related Key-IV pair (K', IV')

1 Run $KSA_{256}(K\|IV)$ and $PKSA_3(K\|IV)$ routines to obtain an initial state $X_0 \in \{0,1\}^{256}$
2 Set the integer $j \leftarrow 0$ and the state $\delta = 0$
3 **while** $j \neq 256$ **do**
4   Set the bit $\delta_j = 1$ and compute $j \leftarrow j + 1$
5   **for** $i \in [0, 255]$ **do**
6   Compute $\varphi \leftarrow Algorithm\ 1(\delta, 160, 160)$
7   **if** $|\varphi| < \ell$ **then**
8   Skip the next instructions and go to the next i
9   Compute the state $X_{0,\Delta} = X_0 \oplus \delta$
10   Run $PKSA_3^{-1}(X_{0,\Delta})$ and $KSA_{256}^{-1}(X_{0,\Delta})$ routines to produce state $X_{0,\Delta}^k = K'\|IV'\|P'$
11   **if** $P' = \texttt{0xffffffffe}$ **then**
12   Set $s \leftarrow 1$
13   **return** (K', IV')
14   Rotate to the right $\delta = \delta \ggg 1$

Table 1. Number of valid possibilities for $\ell = 16$

Cipher	ω											
	1	2	3	4	5	6	7	8	9	10	11	12
Espresso	239	137	110	69	56(18)	51	49	48	47	0	0	0
Grain-128a	256	256	256	256	256	247	233	185	164	158	133	121

4   Key-IV Pairs That Produce Shifted Keystreams

In this section, we will show how an attacker can obtain related Key-IV pairs that produce 4-bit shifted keystreams. Our algorithm's main idea is that we can obtain a valid padding after running KSA^{-1} for 4 clocks if we fix the last four bits of the IV. We also provide a slower algorithm that uses the KSA routine, which will be useful in the next section. Our results are presented in Theorem 2. To increase the complexity of these attacks and consequently increase the security of the Espresso cipher, we recommend using the padding 0x7fffffff instead of 0xfffffffe. To support our claim we adapted Theorem 2 to the 0x7fffffff padding and we presented the attacks' complexity in Theorem 3. Note that in all the attacks the $PRNG$ routine is composed of PKSA and PRGA.

Algorithm 4: Constructing Key-IV pairs that generate 4-bit shifted keystream (forward construction)

Output: Key-IV pairs (K', IV') and (K, IV)
1 Set $s \leftarrow 0$
2 **while** $s = 0$ **do**
3   Choose $K \in_R \{0,1\}^{128}$ and $IV \in_R \{0,1\}^{96}$
4   Run KSA$(K\|IV)$ routine for 4 clocks to obtain a state $X'_0 = K'\|IV'\|P'$
5   **if** $P' = $ 0xfffffffe **then**
6   Run KSA$(K'\|IV')$ and PRNG routine for 252 clocks and 4 clocks, respectively, to obtain bits $z_{257}, z_{258}, z_{259}, z_{260}$
7   **if** $z_{257} = z_{258} = z_{259} = z_{260} = 0$ **then**
8   Set $s \leftarrow 1$
9   **return** (K, IV) and (K', IV')

Table 2. State evolution of bits 255 to 224 after applying the KSA routine (Algorithm 4)

```
0 1 1 1 1 1 1 1 1 1 1 1 1 1 1 1 1 1 1 1 1 1 1 1 1 1 1 1 1 1 1 1
? 0 1 1 ? 1 1 1 ? 1 1 1 ? 1 1 1 ? 1 1 1 ? 1 1 1 ? 1 1 1 1 1 1 1
? ? 0 1 ? ? 1 1 ? ? 1 1 ? ? 1 1 ? ? 1 1 ? ? 1 1 ? ? 1 1 1 1 1 1
? ? ? 0 ? ? ? 1 ? ? ? 1 ? ? ? 1 ? ? ? 1 ? ? ? 1 ? ? ? 1 1 1 1 1
? ? ? ? ? ? ? ? ? ? ? ? ? ? ? ? ? ? ? ? ? ? ? ? ? ? ? ? 1 1 1 1
```

Theorem 2. *There are two attack strategies that an adversary can use to produce 4-bit shifted keystreams. He can use either the KSA algorithm (see Algorithm 4) or the KSA^{-1} algorithm (see Algorithm 5). The algorithms' have an average running time of 2^{32} and 2^{28} iterations, respectively.*

Proof. In the first case, the attacker can use the algorithm described in Algorithm 4 to obtain 4-bit shifted keystreams. For simplicity, we present in Table 2 the evolution of bits 255 to 224 of state X_0 after each run of the KSA routine. We highlighted with red the positions that are updated after each run[4] and we denote by ? the bits that are unknown to the attacker. We can easily see that after 4 clocks the bits from 255 to 228 are unknown to the attacker and are randomly distributed[5]. Hence, we should obtain a correct padding after 2^{28} iterations.

To obtain a shifted keystream we need an extra restriction. More precisely, when we run the KSA routine for 256 clocks state X_0 evolves to state X_{256}, but state $X_0' = X_4$ evolves to state $X_{256}' = X_{260}$. Hence, to obtain the shifted keystream we need $z_{257} = z_{258} = z_{259} = z_{260} = 0$. The probability of this happening is $1/2^4$. Therefore, the average running time of Algorithm 4 is $2^{28} \cdot 2^4 = 2^{32}$.

Algorithm 5: Constructing Key-IV pairs that generate 4-bit shifted keystream (backward construction)

    Output: Key-IV pairs (K'', IV'') and (K, IV)

1 Set $s \leftarrow 0$
2 **while** $s = 0$ **do**
3   Choose $K \in_R \{0,1\}^{128}$ and $V \in_R \{0,1\}^{92}$
4   Set $IV \leftarrow V \| 0\mathrm{xf}$
5   Run $KSA^{-1}(K\|IV)$ routine for 4 clocks to obtain a state $X_0'' = K''\|IV''\|P''$
6   **if** $P'' = 0\mathrm{xffffffff}$ **then**
7   Run $KSA(K\|IV)$ and PRNG routine for 252 clocks and 4 clocks, respectively, to obtain bits $z_{253}, z_{254}, z_{255}, z_{256}$
8   **if** $z_{253} = z_{254} = z_{255} = z_{256} = 0$ **then**
9   Set $s \leftarrow 1$
10   **return** (K, IV) and (K'', IV'')

Table 3. State evolution of bits 255 to 220 after applying the KSA^{-1} routine (Algorithm 5)

```
0 1 1 1 1 1 1 1 1 1 1 1 1 1 1 1 1 1 1 1 1 1 1 1 1 1 1 1 1 1 1 1 | 1 1 1 1
1 1 1 ? 1 1 1 ? 1 1 1 ? 1 1 1 ? 1 1 1 ? 1 1 1 ? 1 1 1 1 1 1 1 1 | 1 1 1 ×
1 1 ? ? 1 1 ? ? 1 1 ? ? 1 1 ? ? 1 1 ? ? 1 1 ? ? 1 1 1 1 1 1 1 1 | 1 1 × ×
1 ? ? ? 1 ? ? ? 1 ? ? ? 1 ? ? ? 1 ? ? ? 1 ? ? ? 1 1 1 1 1 1 1 1 | 1 × × ×
? ? ? ? ? ? ? ? ? ? ? ? ? ? ? ? ? ? ? ? ? ? ? ? 1 1 1 1 1 1 1 1 | × × × ×
```

---

[4] 255, 251, 247, 243, 239, 235, 231
[5] due to the key bits involved in their computation

A more efficient strategy is described in Algorithm 5. In this case, we set the last four bits of the initialization vector to 1. In Table 3 we can see the state evolution of bits 255 to 220 after running the KSA^{-1} routine. We separated the extra four bits of the IV by a straight line and we denoted by $\times$ the bits that are unknown to the attacker, but are irrelevant for our attack. In this case, the updated positions are 252, 248, 244, 240, 236, 232. We can easily see that after 4 clocks we have 24 unknown positions. Thus, the expected running time until we obtain a correct padding is 2^{24}.

As in the first case, we need some additional restrictions. We can see that after running the KSA routine for 256 clocks state X_0 evolves to state X_{256}, but state $X_0' = X_{-4}$ evolves to state $X_{256}' = X_{252}$. Hence, to obtain the shifted keystream we need $z_{253} = z_{254} = z_{255} = z_{256} = 0$. Therefore, the average running time of Algorithm 5 is $2^{24} \cdot 2^4 = 2^{28}$. $\square$

We further consider the padding 0x7fffffff and we study its impact on the average time needed to obtain shifted keystreams. We can easily see that this small change increases the complexity of finding shifted keystreams. Hence, we suggest using this padding instead of the classical one. Note that due to the attacks presented in Sect. 3, it is sufficient to devise a padding scheme that induces an average running time greater than 2^{32}.

Theorem 3. *There are two attack strategies that an adversary can use to produce 8-bit shifted keystreams. He can use either the KSA algorithm (see Algorithm 6) or the KSA^{-1} algorithm (see Algorithm 7). The algorithms' have an average running time of 2^{40} or 2^{34} iterations, respectively.*

Algorithm 6: Constructing Key-IV pairs that generate 8-bit shifted keystream (forward construction)

Output: Key-IV pairs (K', IV') and (K, IV)

1 Set $s \leftarrow 0$
2 **while** $s = 0$ **do**
3   Choose $K \in_R \{0,1\}^{128}$ and $IV \in_R \{0,1\}^{96}$
4   Run $KSA(K\|IV)$ routine for 8 clocks to obtain a state $X_0' = K'\|IV'\|P'$
5   **if** $P' = $ 0x7fffffff **then**
6   Run $KSA(K'\|IV')$ and PRNG routine for 248 clocks and 8 clocks, respectively, to obtain bits $z_{257}, \ldots, z_{264}$
7   **if** $z_{257} = \ldots = z_{264} = 0$ **then**
8   Set $s \leftarrow 1$
9   **return** (K, IV) and (K', IV')

Table 4. State evolution of bits 255 to 224 after applying the KSA routine (Algorithm 6)

```
1 1 1 1 1 1 1 1 1 1 1 1 1 1 1 1 1 1 1 1 1 1 1 1 1 1 1 1 1 1 1 0
? 1 1 1 ? 1 1 1 ? 1 1 1 ? 1 1 1 ? 1 1 1 ? 1 1 1 ? 1 1 1 1 1 1 1
? ? 1 1 ? ? 1 1 ? ? 1 1 ? ? 1 1 ? ? 1 1 ? ? 1 1 ? ? 1 1 1 1 1 1
? ? ? 1 ? ? ? 1 ? ? ? 1 ? ? ? 1 ? ? ? 1 ? ? ? 1 ? ? ? 1 1 1 1 1
? ? ? ? ? ? ? ? ? ? ? ? ? ? ? ? ? ? ? ? ? ? ? ? ? ? ? ? 1 1 1 1
? ? ? ? ? ? ? ? ? ? ? ? ? ? ? ? ? ? ? ? ? ? ? ? ? ? ? ? ? 1 1 1
? ? ? ? ? ? ? ? ? ? ? ? ? ? ? ? ? ? ? ? ? ? ? ? ? ? ? ? ? ? 1 1
? ? ? ? ? ? ? ? ? ? ? ? ? ? ? ? ? ? ? ? ? ? ? ? ? ? ? ? ? ? ? 1
? ? ? ? ? ? ? ? ? ? ? ? ? ? ? ? ? ? ? ? ? ? ? ? ? ? ? ? ? ? ? ?
```

Proof (sketch). The proof is similar to the proof of Theorem 2 and thus we omit some details.

In the first case, the attacker can use the algorithm described in Algorithm 6 to obtain 8-bit shifted keystreams. The evolution of bits 255 to 224 of state X_0 is presented in Table 4. We can easily see that after 8 clocks the bits from 255 to 224 are unknown to the attacker and thus he will obtain a correct padding after 2^{32} iterations. Note that, when we run the KSA routine for 256 clocks state X_0 evolves to state X_{256}, but state $X'_0 = X_8$ evolves to state $X'_{256} = X_{264}$. Hence, to obtain the shifted keystream we need $z_{257} = \ldots = z_{264} = 0$. Therefore, the average running time of Algorithm 6 is $2^{32} \cdot 2^8 = 2^{40}$.

The second strategy is described in Algorithm 7. In this case, we set the last six bits of the initialization vector to 1. In Table 5 we can see the state evolution of bits 255 to 218. Note that we also have position 218 updated. We can easily see that after 8 clocks we have 26 unknown positions. Thus, the expected running time until we obtain a correct padding is 2^{26}. Note that, after running the KSA routine for 256 clocks state X_0 evolves to state X_{256}, but state $X'_0 = X_{-8}$ evolves to state $X'_{256} = X_{248}$. Hence, to obtain the shifted keystream we need $z_{249} = \ldots = z_{256} = 0$. Therefore, the average running time of Algorithm 7 is $2^{26} \cdot 2^8 = 2^{34}$. □

Algorithm 7: Constructing Key-IV pairs that generate 8-bit shifted keystream (backward construction)

    Output: Key-IV pairs (K'', IV'') and (K, IV)
1 Set $s \leftarrow 0$
2 **while** $s = 0$ **do**
3   Choose $K \in_R \{0,1\}^{128}$ and $V \in_R \{0,1\}^{90}$
4   Set $IV \leftarrow V \| 0x3f$
5   Run $KSA^{-1}(K\|IV)$ routine for 8 clocks to obtain a state $X''_0 = K''\|IV''\|P''$
6   **if** $P'' = $ 0x7fffffff **then**
7   Run $KSA(K\|IV)$ and PRNG routine for 248 clocks and 8 clocks, respectively, to obtain bits $z_{249}, \ldots, z_{256}$
8   **if** $z_{249} = \ldots = z_{256} = 0$ **then**
9   Set $s \leftarrow 1$
10   **return** (K, IV) and (K'', IV'')

Table 5. State evolution of bits 255 to 218 after applying the KSA^{-1} routine (Algorithm 7)

```
1 1 1 1 1 1 1 1 1 1 1 1 1 1 1 1 1 1 1 1 1 1 1 1 1 1 1 1 1 1 0│1 1 1 1 1 1
1 1 1 ? 1 1 1 ? 1 1 1 ? 1 1 1 ? 1 1 1 ? 1 1 1 ? 1 1 1 1 1 1 0 1│1 1 1 1 1 ?
1 1 ? ? 1 1 ? ? 1 1 ? ? 1 1 ? ? 1 1 ? ? 1 1 ? ? 1 1 1 1 0 1 1│1 1 1 1 ? ?
1 ? ? ? 1 ? ? ? 1 ? ? ? 1 ? ? ? 1 ? ? ? 1 ? ? ? 1 1 1 1 0 1 1 1│1 1 1 ? ? ×
? ? ? ? ? ? ? ? ? ? ? ? ? ? ? ? ? ? ? ? ? ? ? ? 1 1 1 0 1 1 1 1│1 1 ? ? × ×
? ? ? ? ? ? ? ? ? ? ? ? ? ? ? ? ? ? ? ? ? ? ? ? 1 1 0 1 1 1 1 1│1 ? ? × × ×
? ? ? ? ? ? ? ? ? ? ? ? ? ? ? ? ? ? ? ? ? ? ? ? 1 0 1 1 1 1 1 1│? ? × × × ×
? ? ? ? ? ? ? ? ? ? ? ? ? ? ? ? ? ? ? ? ? ? ? ? 0 1 1 1 1 1 1 ?│? × × × × ×
? ? ? ? ? ? ? ? ? ? ? ? ? ? ? ? ? ? ? ? ? ? ? ? 1 1 1 1 1 1 ? ?│× × × × × ×
```

5 Key Recovery Algorithms

According to the results presented in Sect. 4, we know that related IV's exist. Note that we also know the average running time τ needed to find such a pair (IV, IV') and the keystream shift σ that they produce. Since we do not have access to the secret key, a simple strategy to finding such a pair is to choose a random IV and use it to generate α bits that are stored in memory. Then clock the NFSR either forward or backwards, and then randomly generate[6] IV' until we obtain a keystream with the desired shift σ. Note that the probability of randomly obtaining the desired shift is $1/2^{\alpha-\sigma}$. Therefore, if we choose a large enough α the probability is small enough.[7]

We further assume that we are in possession of two related IV's and we want to recover the secret key. Using a related IV pair, we can use a guess and determine attack[8] to recover the secret key. We propose three key recovery attacks. The first one (forward construction) uses IV pairs generated using the KSA routine, while the second (backward construction) use IV-pairs created using the KSA^{-1} routine. The last attack (mixed construction) assumes that we are in possession of two IV-pairs and is a combination of the forward and backward constructions.

---

[6] an average of τ IV's are generated

[7] e.g. $\alpha = 100$ *since* $\sigma = 4$ *or* 8

[8] An attacker starts by brute-forcing parts of a cryptographic key and then uses various methods to determine the remaining unknown portions, often relying on prior knowledge or observations about the encryption process.

Table 6. Modified cells after running the KSA routine

Clock	Cells
1	193, 197, 201, 205, 209, 213, 217, 231, 235, 239, 243, 247, 251, 255
2	192, 193, 196, 197, 200, 201, 204, 205, 208, 209, 212, 213, 216, 217, 230, 231, 234, 235, 238, 239, 242, 243, 246, 247, 250, 251, 254, 255
3	$191 - 193,\ 195 - 197,\ 199 - 201,\ 203 - 205,\ 207 - 209,\ 211 - 213,$ $215 - 217,\ 229 - 231,\ 233 - 235,\ 237 - 239,\ 241 - 243,\ 245 - 247,$ $249 - 251,\ 253 - 255$
4	$190 - 217,\ 228 - 255$
5	$189 - 217,\ 227 - 255$
6	$188 - 217,\ 226 - 255$
7	$187 - 217,\ 225 - 255$
8	$186 - 217,\ 224 - 255$

5.1   Forward Construction

Before presenting our attack, we want to see which NFSR positions are modified[9] by the KSA routine after each clock. These positions are presented in Table 6.

In this subsection, we study the classical Espresso cipher, while in the full version of the paper [12] we develop a key recovery algorithm for our proposed version of Espresso.

Looking at the KLA and KSA routines, we can see that on clock $i+1$ K's bits used by the feedback functions and the output function are found on positions $0 - (127-i)$, where $i \in [0,3]$. According to Table 6, none of K's bits are modified. Similarly, we can see that IV's bits used by the feedback functions are not modified. In the case of the output function, we can see that the only positions that are modified are 213 and 217 at clocks $2 - 4$. Luckily we can recover them from IV'''s bits. Also, note that for $i = 2, 3$ the value found on position 222 is 1 (due to the shifting of the initial padding).

As stated in Table 6, some positions between 223 and 255 are modified. But we are working with two related IV's that produce 4-bit shifted keystreams. Hence, we know that after 4 clocks we end up with a valid padding. Hence, we know their values.

Rewriting the feedback functions we obtain

$$g_{255}(X_{i+1}) = k_i \oplus k_{i+41}k_{i+70} \oplus z(X_{i+1}) \qquad g_{247}(X_{i+1}) = 1 \oplus k_{i+44}k_{i+102} \oplus k_{i+40}$$

$$g_{243}(X_{i+1}) = 1 \oplus k_{i+43}k_{i+118} \oplus k_{i+103} \qquad g_{239}(X_{i+1}) = 1 \oplus k_{i+46}iv_{i+13} \oplus k_{i+117}$$

$$g_{235}(X_{i+1}) = 1 \oplus k_{i+67}k_{i+90}k_{i+110}iv_{i+9} \qquad g_{231}(X_{i+1}) = 1 \oplus k_{i+50}iv_{i+31} \oplus iv_{i+61}$$

$$g_{217}(X_{i+1}) = iv_{i+90} \oplus k_{i+3}k_{i+32} \oplus z(X_{i+1}) \qquad g_{213}(X_{i+1}) = iv_{i+86} \oplus k_{i+4}k_{i+45}$$

$$g_{200}(X_{i+1}) = iv_{i+82} \oplus k_{i+6}k_{i+64} \qquad g_{205}(X_{i+1}) = iv_{i+78} \oplus k_{i+5}k_{i+80}$$

$$g_{201}(X_{i+1}) = iv_{i+74} \oplus k_{i+8}k_{i+103} \qquad g_{197}(X_{i+1}) = iv_{i+70} \oplus k_{i+29}k_{i+52}k_{i+72}k_{i+99}$$

$$g_{193}(X_{i+1}) = iv_{i+66} \oplus k_{i+12}k_{i+121}$$

---

[9] and hence, unknown to an attacker

and

$$g_{251}(X_{i+1}) = \begin{cases} 1 \oplus k_{i+42}k_{i+83} \oplus k_{i+8} & \text{if } i \neq 3 \\ k_{i+42}k_{i+83} \oplus k_{i+8} & \text{if } i = 3 \end{cases}$$

where

$$z'(X_{i+1}) = k_{i+80} \oplus k_{i+99} \oplus iv_{i+9} \oplus iv_{i+59} \oplus iv_{i+53} \oplus iv_{i+46}k_{i+44} \oplus iv_{i+36}k_{i+29}$$

$$z(X_{i+1}) = \begin{cases} z'(X_{i+1}) \oplus iv_{85}iv_{89} \oplus iv_{94+i} & \text{if } i = 0 \\ z'(X_{i+1}) \oplus iv'_{81+i}iv'_{85+i} \oplus 1 \oplus iv'_{81+i}iv_{53+i}iv_{46+i} \oplus iv_{94+i} & \text{if } i = 1 \\ z'(X_{i+1}) \oplus iv'_{81+i}iv'_{85+i} \oplus iv'_{81+i}iv_{53+i}iv_{46+i} & \text{if } i = 2 \\ z'(X_{i+1}) \oplus iv'_{81+i}iv'_{85+i} \oplus iv'_{81+i}iv_{53+i}iv_{46+i} & \text{if } i = 3 \end{cases}$$

From Espresso's feedback functions we can see that the only functions containing retrievable key bits are $g_{255}, g_{251}, g_{247}, g_{243}, g_{239}$ and g_{217}. Note that all positions, except 217, can be recovered from the padding (see Table 2). In the case of g_{217}, the value can be recovered from IV's bits. Therefore, we obtain Algorithm 8 for recovering some of K's bits. To ease understanding, in Algorithm 8 we marked at each step the recovered key bits %rec and the used key bits %use.

5.2   Backward Construction

In this case, we want to see how the KSA^{-1} routine affects the NFSR positions after each clock. The results are presented in Table 7.

With respect to the classical Espresso[10], we can see that the KSA^{-1} routine on clock $i - 1$ K's and IV's bits used by the feedback functions are unchanged, where $i \in \{0, -1, -2, -3\}$. Moreover, we can see that the first 4 bits of IV' coincide with the last 4 bits of K. The only problem that we encounter is on position 218. Here on the last clock the feedback function uses x_{-1}, but the value can be easily obtained from k_{40}, k_{69} and the output function.

In the case of the output function, the only problematic positions are 213 and 217 from the -4 clock. The two bits coincide with bits 210 and 214 from clock -1. Lastly, for positions 232 to 255 we know the exact values due to related Key-IV pairs used by the algorithm. Therefore, we obtain

$$g_{252}^{-1}(X_{i-1}) = 1 \oplus k_{i+41}k_{i+82} \oplus k_{i+7} \qquad g_{248}^{-1}(X_{i-1}) = 1 \oplus k_{i+43}k_{i+101} \oplus k_{i+39}$$

$$g_{244}^{-1}(X_{i-1}) = 1 \oplus k_{i+42}k_{i+117} \oplus k_{i+102} \qquad g_{240}^{-1}(X_{i-1}) = 1 \oplus k_{i+45}iv_{i+12} \oplus k_{i+116}$$

$$g_{236}^{-1}(X_{i-1}) = 1 \oplus k_{i+66}k_{i+89}k_{i+109}iv_{i+8} \qquad g_{232}^{-1}(X_{i-1}) = 1 \oplus k_{i+49}iv_{i+30} \oplus iv_{i+60}$$

$$g_{214}^{-1}(X_{i-1}) = iv_{i+85} \oplus k_{i+3}k_{i+44} \qquad g_{210}^{-1}(X_{i-1}) = iv_{i+81} \oplus k_{i+5}k_{i+63}$$

$$g_{206}^{-1}(X_{i-1}) = iv_{i+77} \oplus k_{i+4}k_{i+79} \qquad g_{202}^{-1}(X_{i-1}) = iv_{i+73} \oplus k_{i+7}k_{i+102}$$

$$g_{198}^{-1}(X_{i-1}) = iv_{i+69} \oplus k_{i+28}k_{i+51}k_{i+71}k_{i+98} \qquad g_{194}^{-1}(X_{i-1}) = iv_{i+65} \oplus k_{i+11}k_{i+120}$$

---

[10] See the full version of the paper [12] for an analysis of our proposed version.

Algorithm 8: Key bits recovery algorithm for the 0xfffffffe padding (forward construction)

1   scriptsize **Input:** Chosen IV's IV and IV' and key bits k_j, where
$$j \in \{4-6, 29-35, 44-49, 70-72, 84-86, 99-102, 121\}$$
Output: 24 key bits k_j, where
$$j \in \{0-3, 8-11, 40-43, 80-83, 103-106, 117-120\}$$
2   **for** $i \in [0,3]$ **do**
3     $k_{i+117} \leftarrow k_{i+46}iv_{i+13}$ $\%rec: 117-120$ $use: 46-49$
4   $k_{105} \leftarrow k_{45}k_{120}$ $\%rec: 105$ $use: 45, 120$
5   $k_{43} \leftarrow k_{47}k_{105}$ $\%rec: 43$ $use: 47, 105$
6   **for** $i \in [0,3]$ **do**
7   **if** $i \neq 2$ **then** $k_{i+103} \leftarrow k_{i+43}k_{i+118}$
    $\%rec: 103, 104, 106$ $use: 43, 44, 46, 118, 119, 121$
8   **for** $i \in [0,2]$ **do**
9     $k_{i+40} \leftarrow k_{i+44}k_{i+102}$ $\%rec: 40-42$ $use: 44-46, 102-104$
10   $o_3 \leftarrow$
$k_{102} \oplus iv_{12} \oplus iv_{62} \oplus iv'_{84} \oplus iv'_{88} \oplus iv_{56} \oplus iv_{49}k_{47} \oplus iv_{39}k_{32} \oplus iv'_{i+81} \oplus iv'_{i+81}iv_{i+53}iv_{i+46}$
$\%use: 102, 47, 32$
11   $k_{83} \leftarrow o_3 \oplus iv'_{89} \oplus iv_{93} \oplus k_6 k_{35}$ $\%rec: 83$ $use: 6, 35$
12   $k_3 \leftarrow o_3 \oplus k_{83} \oplus k_{44}k_{73}$ $\%rec: 3$ $use: 83, 44, 73$
13   **for** $i \in [0,2]$ **do**
14     $o_i \leftarrow k_{i+99} \oplus iv_{i+9} \oplus iv_{i+59} \oplus iv'_{i+81} \oplus iv'_{i+85} \oplus iv_{i+53} \oplus iv_{i+46}k_{i+44} \oplus iv_{i+36}k_{i+29}$
    $\%use: 99-101, 44-46, 29-31$
15   **if** $i \neq 0$ **then** $o_i \leftarrow o \oplus 1 \oplus iv'_{i+81} \oplus iv'_{i+81}iv_{i+53}iv_{i+46}$
16   **if** $i = 2$ **then** $o_i \leftarrow o \oplus 1$ **else** $o_i \leftarrow o \oplus iv_{i+94}$
17     $k_{i+80} \leftarrow o_i \oplus iv'_{i+86} \oplus iv_{i+90} \oplus k_{i+3}k_{i+32}$ $\%rec: 80-82$ $use: 3-5, 32-34$
18   **for** $i \in [0,2]$ **do**
19     $k_{i+0} \leftarrow o_i \oplus k_{i+80} \oplus k_{i+41}k_{i+70}$ $\%rec: 0-2$ $use: 80-82, 41-43, 70-72$
20   **for** $i \in [0,3]$ **do**
21     $k_{i+8} \leftarrow k_{i+42}k_{i+83}$ $\%rec: 8-11$ $use: 42-45, 83-86$
22   **if** $i = 3$ **then** $k_{i+8} \leftarrow k_{i+8} \oplus 1$

and

$$g_0^{-1}(X_{i-1}) = \begin{cases} x_{i+40}x_{i+69} \oplus z^{-1}(X_{i-1}) & \text{if } i = 0 \\ 1 \oplus x_{i+40}x_{i+69} \oplus z^{-1}(X_{i-1}) & \text{if } i \neq 0 \end{cases}$$

$$g_{218}^{-1}(X_{i-1}) = \begin{cases} iv_{i+89} \oplus k_{i+2}k_{i+31} \oplus z^{-1}(X_{i-1}) & \text{if } i \neq -3 \\ iv_{i+89} \oplus g_0^{-1}(X_{-1})k_{i+31} \oplus z^{-1}(X_{i-1}) & \text{if } i = -3 \end{cases}$$

Table 7. Modified cells after running the KSA^{-1} routine

Clock	Cells
-1	0, 194, 198, 202, 206, 210, 214, 218, 232, 236, 240, 244, 248, 252
-2	0, 1, 194, 195, 198, 199, 202, 203, 206, 207, 210, 211, 214, 215, 218, 219, 232, 233, 236, 237, 240, 241, 244, 245, 248, 249, 252, 253
-3	$0-2$, $194-196$, $198-200$, $202-204$, $206-208$, $210-212$, $214-216$, $218-220$, $232-234$, $236-238$, $240-242$, $244-246$, $248-250$, $252-254$
-4	$0-3$, $194-221$, $232-255$
-5	$0-4$, $194-222$, $232-255$
-6	$0-5$, $194-223$, $232-255$
-7	$0-6$, $194-224$, $232-255$
-8	$0-7$, $194-225$, $232-255$

where

$$z'^{-1}(X_{i-1}) = k_{i+79} \oplus k_{i+98} \oplus iv_{i+8} \oplus iv_{i+58} \oplus iv_{i+52} \oplus iv_{i+45}k_{i+43} \oplus iv_{i+35}k_{i+28}$$

$$z^{-1}(X_{i-1}) = \begin{cases} z'^{-1}(X_{i-1}) & \oplus iv_{i+88} \oplus iv_{i+84} \oplus iv_{i+84}iv_{i+52}iv_{i+45} \\ & \text{if } i = 0 \\ z'^{-1}(X_{i-1}) & \oplus iv_{i+88} \oplus iv_{i+84} \oplus iv_{i+84}iv_{i+52}iv_{i+45} \\ & \text{if } i = -1 \\ z'^{-1}(X_{i-1}) & \oplus iv_{i+88} \oplus iv_{i+84} \oplus iv_{i+93} \oplus 1 \oplus iv_{i+84}iv_{i+52}iv_{i+45} \\ & \text{if } i = -2 \\ z'^{-1}(X_{i-1}) & \oplus iv_{81} \oplus k_5 k_{63} \oplus iv_{85} \oplus k_3 k_{44} \oplus iv_{i+93} \\ & \text{if } i = -3 \end{cases}$$

From Espresso's reverse feedback functions we can see that the only functions containing retrievable key bits are $g_{252}^{-1}, g_{248}^{-1}, g_{244}^{-1}, g_{240}^{-1}$ and g_{218}^{-1}. Note that all positions, except 217, can be recovered from the padding (see Table 3). In the case of g_{218}^{-1}, the value can be recovered from IV'''s bits. Therefore, we obtain Algorithm 9 for recovering some of K's bits.

5.3 Mixed Construction

Once we have constructed two pairs of related IV's using the KSA and the KSA^{-1} routines, we can simply apply both the forward and the backward construction. Note that there might be better approaches when combining the forward and backward type constructions (*i.e.* constructions that recover different bits compared to ours).

In the classical case, we can recover 41 key bits. More precisely, the mixed construction takes as input the two pairs and the key bits k_j, where $j \in \{3 - 6, 25 - 35, 44 - 49, 63, 69 - 72, 76 - 79, 84 - 86, 98 - 102, 121\}$. Then it runs the forward construction and then it runs the backward one. Finally, the algorithm outputs k_j, where $j \in \{0 - 3, 7 - 11, 36 - 43, 80 - 83, 95 - 98, 103 - 106, 113 - 120, 124 - 127\}$.

Algorithm 9: Key bits recovery algorithm for the `Oxfffffffe` padding (backward construction)

Input: Chosen IV's IV and IV' and key bits k_j, where
$\qquad j \in \{0-3, 25-31, 40-45, 63, 69, 76-82, 117\}$
Output: 24 key bits k_j, where $j \in \{4-7, 36-39, 95-102, 113-116, 124-127\}$

1 **for** $i \in [0, -2]$ **do**
2 $\quad$ $k_{i+116} \leftarrow k_{i+45} iv_{i+12}$ $\%rec : 116-114\ use : 45-43$
3 $\quad$ $k_{i+102} \leftarrow k_{i+42} k_{i+117}$ $\%rec : 102-100\ use : 42-40, 117-115$
4 $k_{113} \leftarrow k_{42} iv_9$ $\%rec : 113\ use : 42$
5 $k_{99} \leftarrow k_{43} k_{101} k_{114}$ $\%rec : 99\ use : 43, 101, 114$
6 **for** $i \in [0, -3]$ **do**
7 $\quad$ $k_{i+127} \leftarrow iv'_{i+3}$ $\%rec : 127-124$
8 $\quad$ $k_{i+7} \leftarrow k_{i+41} k_{i+82}$ $\%rec : 7-4\ use : 41-38, 82-79$
9 $\quad$ **if** $i = 0$ **then** $k_{i+7} \leftarrow k_{i+7} \oplus 1$
10 $\quad$ $k_{i+39} \leftarrow k_{i+43} k_{i+101}$ $\%rec : 39-36\ use : 43-40, 101-98$
11 $\quad$ $o \leftarrow k_{i+79} \oplus iv_{i+8} \oplus iv_{i+58} \oplus iv_{i+52} \oplus iv_{i+45} k_{i+43} \oplus iv_{i+35} k_{i+28}$
   $\quad \%use : 79-76, 43-40, 28-25$
12 $\quad$ **if** $i = 3$ **then** $o \leftarrow o \oplus iv_{81} \oplus k_5 k_{63} \oplus iv_{85} \oplus k_3 k_{44} \oplus iv_{90}$ $\%use : 5, 63, 3, 44$ **else**
   $\quad o \leftarrow o \oplus iv_{i+88} \oplus iv_{i+84} \oplus 1 \oplus iv_{i+84} iv_{i+52} iv_{i+45}$
13 $\quad$ **if** $i = 0$ **or** $i = 1$ **then** $o \leftarrow o \oplus 1$ **else** $o \leftarrow o \oplus iv_{i+93}$
14 $\quad$ $k_{i+98} \leftarrow o \oplus iv'_{i+93} \oplus iv_{i+89} \oplus k_{i+2} k_{i+31}$ $\%rec : 98-95\ use : 2-0, 31-28$
15 $\quad$ **if** $t = 0$ **then** $k_{-1} \leftarrow o \oplus k_{98} \oplus k_{40} \oplus k_{69}$ $\%use : 98, 40, 69$

Table 8. Attack Complexity

Construction	Padding	
	`Oxfffffffe`	`Ox7fffffff`
Forward	$2^{104} + 2^{32}$	$2^{101} + 2^{40}$
Backward	$2^{104} + 2^{28}$	$2^{99} + 2^{34}$
Mixed	$2^{87} + 2^{32} + 2^{28}$	$2^{89} + 2^{40} + 2^{34}$

Regarding our proposal, the mixed construction can recover 39 key bits. More precisely, the mixed construction takes as input the two pairs and the key bits k_j, where $j \in \{4-12, 21-31, 36-53, 60-82, 86-90, 95-97, 99-103, 106-108, 117\}$. Then it runs the backward construction and then it runs the forward one. Finally, the algorithm outputs k_j, where $j \in \{0-3, 13-15, 32-35, 83-85, 91-94, 98, 104, 105, 109-116, 118-127\}$.

Remark 2. Note that we also studied the backward and forward combination for the classic case. However, this combination performed poorer than the one we presented. Thus, we omitted it. The same happened for the forward and backward combination for our proposed padding scheme.

5.4   Complexity

To summarise, we provide in Table 8 the complexities of the key recovery attacks. We can see that when we take the attacks separately, the original padding has a better security margin. However, in the mixed case our proposal performs better.

6   Conclusions

In this paper, we have shown that given any Key-IV pair, one can easily construct another pair, with expected 2^{32} time complexity, that produces the same bits as the initial keystream on a significant amount of positions.

Furthermore, we have studied related Key-IV pairs that produce shifted keystreams. We have shown how one can obtain two related Key-IV pairs, in expected 2^{28} trials, such that the pairs generate 4-bit shifted keystreams. To increase the complexity of these attacks, we have proposed a new padding scheme and have proven that the complexity increases to 2^{34}.

Additionally, we managed to describe several attacks that recover some of the key bits and requires only two/four related IV's. Hence, we can decrease the complexity of conducting a brute force attack on the key to 2^{87} in the classical case and to 2^{89} for our proposal.

A   Examples

A.1   Propagation of a Single Bit Differential

Based on Algorithm 1, in Table 9 we present some examples. More precisely, two initial states X_0 and $X_{0,\Delta}$ which differ only in the position presented in Table 9, Column 1, produce identical output bits in the positions found in Table 9, Column 3, among the initial 160 key stream bits obtained during the PRGA.

Table 9. Propagation of a Single Bit Differential

Flipped Bit Position	Number of Identical Keystream Bits	Positions of Identical Keystream Bits
31	25	0-15, 19, 22, 23, 27, 34, 42, 55, 58, 71
47	10	0, 1, 25, 36, 39, 43, 47, 51, 66, 82
71	21	0, 1, 3, 4, 7, 8, 11, 12, 15-17, 19, 20, 21, 24, 25, 49, 60, 67, 71, 75
95	32	0-5, 7-9, 11, 12, 16, 18, 20, 22, 23, 27, 31, 32, 35, 36, 39, 41, 43-45, 48, 49, 73, 91, 95, 99
119	22	0, 1, 4, 5, 8, 9, 12, 13, 16, 19, 24, 27, 35, 36, 40, 42, 46, 51, 56, 59, 65, 67
143	32	0-2, 4, 5, 8-10, 12-14, 16-19, 21-24, 33, 36, 40, 43, 48, 51, 59, 60, 64, 66, 70, 83, 91
167	51	0-2, 4-8, 10-12, 14-17, 19-22, 24-26, 28, 29, 32-34, 36-38, 40-43, 45-48, 57, 60, 64, 67, 72, 75, 83, 84, 88, 90, 94, 107, 115
191	58	0-2, 5, 6, 8, 9, 11, 13-16, 18-20, 22-26, 28-32, 34-36, 38-41, 43-45, 48, 49, 52, 56-58, 61, 62, 65-67, 69, 71, 72, 81, 84, 88, 91, 99, 108, 112, 114, 131
215	81	0, 1, 3-26, 29, 30, 32, 33, 35, 37-40, 42-44, 46-50, 52-56, 58-60, 62-65, 67-69, 72, 73, 76, 80-82, 85, 86, 89-91, 93, 95, 96, 105, 108, 112, 115, 123, 132, 136, 138, 155
239	96	1-3, 5-7, 9-11, 13-16, 18-21, 23-25, 27-50, 53, 54, 56, 57, 59, 61-64, 66-68, 70-74, 76-80, 82-84, 86-89, 91-93, 96, 97, 100, 104-106, 109, 110, 113-115, 117, 119, 120, 129, 132, 136, 139, 147, 156

A.2   Multiple Key-IV Trials with a Fixed Differential

In Table 10 we provide an examples for Algorithm 2.

Table 10. Key-IV pairs which differ only in the 239th position

Key	IV	State
0xd17117b8c5f9042 43a69b7db0a535d2b	0x96a2736a408 208e40e4ce2e9	0x7a53d74a086602e4943e052d9fc6865 b37d9c35fb68b0cf78e8b5bcba7f0a273
0xcee2d9eee6c6da3 625309eb7737e3f4d	0x52385c5ecfd 2fa898bf48b67	0x7a53d74a086602e4943e052d9fc6865 b37d9c35fb68b0cf78e8b5bcba7f1a273

A.3   Key-IV Pairs that Produce Shifted Keystreams

In Table 11 we present a set of examples for Algorithms 4 to 7.

Table 11. Key-IV pairs that produce shifted keystreams

	Key	IV	Keystream
Algorithm 4	0x2a13a9539900630 f7a721a25e2193026	0x2c112eb15ad d58ec3a99599a	0x6757b665d8a3e72 bd2bdfdc326a93404
	0xa13a9539900630f 7a721a25e21930262	0xc112eb15add 58ec3ad959aef	0x757b665d8a3e72b d2bdfdc326a934043
Algorithm 5	0xb1d331f900270d5 f6a43069b404888cf	0x7e8b7fd12fe bf7c2f17d86ff	0x6172f847028df4f eb0906ea001fc6d1f
	0xfb1d331f900270d 5f6a43069b404888c	0xf7e8b7fd12f ebf7c2b17684f	0x56172f847028df4 feb0906ea001fc6d1
Algorithm 6	0xb64e24eddec37cf 8a30970c2155d30cf	0xaee197ec26b 76484bceb639d	0x0261c57c8b0238e 469f8e67299c3ed57
	0x4e24eddec37cf8a 30970c2155d30cfae	0xe197ec26b76 4849c49c2f33f	0x61c57c8b0238e46 9f8e67299c3ed5742
Algorithm 7	0xd90e03c9fdcf7ce 231f9ac4c322ad987	0xb6a7a25b255 b956c9672467f	0xca75acab22d4c9e e1fb6c9045f1379e0
	0xd7d90e03c9fdcf7 ce231f9ac4c322ad9	0x87b6a7a25b2 55b954817ee18	0x05ca75acab22d4c 9ee1fb6c9045f1379

References

1. NIST SP 800–22: Download Documentation and Software (2014). https://csrc.nist. gov/Projects/Random-Bit-Generation/Documentation-and-Software
2. NIST SP 800-90B: Entropy Assessment (2018). https://github.com/usnistgov/ SP800-90B_EntropyAssessment
3. The GNU Multiple Precision Arithmetic Library (1991). https://gmplib.org/
4. Banik, S., Maitra, S., Sarkar, S.: Some results on related key-IV pairs of grain. In: Bogdanov, A., Sanadhya, S. (eds.) SPACE 2012. LNCS, pp. 94–110. Springer, Heidelberg (2012). https://doi.org/10.1007/978-3-642-34416-9_7
5. Banik, S., Maitra, S., Sarkar, S., Meltem Sönmez, T.: A chosen IV related key attack on grain-128a. In: Boyd, C., Simpson, L. (eds.) ACISP 2013. LNCS, vol. 7959, pp. 13–26. Springer, Heidelberg (2013). https://doi.org/10.1007/978-3-642-39059-3_2
6. De Cannière, C., Küçük, Ö., Preneel, B.: Analysis of grain's initialization algorithm. In: Vaudenay, S. (ed.) AFRICACRYPT 2008. LNCS, vol. 5023, pp. 276–289. Springer, Heidelberg (2008). https://doi.org/10.1007/978-3-540-68164-9_19
7. Ding, L., Guan, J.: Related key chosen IV attack on grain-128a stream cipher. IEEE Trans. Inf. Forensics Secur. 8(5), 803–809 (2013)
8. Dubrova, E., Hell, M.: Espresso: a stream cipher for 5G wireless communication systems. Cryptogr. Commun. 9(2), 273–289 (2017)
9. Küçük, Ö.: Slide resynchronization attack on the initialization of grain 1.0, Tech. rep. (2006)
10. Maimuţ, D., Teşeleanu, G.: New configurations of grain ciphers: security against slide attacks. In: Ryan, P.Y., Toma, C. (eds.) Innovative Security Solutions for Information Technology and Communications. SecITC 2021. Lecture Notes in Computer Science, vol. 13195, pp. 260–285. Springer, Cham (2021). https://doi. org/10.1007/978-3-031-17510-7_18
11. Olsson, M., Cavdar, C., Frenger, P.K., Tombaz, S., Sabella, D., Jäntti, R.: 5GrEEn: towards green 5G mobile networks. In: WiMob 2013, pp. 212–216. IEEE Computer Society (2013)
12. Teşeleanu, G.: Some results on related key-IV pairs of espresso. IACR Cryptology ePrint Archive 2023/1691 (2023)
13. Wang, M.X., Dai Lin, D.: Related key chosen IV attack on stream cipher espresso variant. In: CSE/EUC 2017, vol. 1, pp. 580–587. IEEE Computer Society (2017)
14. Yao, G., Parampalli, U.: Generalized NLFSR transformation algorithms and cryptanalysis of the class of espresso-like stream ciphers. CoRR abs/1911.01002 (2019)

Author Index